Non-detention System in School Education

Non-detention System in School Education

By

Dr. M. Nirmala Jyothi

Associate Professor
Department of Eudcation
Sri Padmavathi Mahila Viswavidyalaya
Tirupati—517502 (A.P.)

Editor

Dr. Digumarti Bhaskara Rao

R.V.R. College of Education
D-43, S.V.N. Colony
Guntur—522006 (A.P)

DISCOVERY PUBLISHING HOUSE
NEW DELHI-110002

First Published-2003
Reprinted: 2013
ISBN 81-7141-654-3

Published by
DISCOVERY PUBLISHING HOUSE
4831/24, Ansari Road, Prahlad Street,
Darya Ganj, New Delhi-110002 (India)
Phone: 3279245 • Fax: 91-11-3253475
E-mail:dphtemp@indiatimes.com

Printed at:
Dynamic printers, Delhi

Preface

The Government of Andhra Pradesh has introduced the non-detention system, a system of automatic promotion, at school level realising that education is best imparted in an atmosphere of free progress where the incentive and urge to improve spring from within the educational process rather than from the terror of examinations and detentions. Under this system, the students will be automatically promoted to the next class provided they put in a stipulated percentage of attendance. However, there will be two common/public examinations during the school career, one at the end of the upper primary stage (7th class) and the other at the end of the secondary stage (10th class). This non-detention system evoked a mixed reaction from the educational elite and common men. A study, hence, was undertaken to evaluate the non-detention system and the results of the study were quite interesting. This research monograph on the non-detention system will be of great use to the educational planners, administrators, researchers and teachers.

Nirmala Jyothi
Bhaskara Rao

Contents

1

Introduction

A nation's assets are built up in ever so many ways of which the most fruitful and productive is education. As such it is but natural that education and problems associated with it are the major topics of deep thinking today, especially, in a developing country like India. Teaching, learning and evaluation are the three pillars on which any sound system of education rests. It is needless to mention, that examinations in one form or other were known to the people ever since the days of early civilization. Since their inception they have been undoubtedly playing a vital role enabling the educational authorities, the society and the parents to know about the progress of the school and the teacher and taught to know about their own efficiency.

Being a vital organ of the process of education, one naturally expects that the examination system serves its role effectively and perfectly. But far from being perfect, the essay type, year and examinations that we have today have been found to be the most imperfect, least objective, most unreliable and least valid. The reasons may be many and varied, who the culprits are is a most question; it may be the students, or teachers or paper setters or examiners or even the parents. The fact remains that the present day examination system is infested with innumerable defects.

It is no wonder, therefore, that the *University Education Commission* (1948) was very critical of the system of examinations and remarked, that if we are to suggest one single reform in our education it should be that of examinations. The *Secondary Education Commission* (1954) observed that 'the (present) examinations do not help us in evaluating the real intellectual achievements of the pupils'. The *Education Commission* (1966) recommended for the abolition of set syllabi and the external examinations based upon them and emphasised that they should be replaced by system of internal and continuous evaluation by teaches themselves.

The report of the *University Grants Commission* (1962) entitled 'Problem of examination reform', stressed the need for improvement of the methods of teaching, and learning, and that examinations should periodically reveal to the students his progress in learning.

According to *Bora* (1974) examinations are as important in education as the test conducted by a doctor before treating a patient. If all examinations are set aside, all consequences of education will also be flung away and teaching and learning becomes a meaningless enterprise.

The Government of India in its *National Policy on Education* (1986) laid down that a major goal of examination reform should be to improve the reliability and validity of examinations and to make evaluation a continuous process aimed at helping the student to improve his level of achievement rather than at certifying the quality of his performance at a given moment of time. It sought to de-emphasise the role of examinations in the field of education. The policy stressed that assessment of performance is an integral part of any process of teaching and learning. As a part of sound educational strategy, examinations should be employed to bring about qualitative improvement in education. The objective will be to recast the examination system so as to ensure a method of assessment that is a valid and reliable measure of student development and a powerful instrument for improving teaching and learning.

According to the Report of a seminar held at *Sourashtra University* (1985), examinations should not be looked at in isolation. They should be treated as a means to improve the teaching-learning process and should serve as an instrument of improving the quality of education.

It is no wonder that many an educationist and many a commission of education suggested many a reform. There are probably as many, if not more, suggested reforms, as there are defects. Yet nothing tangible and substantial has been done to bring about improvement in the system. This is what surprises one concerned with the Indian education system. The Education Commission aptly remarked in this context that one need not be surprised to note, in this type of situation, that there have been cries at times to abolish all examinations. In fact vexed with the faulty evaluation system many western countries indeed have taken steps to reduce their dependence on public examination as a basis for issuing school leaving certificates. In Canada, Ontaria, abolished its examinations in 1967; Mantaba did so in 1970 (*Singha,* 1984).

The modern philosophy of education aims at bringing to light the many hidden talents of the students and full play of their intellectual faculties. It lays more emphasis on the all round development of his emotional and social life and for the complete building up of his personality. This change in the techniques of education should necessarily bring a change in the system of examination. New methods should be adopted for assessing the progress and development at every stage instead of the old system of examining the students at the end of the course.

Andhra Pradesh state has been pursuing many progressive educational ventures. So is the case with reform of examinations. The state has been implementing all the national policies in the field of education. As a drastic step in reforming its system of education the Government of Andhra Pradesh has introduced the non-detention system in 1971. According to this system any student will be automatically promoted to the next class during his school career, irrespective of his academic achievement provided he puts in a stipulated percentage of attendance at the school. However, there will be two common examinations, one at the end of the upper primary level corresponding to class VII and the other at the end of secondary level corresponding to class X. A student may be detained in these classes if he does not pass the respective common examinations. In all other classes he will be automatically promoted whatever may be his achievement provided he puts in the required attendance at the school.

This innovative reform has indeed evoked a mixed reaction from the public and the educational elite of the nation. Even prior to the introduction of this system by the Government of Andhra Pradesh certain commissions did not favour complete abolition of examinations from the total spectrum of education. For example, the *Hartog Committee* (1936) was clearly opposed to the policy of abolishing examinations altogether and pointed out the need for careful and systematic experiments to improve the examinations.

Similarly, the *University Education Commission* (1948) said that, even though in India as elsewhere in the world, dissatisfaction with examinations has been so keen that eminent educationists and important educational organisations have advocated the abolition of examinations, 'they did not share that extreme view' and felt that examinations rightly designed, intelligently used could be a useful factor in the educational process. In the same vein they emphasised that, if examinations were necessary, a thorough reform of them was still more necessary.

The *Secondary Education Commission* (1954) also felt that a constant and realistic appraisal of the pupils progress should be made throughout his school career and that efforts should be made to design new evaluation programmes which would not be a test of memory only, but a measure of the pupil's educational growth.

The *Education Commission* (1966) recommended for 'abolition of set syllabi' and the 'external examinations based upon them' and emphasised that they should be replaced by a system of internal and continuous evaluation by the teachers themselves.

Different shades of opinion have been expressed on the non-detention system introduced by the Government of Andhra Pradesh. Some condemned the government's actions, while others commended it. Some reacted very sharply and assailed the Government that it has taken as 'very un-academic decision on an academic matter', and 'abolished detentions with a stroke of the pen' (Editor, *The Educational Review,* 1971; *Venkata Rao,* 1971). There were others who hailed the Government for its 'bold step in the right direction' (*Sarabhachari,* 1971; *Krishnamoorthy,* 1977).

Krishnamoorthy (1971) observed that detentions were negative incentives. They did not promote learning, on the other hand they led to unlearning of what has been learnt. Further, they developed inferiority complexes and unfavourable attitude towards the school, the teachers and the system of education as a whole. *P.V. Narasimha Rao* (1971), (the present minister of external affairs, Government of India) who was then minister of education, Government of Andhra Pradesh who piloted this reform contended that education was best imparted in an atmosphere of free progress when the incentive and urge to improve sprang from within the process of education rather than from the terror of examinations and detentions. Kabra (1971) also expressed a similar view.

It was felt by many that this system would reduce wastage and stagnation (*Kabra,* 1971; *Krishnamoorthy,* 1971; Venkata Reddy 1971; Rao, 1977). Further, it was opined that this reform would allow teachers to use better methods of teaching and evaluation in the place of the outmoded methods of teaching and evaluation that were in vogue. The teachers would have ample time and freedom to try new and innovative methods as they were released from the cruel grip of early examinations and the like (*Sarabachari,* 1971; *Satyanarayana,* 1971).

However, the system was criticised by many others. The Editor, *Educational India* (1971), while agreeing that fear of detentions was not good for education and for acquisition of knowledge, questioned wheather students, especially adolescents, would make genuine efforts to study, if they knew that whatever their progress—good or bad—it was not going to matter much for their promotion. According to him incentives should be there for learning. Without some compelling circumstances students would not care to keep up to date.

According to the Editor, *The Educational Review* (1971) the students belonging to the backward classes who were supposed to be most benefited by the 'testless schools' would indeed be deprived of the chance to improve themselves because they would not be regular in their school work, as there was no incentive for the same, and they would not be able to cope up with the task of studying hard and assimilating knowledge all of a sudden at the VII class or X class level. The net result would be instead of detaining them in different classes, the 'judgement day' was only postponed and there would be large scale detentions in the VII and X classes (*Vankata Rao,* 1971).

It was also felt that as a side effect discipline would be seriously affected in the schools (Editorial, the *Educational Review,* 1971; *through different states,* 1971). *Bullayya* (1977) also opined that this system would not be successful with the understaffed schools and insincere teachers.

Apart from these 'opinions' expressed by different educationists about the non-detention system very few empirical studies have been conducted on its merits and demerits especially in India. A few studies conducted in the USA by *Keye* (1911), *Klene* and *Branson* (1929), *Arthur* 1936), *Coffield* and *Bloomers* (1956), *Kowitz and Armstrong* (1961); *Gaite* (1969); and *Otto and Melby* (n.d.) found that students who were promoted did well in tests compared to those who were not promoted. Studies by *McCullers* (1978), *Gayen* and *Lyle* (1971), *Glucksberg* (1962) and *Dornbush* (1965) have shown that rewards facilitate performance.

In a study conducted in 11 schools, *Venkata Rami Reddy* and *Bhaskara Naidu* (1981) observed that the achievement of students reduced significantly in the non-detention system in all subjects except mathematics. This was true irrespective of the locality, sex or social class of the students.

There is no gainsaying that no system should be just overthrown labelling it as useless without making honest efforts to evaluate it. In fact, every human activity requires to be evaluated over a period of time, to provide for introspection growth and direction. It is more pertinent to education and to its innovative reforms especially in the field of examinations as they form an essential element of any structure of education.

The non-detention system was introduced in Andhra Pradesh in the year 1971-72., It is high time that a systematic study of the effect of the system in all aspects like achievement, rate of dropouts, etc., is made, so that the system may be introduced in other states also if the results are in the desired direction. It will be worthwhile for Andhra Pradesh also to know where it stands, whether the scheme is working on right lines yielding the desire results, or whether drastic modifications are required and if so in what direction.

The present study was therefore, designed to make a comparative study of the achievement of students under the detention and non-detention systems. Further it was, opined that the new system would reduce the rate of dropouts. Thus the study intends to compare the rate of dropouts also under the detention and the non-detention systems. As mentioned earlier, it was opined by the advocates of this system that the new system would allow teachers ample time to try new methods of teaching, and that students learn better in this system, in a natural setting, free from fear of detentions, etc. It was contended by others that students lose interest in studies and that indiscipline will increase. How do the teachers, students and administrators react to this system? Do they have a positive or negative attitude towards it? Students are the undergoers of the system. Teachers are its implementors, while administrators are the supervisors of its proper implementation. As such, an analysis of their attitude towards the system, may go a long way to improve its functioning. Hence, the study aims to probe into this aspect also.

2

Review of Related Literature

History of Achievement Testing

Evaluation is an integral part of teaching-learning process. Hence, the some kind of evaluation is inevitable in any education system. Thus the history of achievement testing can be traced back to antiquity. However, it is only in the present century that testing methods themselves have been subjected to systematic and critical analysis using scientific methods. Modern achievement testing is generally considered to have begun with the publication of J.M. Rice's study of achievement in spelling in 1897 (*Scates,* 1947). This does not mean, however, that there had been no systematic evaluation of learning prior to that time. The most dramatic use of formal testing in the service of the society is the 300 years history of civil service examination in imperial China (*Du Bois,* 1965).

Examinations in one form or another were known to people ever since the days of early civilization. Crassey, an eminent sociologist, attributes the remarkable stability of the old Chinese civilization, among other things, to her highly organised examinations system (*Mookerji,* 1951).

Examinations in India

Examinations have a long history in our country also. In the traditionally rich ancient India, to mark the end of formal education for any individual 'samavartana' ceremony was performed which included a final rigorous evaluation of his accomplishments. The unique method of assessment in those days was oral-aural. The stress was on correct pronunciations of vedas and other sacred texts. The examinee who mispronounced one word from the sacred texts was 'Aikanyika' or 'pupil of one error'. Similar epithets which were based on the number of mistakes made by the pupils were used. These epithets were so common during that period that they attracted the attention of Panini (*Mookerji,* 1951). A mention of practical examination was made for the first time in the Buddhist educational system.

Taxila and Nalanda were two major centres of learning in India. In these two universities a sound system of assessment was developed by the famous teachers who worked there. The University of Nalanda had an entrance test, which was considered to be of a very high standard. Hieun Tsang observed that only 20 per cent of the applicants could seek admission to the above university by passing its entrance text. The University of Taxila, the most renowned seat of medical education in the country attracted students from various parts of the world. At the end of a seven-year course of medical studies, a practical examiantion was held as a test of the students' knowledge of medical plants, their properties and uses (*Mookerji,* 1951).

With the advent of the British on the Indian scene, the older type of educational institutions in India were replaced by the British type of schools in the 19th century. Written examinations became the main tool of educational assessment as against oral tests or viva-voce that was prevalent in the earlier period, because it could be used on a larger number of students at the same time. The modern type of examination came into the educational scene in our country after the establishment of the three universities at Calcutta, Bombay and Madras as per the recommendations of the Wood's Despatch of 1854 (*Krishnamoorthy,* 1977).

The Necessity of Examinations

Every human activity requires to be evaluated over a period of time to provide for introspection, growth and direction. It is all the more pertinent in educational arena. Evaluation is as important as instruction in the process of education. It forms an essential element of any structure of education. However, the methods of evaluation may change from time to time to suit the objectives of the educational philosophy of the society (*Venka Reddy,* 1977).

In ancient times, pupils used to go to the gurus (Rishis) and studied what they were taught. They were tested amongst scholars. They had to answer what they were asked, and if they failed in doing so, they were not allowed to leave the ashram. Thus perfection was brought about, and education was fruitful (*Mookerji,* 1951).

Examinations serve mainfold purposes, directly or indirectly. They are used to test the achievement of pupils, the efficiency of teaching and to evaluate the whole school system. They are used for helping parents and the employers to know the calibre of their wards or applicants. They are also used for deciding the eligibility of students for different courses of higher studies in colleges and universities. They help us to know the helpful and regressive factors in education. They also help in marking a definite stage of education where a student who cannot or does not wish to pursue further studies, enters into a vocation or seeks self-employment. It is obvious examinations are extremely important in the entire educational system (*Kochhar,* 1982). Further, the quality of a school is also judged by the number of pupils of that school who have successfully passed or distinguished themselves in examinations (*Trivedi,* 1968).

According to *Krishna Moorthy* (1971) examinations play a vital role as an important organ of the educational system permitting the educational authorities, society, the parents, the teachers and the students to know about the work of the school and the progress of the students. The work of the educational institutions, the worth of the teachers and the progress of the students are being assessed with the help of the results of the examinations.

According to him examinations are important because:

1. they enable the teachers to know the level of progress of their students for improving their teaching;
2. they permit the students to realise their weakness in order to overcome them and to improve their learning;
3. they give scope to the educational administrators to assess the work of the schools and the teachers; and
4. they enable the public to know how advantageously the public funds are utilized on education.

Considering the contributions of examinations to the life of the nation, it is interesting to note that great reformers, politicians, statesmen, philosophers, educationists, scientists and literary saints of our nation are the product of our examination system (*Krishna Moorthy,* 1971).

Hill (1972) defined evaluation as the process by which we form judgements about the value of the educational status or achievement of students. To form such judgements, we most determine what their level of achievement is—which requires some kind of measurement. And we must decide to what extent we find that level satisfactory—which means placing a value upon it. To judge the value of any educational achievement, we must relate it to the goals and objectives of education. Evaluation requires, then that we have a clear concept of the goals we wish to reach by means of instruction and that we have ways of measuring the extent to which these goals are realised in our students.

Since any meaningful objective of education implies some change in the characteristics or competencies of students it is to the students that we must look for evidence of its achievement. And in order to find such evidence, we must in the first instance, know what we are looking for. We must determine what characteristics we should expect to find in the students. Having thus formulated our goals in concrete terms, we can plan learning experiences which seem likely to lead to development of these characteristics; and we can devise means of assessing that extent to which they have been developed (*Hill,* 1972).

The key to effective teaching and learning lies in their planning in relation to clearly conceived goals—goals conceived in terms not of what the teacher does, but what the student becomes. A sound programme of evaluation is an important aid to this kind of planning, for it forces us to focus our attention on the meaning of the goals. Both the instructors and the students need to know, how well the goals of instruction are being achieved. This knowledge helps the instructor to do his job better. When he tests his students periodically, he finds out what they are learning well and what they are failing to learn. This gives direction to his teaching, enabling him to emphasise the topics and teh objectives which are shown to need more emphasis. This kind of knowledge is needed by students also. It enables them to see the progress they are making, and thus gives them a sense of purpose in their learning (*Hill,* 1972).

Achievement tests can also be used according to *Hill* (1972) for grading students, in reviewing a unit of study and for diagnosing specific strength and weaknesses of students' learning. Tests of various kinds may be used at the beginning and at the end of the term or year to measure the progress made by students during that period.

According to *Dressel* (1976) evaluation involves judging the worth of an experience, idea, or process. Education is a complex process involving the selection of ideas (concepts, values, skills) and planning of experiences designed to foster mastery of these ideas in the people subjected to the educational process. Choices must be made in planning and educational programme and the effectiveness of the programme must also be studied. Evaluation is therefore, inevitable in education.

'Evaluation', according to Wriststone, 'is a relatively new technical term, introduced to designate a more comprehensive concept of measurement then is implied in conventional tests and examinations'. Monroe has distinguished between measurement and evaluation by indicating that the emphasis in measurement is upon a single aspect of the subject matter, achievements of specific skills and abilities, but the emphasis in evaluation is upon the broad personality changes and major achievements of an educational programme. These include not only subject matter achievements, but also attitudes, interests, ideals, way of thinking, work habits and personal and social adaptabilities (*Sharma*, 1983).

According to *Knowles* (1971), educational evaluation is the process of determining the value of an activity, object or problem. The process of evaluation is continuous and inevitable.

According to the *National Education Policy* (1986), the examination system has to ensure a method of assessment that is valid and reliable measure of student development and it should be a powerful instrument for improving teaching and learning.

Writing on reforms in examinations *Kannababu* (1970) observed that evaluation is an effective scheme of examination reform, improvement of instruction and curriculum. It is not simply a process of testing and estimating attainments, but it is a process which leads directly to the improvement of instruction. Replacing the essay type by the objective and more comprehensive method is not all that is meant by examiantion reform. There should be more examinations. All aspects of the child's mind or personality must be measured. But it is not possible to measure the all round growth of the pupils by objective tests. Many important traits of personality cannot be easily assessed by ordinary tools of measurement; subjective techniques are also needed at times in measuring the all round growth of pupils.

Stressing the need for continuous comprehensive evaluation the Editor, *Journal of Education and Psychology* (1988) criticised the present day examination system as it does not fully evaluate all the objectives concerned with academic achievement and totally ignore the evolution of non-academic achievement. It is in this context that comprehensive evaluation covering different aspects of pupils personality has been conceived.

Barnette (1957) has reported that students who entered college with advanced standing based on performance on achievement tests have generally had better records in college than students admitted under regular procedure. There appears to be a general agreement that achievement tests serve a number of purposes. Historically, they have been recognised as motivators of students and as one basis for assigning grades. Their uses in providing teachers with feedback regarding the effects of instructional procedures has also been recognised. Their use in certification and in selection has also been well established.

According to *Venkata Rami Reddy* (1977), that some sort of examination or other is an essential aspect of any educational system, is an undisputed fact because teaching, learning and evaluation should go hand in hand, each contributing to the other in any sound system of education. But the controversy is about which of several types of emanation systems we should have.

According to the *Editor, Educational India* (1978) measurement of educational standards and abilities is important for the pupils to know the pace of their progress, for the teachers to determine the capacity of the pupils to grasp and their own ability to impart the knowledge for the authorities to find out the value and relevance of the curriculum, and for the employer for selecting 'round pegs' for round holes and 'square pegs' for square holes. Therefore educationists all over the world have applied themselves to the task of evolving testing techniques which may give a reliable assessment.

Defects in the Present day Examinations

Despite their long history and large contribution to the development of individual and national life, they have been and are being subjected to serious and severe criticism by one and all. It has been remarked that the defects of the examinations out weigh the good effects. Subjectivity and unreliability of evaluation procedures in the existing system of examinations have remained a point of severe criticism and comment (*Starch* and *Elliot,* 1913; *Starch,* 1913; *Ruch,* 1924; *Burt,* 1949; *Balard,* 1949; *Salamatullah,* 1958; *Charwood,* 1959).

M.C. Chagla, the then Union Minister of Education, addressing a conference at New Delhi said that 'he was naturally, temperamentally and constitutionally averse to examinations, which in his view, did not test the ability or capacity of students'.

The charge was made that examinations tested only the knowledge of the candidates in certain subjects, but failed to take into account the entire personality of the candidate. This is no doubt true. But the present day examinations are not intended to vouch for the personality or character of the candidates. They deal only with their intellectual equipment and training. Evaluation on this basis is needed for many purposes. Other aspects of the examinees personality can be judged by the persons who need to judge them according to the Editor, *The Educational Review* (1970).

The process of measurement in education cannot be rated very high in reliability, especially when abilities of different individuals have to be compared, because there is a subjective element involved (*The Editor, Educational India,* 1978).

Examinations cannot be abolished. They must be mended to suit the needs of our times. But they have now been institutionalised to such and extent that they have become a Frankenstein's Monster ready to eat its own creator (*Singha,* 1984). *Mehta* in his foreword to Empirical studies in examination research (1961) remarked 'If there is any one thing which has so completely dominated our educational process, it is the examination system. The whole process of education is geared round examinations and it looks as if the object of learning is to satisfy the test of examination. There can be no improvement in our education structure, unless something is done to get rid of this straglehold of examinations'. Obviously the individual child can hardly be adequately evaluated under the existing pattern of education and examination for the integrated growth of his personality (*Sharma,* 1985). Ryburn strongly criticises them and says 'It goes without saying that examinations are the enemies of creative work, at least as they are usually conducted' (*Kannababu,* 1970).

Raghuram Singh (1971) listed the following defects of the traditional system:

1. The real goals of teaching and learning a subject are ignored by the teachers and students;
2. Acquisition of knowledge, memorization and reproduction in the examination are the chief purposes of present day education;
3. Examinations are found to be lacking in adequacy, validity and reliability as educational tools;
4. Teachers are unable to identify the strength and weakness of their teaching from the way pupil performance is reported at present;
5. Pass or attainment of high marks at the public examination is the only goal which a majority of students attempt to reach:
6. Educational institutions are assessed by the percentage of passes at public examinations.

According to *Wango* (1972) an examinee gaining high score in the present type of examinations is not decidedly a bright student and the one gaining a low score in the same examinations is not wholly a dull student. Present day examinations are nothing but 'tricks of the trade' meant to throw dust in the eyes of examiners and to test one's memorisation of facts and figures without actual understanding of the same. The examinations fail to assess the personalities of the examinees.

According *Dandekar* and *Vidya* (1972) examinations exercise an unwholesome and unhealthy influence on our education at all levels so much so if any school activity is not related to examinations, it miserably fails to interest the teacher no less than the pupils.

The drawbacks of the examination system were listed as follows by the *Editor, Educational India* (1977):

1. More subjectivity in awarding marks and great variation from examiner to examiner;
2. Chance played a more important part to determine the success or failure of a candidate;
3. It did not test the important abilities of the pupils and encouraged cramming;
4. The questions were mostly stereotyped and repetitive;
5. Questions were often too easy or too stiff;
6. No weightage was given to internal assessment;
7. The coverage of syllabus was not adequate;
8. Question papers were set by paper-setters who had no experience of teaching higher secondary classes thus ignoring the level of competence of the students;
9. It encouraged selective studies;

10. The time allotted to the chief examiner was inadequate and the number of answer books allotted to examiners was sometimes more than they could examine during the time allotted for the purpose, which contributed for irrational valuation.

Weakness in the school administration i.e., ineffective guidance, supervision and administration of schools had been unanimously rated as contributing to the incidence of failure. It was also noted that good teachers professionally well qualified, were not available in large numbers (*Editorial, Educational India,* 1977).

According to *Srivastava* (1979), examinations were instituted for realising the purposes of valid and reliable evaluation and of acting as instruments for improving teaching and learning. But the traditional education strategies have only concentrated on the former of these at the cost of the latter.

The history of eduction in ancient India and elsewhere shows that debates, discussions and oral tests were the major tools of assessment in the olden days. But with the advent of the British on the Indian scene, written examination and terminal system of testing came into vogue. The defects of this types of examinations are too many. The various committees appointed to go into the problems of education in general or examinations in particular have been unequivocal in their wrath against the system of one examination at the end of the year where, in just three hours, what has been learnt in over 300 days is tested and the candidates' fate is sealed (*Venkata Rami Reddy,* 1978a).

Research at the university of Essex revealed that students says: 'you despite yourself for waning to do well in examinations; it's a conflict inside yourselves', or 'writing 4 questions in a 3 hours examination paper is a total contradiction of what you have been training yourself to do throughout the year' or 'the more cold blooded you can become the better; you have got to make yourself like a machine', or

'I don't think without distorting my personality and recognition I could get a 2 (1) in this place. I could have to conform to the right model', or 'It is a great mistake to be over sophisticated in excesses it's part of the technique not to be; one has to limit oneself'.

These may be rather exaggerated reactions but they draw attention to the life stage of students where control, independence and autonomy are crucial and influence the development of personal and professional identity. Assessment, the dominating instrument of control in higher education, gets band up with this struggle for independence. Conformist students may lose in this battle and become passive learners whose view of education is dominated by memorising. Other students become rebellious and find their energies are dissipated in hostility or apathy and withdrawal. Only the more motive and independent students cope with the system and maintain a sense of integrity (*Cox,* 1975).

Venkata Rami Reddy (1977) observed that the present system of examination at the end of the year or at the end of the course is very much criticised for its many lapse. To put it in one word, it had reduced teaching to mere coverage of a given syllabus; and learning to a part-time activity where the student tends to postpone sincere study until the end of the course and crams desperately with little understanding at the eleventh hour, burning the mid-night oil, as the spectre of examination hovers over his head. The teaching learning process has, therefore, become a drab, mechanical and meaningless activity and education has been reduced to mere passing of examinations where chance, luck and many other factors play no mean role in getting marks and also in the occurrence of questions.

There is today a veritable crisis in public examinations. They were never so much called in question. Their contradiction were never so glaring. The result is that the public has lost faith in the present system of examinations. Students and teachers feel that they can be manipulated and misused. There is no denying the fact that malpractices in examinations are too rampant. They seem to defy any solution (*Singha,* 1984).

Singha conducted a survey of the unfair means used in university examination in 1974. He found that nearly 10 per cent of the students taking under-graduate examinations were reported to use unfair means. The NCERT established similar statistics for school board examinations. In addition to this there is faking of degrees, certificates and marks sheets, large scale leakage of papers, mass copying, etc. The system seems to be breaking down under its own weight. The system has become disfunctional and is doing more harm than good in socio-academic areas.

In his editorial entitled 'Examination Politics' the Editor, *The Educational Review* (1970) made some interesting observations. He pointed out that with the intrusion of politics into education, the teaching profession, the experts and also the administrators lost control. Those who seek to change policies now do so, for the most part, with a view to exploit education for vote catching. Side lights on the reactions of politics to educational problems are finished in the brief press report of the proceedings of a meeting of the consultative committee of the members of parliament for the Ministry of Education and Youth services.

Various committees and commissions appointed by the Government of India for evaluating the Indian examination system, have bitterly denounced the monarchical control and undifferentiated regimentation of examinations as the sole means of evaluation (*Report of the Bhopal Seminar on Examination,* 1956; *Report of the Committee on Indian Examination Reform Project,* 1958; *Examination in Higher Indian Education, Charwood, et al.,* 1959; *Report of the University Education Commission,* 1948; *Report of the Secondary Education Commission,* 1954; *Report of the Education Commission,* 1966).

The report of the *Secondary Education Commission* (1954) says that 'the examinations do not help us in evaluating the real intellectual achievements of the pupils'. The commission also observed that examinations have succeeded in reducing the whole process of education into mechanical routine of imparting and memorising facts.

Bloom (1961) remarked that the examinations, as they are today, have reduced learning to a part time activity, teaching to the coverage of syllabus and education to a relatively drab and meaningless activity. Taking examinations is viewed as a dreaded experience with great anxiety and emotional tension being developed by a majority of students. Luck and chance are regarded as powerful factors in determining the questions asked, the marks received. In the same vein *Prof. Narul Hasan* (1975), the then Union Minister of Education, pointed out in the Lok Sabha that the examination system in India has virtually collapsed and there is no use of trying to resurrect it even if we so desired. He added that the tension it creates on the nerves of the students is good enough justification for bringing about changes in the examination system.

The following drawbacks of the system of judging the students only by the final examination have been observed by *Chacho* (1964):

1. Due to some mishap or accident one may spoil the paper and thereby he will be doomed in his educational career.
2. The final testing is not the real index of the true quality or merit of the student. At present the method of instruction is aiming only at the final examination. This leads to many unhealthy trends.

Subbaiah Naidu (1964) listed a series of defects of the present day examinations. He observed that so far as students are concerned they feel that its is enough if they pass the final examination and that they must pass the examination somehow or other. Thus the present system of education has adversely affected their method of study and their attitude to education. It is common knowledge that most of the students just attend the college only for the sake of attendance. It is true that colleges conduct periodical tests, terminal examinations etc., to gauge the progress of students, to advise them accordingly and to instill in them the habit of regularity in studies. But knowing that the performance in the class tests, etc., is not going to be considered and that only their performance in the final examination is that which really counts most of the students, no wonder, are indifferent to the class tests. They even do not hesitate to absent themselves from these tests without any valid reason. They begin there studies about a month or two before the final examination.

It is natural that having begun their studies at the eleventh hour, they find no time for reading through the prescribed test books. They run after any cheap notes, wrongly called guides. The guides indeed do not guide but only misguide. The students have no time for understanding. They can not study the whole subject; and so merely cram some topics which they select and try to reproduce in the examinations. Several types of malpractices adopted by students during the examination are the direct result of their having neglected their studies during the greater part of the year and their anxiety to somehow pass the examinations (*Subbaiah Naidu,* 1964).

It is reported by him that teaches are being taken to task for the results in examinations in certain places. It is true that a teacher must teach and one direct result of good teaching may be large number of students passing an examination. But it is not fair to punish a teacher for poor results specially because he has practically no say in the matter of selecting his pupils, apart from the most important fact that the system of examination, as it is, is highly defective. If this tendency to punish teachers for poor results grows, it may result in teachers themselves resorting to malpractices to make their students pass their examinations, so that they may retain their jobs.

It is agreed by one and all that examinations cannot be dispensed with altogether. But the type of examination should be such that it implants habits of mental discipline among that students and brings out their latent abilities so that they grow to their full and natural stature (*Sabbaiah Naidu,* 1964).

According to *Kabra* (1971) our present educational set up is faulty and is affecting the society badly. Our whole education has become examination centred weekly, monthly, quarterly, half-yearly and annual—so many examinations are always there, keeping the heads of our youths occupied and encumbered, leaving little taste for free, independent and creative thinking. *Partha Sarathy* (1980) also expressed a similar opinion about too many examinations.

The Vice-Chancellor of Gandhigram Rural Institute in his introductory speech at a two day workshop on 'New concepts in teaching and evaluation at the University level' (1988) highlighted the problems of students related to examinations like judging the abilities of students in a 3 hour examination, ever soaring examination fees, only 50 per cent to 60 per cent passes, etc., and pleaded for examination reforms with checks and balances.

According to *Sudha Rao* (1987) it is right to allege that one shot evaluation at the end of school year aiming at passing judgements on the performance of pupils and placing them under different categories like pass, fail, first division, etc., cannot be viewed as an integral part of the total teaching learning process.

According to the *Editor, Journal of Education and Psychology* (1988), the major drawback of the present day examination is that it doesnot fully evaluate the objectives concerned with the academic achievement and totally ignores the evaluation of the non-academic achievement.

The most dreadful of the examinations are the Board and the University examinations. These are a fever in themselves and a disease. Yet they are given the top importance. The student's future life, his success, profession and his whole destiny depends on this. A little derailment may cause havocks. All ambitions and aims are broken and all cherished dreams shattered within one stroke and the boy who was to become and engineer becomes an overseer or a teacher and the one aspring to become a doctor has to be content with a compounder's job, howsoever, better personality traits he might otherwise be possessing. The marks obtained at the external examinations are destiny makers so far as seeking of professions, admissions and scholarships are concerned (*Kabra,* 1971).

Khan (1971) contends that the examination system, as it is prevalent in India, has proved to be useless and it has been reduced to a mere farce. It does not help any more to know the merit of a student. It only helps the students to get some scraps of papers named degrees. From all parts of the country there have been reports regarding increasing malpractices in the examinations day by day. Sometime back it was reported that the students even demanded back it was reported that the students even demanded copying to be their birth right. This state of affairs now demands an immediate change in the system of examination.

The various defects and their remedies and the facts that lead or prove to abate the cause of evils in the examinations system are dealt with by *Khan* (1971). According to him, in the first instance, the present system is neither helping a student to earn his daily bread, nor helping him to acquire true knowledge. This system was evolved long back. With the erosion of standards, the same system now proves a failure. This erosion or lowering of standard has creeped in stealthily into our education because of the lenient formulas adopted by the universities and educational institutions to pass the students to higher class. Today even a graduate does not have the standard equal to a matriculate of 1940. As a result of this low standard the students fail to cope with the courses of studies and at the end of the year they resort to all sorts of malpractices in the examinations.

Secondly, cheap guides and key books in all spheres have reduced the education to a mere flop. They are available in such abundance and variety that the students care less for the teachers' teaching in the classroom whatever may be the standard of teaching. They come to the college only for attendance sake. These guide books also make it easier for students to copy in the examination hall by giving questions and answers in an elaborate manner. This has facilitated a student not to read for the whole year and at the time of examination, he just skips over the guide books to remember the page numbers of different answers. Some examinees do not know even this and they are supplied with copies from outside the examination hall. Khan described an incident when he came across a student in the examination hall with a big volume of condensed guide books and being asked why he had brought such a big book into the hall, he replied that the index of that volume was exhaustive and one could easily sort out the answers. From this it can be easily ascertained the utility of the present examination system. For this our half educated, money minded but experienced (as they put it) professors are mainly to be blamed. It is they who prepare these guide books, only to misguide the young students. Therefore, it is high time that these cheap, easy guide books should be kept out of publication.

Thirdly, copying has become so easy now-a-days that many students do not waste their time on such useless (?) pursuits like reading, but spend their time in visiting movies and taking part in cheap college romances. Blind copying of western civilization and unclean cults is also taking away much of their valuable time. Further, to detect or prevent them from copying in the examination hall, the invigilators are afraid and petrified, because they know the consequences of this vicious circle. They know they would unnecessarily be man handled and even the police and judiciary forces at times do not come to their rescue.

Forthly, according to Khan the mode of examination is to be blamed. In this country, we depend solely on one type of examination. In the examination, out of the whole syllabus, 10 questions are asked and if a student can answer 5 of them correctly it is assumed that he knows 50 per cent of the facts taught to know the merit of a student. Therefore, a mixture of both internal and external examination should be followed to gauge both the written and spoken capability of a student. According to Khan, 50 per cent of the marks should be with the internal teacher who would watch, judge and gauge the standard of a student both in the classrooms by way of oral and written question answers and outside the classroom to know his behaviour to give marks and the rest 50 per cent would be written examination, where essay type questions should be replaced by objective and witty questions. The number of questions should be so many that a student would not get time to search their answer in the examination hall. The pass marks should not be 30 per cent but should be increased to 50 per cent both in the internal and external examinations and 70 per cent would be a distinction.

Khan further observed that the time was ripe and unless immediate attention was given to this long standing problem by our educationists to eradicate these evils of examination system, the future generations would only be reduced to more dullards and parasites of this society and country.

Kuruvilla Jocob (1964) observed that though the system of examinations is an important part of educational process, examinations and evaluation techniques, which should be only tools in the hands of teachers, had during these days become the masters of education process that led to the present confusion. Commenting about the system of marking he contended that the minimum of 35 per cent for pass is another thing to be considered. Too low a minimum, according to him, had a very bad effect.

According to the *Editor, Educational India* (1977) examinations are an integral part of the educational system. However, to many a student education has become to more than passing an examination as a crowning glory. Examinations meant many sleepless nights to millions of youth whose number was swelling with the passage of time. It was no less disturbing to thousands of teachers whose efficiency was judged by the man in the street, was well as authorities, by the yard stick of the percentage of passes. The examination tested only the scholastic attainments of the examinees leaving aside the more important aspects.

In the same vein *Sarabachari* (1971) observed that a study of the institution and growth of the examination system in our schools will reveal several heinous and abnoxious bye-effects on our children, besides customary failures. As P.C. Wren has put it: 'From small beginnings the examination has grown and grown until it has overshadowed all education in this country' and 'as soon as the examination becomes the great end, cramming becomes the Royal Road'.

Sarabhachari opined that now his warning came true. What are the teachers and pupils doing in schools? Practically most of the work that teachers do, (and it is not quite their fault alone), is coaching the pupils for some year-end big event of either an annual examination of their own, or public examination of the government. Education in the institutions is assessed by the yard stick of percentage of passes. It is saddening to note that some managements and some educationists have begun to applaud the heads of institutions who secured high percentage of passes under the present type of public examinations. So much so the entire teaching body is bent towards mounting up their results higher and higher by (1) careful weeding out the undesirables in the lower classes (2) calculated selection of probable questions in the subjects (3) dictation of full answers to the expected questions (4) getting answers or passages memorised from guide books (5) and insisting on repeated correct reproduction of these answers. The slip tests instituted by the department are termed as mini examinations to train them in writing answers got by rote, in an instalmental basis, for the final show. Thus the whole machinery in the school is practically geared up to meet the big event at the year end. The pupils, in this frenzied drive of memorization of set answers, quite often understand very little of what they are doing. For the pupils, the guide book has become the supreme Goddess before whom the teacher and the institution pale into insignificance. Pupils have become mere horses that are doped and trained to win the final race. Their luck is cast in the balance in March or April of every year and schools have been virtually reduced to coaching institutions. Sarabachari epitomized this situation in his book 'Toward brighter schools' as follows:

> "Mug up mug up is your 'mantra',
>
> To cram the notes is their 'Tantra',
>
> The entire school is one big 'yantra' of malpractice.."

According to *Singha* (1984), public examinations have become irrelevant in modern society. Padagogically, the present system is based on misconceived assumptions which have led students and teachers to have an inverted perspective about academic work. In this perspective examination results and grades have become the chief reform of institutionalised value. The result is that learning has become misdirected, teaching is unprincipled and curriculum is eroded. It is a total inversion of pedagogy.

Examinations have become counter productive in the field of learning as they provide disincentives rather than incentives for it. 'What is the use of working hard'? is a common question asked from principals. The teacher's attention is being diverted away from the real objectives which are important for an all-round development of children. It even curbs the teacher's initiative or originality. As far as the curriculum is concerned, the present system becomes self eroding. The instructional objectives that are initially laid down can not be pursued because of the system. They have become tools for trivializing, de-individualising, de-personalizing and even de-humanizing man. Their real bane, therefore, is the enslavement of man (*Singha*, 1984).

There can be no doubt according to *Hill* (1972) that methods of teaching and learning are very much influenced by examination. The criticisms of the traditional system of examinations of which there have been so many are based largely on the belief that examinations have a 'baneful effect' on education. It is natural that both students and teachers are interested in that kind of instruction, and those habits of study, which help students perform well on examinations. It can readily be pointed out that much of the work in schools in devoted to memorisation of information. Students are not interested in learning to understand the facts and principles of the subjects they study, to apply their knowledge to significant problems or to think, or reason.

A related complaint is that students do not devote themselves to sustained study throughout the school year, but prefer to concentrate on craming in the last few weeks before the examinations. Another criticism is that students do not study, and many teachers do not teach the entire content of their courses. Selective study is common. Mastery of limited portion of the syllabus is considered more important than comprehensive coverage. Again the reason can be found in the nature of examinations. The questions do not cover the whole syllabus. The portions which they do cover are often the same from year to year, and so they can be predicated by teachers and students. The opportunities given to the students to choose the questions make it possible for them to get full marks by preparing for questions on one fourth to one third of the topics in the syllabus (*Hill,* 1972).

Gayan, et al., (1961-70) found the reliability and validity of most of the present examination systems to be very low and this was so because the performance of students was assessed in a single final examination, by a large number of examiners, on a set of questions mostly of the essay type and comparatively small in number from which, again, students were given option to select alternatives.

Harpar (1970) in his experiment on ninety marking ten took ten history answer-books in which the candidates had answered the same five (out of ten) questions. It was found that the marks given by the examiners for these ten answer-books ranged from 2 to 38 out of 50, while for the four it was only 10. pass percentage was 50, while for the four it was only 10. The average marks for the ten answer books as given by the different examiners ranged from 8.8 to 27. It was found that inter examiner reliability was very low.

Tayler (1963) made an extreme comment that an examiner's marks had neither the sanctity nor the precision which was usually attached to them. Different examiners showed a large variation in the mean and standard deviation of their evaluation. *Tayler* (1964) in his study, an examination of examiners, emphasised the same point of low inter-examiner reliability. *Gunasekaran* and *Jayanthi* (1980) conducted a study of the revaluation cases. It was found that about 25 per cent of the applicants benefited as a result of revaluation. On the aspects of multiple examiners, *Tluange* (1974) suggested that there was no justification for referring the scripts to a third examiner on the ground that the first two examiners gave divergent marks.

In a study related to the university examination system *Chauhan* (1967) found that of the students who failed, a large proportion failed not because of not knowing the subject matter but because of some external factors like defective question papers, carelessness of examiners in evaluating answer books and evaluation by incapable examiners.

Malhotra (1972), while studying the effectiveness of question papers of matriculation examinations, observed that the question papers had many defects with respect to difficulty level, coverage and weightage. *Lele, et al.,* (1962) found that only one-fifth of the total questions were good, whereas the rest were poor discriminators. *Rao* (1968) found that in many cases question papers were not properly balanced as far as the difficulty value of the items was concerned. They failed to discriminate pupils of high and low ability. In a similar context, *Bhola* (1978) also found that question papers were not well balanced in respect of attributes of discriminative power, difficulty level, reliability and validity of the question items. He further found that alternative question papers set for the morning and evening sessions were not analogous and of same standard. Further note, *Lele, et al.*, (1963) found that in essay type examinations teachers and students did not agree as regards the difficulty level of the questions and the selection of questions on the part of students varied with their nature.

Sali (1978) conducted a survey to analyse student's achievement in each constituent question of mathematics in secondary school leaving examination. He found in his study that out of 45 sub-items in nine questions, three sub-items were responded to by more than 80 per cent candidates. 14 sub-items were answered by only 20 per cent candidates and the remaining 28 sub-items were attempted by 80 per cent candidates.

EXAMINATION REFORM

Need for Reform

The modern philosophy of education aims at bringing to light the many hidden talents of the students and a full play of his intellectual faculties. It lays more emphasis on the full development of his emotional and social life and for the complete building up of his personality. This change in the technique of education should necessarily bring change in the system of examination. New methods should be adopted for assessing the work, progress and development of the students at every stage instead of the old system of examining the student only once at the end of the course (*Chacho,* 1964).

Referring to the urgent need for reform in the examination system, the Union Minister of Education observed that it was necessary to stimulate the students to a proper study of their subjects, to remove the fear of examination from their minds, and at the same time to have some sort of evaluation (*The Editor, The Educational Review,* 1970).

Sincere parents and serious educationists do not favour abolition of examinations altogether, but they strongly plead for their reform. Hence, the reform of examinations has become the key note of the educational policy of the centre and state governments in our country (*Krishna Moorthy,* 1971).

The University Grants Commission appointed a committee in 1958 to make a thorough study of the problems involved in the task of examination reform and to propose remedial measures. Dr. Benjamin Bloom of the University of Chicago was invited by the Ministry of Education to direct several workshop on evaluation. His services were utilised by the UGC to organise workshops or seminars at Osmania, Poona, Patna and Aligarh Universities. His report revealed how the specific objectives of teaching would be formulated and how test materials could be prepared to assess the extent to which the objectives were fulfilled. Dr. Bloom located the high rate of failure in the examination in (1) the selection or admission procedures (2) the types of learning experiences provided and (3) the types of examinations used to determine success or failure.

He further said that examination reform is really a complex one involving the whole of the teaching-learning process and would be largely solved if we could somehow improve the quality and methods of teaching and the responses and learning habits of students. According to him examinations do much to control the behaviour, thoughts and attitudes of students and teachers alike. But no living individual group has control over the examinations which are only a body of traditions and practices which have accumulated over the years. The syllabus usually contains a detailed list of topics. This shows that education is equated with the acquisition of some detailed information on each topic, which has naturally become the major purpose of instruction for the teachers, the major objectives emphasised by the examiner, and consequently, cramming of such information has become the major task undertaken by the student. A comparison of the question papers over several years reveals a highly stereotyped character in the questions set. Originality in setting questions is not valued. The necessary material for setting the papers are the syllabus and the old question papers, the same tools as the student uses in his preparation for the examination. The teachers, since their efficiency is judged by the percentage of passes, are motivated to dictate notes on the probable questions which can easily be reproduced in the examination hall (*Editorial, Educational India,* 1977).

There is no doubt about deep rooted defects in the present system of examination, but the important question to answer is what do the examinations seek to do? Do they achieve what they set out to achieve? If so, they may be retained. If not, they are to be modified to achieve the end. The inevitable imperfections of a system do not by themselves justify its abolition. But they certainly point to the necessity of thinking about other alternatives (*Gopal Krishna Moorthy,* 1964). The University Education Commission also held this view. In their report they said examinations rightly designed and intelligently used can be a useful factor in the educational process. Thus, if the examinations are necessary, a thorough reform of the examinations is still more necessary.

History of Reform

Examination reform has become a problem, a thorn in the bed for the educational administrators. Many attempts were made to reform the examination system in India, especially after 1948 in line with the University Education Commission's remark that reform in examination is of utmost importance in reconstructing Indian education.

Krishna Moorthy (1971) traced the history of examination reform in India as follows:

In 1958, the All India Council for Secondary Education (AICSE) made the first major attempt to reform examinations on a large scale by setting up the Central Examination Unit (CEU) for the purpose of reforming examinations at the secondary stage of education.

In 1961, with the establishment of the NCERT in New Delhi, the responsibility of reforming examinations was pushed on its shoulders, as the AICSE and CEU became a part of NCERT. The CEU was merged with the department of curriculum and evaluation.

At the state level, state evaluation units have been established in different states which have been entrusted with the task of reforming examinations. These SEU's came into existence during the first part of the last decade.

In Andhra Pradesh the state evaluation unit was established in 1964, with the establishment of State Council of Educational Research and Training (SCERT) in 1967, it became one of its chief departments.

Type of Reform

Commenting on the hapazard way of tinckering with examination system in different parts of the country, the Editor, *The Educational Review* (1975) observed, no doubt examination reform is being debated all over the world. But here the pressure for reform has come not from psychologists and educationists, but from students who want an easy pass without adequate preparation or study. Education without evaluation is no education at all. What is needed, therefore, is a concrete drive to change the psychology of the students, to make them more responsive to discipline, to inculcate in them habits of regular study and a sense of examination ethics; and to make them understand that examination cannot be sabotaged or downgraded without hurting their own interests.

The reform of examinations is not a simple task. If it is to be successful, all the concerned agencies should develop a favourable attitude towards examinations, according to *Krishna Moorthy* (1971). The students should be educated as to the desirability of educational measurement in their own interests. Parents should also consider examinations as a necessary phase of the educational career of their children. Administrators should see that examination phobia is not developed in the students by imposing too many restrictions and too much rigidity. The administration of examinations should take pace in a calm, peaceful and graceful environment where mutual trust pervades all through. It should be remembered that examinations are a means for the end of acquisition of knowledge—and that they are not an end in themselves.

A number of suggestions can be given to improve examinations according to *Wangoo* (1972). According to him, examinations cannot be abolished altogether but they need immediate reforms. They are useful provided their scope and utility is overhauled to suit our soil. In the first place an external examination at the end of the year or session should not be 'fate determining' factor. There should be frequent periodical examinations during an year or a session, to assess and properly modify the progress of the student in the course which he has undertaken. This may be done on monthly, quarterly, or six monthly basis depending upon many factors including the number of lectures successfully delivered by the concerned teacher and the amount of fruitful practical work done in the field or lab.

Secondly, semester system can gain popularity in our educational institutions, provided the scheme is well engineered. It is most useful in the post school period when students are comparatively matured and some specialisation has started.

In the schools monthly tests are a boon to serve as pointers for both the teacher and the taught to adjust their teaching-learning programme. Periodical examinations of the semester type, should not be wholly essay type or wholly objective type, so as to minimise the possibility of having a telescopic view of a topic, a portion or a chapter by examinees. Both types should be given their due share to assess the total performance of a class or group. Frequent examinations help to assess the progress of both the teacher and the taught.

Satyamma Srinath (1964) observed that measurement of knowledge and also evaluation of all-round development of the student should be given equal importance. Annual examination should be coupled with periodical short and objective tests. *Subbaiah Naidu* (1964) also suggested that internal assessment based on the students' performance in periodical tests must be introduced.

Internal assessment has certainly many advantages according to *Raghuram Singh* (1971). The are:

1. Internal assessment can attempt the overall appraisal of educational development of the pupils. It can cover academic and non-academic areas as well;

2. It gives a reliable picture of students' progress in the classroom from time to time;

3. It promotes regularity and punctuality in pupils' attendance and gives them a greater sense of purpose in their learning;

4. It enables teachers to improve their teaching techniques and mount remedial teaching wherever and whenever necessary;

5. It enables teachers to give periodic educational guidance and when necessary vocational guidance;

6. The chance element or element of luck associated with the traditional examination, is eliminated because assessment is spread over the full length of a course;

7. Internal assessment system develops valuable records or files of student work that may be useful for a prospective employer;

8. Internal assessment gives teachers who are incharge of courses the much needed satisfaction of 'decision making' on pupil's progress.

Hill (1972) also observed that many kinds of improvements can and should be made in examinations both internal and external. Tests, many of which may be short ones, should be used frequently in order that the instructor and the students may know how well they are doing.

Sukha Dev Singh (1985) stressed on the need to follow the 'evolutionary mode to change the conventional examination system into the internal evaluation system to avoid conflicts and subsequent pressures'. According to him the internal evaluation system is a process of telling a student what he lacks in his learning of a particular course. Since it guarantees absolute freedom to the students to 'cross examine' their teachers, by implication, it makes the teachers more responsible and more alert about the latest developments relevant to their subjects.

Sukha Dev Singh advocated a system of 'un-announced' scheduled of examinations also to keep the students all the time on their toes. This will also minimise the irregular attendance at the classes by the students. According to him, teacher's integrity of character was a prerequisite to the success of internal evaluation system.

It is argued that one examination cannot adequately assess a student's achievement of the objectives of education or his ability to pursue his education further. The certification of students, according to these arguments, should be based at least in part, upon periodic internal assessment of their work. Combination of the results of internal and external assessment was advocated by the three well known educational commissions headed by *Radhakrishnan* (1948), *Mudaliar* (1954) and *Kothari* (1966).

Satyamma Srinath (1964) compared the system in the U.S.A. with our system and observed that the system of examination in U.S.A. is quiet different from that of ours and it has some advantages. There are usually intensive courses of short duration. Evaluation is not done by a single final examination, but by 2 or 3 mid term tests and often a term paper and a final examination. Marks in all these make up the grade and not one final examination. Study of an intensified course over a short period and gaining a thorough knowledge in it is much better than a diversified study of many courses for a longer period. Assessment of a candidate's standard by the teacher himself (i.e.) one who has taught, will give a clear and exact position of the student, than if assessed by some other teacher.

According to her the abolition of final examination is not possible. It is necessary to evaluate in some way or other the student's progress and development resulting from the educational process which he has undergone. The right type of internal assessment would stimulate the students to develop better methods of study, habits of continuous work and the right attitude to learning. A method of combining the results of final examination with the internal assessment of the work of students based on a cumulative record maintained by teachers has been experimented and its is still continued in schools. However, this has not proved of much value as it requires a lot of integrity and sincerity among the teachers and students as well. Further, improvement of the examination system implies a parallel improvement in the process of teaching and learning.

In Soviet Higher educational institutions, examinations are held twice a year—in winter and summer. They are intended to reveal the level of student preparedness and their ability to deal with questions coming with in the scope of the studied material, and determine their ability to systematise their knowledge and to put into actual practice. As a rule, in winter the examinations and tests cover the matter studied in the first half of the academic year, and in summer the examinations are twice as hard—firstly, because the volume of material is much greater and secondly because summer is summer (*Ilyukhin* and *Tsimirinova,* 1971).

Now-a-days the concept of evaluation has changed in Russia also. The previous process of evaluation was the external examination, which was considered as a defective process, or a one way process. Evaluation should be continuous, comprehensive and is inseparable from the instructional programme. There is a no one better than the teacher himself to execute the programme of evaluation in an effective way, since he alone is in constant touch with the students. Education is a bipolar process. Since evaluation and instruction go hand in hand, there is little justification in passing judgements about the outcome of instruction on the basis of a single examination of doubtful validity and reliability (*Ilyukhin* and *Tsimirinova,* 1971).

According to *Jagadeesan* (1979) though the semester system has been conceived to fulfil some sound academic objectives, mis-givings about its efficiency has arisen particularly in respect of internal assessment. In the old system the day of judgement was a distant prospect and the preparation for the examination could wait till a month or so before the day of reckoning. Portions are accumulated to be examined at the end of two or three years. But in the new system, the teacher is engaged in a simultaneous job of teaching and judging. The students can pass their examinations in convenient instalments instead of carrying a heavy load over a period of two or three years. Limited portion facilitates intensive study. The system encourages student involvement in the learning process on their own, in addition to being at the listening end. It seeks to encourage the student in participation and independent search for knowledge, rather than passive reception.

The *Secondary Education Commission* (1954) recommended that the final assessment of the students should not be based on the results of external examination alone and that things such as school records and internal tests should be taken into consideration. The findings of the Commission and its recommendations were fully endorsed by the Central Advisory Board of Education at its meetings in 1953 and 1954. The *Education Commission* (1966) also recommended abolition of set syllabi and the external examinations based upon them and emphasized that they should be replaced by a system of internal and continuous evaluation by the teachers themselves. In the report of the *University Grants Commission* (1992) on the problem of examination system, *Dongerkery* stressed the need for improvement of the methods of teaching and learning and that examinations should periodically reveal to the students his progress in learning. This naturally serves as a basis for motivation and makes the students take appropriate steps to maintain or improve his mastery of the subject.

Three facets of examination reform, viz., internal assessment, question banking and grading have been emphasised by the University Grants Commission also (*Examination Reform: A Plan of Action,* 1976).

Shah (1972) surveyed the pattern of internal-external assessments in arts, commerce and science colleges. He found that there was a tendency to decrease weightage of internal assessment in art, science and commerce colleges, while in colleges of eduction the tendency was in favour of increasing the weightage of internal assessment. He found significant correlation between internal and external assessments. *Deshpande* (1972) also found a positive correlation between internal and external assessments, but it varied from school to school. *Gunasekaran* and *Jayanthi* (1980) also found significant correlation between the marks of continuous internal assessment and the University examination. *Nath* (1980) found that the internal assessment marks possessed some predictive value for the external assessment marks, but there was a tendency towards over making in internal assessment. *Rasool et al.,* (1981) while studying internal and external awards at the Post-graduate level in Jammu University, found that the majority of the teachers adopted a lower range for the marks in internal evaluation than that was found in external evaluation. Most of the coefficients of correlations between internal and external examiners were positive. In another study, *Rasool, et al.,* (1981) studied the trend of marking in internal and external assessments and found that marking was highly liberal under internal assessment.

Educationists and examination reformers have been advocating the use of formative evaluation on a continuing basis. They argued that since continuous evaluation is a teaching strategy, it is likely to improve the academic attainments of students. *Sudha Rao* (1987) conducted a study to study the effect of continuous evaluation on school learning and constructed tests for the study on the basis of Bloom's taxonomy of educational objectives. The study has established that continuous evaluation had a positive influence on learning under normal school situation.

To remedy the ills of the traditional examination many an expert has suggested as early as in 1940's introduction of internal assessment as a substitute for public examination. This system, where the teacher who teaches also evaluates the students progress in learning, though undeniably sound, both psychologically and pedagogically, has many difficulties in its implementation under the present day Indian conditions. It has been tried at different levels of education in different institutions by enthusiasts, but was given up due to various problems that have cropped up in its implementation (*Venkata Rami Reddy,* 1977).

According to the *Editor, Educational India,* (1971) though there is no doubt that internal assessment offers a better criteria than an annual examination in measuring the progress of a student, the question is how is this internal assessment to be made? And, if it becomes too subjective as it would, the promotion of a student will depend on the whims and fancies of the teachers. As if to overcome this objection, it is recommended by certain Committees that internal assessment should be on the basis of norms laid by a board or a university. such assessment should be subjected to external moderation by the board or the university. To say the least, this is an extremely cumbersome process which might lead to distorations and discrepancies. It is a well known fact that the universities and boards which now conduct examinations are not free from officials indulging in corrupt practices and as such, how can they be trusted with the task of formulating norms for even internal assessment? If examinations are an obsession with the present day students, and therefore, they should be minimised, under the new scheme, internal assessment would also become an obsession. At least, examinations have the advantage of being impersonal and whoever is able to write well can hope to get through. If on the other hand, they are substituted by internal assessment, students would start pleasing the teachers which could be done in more than one way. The entire system will be filled with corruption and the resultant benefit would be much less and more obnoxious than the evil effects which the present system is supposed to breed.

In has the other side of the picture also. Student stay away enblock from a test or seminar and challenge the teachers to refore their marks. They literally besiage the teachers demanding attendance, marks and the teachers have to remember that discretion is the better part of valour. They have to send for, or themselves go in search of, the students who do not write their tests/exercises/assignments in time and get them to write in order to have records for assessment failing which an explosive situation need not be ruled out.

A massive programme of training has been launched for the last two years by the Government of India and the State Governments, in order to train and orient the teachers towards a comprehensive programme of evaluation in line with the National Policy on Education (1986) which emphasises continuous and comprehensive evaluation. The continuous comprehensive evaluation encompasses the personality development of the learner also. Hence, this includes academic and non-academic achievement together with the acquisition of desirable personal and social qualities, interests, attitudes, skills, etc.

The seminar on Examination Reform at *Saurashtra University* (1985) felt that:

1. Reform of examinations was an urgent need and suitable measures should be taken to mitigate the evils of the system;
2. Short term measures as well as long term measures should be adopted in order that examinations serve their purposes in an appropriate manner;
3. As a short term measure, techniques of evaluation should be improved and new and innovative methods of evaluation should be employed so that quality of question papers is improved. Possibility of introducing question banks and grading may be explored;

4. In view of the large number of students taking public examination process may be explored;
5. As a long term measure, examinations should not be looked in isolation. They should be treated as means to improve the teaching learning process and thereby serve as a instrument of proving the quality of higher education;
6. The University has a very important role to play in improving evaluation and teaching-learning process. It should organise training of teachers and examiners on a large scale to improve their professional competencies in areas of item/question writing, internal assessment and grading;
7. Workshops and refresher courses should be organised with the help of various national level institutions of teacher training for the sole purpose of improving the quality of question papers;
8. Not only teachers but also the community including the employers should be oriented to the new concept of evaluation.

According to *Dressel* (1976), only when the students become competent evaluators of their own goals, experiences and accomplishments, they become truely educated (liberally educated) and capable of engaging in the fundamental processes essential in a democratic society'.

A one day seminar on curbing malpractices at the examinations was organised by South Gujarat University (1987-88). Students, teachers, invigilators and all those who perform duties at the time of examination participated in this seminar. Why students resort to malpractices was the main thrust of discussion. It was felt that irregularities in academic terms, and inadequate coverage of prescribed syllabus, non-availability of prescribed text books, etc. motivated students to indulge in malpractices.

The students also emphasised urgent need to change the present examination system and suggested 'open book examination system'. They also emphasised compulsory supervision by teachers and preferred centralised assessment along with dummy numbers. With regard to punishment they said publicity be given to the rules regarding punishment and all those who are connected with malpractices should be punished.

A two day workshop on *'New Concepts in Teaching and Evaluation at University level'* (1988) came out with several recommendations in teaching-learning-evaluation process. They suggested:

1. restructuring the syllabus;
2. teaching methods;
3. examination reforms with checks and balances; and
4. teacher evaluation.

No Examination?

To eliminate the psychology of fear, the union minister of Education suggested 'continuous internal evaluation' and the 'abolition of external examinations' in the primary classes. He felt that internal evaluation must be combined with public examinations. The element of gamble and arbitrariness in examinations must be reduced (*The Editor, The Educational Review,* 1970).

The suggestions to do away with examination in elementary schools appear to have been widely welcomed at the meeting. However, experienced teachers and authorities on primary education must be consulted before any decision is taken in this matter according to the *Editor, The Educational Review* (1970). Children learn many basic skills, and the foundations for all their future studies are laid there at the primary level. For example, the fundamental operations of arithmetic have to be learnt there. How is the teacher to be sure whether the pupils have mastered addition, substraction, multiplication and division, if there is to be testing? Surely, pupil's who have automatically come upto, say, standard VII can not be taught addition from the scratch.

People are some times noticed condemning the very principle of examination, while condemning examinations of a particular kind. Such people believe that examinations are superfluous adjuncts and of no consequence in the process of education. This is a completely erroneous estimation of the whole process and in fact, the very essence of science and culture is renounced by such outright rejection. It has long been established that examinations are that part of the teaching-learning process by means of which teaching and learning are assessed and evaluated.

Educational examination is as important as a medical examination conducted before treating a patient, or a geological survey which is also a kind of examination carried on before successful mining operations are undertaken. If all examinations are set aside, all consequences of education are also flung away and the question of teaching or learning becomes a meaningless enterprises. For, even asking simple questions to know about teaching or learning is nothing more or less than what is virtually meant by the term examination (*Bora,* 1974).

As mentioned earlier, M.C. Chagla, the then Union Minister of Education said that 'he was neutrally, temperamentally and constitutionally averse to examinations, but in this imperfect world there was no other device we could think of except examinations'.

Gautam (1964) observed that he did not share the opinion expressed by some people that the examinations should be got ride of because they are capricious, in valid, unreliable and inadequate and tend to corrupt the normal standards of university life. The fact remains that examinations cannot be dispensed with. The psychology of fear alleged to be prevalent among students is often depicted in frightful colours for purposes of propaganda. Some element of nervousness is undoubtedly present, and the best way of dealing with it is to infuse self-confidence in the students and to pursuade them to look upon examinations as an opportunity for achievement. A great deal of thought has to be bestowed on the element of arbitariness in setting question papers or evaluation of answer papers. All the can be said is that no one with reasonable competence must be denied a pass.

According to *Singha* (1984) public examinations will not be abolished but will only be de-emphasized. They will possibly be metamorphasised and will be supplemented by alternate strategies which are already under way. The metamorphosis of examinations according to him are as follows:

1. There will not be too many external examinations—not more than 3 examinations upto the end of the under-graduate stage as laid down by the National Policy on Education (1979);
2. The passing of a public examination or the securing of appropriate grades in that examination may be utilised as a criterion for permitting candidates to appear at such competitive examinations as suggested by *CABE* (1970): that all the state governments and the Government of India should agree that all recruitment to the service would be made in future on the basis of results of competitive examinations held purpose-wise by the appropriate authorities. So we may expect recruitment for jobs to be gradually de-linked from educational examinations;
3. There will be attempts to improve their measurement value. Apart from the improvements in questions and question papers, many other procedures of external examination will be made more systematic and scientific;

4. Statistical scaling of marks with a view to controlling inter-examiner and inter-subject variability may find favour with the examining agencies. The adhocism in the determination of cut-off points and the award of grace marks may be replaced by some sound rationale.

According to him public examinations will not be abolished even by 2001. They will continue to be used and continue to be modified by socio-economic factors.

REPORTS OF VARIOUS COMMITTEES AND COMMISSIONS

Several Commissions and Committees that have gone into the system of education in general and examination in particular have given their opinion about the examination system and suggested measures to improve it. The observation of some of the Commissions and Committees are briefly presented in the following pages:

1. Calcutta University Commission (1920)

The Calcutta University Commission while giving a number of suggestions for improvement of education in India defined the purpose of examinations as a general test of fitness for a course of university students.

2. Hartog Committee Report (1936)

Hartog Committee was formed with Sir Philip Hartog as its Director to test the concurrence of making a number of examination scripts by a number of independent examiners. It was found that when fourteen experienced examiners valued a second time independently fifteen scripts, these examiners between them allotted over forty different marks to several scripts.

However, the committee was clearly opposed to the policy of abolishing examinations altogether and pointed out the need for careful and systematic experiments to improve the methods of examinations (*Hargog* and *Rodes,* 1936).

2. Norwood Committee Report on Curriculum and Examination (1943)

This committee was appointed was by the President of the Board of Education in England to study the curriculum and examination practices in the secondary schools in that country. It condemned the whole system of examinations and envisaged the substitution of internal for external examinations. It also recommended abolition of the external examinations in grammar schools at the age of 16.

4. University Education Commission (1948)

The commission was appointed by the Government of India under the chairmanship of Dr. S. Radhakrishnan. The commission said that we are convinced that if we are to suggest one single reform in university education it should be that of the examinations. We advisedly say 'reform' although we know that in India, as elsewhere in the world, dissatisfaction with examinations had been so keen that eminent educationists and important education organizations have advocated the abolition of examinations. We do not share that extreme view and feel that examinations rightly designed and intelligently used can be a useful factor in the educational process. If examinations are necessary a thorough reform of these is still more necessary.

5. The Secondary Education Commission (1954)

The Secondary Education Commission which was appointed under the chairmanship of Dr. A. Lakshamana Swamy Mudaliar expressed the view that the traditional examinations which were restricted in their scope, mechanical in their techniques and unreliable in their conclusion constituted a serious educational problem. It therefore suggested that a constant and realistic appraisal of the pupil's progress should be made throughout this school career and that efforts should be made to design new evaluation and testing procedures which would not be a test of memory only, but a measure of the pupil's educational growth.

6. Central Examination Unit (CEU) (1960)

An examination unit was set up in 1958 for the specific purpose of improving the quality of secondary education. It realised that the crux of the problem lay in the undue importance given to examinations and that no worth while changes could be effected with out a reform of the examination system. At the same time, it observed that, reform in examinations, can not be brought about with out improving the methods of teaching and learning.

7. The Education Commission (1966)

The Commission observed that this is one of the areas in education about which one can say that the problem is known, its significance is realised the broad lines of the solution, at least to begin with, are known. But for some reason or other an effort to implement it on a worth while scale or in a meaningful manner has not yet been made.

'One line of attack would be to abolish set syllaby and the external examinations based on them altogether and to replace them by a system of internal and continuous evaluation by the teachers themselves. This is already being done in some institutions like IITs and the Agricultural universities and it could be increasingly extended to others as soon as the necessary facilities and conditions can be provided. We hope that at no distant date, it will be adopted by all teaching universities and that the major universities, would give a lead in this matter. We realise, however, that external examinations will remain with us for a long time, especially in universities which have large number of affiliated colleges of very unequal standards. The main strategy here would be to attack the problem on two fronts: introduction of more frequent, assessment so that the undue emphasis on the final examination as the sole determinant of success is reduced, and reform of evaluation techniques'.

A committee of the members of the parliament which considered the recommendations of the Education

Commission, recommended that in the matter of examination reform attention should be concentrated on three major areas:

1. reduction of the dominance of external examinations;
2. introduction of reforms which would make them more valid and realistic measures of educational achievement; and
3. the adoption of a good system of internal evaluation.

8. The National Policy on Education (1968)

The policy laid down that a major goal of examination reform should be to improve the reliability and validity of examinations and to make a continuous progress aimed at helping students to improve his level of achievement rather than at certifying the quality of his performance at a given moment of time.

9. University Grants Commission's 'Examination Reform—A Plan of Action' (1973)

The report stated that examinations have dominated the educational process and that external examinations have encouraged selective study and cramming. Examination marks have lacked reliability and validity and unfair means in examinations have increased tremendously. The crippling effect of external examinations on the quality of instruction has compelled various agencies to bring improvement in the present system. In this context the UGC has proposed the implementation of innovative programmes like internal assessment, grading system, etc.

10. University Grants Commission's Examination Reform—A Plan of Action' (1976)

In its document on the plan of action in examination reform, the University Grants Commission re-emphasised three facts of examination reform in the universities. They are (1) internal assessment, (2) question banking and (3) grading.

11. The National Policy on Education (1979)

The National Policy on Education (1979) sought to de-emphasise public examinations. It was against abolition of examinations. The policy laid down that there should be not more than 3 examinations upto the end of the under-graduate stage.

12. The National Policy on Education (1986)

According to the National Policy on Education, 1986, the 'existing mode of evaluation of pupils is recognised as out of tune with the professed educational goals. The suggestions offered focus on the need for continuous evaluation on the basis of observations, discussions, diagnostic studies, system analysis and simulation exercises, etc.

'At the elementary level it is suggested that evaluation may be undertaken on the basis of direct contact and oral observations except in the case of mathematics and languages'.

'At the secondary level the evaluation should include attendance, regularity, punctuality, home work, class work, practical work, socially useful work, participation in games and sports, etc. The evaluation should be of the total work transacted including the subject areas. It should be necessary to obtain a minimum prescribed pass mark. It is emphasised that the subjectivity in evaluation must be done away with'.

'The result may not be declared on the basis of marks and children should not be classed as I, II and III divisions. The graded scales may be adopted for evaluation.

'The process of evaluation should be a continuous one confining to total work and activities of students rather than undertaking it once or twice in a year'.

DETENTIONS OR NO DETENTIONS?

The traditional examinations have become tools for trivializing, de-individualizing, de-personalising and even dehumanizing man. Their real bane, therefore, is the enslavement of man (*Singha,* 1984).

Will the new society and its education system go on tolerating the irrelevance of public examinations? Reviewing the thinking in different countries on this aspect, Singha states that authorities in many western countries are taking, or are about to take, steps to reduce their dependence on public examination as basis for issuing school leaving certificates. In Canada, Ontario abolished its examinations in 1967, Manitoba did so in 1970, Queensland has announced plans to terminate all its secondary school examinations and other Australian states have given notice of similar moves. Sweeden has abolished all external examinations and Norway is reported to be moving in the same direction. Great Britain is experimenting with school based examinations and reference tests, while the U.S. has for many years operated an elaborate system of attitude and achievement testing not tied to any particular school prescription (*Singha,* 1984).

Andhra Pradesh never lagged behind in any kind of progressive educational venture. So is the case with reform of examinations too. The state has been implementing all the national policies in the field of education and in addition, has gone a step forward in introducing the 'non-detention system', in line with the international thinking on the philosophy of evaluation as propounded by Dr. Bloom and his associates.

Against the historical background of unequivocal criticism of the traditional system of examinations and its baneful effects, the State of Andhra Pradesh plunged into this type of examination reform and introduced the non-detention system in the year 1971-72. However, during the period from 1970 to 1973 the State was in a great turmoil and witnessed two agitations unparalleled in history and virtually the follow up measures of the non-detention system could not be thought of until August 1973 though the educational set up at the top had already devised a programme. Peace had been completely restored by September 1973 and as a measure of orientation to all the inspecting staff, 3 state level conferences were held in the 3 state level conferences were held in the 3 regions of the State. The last of the series was held on September 5, 1973. Thus Andhra Pradesh State's measure of examination reform may be said to have been started in right earnest from 5th September, 1973 (*Editorial, Educational India,* 1977).

It is worth while to note the salient points of the new evaluation scheme of Andhra Pradesh. It is well known that examinations have completely dominated the education system. Further, the fear of detention sometimes acts as a powerful factor damping the enthusiasm of the pupils preparing for the examination. To avoid this deterant factor, evaluation procedures are devised to assess the achievement of pupils. The evaluation, according to the new procedures, should be made in an atmosphere free from fear of detention, by merely grading the students' progress without indicating pass or fail. Thus the stigma of failure is taken away and with it the fear of detention. Under this scheme there will be two public examinations one at the end of the upper primary level corresponding to the 7th class and the other at the end of the secondary level corresponding to the 10th class, where there will be detentions. In all other classes students are automatically promoted to the next higher class irrespective of the level of their achievement, provided they put in a stipulated percentage of attendance.

All those concerned were given orientation on the new evaluation policy and procedure, as a follow-up of the policy of non-detention system with stress on objective based teaching techniques. These were dealt with in the broad spectrum of evaluation. All-round development of the pupils and their growth was sought to be carefully assessed continuously throughout the year. Various recording instruments were also devised for effective evaluation. The 'annual plans', 'unit plans' and 'lesson plans' were suggested to improve instructional activities along with 'unit test's, 'standardised tests' and 'assignments' which were suggested to strengthen the assessment programme. Cumulative records should also be maintained for recording the allround development of the child along with progress cards which were used to indicate the scholastic attainments of the children.

Emphasis is asked to be given on the 'design and preparation' of individual tests to measure the 3 domains of human life—cognitive, psycho-motor and affective. In the cognitive domain attempts are made for comprehensiveness in the child's understanding, judgement, ability to remember, to assess his capabilities in knowledge, comprehension, application, analysis and judgement. The child's skills are asked to be measured in the psycho-motor domain—skills are asked to be measured in the psycho-motor domain-skills in such things as music, tailoring, type writing, reading a map, etc.—to focus how his thinking faculties function through neuromuscular coordination. In the affective domain his capabilities as well as attitudes in appreciating things are asked to be assessed and developed.

The headmasters have been asked to utilise their institutional plans and all other ancillary services such as school complex, scouting, science club, etc., to strengthen the endeavour of the teachers in implementing the new evaluation procedures. In the institutional planning they are asked to work out the minimum academic programme and the school improvement programme. They are asked to work out improvements with resources already available and those that can be improvised locally. In-service programmes for all teachers to effectively reorient them to the new ideas in education and to equip them with the necessary dynamism and school complex have been stressed so that the primary and upper primary schools can have access to facilities available in the secondary schools and also to bridge the gaps in the attainment of pupils expected of then in higher standards (*Editorial, Educational India,* 1977).

After outlining the background and the new setting of the ambitious programme, the Editor observed that it was high time that the Andhra Pradesh Government or National Council for Educational Research and Training should make a system analysis and then move further in the programme.

In effecting reforms in the field of education in general and examinations in particular the Andhra Pradesh State Department of Education has been taking into consideration the international thinking like the philosophy of education propounded by Dr. Bloom and his associates, the automatic promotion policies adopted elsewhere and so on (*Krishna Moorthy,* 1977).

Such a policy has been introduced with the objectives of rooting out stagnation at the primary stage of education, fulfilling the constitutional obligation of compulsory, primary education, minimising the wastage, replacing the fear of examinations by real love for education and to undo all the factors that are responsible for annual detentions by undertaking remedial educational programmes and the like (*Krishna Moorthy,* 1977).

According to *Sarabhachari* (1971), the Andhra Pradesh State's non-detention system is a very bold and salutary reform which though belated is welcome; as it is 'better late than never', On this issue various opinions have been expressed; some admiring the measure and some denouncing the same. While every reform or change has its shortcomings, and is open to abuse in practice, the present action of the government deserves to be congratulated upon for this exemplary step.

As a result of research, perhaps done in the wing of the Directorate on Examination, or on becoming aware of the defects of the examination system coming to the fore in a larger and larger measure year after year, the government has duly abolished the yearly detentions and made 2 years of study as first unit, and a further study of 3 years as the next unit to sit for the final examination. The teachers under this set up have gained ample time and room to teach, and the pupils to learn. Till recently they were caught in the tentacles of the octoped like yearly examination and the like, and now they are freed from its cruel grip. They have to turn to methodical work of instruction through play-way, projects, self study and development of interests, emotions and skills through auto-learning in full spirit in which they were trained years ago. They have now peace and leisure to watch the aptitudes of pupils as envisaged by the cumulative records.

The Director of Public Instruction has stated that in the changed set up, the teachers will be given refresher courses at district levels in certain subjects. This reform, it is hoped, would lead to better conditions, where true learning and true teaching take place; the teacher becomes trusted and honoured a philosopher, friend and guide, to his pupils. Honest and planned work under the aegis of this reform can be believed to yield true fruits of education, contentment has to take the place of greed, and adoration of truth to blind mammon worship, first in the sphere of education. But it should also be realized by the powers at the helm of affairs that the teacher, just like the cow, should be kept healthy and happy both in the body and mind and as such should be fed well for yielding good milk to the children gathered in the school. This measure may be adopted by other states too, as necessary (*Sarabhachari,* 1971).

According to *Krishna Moorthy* (1971), the main aim of examinations should not be to detain children in their old classes but to measure their strengths and weaknesses so that strong points can be further strengthened by special instruction and guidance, and weak points can be eliminated by remedial instruction and incentive motivation.

Failure in examination has a great and distressing effect upon the minds of young children. Hence, detaining a child for one full year in his old class for not getting through in one of the subjects is quite unwarranted. Instead, such children may be given special coaching in the weak subjects for some time and tested again so as to proceed to the next class or grade (*Krishna Moorthy,* 1971).

Experimental studies of *Keyes* (1911), *Klene* and *Branson* (1929), *Arthur* (1936), *Coffield* and *Bloomers* (1956), *Gaite* (1969) and *Holmes, et al.,* (1983) have proved beyond doubt that non-detained students did better than the repeaters. Detention is a negative incentive which does not promote learning but only leads to unlearning of what was learnt and also develops inferiority feeling and unfavourable attitude towards the teacher, the school and education in general. *Hence, Krishna Moorthy* (1971) observed that examinations should be taken to serve as the means of educational measurement for improving the learning of children and not for punishing the children by declaring them as having failed. Numerous factors beyond their control contribute to failure in examinations. A number of studies have been conducted to find out the factors which contribute to failures in examinations. According to Bokil (1956b) the size of the school influenced the number of candidates scoring less than twenty per cent of the total marks, Directorate of Extension Programmes for Secondary Education (DEPSE), (1964) found that teacher's qualifications and background, teaching methods, working conditions and location of school, transfers, building, equipment, clerical work done by teachers, pupils previous attainment, pupils' attendance, media of instruction, examinations, etc., were factors which were related to pass-fail percentage of schools. The Government Central Pedagogical Institute (GCPI), Allahabad, (1964) found that many social, economic and educational factors were responsible for failure in schools. NCERT (1965) conducted a sample study of failures in boards of secondary examinations taking the sample from Bihar, Delhi, Gujarat, Kerala,

Maharashtra, Mysore, Rajasthan and Uttar Pradesh. It was found that the majority of failures were not due to failure in English alone. It was found that the compartmental examination conducted by certain Boards did not seem to make much difference to the large scale failures. The Directorate of Higher Education, Hyderabad (1966) found that the high percentage of failures in the examination at the secondary stage was mainly due to inadequacy of library and laboratory facilities and untrained teachers. *Gadgil* (1978, 1979a, 1979b) found that a large number of failures were mainly due to inadequacy of mastery over the subject on the part of the teachers.

The Committee of Members of Parliament on education has recommended that examination results at the end of 10 or 11 years period of schooling should merely indicate the performance of the student in different subjects and not declare whether he has passed or failed. Under this system, no student would be detained but whether he should be admitted to the specialised higher course which he opts will depend on whether his performance in the subject concerned was considered satisfactory or not by the admitting authority (*Kabra,* 1971).

Commenting upon this proposal, *Kabra* (1971) observed that the committee expects that this system will eliminate wastage and stagnation in the present system which stipulates that unless a student has secured a certain minimum in all the subjects he is not eligible to proceed for higher education. The proposed system will not prevent a student from going to the next class, even if his performance was not uniformly good in all subjects. Prof. J.P. Naik, Educational Adviser, to the Government of India, explaining the committee's recommendations to newsmen, admitted that if this suggestion was accepted, it would need an amendment to government rules which specify qualifications for employment. Instead of stipulating that a candidate should have passed the school leaving examination, as is being done at present, the government would have to specify the minimum standards of performance it expects from a candidate for particular jobs.

Imperceptibly, without the student feeling that he is being examined, the teacher should assess and evaluate his comprehension and grasp of the subject. This evaluation may be weekly. Whatever has been taught during the week, that and only that, must be evaluated by seeking answers to questions either orally or in written tests, or by assessing the assignment work, and thus the regularity of progress and achievement may be estimated. This weekly assessment should have some grading which the teacher may note against every student and may read just his teaching accordingly. Obviously, this assessment should be a part of teaching and nothing in itself. Through such assessment, the teacher will himself know whether his teaching is in accordance with the mental level of his pupils and how far they could grasp it. Thus the teachers will get every opportunity to adjust their teaching accordingly. The teacher and the student will both feel keen, animated and enthusiastic. This assessment is the real examination of the student in which the student will find spontaneous development, without being tortured and tormented by the external formal examination. The outcome will be students will have better comprehension of the subject than those who simply pass the examination.

It is true, to do all this, the teachers will surely have to work sincerely. In the existing scheme a student has an examination at the end of the session. This is based on his study of the whole syllabus covered during the academic year. This is quite unnatural, unpsychological and illogical. It is not at all related with actual life situations because no occasion ever comes in life when one's total knowledge is put to test (*Kabra,* 1971).

The plan of education free from the so called examination is workable in fulfilling the following view-points according to Kabra:

1. Total liberation from the phobia of examination;
2. Imperceptible, indirect and internal assessment of the student;
3. Direct relation between teaching and testing and to readjust and modify accordingly;
4. Cumulative effect of evaluation is the standard of progress;
5. Sense of duty, hard work, sincerity and dynamic enthusiasm desirable on the part of the teacher;
6. Inculcation of regular study habits;
7. Learning becomes an interesting experience;
8. Coordinated and balanced knowledge of the subject;
9. Evaluation and assessment is fairly balanced while examination is imbalanced;
10. Examination aims at testing the memory while evaluation informs about the scholar's comprehension;
11. Assessment tells about the eligibility of the student to accept the next unit and promotion to the next stage;
12. The teacher has also to assess and evaluate his own teaching;
13. The economic status of the teachers be improved and recognition from the society;
14. The innate mobility and grace of the teacher be awakened, animated and enlivened so that correct and honest judgement be available;
15. Timely knowledge of the individual difficulties for immediate remedy;
16. Testing the pupils' span of knowledge;

17. Regular record keeping of the pupils' activity and progress.

According to Kabra, assessment is comprehensive and broad based. Therefore, in assessment not only essay type of tests but also interviews, inspection, opinionnaire and questionnaire, etc., are used. As the values of life are changing, corresponding modification in education is essential. This scheme accepts the demand and challenge of the time.

Education without examinations will be free from terror and tension. Then the students will be able to learn in a natural set up. The comprehension of the subject will be clear and intense. Not only the retaining power of the mind but also its broad spectrum of understanding will be tested and developed and there will be natural and spontaneous learning on the part of the child (*Narasimha Rao,* 1971).

There has been criticism against the methods of education and also the system of examinations conducted, the essence of this criticism being the unsuitability of these methods of education and examination procedures to a harmonious development of pupils' personality and its moulding to meet the requirement of the nation. According to *Satyanarayana* (1972) it is hoped that the non-detention system would allow the schools to try out better methods of education for achieving the desired development on the intellectual as well as many other aspects of the personality of the pupils.

Commenting on the decision of the Government of Kerala that the pass percentage in the primary and secondary classes in schools should be a minimum of 90 and 80 respectively, a spokesman from the education department pointed out that the detention of a student, did more harm than good as he would neither attend the class nor take interest in the studies. He becomes a problem and may even organise a group to defeat the education programmes (Through different states, *Educational India,* 1973).

It would not be correct to declare that a student had failed in the absence of scientific method to find out intelligent and efficient students. Unless diagnostic tests are made to find the weak points in a student and measures taken to rectify these defects, it will not be proper to say that a student has failed and that he should study in the same class. A majority of the students who fail belong to the socially and economically backward sections. Requiring them to study in the same class for one more year will only force them to leave the school. Due to financial problems the parents of these children may also ask them to discontinue the studies (Through different states, *Educational India,* 1973).

Rao (1977) opined that the non-dentention policy is basically a sound educational policy and Andhra Pradesh is the only State to take the initiative to implement this policy in a bold and imaginative way. Of course there might be some drawbacks and they are inevitable, in any kind of educational reform worth the name, in the initial stages. The educational philosophy behind the policy is that if a pupil is regular to the school he will, at least acquire the minimum attainments in a normal school situation.

He further observed that, if a pupil who is regular is not able to acquire the minimum attainments, the fault is somewhere else, not necessarily in the pupil and the pupil should not be penalised by declaring him as failed for the fault which is somewhere else. It is the duty of the school and the teaching community to locate the fault and take corrective measures to ensure the normal school situation rather than making the pupil a scapegoat. Any one can hardly dispute this philosophy.

The education department of Andhra Pradesh has done a lot of work for the successful implementation of this policy. Through a massive statewide academic programme, all the teachers were trained in the concept and techniques of continuous evaluation and to utilise the feedback of evaluation for better teaching and learning in the classrooms. A lot of literature was published for the benefit of teachers. The non-dentention policy has greatly helped in arresting wastage and stagnation which is one of the very serious problems of Indian Education today (*Rao,* 1977).

While the above are opinions expressed commanding the non-detention system, there were others who denounced the policy. For example the *Editor, The Educational Review* (1971) observed that the policy is indeed something of a revolutionary experiment in education. Old fashioned people both parents and teachers, may well feel dismayed and consider this experimentation with a vengeance. It boils down to this: that there will be automatic promotions throughout the school years except for the two exceptions.

In academic terms this seems to mean education without evaluation. The reasons against it may be old, they are as valid now as much as they were hundred years ago. Without testing neither the teacher nor the pupils know where they stand. It is good for the teacher to know how far the students have understood and assimilated what they have been taught, and it is good for the pupils also to know this. There is a great deal in academic studies which may be dull or difficult to grasp. Testing provides necessary incentive to study this and it helps the teacher to put them across to the pupil. Both the pupil and teacher are deprived of motivation where testing is not permitted.

It may be that even under the new dispensation teachers are to hold tests and that the only essential reform is that promotions are no longer dependent on testing. But when the pupil knows that it matters nothing to his school career, whether he does well or ill in his tests, can we expect him to take the trouble to study hard and understand? It is only human nature to take things easy, and for children, studying is not so pleasant as playing. Inspite of tall talk about the play way methods of learning, school subjects indeed, at least as things stand in our country, is not the same as playing.

According to the Editor, the educational authorities of Andhra Pradesh may have been persuaded to take this step in the belief that the tender minds of young people should be spared the nervous strain of examinations and the frustration of occasional failures. For a normal child the strain is a healthy way of toughening up his mental fibre and it is wrong to think that children brood very much over occasional failures. To be spared these strains and frustrations may make them live in a make believe world where there is never any hard task of any disappointment.

We must anticipate also another unfortunate consequence of the new set up. It is not unreasonable to apprehend that discipline will be seriously affected. Already there has been a considerable amount of political pressure with regard to admissions and promotions in schools. This had eroded the moral authority of teachers and headmasters who find it difficult even now, to run the school decorously and effectively. One can easily visualise the encouragement to indiscipline when automatic promotions are guaranteed. Students from backward classes who are probably expected to be the main beneficiaries of the testless school are actually being deprived of opportunities of proceeding to higher studies and raising their status, according to him.

Another undesirable consequence is that the failures even at the semi-public examination at lower secondary level (VII class) will run to staggering proportions. Most of those who fail may choose to bid goodbye to their studies and become permanent dropouts.

According to the Editor, the decision appears to have been taken hastily without due consultation with academic experts. One can understand the Parliamentary Advisory Committee to the Union Minister of Education considering tentatively a suggestion to have no examinations in the primary schools. It was a non-academic approach to an academic problem. But to abolish all school evaluation throughout a State is to undermine the foundations of the very process of learning. It is not too late to reconsider the order. If necessary, the experiment may be tried in a few selected schools and results watched (*The Editor, The Educational Review,* 1971).

Commenting on the observations made by the Education Commission (1966) the Editor, the Educational Review (1967) observed that one of the most ill conceived recommendations of the Kothari Commission was that the school leaving examination should be abolished. Every school, it was suggested, should issue its own certificate about the performance of each student. The world of make believe to which this seemed to lead, has cast its spell on those who must have advised the Committee of Members of Parliament on Education. The Committee has agreed that the school leaving certificate should state the performance of the student in each subject without declaring him passed or failed. It should also be open for a student to repeat the examination in one or more subjects, according to his needs so as to improve his performance. However, the Committee did not recommend that schools should stop failing students in internal examinations.

What must have promoted the Parliamentary Committee is perhaps the spectacle of the appalling wastage in failures at the school leaving examination. But merely to refrain from declaring the failures as such is not going to make them succeed. It is necessary both for students and teachers to know where they stand.

The remedy for the failures lies in raising the standards of teaching right from the primary stage. A high teacher-pupil ratio, leniency in promotions in the lower classes, the abolition of the selection examination in the school final class—these are some of the causes behind the vast numbers of failures in the school leaving examination. It should also be remembered that even the majority of those declared successful are really qualified neither for higher studies nor for employment.

The criticism has been made that the examinations are rigid, and that the case of Srinivasa Ramanujam, the famous mathematician, justified the present decision and that Madras State has already anticipated it. Examinations have to be rigid to a minimum extent at least. They have to test the attainments of pupils in reading, writing, arithmetic, elementary science, history and geography (*The Editor, The Educational Review*, 1967).

The *Editor, Educational India* (1977), observed that the main point made out by the Committee appointed by the Central Advisory Board of Education to go into the problems of examinations was that public examinations should not be frequent and they should be reduced to the minimum. Secondly internal assessment of students by teachers of the institution concerned should be given greater weight in deciding the fact whether a student should be promoted to the higher class. In other words, the Committee has taken for granted that examinations as are now conducted do not do justice in assessing the real capacities of students. It is this point that Mr. P.V. Narasimha Rao, the then Education Minister of Andhra Pradesh, who was also a member of the committee, stressed when he said that education is best imparted in an atmosphere of free progress where the incentive and urge to improve spring from within the educational processes rather than from the terror of examination and detention.

This takes us to the question whether the fear of detention really retards the progress of a 'good' student. To some extent it does, but the factor to be considered is, whether the student would make any genuine effort at study if he knows that whatever be his progress, he will not be detained. While every one agrees that the student should have all the incentives necessary to go ahead with his studies, it must also be remembered that unless there is some compelling circumstance, he would not bother to keep up-to-date. He would rather postpone and accumulate arrears than be prompt. Ultimately, he will find every thing has grown beyond his capacity to assimilate and the net result would be even worse.

To give up detentions and reduce the number of examinations without adequate preparation, according to the Editor, would certainly lead to negligence on the part of students. Mr. Narasimha Rao is too optimistic to believe that this is not so, but unless the character of the students and the teachers show visible signs of improvement, it would be dangerous to meddle with the present state of affairs. It is nobody's case that backward students should not be helped, but to introduce drastic reforms without making sure of the consequences would be most undesirable. If one sees the condition of colleges and the general tenor of students, one would realise that all is not well with them. And take away the only fear, that of examination, the result will be obvious. While one must agree that much needs to be done in the sphere of examinations, the first emphasis should be on promoting quality, both of the teacher and the student. When once that is done it will be time for drastic changes in the examination system (*Editorial, Educational India,* 1971).

The resolution of the seminar of aided and private school teachers held at Hyderabad on July 16, 1971 stated that abolition of annual examinations for promotions and detentions without preparing the teachers for a reformed system of evaluation through orientation programmes and schemes, may given rise to a new situation of student indiscipline for which the teacher community may have to bear the brunt of responsibility (*Editorial, Educational India,* 1971).

The seminar discussed the implication of the Government's decision to abolish detentions and felt that in taking such a decision of far reaching consequences, the teaching community was not given an opportunity to express its view.

Its implementation as an isolated educational reform to the exclusion of other urgent reforms as recommended by the Kothari Commission was felt to be rather 'uneducational'.

Without reforming the educational system and improving the quality of education imparted, implementation of such a far reaching measure, the seminar felt, would devote on the teachers a very heavy responsibility which they would have to carry out under abnormal conditions like crowded classrooms and lack of proper teaching aids (Through different states, *Educational India,* 1971).

The whole hearted and psychological participation of students, teachers and parents was essential for maintaining the standards of education, where a major reform of abolition of detentions in school had been introduced. This view was expressed by a spokesman of the Education department when his attention was drawn to a report that almost every other student in the sixth, eighth and ninth classes in a Municipal High school at Vijayawada returned blank answer papers in the annual examinations. The spokesman said that the department was embarking upon major steps to create a conducive climate for the proper working of this reform of abolition of detentions except at the 7th and 10th class levels where government examinations are held (Through different states, *Educational India,* 1972).

Venkata Rao (1971) observed that the government, with a stroke of the pen had abolished every kind of testing for the purpose of promotion in schools. According to him, abolition of examinations is no solution to the grave defects of the system, as examinations test the efficiency of teaching and learning.

In the words of the *Secondary Education Commission* (1954) examinations 'have a stimulating effect on the pupils and the teachers by providing well defined goals and objective standards of achievement.' They help in setting up an aim before the pupils and the teachers. In the case of a common external examination, when the performance of the pupils is assessed on the basis of a common criteria, they help in comparing the soundness of instruction obtaining in the different institutions. By means of examinations the pupils know where they are and teachers know where their pupils are, how much knowledge imparted to them has been assimilated what attitudes they have developed and what social skills they have learnt (*Kochar,* 1983).

According to *Venkata Rao* (1971) the only beneficial outcome of this reform is the disappearance of the malpractices both by the pupils and the teachers in the examination hall and elsewhere. But abolition of the examinations with a view to eradicate the abuses of the system is a remedy worse than the disease. As a matter of fact no serious endeavours have been made to eliminate these malpractices. They will disappear if external examiners are appointed for final evaluation. This entails additional expenditure. If education is to be given its due, we should not grudge this additional expenditure. Most problems plaguing education are the direct outcomes of an extreme reluctance to earmark the requisite funds for educational development.

According to him the likely outcomes of this measure are the following:

1. Teachers are assured of the promotion of the pupils whether they teach well or not. So teaching suffers;
2. The pupils are given a boon. They will be promoted to the next higher class on the basis of 75 per cent of attendance. They need not study hard for good marks or promotion;
3. The pupils face external examinations at the end of the VII and X classes. Having not been trained all the while to face serious examinations of any kind, they will find these external examinations, insurmountable barriers in their educational march. They will be overwhelmed, confused and perplexed, the effort required being entirely new to them, resulting in stagnation of unprecedented dimensions;

4. To solve this the government will be impelled by the logic of circumstances to abolish these examinations too like the Bagalpur University abolishing the P.U.C. examinations yielding to the clamour of the students;
5. The government will become highly popular with the secondary school pupils, but unpopular with the teachers, headmasters and those who value education in its right sense.

The government's non-detention policy in schools is intended to eliminate wastage and stagnation according to *Bullayya* (1977). Rules of attendance are not rigidly enforced in the schools, VII common examination and the counter X class common examination constitute the very anti-thesis of the policy. According to him all schools do not conform to the required standard. Some are fully staffed, while many are not. Where the staff is adequate it may not be suitable, if suitable, instruction is neglected. A number of recognised but unaided private schools which do not feel obliged to follow the instruction of the education department also exist. The solution to the problem lies in a two fold strategy:

1. Till such time as adequate staff is provided for all schools with minimum teaching aids, there should be need based rational distribution of staff. There should be provision for part-time staff whenever necessary;
2. A programme should be laid down for the coverage of syllabus (class-wise) and for tests in each individual school before the commencement of the school year. A teacher-wise performance register should be maintained by the headmaster. The inspector/supervisor should watch implementation of the programme and report on the work of each individual teacher and the head-master to his immediate higher authorities.

He observed that on the basis of the record of continual tests students can be promoted and detentions avoid. Without recourse to such systematic work it will not be possible to make school education a success.

The Editor, Educational India, 1977, was very critical of the new system. He observed that:

1. 'Take it easy' attitude is growing among children which will spoil generations to come;
2. The community shares with Dewey a faith in the healthy capabilities of children and with Rousseau a belief that everything is good as it comes from the hands of the creator, every thing degenerates in the hands of man. It may be true what John Holt said 'Nobody is born stupid but we encourage children to act stupidly';
3. Contemporary society and the educational system are hostile to the process of learning and maturation;
4. What we have now is compulsory mis-education;
5. Chance still plays a more important part to determine the success or failure of a candidate—but that is postponed till class VII examination and SSC examination. In the intervening classes promoting pupils with very little, or no learning at all, takes places;
6. The only two public examinations do not test the important abilities of the pupils;
7. No weightage is given to internal assessment even in this new evaluation scheme in the only two public examinations one at class VII and the other at Class X;
8. Even the new scheme is encouraging selective studies;

9. The time allocated to examiners is still inadequate and the craze for valuing more answer scripts to earn a few paise more still looms large;
10. The weakness of the school administration still persists in guidance, supervision and administration;
11. The teachers are still judged of their efficiency only by the percentage of passes and the threat to the teachers is now all the more greater today than it was before, with stoppage of increments in their salaries;
12. The alarming percentage of failures in the public examinations even in the new system is an eye opener to the fact that the new system is no better than the previous one.

Why did the new evaluation scheme fail even though it has been claimed to be an educational innovation? Why did not the expected changes materialise? Are important questions (*The Editor, Educational India,* 1977). The failure is attributed to some of the circumstances which are as under:

1. Departments' failure to anticipate problems which teachers encountered and the lack of feedback mechanism which made it impossible to deal with problems as they arose;
2. Failure to modify the established practices;
3. The teachers inability to carry out their new roles due to lack of understanding and inadequately developed skills;
4. Instructional procedures and materials lacked specificity and were often unavailable;
5. A deep frustration on the part of the teachers as they become aware of their inability to handle the situation in the prescribed manner;

6. Too much work load with too many working hours;
7. Although the ultimate criterion for a successful change strategy is the performance of the students—short term criteria are needed as a means for guiding the change process to ensure that continuous progress is made;
8. The necessary dynamism and the follow-up work is not there with the change of men and authority who conceived of the new evaluation scheme;
9. Promotions and the performance of the students should not have been separated.

Andhra Pradesh seems to be where it was previously and the alarming percentage of failures at both the public examinations and even at the intermediate level pinpoint the above education. Hence the Andhra Pradesh Government should take immediate steps for a proper system analysis of its new evaluation scheme with no further loss of time and precious years for the students (*Editorial, Educational India,* 1977).

Commenting upon the examination system and necessity of examinations *Narayana Rao* (1970) observed that in 1917 the Soviet Government did away with all forms of examinations. After 15 years of experience the Central Committee of the Communist Party found the system ineffective and undesirable and recommended the re-introduction of a rigid system of examination.

According to *Singha* (1984) as special tests for recruitment or admission may not be possible, public examinations will continue to play their role with importance being attached to their certificates. All that can possibly happen is that, there will be a greater tendency at the elementary level to drop examinations altogether and to substitute them by automatic promotions. But at the higher stages of education, they will not be able to do away with them completely.

EMPIRICAL STUDIES

1. Effects of Promotion Vs Non-promotion on Achievement

The general assumptions underlying the non-detention system are that learning effectiveness, motivation to learn, and mental health of the students will be enhanced. The justification for non-promotion is that, the threat of failure will cause a student to work harder and therefore achieve better results, and that repetition of a subject will lead to a mastery of that subject. To determine whether this was true, Otto and Melby (n.d.) tested equated groups of 192 pupils in grade 2A and 160 pupils in grade 5A taught by 18 teachers in four school systems. They found that children in the experimental groups who were told that they would be promoted regardless of their efforts made slightly more progress than those in control groups who were told they would not be promoted if they did not work diligently.

Keyes (1911) studied the achievement of approximately five thousand repeaters by comparing their performance before and after non-promotion. He reported that 21 per cent of the pupils did better after repeating, 39 per cent did worse and for 50 per cent nonpromotion had no effect. *Klene* and *Branson* (1929) reported the findings of an experimental study that compared promotion and non-promotion. The authors matched the mental age, chronological age, IQ and grade placement of elementary school pupils who were expected to repeat a grade. The students were randomly assigned to non-promotion or trial promotion. The experiment lasted for one semester, and the students were tested at the beginning and end of that semester. The study concluded that the promoted group showed greater academic progress than the repeaters.

The study of *Gaite* (1969) attempted to determine if non-promotion improves high school pupil's grades. Student grades were analysed in all the subject matter areas, prior to non-promotion and at the end of the repeated years, since students failing one subject area had to repeat all subjects.

Although Gaite found statistically significant differences in some areas, he concluded that the amount of growth was not justified by the extra time spent in the grade.

Otto (n.d.) has stated, 'The closely associated activities of marking (giving grades), reporting to parents and determining promotion or non-promotion are probably the most disagreeable, disheartening, frustrating and confusing duties of a teacher'. This is particularly true in the light of recent community demands to upgrade pupil education. The percentage of grade failure has sometimes been constructed as an indication of a school's desire for quality and insistence on high standards, and many educators have given credence to this proposition. Yet, evidence indicates that the schools that have the smallest failure rate have the highest degree of measurable pupil achievement.

Coffield and *Blommers* (n.d.) compared the achievement test scores of 25 schools having a rigid promotion policy and 28 schools having a lenient policy (as judged by the percentage of non-promoted pupils). The average achievement of the seventh grade was slightly higher in the schools with a lenient promotion policy, although not sufficiently higher to be statistically significant.

Coffield and *Blommers* (1956) used test scores collected each January in the annual Iowa testing programme. By writing to the school superintendent, they located 190 pupils in grade seven in 1953-54 who had been promoted normally from grade one and grade two, but had repeated one grade in going from grade three to grade seven. No one can know what progress these children would have made if they had been promoted regularly in study without being required to repeat one grade, but one clue is to study the progress of similar pupils. For 93 repeaters, promoted class mates, who matched them initially in test scores, were identified and for the remaining 57, a similar match was made in another school system. These promoted children who achieved before promotion as low as that of 190 repeaters, made substantially greater progress when promoted than did those who repeated a grade.

Grade 3 had been the stumbling block for almost a third of the repeaters—55 in all. Their average achievement in tests of reading, study skills, language was five months below grade standards when they were first tested in grade three. Twelve months latter, still in grade three, they had advanced only three months over their previous achievement. Instead of being on par with matched former class-mates who had been promoted, they were now six months behind them. Those matched with outsiders were now five months behind in test scores.

By the time these repeaters of the third grade reached the seventh grade, the promoted children simultaneously reached the 8th grade, the repeaters matched with classmates averaged 13 months behind, and those matched with outsiders averaged 8 months behind.

The number of children who repeated grades four, five, six and seven was smaller than the number repeating grade 3, and the results were less striking, but the general picture was one of less than a full year of progress when repeating a grade and of failure to catch up with promoted classmates or outsiders who were once equal with them in achievement.

Failing, or the threat of failure, has been considered to spur learning. Apparently, the reverse is more often, true. The adage nothing succeeds like success' is demonstrated in learning activities. Failure, especially repeated failure, is likely to kill the pupils' incentive to learn, further, is likely to kill the pupils' incentive to learn, Further more, pupils who are encouraged and whose work is praised achieve more than those who are warned that they will fail unless they keep their work upto standard.

Hillson and others (1964) reported a controlled study of non-graded reading in the primary school. The commonest finding was that non-graded programmes at the elementary level resulted in gains in the skill subjects that are made the foci of the programmes.

Bir Singh (1971) conducted a study to know the progress in terms of marks and percentages made by pupils making more than one unsuccessful attempt for passing an examination. Those who fail at an examination for the first time almost under percentage of chances are that they will fail at second attempt as well. This, however, indicates a tendency that the chances for passing an examination at the second attempt are not very bright. The chances for passing an examination are better at the third or fourth attempts than at the second attempt when a pupil fails. In most cases, either he leaves school in disappointment or fails if he appears the next time. Some pupils no doubt pass the examination at the second attempt.

Thus it is no use keeping a pupil in the same class for one extra year. If at all we require him to improve, keep him in the same class for three years, and then alone we can find some improvement in his achievement. This will happen only if the pupil dares to afford to study for three years in the same class.

The range of marks obtained was highest in the case of those pupils who failed at their first attempt. It is lowest in the case of those who fail at their fourth attempt. The tendency is that the range of marks awarded decreases with the number of attempts made by pupils to pass an examination. If the range of marks is high the pupils level of achievement differs greatly.

The data reveals the effect that the consistency in the total number or cards obtained at an examination by failing pupils increases with the number of unsuccessful attempts they make to pass an examination.

The number of marks gained by such failures differs to a great extent, it goes on increasing with the number of unsuccessful attempts made at passing an examination. The mean of the marks gained was only 3 per cent by repeating the same course for another year. The gain at the 2nd attempt was nearly 3.24 per cent. However, the gain at 3rd attempt was nearly 6 per cent over the percentage of marks obtained at the first attempt.

Since total number of marks obtained by failures differs to a great extent, they can not be termed as homogeneous in this respect. It is therefore unwise to keep them in the same class as is done by most of the schools. Almost every failure requires different treatment and hence, every one of them needs to be given individual attention by every teacher of the class.

In a study conducted in 11 schools, *Venkata Rami Reddy* and *Bhaskara Naidu* (1981) observed that the achievement of students reduced significantly in the non-detention system in all subjects except mathematics. This was true irrespective of the locality, sex or social class of the students.

2. Promotion Vs Non-promotion and Social and Emotional Adjustment

For more than fifty years, researchers have attempted to identify the influence of promotion or non-promotion on the social or emotional characteristics of students. An early study of McElwee (1932) sought to compare the degree to which desirable and undesirable character traits were possessed by groups of New York city second-graders, third-graders and fourth-graders who had been retained in a grade, those who had been regularly promoted and those who had advanced in grades ahead of their peers. The children's teachers evaluated the students on a scale of seven positive and seven negative characteristics, ranging from 'gets along well with others', to 'listless'. McElwee found that all groups possessed more desirable than undesirable traits and that accelerated students were judged as having more desirable traits than their regularly promoted peers, who in turn received higher scores than the non-promoted students. The inverse was found to be true for undesirable traits, with the non-promoted judged as most disobedient.

In 1933 *Farley, Frey,* and *Garland* also reported an attempt to identify the personal qualities associated with promotion and retention. Their search was similar to McElwee's. High positive correlations were found between achievement, ability, and grade placement. They also found a correlation between non-promotion and 'poor character'.

In the winter of 1938, principals in St. Paul, Minnesota, identified pupils in grades IB through 8A who were expected to fail at half-year. Pairs of students were matched in each grade for age, intelligence, achievement, and personality traits. One member of each pair was promoted and one was not. The researchers hypothesized that students who are retained have more time to make satisfactory personality adjustments than those promoted. The findings were statistically insignificant, and the hypothesis was rejected, non-pormotion did not seem to lead to improved personality measures. The difference in achievement between the two groups was not significant. The authors concluded, 'the crucial issue appears to be not whether the slow learning pupil is passed or failed, but how adequately his needs are being met' (*Cook* and *Kearney*, 1940).

Anfinson (1941) presented a study of junior high school students that attempted to determine whether non-promoted students are less well adjusted than their peers. Pairs of students were matched for attendance, chronological age, intelligence and socio-economic status, and were given two personality inventories. One member of each pair had failed a grade, or portion of a grade, and the other member had not. The author found that although promoted students seemed adjusted than repeaters to the school curriculum, the two groups did not differ appreciably in other ways.

A study directed by *Sandian* (1944) also dealt with the issue of adjustment and came to conclusions different from those of Anfinson. Sandin compared children who had failed at least once in the first eight grades with their peers who had been promoted. Except for first graders, the study found that non-promoted students were not perceived as an appropriate seatmates by their peers, and the former often chose companions from higher grades. Repeaters were also given significantly more ratings by their classmates as being unfriendly, cruel, or bullying, and teachers to gave them lower ratings on social and personal characteristics. By the time the non-pormoted pupils had been in school for a number of years, they eagerly anticipate the age at which they could leave.

Goodlad (1954) selected two groups of 50 boys and girls, matched for mental age, chronological age, and achievement. The first group was composed of non-promoted first graders, and the second of their promoted peers. At the end of the second year of schooling, the groups were compared in-terms of social and personal development. Students self-perception of adjustment was determined by scores on a self-rating instrument, peer ratings were determined by responses to sociometric questions, and the teacher ratings were determined by responses on a pupil behaviour rating scale. Neither the pupil's self-ratings nor the teachers' behaviour ratings showed significant differences between the groups. The sociometric data did, however, reveal significant differences, the general effect of non-promotion was negative.

Morrision and *Perry* (1956) supported Goodlads' findings that pupils above the typical age in classes were perceived as less popular than their regularly promoted peers.

White and *Howard* (1973) administered a 100 item self-concept inventory to sixth grade boys and girls from six school systems in North Carolina. The students were classified into groups based upon their having been promoted or held back. Fortythree boys and thirty girls and failed to be promoted at least once. The authors correlated nine sub scales of the self-concept inventory with promotion and non-promotion. A positive correlation was found between promotion on eight of the nine sub scales. Conversely, as the number or grades the students failed increased, their self-concept measures declined; the authors found a high correlation between poor self-concept and grade failures.

Finlayson (1977) studied a group of primary school children for a two year period during which a self-concept inventory was administered on four occasions. Groups of promoted, borderline, and non-promoted pupils were identified from a total sample of first graders who had never previously failed a grade. Each group contained twenty five students. It was anticipated that the self-concepts of the borderline and promoted pupils would remain constant, whereas the self-concepts of the non-promoted pupils would decline. The study found that non-promotion did not negatively influence self-concept.

Self-esteem of children who fail in school is also a chief concern. According to the reformated learned helplessness model (*Abramson, et al.,* 1978) the subset of helplessness called failure affects self-esteem. The authors also suggested that teaching individuals to attribute success, internal attributions for success and external attributes for failure contribute to improved self-concept.

Two theories which have contributed to the understanding of motivation and behaviour in achievement situations are social learning theory (*Rotter, et al.,* 1972) and achievement motivation theory (*Atkinson* and *Feather,* 1966). Research based on these theories has demonstrated the necessity of considering value (*Feather,* 1961; *Phares* and *Rotter,* 1956) as well as expectancy (Lefcourt and Ladwig, 1965; *Tyler,* 1958) in predicting behaviour. Lack of either value or expectancy would produce passivity. Value itself is affected by expectancy (*Atkinson* and *Feather,* 1966; *Rotter,* et al., 1972). Researchers in the area of learned helplessness (*Hanusa* and *Schulz,* 1977; *Wortman, et al.,* 1976) have found that when attribution to ability was induced, subjects performed better than when situational attributions for control were induced.

Personality and behavioural consequences of learned helplessness were monitored in children who had experienced extensive failure in school. Controlling for sex, race, age and IQ, three groups of children (falling, average and remedial) performance an experimental task and responded to questionnaire on self-concept and attributions for success and failure. To compare the predictive quality of learned helplessness theory with that of value expectancy theory, children were assigned to one of two reinforcement conditions (Prediction of academic success and this prediction plus monetary reward) on a maze task. As predicted by value expectancy theories, failing children were significantly more persistent in the monetary rewards condition than in the prediction of academic success condition. In agreement with learned helplessness theory, low self-concept was predicted independently and significantly by school failure, internal attributions for failure and external attributions for success ($R^2 = 0.48$) (*Johnson,* 1981).

3. School Drop-outs

It is widely accepted that wastage and stagnation are the greatest corroding agents to education at all levels in India. The latest statistics on wastage and stagnation total educational wastage provided by the Union Ministry of Education (1984) indicate that the incidence of dropouts at the primary stage is 63 per cent, while it is 50 per cent at the secondary stage. The current dorp-out rate in India is 76.6 per cent at the end of the middle class. The high incidence of wastage and stagnation in Indian schools has naturally created a sense of alarm amongst educators and serious efforts are therefore, being made to reduce the same.

One of the aspects of non-promotion that needs exploration is whether a student who has not been promoted or has failed school subjects is likely to drop-out of school earlier. *Nagamani* and *Rajarajeswari* (1988) found that 30 per cent of students gave 'fear of examination' as the reason for their dorpping-out. *Kandekar* (1974) got similar type of findings.

Academic achievement, as reflected in grade point average, courses failed, retention and achievement test scores have been uniformly found to be lower with the drop-outs.

Howighurst et el., 1962; *Combs* and *Cooley,* 1968; *Moritz,* 1977; *Stroup* and *Robins,* 1972; *Lloyd,* 1978). More frequent absence from school has been found an important factor with the drop-outs (*Havighurst, et al.,* 1962; *Moritz,* 1977; *Lloyd,* 1978).

A large proportion of both girls and boys are turned away from the school system as a result of examination and selection mechanism (*Finn, et al.,* 1979).

Intellectual ability and academic achievement of drop-outs are found to be lower than the stayins (*Combs* and *Cooly,* 1968; *Sharma* and *Sapra,* 1969; *Stroup* and *Robins,* 1972; *Broady* and *Broady,* 1976; *Moritz,* 1977; *Lloyd,* 1978; and *Pathy,* 1982).

Lack of interest and motivation and irregular school attendance are rated high for drop-out (*Sharma* and *Sapra,* 1969).

Daly and *Bateman* (1978) report that college withdrawal tends to be tied to academic reasons.

One of the earliest and most thoroughly conducted studies was that by *Thompson* (1969) conducted at Mc Comb Country Community College, Michigan. Of 3,568 students contacted, 1,434 (40%) responded regarding their course withdrawal experience. The four most frequently selected reasons on withdrawal from a list of 17 possible reasons, were job conflict, academic difficulty, change to different programme and lack of interest in course.

Broadbent (1975) examined 2,227 course schedule changes at Leeward Community College, Hawaii. The most frequent reasons given for change in schedule resulting in withdrawl by respondents were inconvenient course time, irrelevant course material and deficient academic background.

Researchers at Roane State Community College, *Tennesee* (1975) found the most frequently selected reasons for course withdrawals to be schedule conflict, fear of a poor grade, cancellation of the course, change in the students' programme, inadequate academic background and dissatisfaction with instruction.

The *Taxas Education Agency* (1977) reported on 4,197 course withdrawals at 10 Texas Community Colleges in the fall of 1976. The most frequently selected reasons for students withdrawl were grade problems, attendance problems a heavy course load, conflicting job hours, dissatisfaction with instruction and course content and other personal reasons.

Daly and *Bateman* (1978) selected a sample of 132 students at Santa Anna College who had drop-out at least one course out of a random sample of 504 students (enrolment 16,500) between the 2nd and 10th week of classes. By deleting withdrawals which took place during the first week of classes, many changes of section within the same course were ignored. 83 per cent of the sample responded. Of the reasons cited for withdrawl, 40 per cent were directly attributable to instructional factors, including excessive course materials, dislike of the instructor, dislike of the class and fear of a poor grade.

Grunes (1974) observed that many withdrawals are due to poor academic advisement and excessive work load.

Renie (1986) investigated factors related to the drop-out of freshman students with particular attention to the difference between drop-outs and persistants. Statistically significant differences were found between drop-outs and persistents in age, gender, home town location, high school records, study habits, first semester college grades, etc.

Brown (1963) asserts that the non-graded programme at Malbourne High School, Malbourne, Florida led to great decrease in the frequency of drop-outs.

An analysis of *Ayre's data* (1909) as well as of more contemporary data suggests that American education has typically practised both promotion and non-promotion. Failure rates of 10 to 15 per cent, which were regularly reported early in the century, have been dropping over the intervening years. Contemporary analysis by the National Centre for Educational Statistics (*Grant* and *Eiden*, 1980), show a steady increase in the number of fifth graders who are graduated by elementary schools and in turn graduate from high school. Whereas 30 per cent of fifth graders in 1924 completed high school, almost 75 per cent of fifth grade students entering in 1969 were graduated by 1977.

Although it is a remarkable increase in the number of fifth graders who finish high school, the point here is that more than 25 per cent, even today, do not graduate. This 25 per cent cannot be considered a population that has been non-promoted in the sense of being held in grade. They have, indeed dropped-out.

In the heat of the promotion versus non-promotion debate, the drop-out rate is often not considered. Nevertheless, the issue of whether these increasing rates of promotion or good or bad or whether a 25 per cent drop-out rate is desirable will not be decided by the numbers themselves. One report indicates that public schools currently do not promote more than 1 million young people, and the National Centre for Educational Statistics bases its retention figures on fifth grade enrollment, because the number of children who spend more than one year in the same grade in the early elementary grades inflate enrollment figures for those grades.

Tyler (1974) has pointed out that more intelligent children tend to get better grades in school, remain in school longer, and have more positive attitude towards school, but it is also true that remaining in school is likely to increase one's level of general ability. Thus, the relationship is probably in which intelligence affects classroom learning and classroom learning intern affects intelligence.

4. 100 Per Cent Promotion or Social Promotion

There are a number of educators who feel that 100 per cent promotion or social promotion can create problems for the learner. *Newhen* (n.e.) suggests that when students without the capacity for achievement are promoted, gaps of information and skill that a student should have received are in evidence, leading to serious failure later. However, if schools maintain small enough classes so that teachers may work with students at their ability and achievement level this should be no problem. *Gordon* and *Elliott* (n.d.) objective to the promotion of slow learning pupils when they have reported a grade and have still failed to improve. Both writers maintain that promotion on the basis of chronological age often places slow learning pupils in situations where even when their individual activities are suited to their capacities the group activities are far beyond their intellectual level.

Padmanabhaiah (1972) found that 75 per cent of the teachers strongly agreed with the statements that: If there were no detentions there would be indiscipline in the classrooms and pupils will not show interest in their studies. Many felt that there should be detentions to maintain good standards in education.

5. Failures

Passing or failing in an examination depends upon the interplay of a large number of variables related to pupils, teachers, subjects, schools, the examination system and parental status. Studies related to failures have been conducted at the school level as well as the University level *Bokil* (1956) found that the school size was not so important a factor which affected the percentage of failures, but the size of school influenced the number of candidates scoring less than 20 per cent of the total marks.

As for the locality of school, rural or urban, *Bokil* (1956) found the rural schools had more variation in failures. While conducting studies in relation to failures in English, *Bokil* (1963) found that one-third of the failures were by a margin of less than 10 per cent marks, overall average score in English was 31 per cent which was less than the pass marks of 35 per cent. While calculating the average percentage of failures in English, *Bokil* (1958) found that there were significant differences from group to group and from year to year.

The Directorate of Extension Programmes for Secondary Education (1964) found that teachers' qualifications and background, teaching methods, working conditions and the location of school, transfers, building, equipment, clerical work done by teachers, pupil's previous attainment, pupil's attendance, media of instruction, examination, etc., where the factors which were related to pass-fail percentage of schools. It was also found that the largest failures at the S.S.C. level were in English and mathematics.

The *Government Central Pedagogical Institute* (1964) found favourable results for regular candidates. It was found that girls failed less than boys. The performance in english, mathematics, science, and civics were responsible for the higher incidence of failure. The study found that many social, economic and educational factors were responsible for failure in schools.

The *National Council of Educational Research and Training* (1965) conducted a sample study of failure from the Boards of Bihar, Delhi, Gujarat, Kerala, Maharashtra, Mysore, Rajasthan and Uttar Pradesh. It was found that the compartmental examinations conducted by certain Boards did not seen to make much difference to the large scale failures. It was further found that the majority of failures were not due to failure in English alone.

The *Directorate of Higher Educational, Hyderabad* (1966), found that the high percentage of failures in the examination at the secondary stage was mainly due to inadequacy of library and laboratory facilities and untrained teachers.

While conducting studies in relation to failures in english, mathematics, and social science, *Gadgil* (1978), 1979a, 1979b) found that a large number of failures were mainly due to inadequacy of mastery over the subject by the teachers.

In a study on important reasons for failures at examinations as given by the examinee themselves, *Bir Singh* (1971) found that 43 per cent of respondents held the school as responsible for the failure of a pupil. The teachers of english and mathematics were held responsible to the extent of 50 per cent each. The poor teaching in all subjects was responsible to the extent of 16 per cent. 2 per cent of responsibility lay on schools for not caring to take steps to teach the pupils a legible and fast hand writing. The teachers' extensive punishment and criticism was responsible for failures to the extent of 3.5 per cent.

Parents were responsible to the extent of 29.79 per cent. This was due to the fact that the parents were poor and had to take the help of their wards in management of home affairs and in their professions. Poor parents fail to provide all essential books, appropriate facilities for study at the home, private coaching at the home, and proper diet and clothing. And some don't recognise the importance of regular punctual attendance of their wards in schools.

The pupils who failed in examinations were ready to admit their responsibility for failure to the extent of 20.014 per cent. Unfavourable social environment caused failure to the extent of 4.9 per cent. Physical surroundings like long distance of two to six miles from the school to the pupils' house and the fact that they had to go to the school on foot was responsible for failure of students to the extent of 1.75 per cent.

Causes for large scale failing in class X examination have been reported in a study made by Zilla Parishad Secondary Schools Common Examination Board, Kurnool, of Andhra Pradesh. It was observed that failures were mainly due to admissions made to classes VI and VIII without proper screening, indiscriminate opening of schools, lack of systematic scrutiny of written work of pupils and over crowding in classes (Through different states, *Educational India,* July, 1971).

6. Studies on Achievement

(a) Achievement Motivation

The need that has attracted the greatest amount of attention in recent years has been the need to achieve (n-Ach). As the term implies in n-Ach relates to accomplishment, mattering, manipulating and organising the physical and social environment, overcoming obstacles and maintaining high standards of work, compelling through striving to excel one's previous performance, as well as rivalling and surpassing others (*Lindgren,* 1979).

The need for achievement commonly known as achievement motivation, has been defined as 'the striving to increase or keep as high as possible one's own capability in all the activities in which a standard of excellence is thought to apply and where the execution of such activities can higher succeed of fail" (*Heckhausen,* 1967).

Mukarjee (1965) states that the need for achievement is characterised by a desire to attain a high standard of excellence and objective accomplishment, to increase self-regard by successful exercise of talent and to select tasks which are difficult and complicated.

Mc Clelland and his associates (1961) have reported that those with high need for achievement scores were concerned more directly with achieving success while those with moderate or low need for achievement scores were security minded and chiefly concerned with avoiding failure or with achieving a minimal level of aspiration. To promote optimum achievement, high need for achievement is a prerequisite. Mc Clelland and his associates have found high correlation between academic achievement and need for achievement as measured by Thematic Apperception Test.

Finlayson (1970), *Bhatia* (1977), *Desai* (1971) and *Reddy* and *Basavanna* (1978), using different measures of achievement motivation, have found in to be positively associated with academic achievement.

The study of *Hemalatha* and *Seetha* (1986) revealed that high and low achievers differed significantly with regard to their need for achievement scores. They found significant positive correlation between achievement motivation and academic achievement.

Some studies have showed negative or insignificant correlation between achievement motivation and academic achievement. *Hundal* and *Jeratha* (1972) obtained almost zero correlation between n-Ach and academic achievement. *Bhatnagar* (1969) and *Smith* (1964) got a negative relationship between the two variables.

According to *Atkinson, et al.,* (1964), the strength of tendency to achieve success is a multiplicative function of the variables, motive to achieve success (Ms), individual's estimate of probability of success (Ps) and the incentive value of that goal for the individual (Is).

Many investigators have reported sex differences in measures of achievement motivation and level of aspiration. Sex differences in favour of boys were reported by *Walter* and *Marzolf* (1951) *Muthaya* (1957) and *Jabar* (1968). On the other hand, superiority of girls in achievement motivation was reported by *Chaudhary* (1971) and *Agarwal* (1974). *Sinha* and *Alika Garg* (1987) have found a slightly higher tendency of girls towards n-achievement. Relationship between n-achievement and masculinity and femininity was studied by *Pillai* (1983) and he found that high masculine subjects irrespective of their sex. He also found a significant positive substantive relationship between achievement motivation and masculinity and femininity even when the effect of intelligence and socio-economic status were partialed out.

According to *Atkinson* (1978) and *Horner* (1978) motivation affects achievement. They found that competitive situations increase mastery motivation for men, whereas for women competitive situations decrease mastery motivation.

(b) Sex Differences and Achievement

In 1873, Herbert Spencer in an article 'Psychology of the sexes' argued interms of the theories of Charles Darwin that the intellectual attributes of women developed differently in course of evolution. Women were thus deficient in the powers of abstract reasoning and in the most Abstract of the emotions, the sentiment of justice. The prevalent views in Germany were even less favourable to women. Women were thus deficient in the powers essential for the survival of the race (*Sherman,* 1978). In 1906, E.L. Thorndike rejected the view that the differences between the sexes which he had observed could be inherent since such differences were too small to be of practical significance. Holligworth, a student and college of Thorndike at Teachers College, Columbia University contended that the small differences observed were due to social influences and not to biological causes and that the true intellectual potential of women would only be revealed with women received a similar education and had the right to choose equivalent careers.

Tyler (1956) in a review of research in the United States reported that in all studies girls achieved consitently higher grades than did boys. When batteries of achievement tests were used to assess achievement rather than using school grades for this purposes, girls continued to exceed boys in performance in languages while boys tended to perform better in mathematics and science. However, the differences between the sexes were small and frequently inconsistent within the same subject area; for example boys performed better on problem solving in mathematics, while girls frequently performed better on computation.

Walker (1976) has reported from the International Association for the Evaluation of Educational Achievement (I.E.A.) a study on sex differences in subjects other than mathematics and science. On reading comprehension tests, boys showed lower performance than girls in a majority of countries, but the differences between the sexes were in general slight. In the cognitive literature tests boys did less well and also showed less interest in literature. Again in the study of English as a foreign language, boys scored below the girls on both reading and listening tests. In the civic education achievement tests boys recorded higher scores than girls.

Moss (1982) reported on sex difference in achievement in mathematics in Australia across an interval of 14 years from 1964 to 1978, during which period the women's liberation movement started to have a significant influence on employment opportunities and on the participation by girls in education at the upper secondary and tertiary levels. The findings from this study, which involved the use of the same tests on the two occasions and across several autonomous state educational systems within Australia, indicated at the lower secondary school level a slightly higher level of performance by girls on subject involving elementary arithmetic and algebra and a higher level performance by boys on subtests involving advanced arithmetic and geometry. Average achievement of girls did not equal that of boys, greater gains were made by girls over the period from 1964 to 1978.

Maccoby and *Jacklin* (1974) concluded that girls, by adolescence; excel at tasks requiring verbal power, including both receptive and productive language, higher level verbal tasks (analogies, comprehension of difficult written material, creative writing) and lower level fluency measures. One factor underlying female superiority in some aspects of verbal ability may be perceptual speed and accuracy since female excelled on this measure in all four studies of sex differences cited by Maccoby and Jacklin.

Girls typically excell in english, spelling, writing at art; boys in mathematical reasoning, history, geography and science (*Terman* and *Tyler,* 1954).

It is a well documented fact according to *Northby* (1958) that girls do better in schools than boys do, at least so far as teachers rated achievement tests were concerned.

Maccoby (1967) also found that girls performed better than boys at elementary and secondary school levels.

Seashore (1962) brought together a large number of validity coefficients for scholastic aptitude tests and found that groups of girl and typically produced significantly higher coefficients than had groups of boys.

Special ability tests typically show feminine superiority of verbal fluency, manual dexterity, rote memory and classical aptitude (*Tyler,* 1965).

Girls tend to out perform boys in reading and verbal skills (*Stand* and *Lindquist,* 1942; *Gates,* 1961 Maccoby 1966; *Asher* and *Gottman,* 1973; *National Assessment of* Educational *progress,* 1972, 1976). *Flanagan, et al.,* (1961), Resenberg and *Sutton* (1964, 1969), *Monday, Hout* and *Lutz* (1966-67), *Droege* (1967) and *Very* (1967) found that girls' greater achievement in reading and verbal skills persists in to high school and beyond.

Griffin and *Flayharty* (1964) found that feminity is positively correlated with grades. *Eysenck* (1969) and others found that sex differences are apparent in English paper, but neither in verbal reasoning nor in mathematics the superiority of the girls in English is equalled by their superiority in reading. *Sevenson* (1971) enunciated that controlling for verbal intelligence, girls score better on verbal achievement tests than do boys after which they are award higher marks than boys for similar achievement test scores.

Cornelius and *Cockburn* (1978) found that there is little difference between the overall performance of boys and girls, but in individual subjects large differences do exist. *Philips* (1979) found in 4th grade sample correlational analysis that sex and residual reading gain was negative. *Tauliatos* (1979) found that achievement of girls was higher than that of boys. *Blattastien* (1981) indicated that sex differences for all achievement measures existed initially and finally.

Maccoby and *Jacklin* (1974) concluded that sex differences were well established with three cognitive constructs: mathematical performance, verbal ability and spatial visualizing ability. These differences appeared failrly consistently (in over 50 per cent of the studies) by early adolescence.

There have been many studies of sex related differences in mathematics (*Aiken,* 1972; *Stafford,* 1972; *Fennema,* 1974; *Callahan* and *Glennon,* 1975; *Fennema,* 1975; *Fennema* and *Sherman,* 1977; Sherman, 1977). As reported in a review of 38 studies by *Fennema* (1974) no significant difference were found between boys and girls mathematical achievement before or during early elementary years. It apparent in the upper elementary and early high school years, any differences were between levels of cognitive tasks. Boys were favoured when the task were at higher cognitive levels and girls were favoured when tasks were at lower cognitive levels.

Data from *National Assessment of Educational Progress* (NAEP, 1975) indicate neither sex has a clear advantage in computational ability.

The results of studies of *Fennema* (1974) support the earlier conclusion of male superiority in mathematics. *Fennema* (1977) has challenged the view that sex differences in mathematics performance exist, once differential course taking on the part of the boys and girls is accounted for. *Benbow* and *Stanley* (1980) argue that course taking alone cannot account for sex differences, because they find more boys than girls among the mathematically precaucious prior to ages when mathematics courses become elective. Although Benbow and Stanley argue that their data support a genetic explanation, they fail to consider experimental factors other than course taking that might explain sex differences in mathematics performances. *Parsons* (1981), for example, finds that parental expectations exert powerful influence on the mathematical performance of boys versus girls.

The International Association for the Evaluation of Educational Achievement (IEA) examined mathematics achievement in twelve high literacy countries during the 1960s (*Finn, et al.*, 1979). Boys at all levels performed better than girls, with the exception of certain aspects like computational problems in the U.S., Sweden and Israel. Sex differences were highest among 13 year olds in Belgium.

A major conclusion of the research was that achievement differences were primarily related to differential opportunity to learn, including equal or unequal exposure to topics, support systems for learning and appropriate models. In IEA surveys of six other school subjects in 21 countries including some underdeveloped once between 1966 and 1973 boys scored higher at all levels in total science achievement. The differences increased from 10 years through 14 years to the final secondary school year. Boys performed markedly better in physical science as compared to biology in U.K., Sweden and Newzealand. Girls out-performed boys in biology at certain ages. Girls generally out-performed boys in literature.

Despite *Jacklin's* (1979) statement that 'when the number of mathematics courses taken by high school students is partialed out, sex related differences in visuo-spatial ability are mitigated or disappear', and that if the trend for more girls to enroll in higher mathematics classes in high school continues, the actual demographic fact of sex related difference in visuo-spatal ability will lessen and perhaps disappear from adolescene (and perhaps well before adolescence) on many task that require so called spatial skills (*Maccoby* and *Jacklin;* 1974; *Wilson, et al.*, 1975; *McGuiness* and *Pribran,* 1978; *Harris,* 1978, 1979, 1981; *Fennema,* 1979; Mc *Gee,* 1979; *Sherman,* 1980; *Bowker* and *Trafton,* 1981; Eliot and *Hauptman,* 1981; *Liben,* 1981).

Keeves (1973) reported from I.E.A. studies of mathematics and science that in general and pattern of results was one of superior performance by male students.

Biley (1981) found that male students performed significantly better than female students on final accounting examination.

The study of *Nongunch and Elements* (1982) revealed that males significantly out-performed females on 25 of 72 occasions, but on no occasion did females significantly out-perform males in spatial tasks.

Leibovich (1880) compared the scholastic achievement of 30 male and 30 female students from the 5th, 6th and 7th grades in Buenas Aires, Argentina, A battery of 35 tests covered perception, general reasoning, space, verbal ability numerical ability, computing speed, memory and attention. A 2 way ANOVA was performed for each test to determine the influence of sex and school level on scores, school level did not significantly influence scores on perceptual tests but it did influence the other. The achievement of males was generally higher than that of the females.

Girls in U.K. generally perform as well as boys in elementary school upto 11 years and their performance dramatically drops at the secondary school level (Bristol *Women's Studies Group,* 1979; *Sharpe,* 1976).

However, *Sherman* (1977) observed no significant differences in the achievement of boys and girls in arithmetic but in reading tests girls achieved significantly higher scores.

Similarly, *Sharma* and *Bhargava* (1980) found that difference between the mean academic attainment of males and females was insignificant. *Lynn* and *Steven* (1983) also found no gender difference in science and mathematics achievement.

Grewal and *Bansbir* (1987) observed that sex had no significant influence on the development of verbal reasoning.

(c) Socio-economic Status and Achievement

Among the several sociological factors, socio-economic status (SES) of a child was examined in a wider perspective.

According to *Curry* (1962) social and economic factors have an effect upon language achievement in the middle intellectual ability groups. Both the upper and middle SES groups achieved better than lower SES groups. *Chopra* (1966) also found that socio-economic background was positively related to success in high school achievement.

In the multifactor study of *Srivastava* (1967), it was found that underachievement was related to poor study habits, low academic motivation, poor health, age, SES, fathers' profession, number of siblings and birth order.

Entwistle and *Welsh* (1969) observed that correlation between attainments and SES rating showed no sex differences, but there was the expected positive relationship between high social class and school attainment. *Halls* (1969) found that students belonging to the lower SES experienced low academic success, while those with middle SES fared better.

Khanna (1980) established a significant and positive relationship between SES and academic achievement.

In an attempt to identify the factors which contribute to school success, *Miner* (1970) concluded that the breadth and quantity of early learning experiences, the type of adult models a variable to children for patterning their own behaviour, the amount and quality of health care and nutrition, the amount of opportunity for intellectual stimulation, the kind of behaviour that was exerted over the child or the youth, are some of the dynamic factors that bear some relation to SES and useful in shaping and predicting academic achievement. *Dave* and *Dave* (1977) found that a higher percentage of rank students belonged to homes having higher parental income, occupation and education.

Varma (1972) observed that the educational opportunities of children whose parents have low status jobs and low incomes are apt to be considerably lessened before they even enter the school door. These children are placed at a disadvantage not only by their homes but unwillingly by the schools as well. *Entwistle* (1972) concluded that in the high intellectual ability group even when measures of intelligence were held constant the richer the SES background the less was the probability of failure. *Dewal* (1974) observed that effective teaching and learning was hampered by poor SES background.

Socio-economic status was related not only to the total achievement but also to achievement in specific school subjects. *Abraham* (1974) found achievement level in English as associated with SES and *Basavayya* (1974) found overall language achievement as influenced by the parental occupation and education.

In the same vein *Rychalk* (1975) concluded that children from lower socio-economic communities are handicapped with certain educational deficiencies like poorly articulated verbal skills and inappropriate learning strategies, which result in an amplified reliance on affective factors in the learning process.

In a *Wisconsin* study (*Fenske,* 1969) gathered information regarding scholastic achievement and socio-economic characteristics of nearly 4,000 high school seniors. It was found that verbal ability, SES and scholastic achievement were correlated with each other at 0.60 level or above in almost every population. All the three of these variables were good predictors of college attendance; however scholastic achievement was a better predictor of subsequent grades than were the other two.

From her study *Saini* (1977) found that the economic status as well as educational standard of parents was having a significant affect on the academic achievement of arts students at the college level, but in the case of science students academic achievement was significantly related to educational standard of parents, but not to economic status.

SES, parental background and attitudes (*Fennema* and *Sherman,* 1977) and the influences of teachers and school systems (*Fennema* and *Sherman,* 1977; 1978) all may affect mathematics related attitudes and behaviour in high schools.

SES can be regarded as an important aspect of student social background (*Kogan,* 1977) as a factor which by determining certain aspects of family environment-indirectly influences students classroom performance (*Marjoribanks,* 1977).

Children from poor and/or non-white homes tend to score at below average levels no tests which purport to measure intelligence (*Babad* and *Coleman, et al.,* 1966).

According to *Coleman et al.,* (1966) and *Mostellar* and *Moyniha* (1972) home and family background variables made a much more significant contribution to student achievement than any school or teacher variables.

Ramoji Rao (1977) observed that poor facilities in their houses as regard to study space, study materials, lighting facilities etc., would deprive the children from attaining good academic standards. *Irwin* (1978) found that approximately a third of the variance in school grades is explained by measures of early intellectual ability and family economic level and intellectual stimulation in the home.

Coleman et al., (1966) found that school facilities, curriculum and teacher characteristics had little correlation with achievement independent of the students socio-economic background. Their study also predicted achievement more effectively with SES characteristics than did school factors.

SES of the pupils is positively and significantly correlated with their actual performance in all the five major school subjects and teacher ratings made by their teachers on their academic achievement (*Ganapathy* and *Singh,* 1981).

Brenstein (1968), *Fraser* (1969), *De* and *Singh* (1970) *Oberlander and others* (1970), *Abraham* (1974), *Harris* (1979), *Katherene* (1975) have all found that family size and achievement are inversely related. That is, larger the family size lesser was the performance and vice versa.

The relationship between parents' education and academic achievement was studiea by *Watson* (1965), *Blan* and *Duncon* (1967), *Fraser* (1969), *Chatterji et al.*, (1971), *Abraham* (1974), *Trivedi* (1974), *Rathnaiah* (1977), who found that parents' education was significantly related to the scholastic achievement of pupils.

Coster (1958), *Gupta* (1968), *Fraser* (1969), *Verma* (1971), *Bulcock et al.*, (1974), Mathew (1975), *Raymond* (1976), Hushak (1976), *Sharma* and *Bhargava* (1980), *Rathnaiah* (1978), *Gupta* (1982) have examined parental occupation and income and these studies have found a high degree of relationship between these SES variables and academic achievement.

High average and low achieving boys and girls in the first and third grades were compared on (a) their expectations for success prior to an anagrams task (b) their subsequent perception of the cause of failure on the task and (c) their expectations for future success. Results indicated that boys with a history of low academic success in school had lower expectations for success on the task and tended to be more likely to attribute failure to lack of ability than boys with a history of average on high academic success. In contrast, the high achieving girls had lower expectations for success than the low-and average-achieving girls. Further more, children who attributed failure to low ability reported relatively low expectations for future success. These findings suggest that children's perception of the causes of past performance outcome mediate their subsequent expectations (*Deborah* and *Joel*, 1980).

Home environment has got a strong association with academic achievement. Investigation conducted by *Harrett* (1957), *Fraser* (1969), *Mishra* (1960), *Mathur* (1964), Henderson and Merritt (1968), *Keeves* (1972), Srivastava (1974), *Marjoribanks* (1976), *Hemakumari* (1977), *Bradley et al.*, (1977), *Varma* (1982, *Jagannadhan* (1986) have all emphasised that family's social and psychological environment has got pervasive influence on the academic achievement of school children.

According to Gottfredson (1981), minority persons from lower class backgrounds have more limiting factors in their social space than do white persons from lower class backgrounds. Gump and *Rivers* (1975) concluded that social status had as strong an influence on mastery as race.

Jensen (1969) maintains that heredity severely limits the ability of back youth to think conceptually. Cultural deprivation was one of the first theories concerned with the education of lower class students to emerge in the 1960s. Bernstein (1994) and Reissman (1962) were two of its major architects. Cultural deprivation theorists assume that lower class youths do not achieve highly academically because of the debilitating effects of poverty and the intellectual and cultural deficits that these students experience during their first years of life.

Cultural difference theorists, notably *Valentine* (1968) and *Baratz* and *Baratz* (1970), reject the arguments of the cultural deprivationists. They maintain that ethnic minority and poor youth have strong, rich and diverse cultures. These cultures, argue the cultural difference theorists, consists of languages and dialects that are rich and elaborate and of values, behavioural styles, and perspectives that can enrich the lives of all students. They argue that these minority youths fail to achieve highly in schools not because they have deprived or deficit cultures but because they have cultures that are different from the schools' middle class culture.

Another group of social scientists (*Green,* 1977) argues that the most effective way to help poor and minority youth to achieve academically is to place them in higher status.

Gaynor (1981) from her ethnographic study of a middle class housing estate in Great Britain and shows that families living there are in the process of moving from working status to one termed the 'new' middle class achieving their newly acquired status through the occupational mobility of men, women of the estate develop a collective estate culture and life style conducive to the academic success of their children.

She concludes her analysis by relating micro level changes in family life style and school achievement to changes in the occupational structure of the society.

Shashidhar (1981) studied the relationship between certain school variables and the achievement of SC and ST secondary school students of Karnataka. The study used a pool of tools to get data. The variables openness of the school, teacher's attitude towards scheduled castes and intelligence were found to be significantly related to the achievement of SC students. *Rani* (1980) in her study on a sample of undergraduate engineering students belonging to five different institutions in India, observed that academic achievement of the SC students was significantly lower than that of non-SC students Aruna's (1981) study also reported similar results.

Sharma (1967) found that among the different caste groups, those from higher castes were better in achievement. *Lalithamma* (1973), in her study found that pupils belonging the scheduled caste and scheduled tribes do not achieve adequately. *Sarala* (1975) inferred that pupils belonging to forward communities are slightly better than pupils belonging to backward communities with regard to their academic achievement. *Ushashri* (1978) found that socially disadvantaged pupils (Harijans) and the socially non-disadvantaged pupils differed significantly in their academic achievement. *Maestas* (1981) quoted from the works of *Coleman and others* (1966) that the assessment of achievement must be sensitive to differences in social class and ethnic caste. He concluded that non-Mexican American students achieved at higher level than Mexican American students. *Blattestrin* (1981) also indicated that ethnic differences were consistently found in achievement. *Jagannadhan* (1986) also found that children from backward communities scored significantly below that of the forward communities.

Jensen and *Figueroa* (1975) and *Reynold* and *Gutkin* (1981) have compared various groups with reference to primary memory ability (Level I) requiring minimal manipulation of the stimulus input, as well as complex cognitive processing (Level II) requiring intentional manipulation of the stimulus input prior to recall. *Nenson* and Inouye (1980) and *Vernon* (1981), *Jachuck* and *Das* (1982), *Radha Syam and others* (1988), have reported significant racial ethnic and contrast genetic group differences in the processing of Level I and Level II abilities.

Kamin (1981) and *Blan* (1981) have criticised that the genetic explanation of the differences in cognitive ability and have emphasised the environmental hypothesis.

Rao (1965), *Coleman et al.*, (1966), *Fenskl* (1969), *Sudhama* (1973), *Reddy* (1973), *Shachdev* (1974) found that achievement was not significantly related to socio-economic status.

The study conducted by *John Hottie* (1984) did not support the commonly held view that home environment exerts direct effects on academic achievement.

Gupta (1968) found that parents' education and pupils achievement are not significantly related to each other.

(d) Locality and Achievement

The locality in which the child resided or where the school is situated is also an important variable affecting the academic achievement of the students. *Chatterjee* (1977) found that at V class level city pupils tend to do better than rurals. *Sharma* and *Bhargava* (1980) also found that rural and urban children differed significantly in academic achievement. However, *Maestas* (1981) findings suggested that region did not influence student's achievement, nor did the size of the community or size of the school.

According to *Benson* (1985) in the lower grades, children in the rural areas and in urban slums may drop out of the school and study poorly on account of the problems of health and diet.

Bokil (1956c) found that rural schools and more variation in failures.

In another investigation *Bokil* (1956b) found that school size was not so important a factor which affected the percentage of failures, but the size of the school influenced the number of candidates scoring less than twenty per cent of total marks.

In their investigation on aspirations of urban and rural youth *Sewell* and *Nenser* (1975) reported lower educational and career aspirations for youth in rural locations, as compared with youth from urban locations. *Farmer* (1980), however, found no significant effect for school location on career motivation.

Educational programmes for people in rural areas are generally seen as a means of compensating for and counteracting the dominance of powerful urban centres over the weaker rural community. Compared with people living in urban areas, country dwellers are in many respects at a disadvantage with regard to essential services, including access to educational institutions and quality of education. This is particularly true for rural masses in developing countries (*Bude,* (1981).

According to *Beedwat* (1976) the intensity of incidence of under achievement was more or less uniform in the urban and rural areas.

Grewal and *Bensbir* (1987) observed that the residential background had no significant influence on the verbal reasoning of boys and girls.

3

Statement of the Problem and Hypotheses

Many an educationist emphasised on the ills of the examination system and recommended several reforms. The university education commission has remarked that if any single reform in the education system has to be recommended that should be that of examinations. Many committees and commissions recommended different types of reforms in the system of education in general and examinations in particular.

The Government of Andhra Pradesh has introduced in 1971 a major reform in the system of school education in the State. According to this reform, which is known as the non-detention system students will be promoted from one class to another, provided they put in a stipulated percentage of attendance. However, at the VII and X class levels they may be detained if they do not get the prescribed minimum marks in a common/public examination conducted at the end of these two classes. In all other classes they will be automatically promoted irrespective of the level of their achievement provided they put in the required percentage of attendance.

In this system, therefore, the stigma of failure, and along with it, the fear of detentions are almost taken away.

The educational philosophy behind this non-detention system or automatic promotion system, as it is some times referred to, is that education is best imparted in an atmosphere of free progress where the incentive and urge to improve spring from within the educational process rather than from the terror of examinations and detentions (*Kabra*, 1971; *Krishnamoorthy*, 1971). If a pupil is regular to the school he will, in all probability, acquire at least the minimum that is expected in a normal school situation (*Rao*, 1977). It was also argued that in the non-detention system the child would be able to study and learn in a natural setting which would help him in grasping the various subjects better. It was felt that detentions were negative incentives. They develop inferiority complexes and unfavourably attitude towards the school, the teaches and the whole education system (*Kabra*, 1971; *Krishnamoorthy*, 1971). The new system on the other hand would allow the teachers ample time and freedom to try new methods of teaching and evaluation (*Sarabhachari*, 1971). This would help the teachers in the development of the desired intellectual as well as various aspects of personality among the students (*Satyanarayana*, 1972). It was also felt that this system would reduce wastage and stagnation (*Kabra*, 1971; *Krishnamoorthy*, 1971; *Rao*, 1977; *Venka Reddy*, 1971).

But there were others who condemned the government for taking this wrong step. They said the government of Andhra Pradesh has abolished detentions with a stroke of the pen. They felt that the only inducement to study has been removed. This system would tell upon the standards of education, which were already low. Though tests and examinations would be conducted in the non-detention system also, students would not evince any interest in the tests as the marks obtained in them were not going to matter much (*Editorial, Educational India*, 1971). According to the Editor, The Educational Review, for a normal child, the strain of examinations and related detentions is a healthy way of toughening up his mental fibre and it is wrong to think that children brood very much over occasional failures. This is indeed a revolutionary experiment in education with 'vengeance' (*Editorial, The Educational Review,* 1971).

Any change that is brought about in any system would invite a mixed reaction. In the same manner this reform was also condemned by some and commanded by others.

Apart from these 'opinions' expressed by different educationists about the system very few empirical studies have been conducted on the merits and demerits of the system. It is high time that the system is evaluated in all its dimensions, so that the system may be introduced in other states also if the results are in the desired direction. It will be worthwhile for Andhra Pradesh also to know where it stands, whether the scheme is working on right lines yielding the desired results, or whether drastic modifications are required and if so in what direction.

1. Statement of the Problem

Thus the present study is designed to evaluate the non-detention system in different aspects like its effect on the achievement of students, percentage of passes, rate of drop outs and the attitude of students, teachers and administrators towards it.

2. Objectives

1. To make a comparative study of the achievement of students under the detention and non-detention systems.
2. To make a comparative study of the percentage of passes in the detention and non-detention systems.
3. To make a comparative study of the rate of drop-outs in the detention and non-detention systems.
4. To assess the attitude of pupils, teachers and administrators towards the non-detention system.

5. To suggest remedies for the defects if any in the system.

3. Specific Questions to be Answered

Answers to questions such as the following were sought to be found out from the study.

1. Is there a significant difference in the achievement of students under the detention and non-detention systems?

   Will the answer to the above question differ from boys to girls, from one social class of students to another, and from students of one locality to another?

2. Is there a significant difference in the percentage of passes under the detention and non-detention systems?

   Will the answer to the above question differ from boys to girls and from locality to locality.

3. Is there a significant difference in the rate of drop-outs under the detention and non-detention systems?

   Will the answer to the above question differ from boys to girls and from one locality to another?

4. How do the students feel about the new system of evaluation? Do they have a negative or positive attitude?

   Will the answer to this question vary with the sex, locality or social class of the students?

5. What is reaction of the teachers towards the new system?

   Does the answer to this question vary with the sex, locality, level of teaching, or experience of the teachers?

6. What do the administrators think about the system? Do they react favourably or unfavourably towards it?

7. Is there any significant difference between the attitude of pupils, teachers and administrators towards the system?

4. Hypotheses

In the light of the above, the following major hypotheses were set up for investigation:

1. There would not be any significant difference between the achievement of pupils under the detention and non-detention systems.

   This would be true irrespective of the sex, social class or locality to which they belonged. The above hypotheses were tested separately for each of the six subjects and the total of all the subjects.

2. There would not be any significant difference between the percentage of passes in the two systems.

   This would be true irrespective of sex or locality of the pupils.

3. The rate of drop-outs in the non-detention system would be significantly less than that in the detention system.

   This would be true irrespective of the sex or locality to which the pupils belonged.

4. Pupils would have a negative attitude towards the non-detention system.

   This would be true irrespective of their sex, locality or social class.

5. Teachers would have a negative attitude towards the new system of evaluation.

This would be true irrespective of their sex, locality, level of teaching or length of experience.

6. Administrators would have a negative attitude towards the system.

7. There would not be any significant difference between the attitude of pupils, teachers and administrators towards the new system of evaluation.

In addition to the above major hypotheses the following related hypotheses were also set up for investigation.

1. There would not be any significant difference between the achievement of boys and girls.

2. There would not be any significant difference between the achievement of pupils belonging to different social classes.

3. Pupils hailing from different localities would not differ significantly with regard to their achievement.

The above hypotheses were tested separately for each of the six subjects and the total of all the subjects.

Variables Studied

Since the problem envisages an evaluation of the non-detention system with reference to achievement, percentage of passes, rates of drop-outs and the attitude of pupils, teachers and administrators towards the system, a brief description of the variables employed in the study is in order.

1. System

As pointed out earlier the Government of Andhra Pradesh introduced the non-detention system in the year 1971-72. Prior to 1971 there were detentions. That system was called detention system. Under that system pupils were promoted to the next higher class based on their performance in tests and terminal examinations. To get promotion one should get 20 per cent of marks in Hindi and 35 per cent of marks in all other subjects. However, if the aggregate was more than 195, for every 10 marks above 195 one mark could be added to the marks in any subject in which the student got less than the minimum required for a pass. The moderation could be upto a maximum of 20 marks in all the subjects put together, subject to a maximum of 5 marks in any subject.

In the non-detention system on the other hand, the student will be promoted to the next higher class irrespective of the quality of his academic progress, provided he puts in 75[1] per cent of attendance at the school. However, at the end of the 7th and 10th classes a common/public examination will be held, and a student can be detained in these classes if he did not secure the specified minimum percentage of marks (which was the same as in detention system).

2. Academic Achievement

According to the Dictionary of Psychology (*Chaplain,* 1961), 'academic achievement is the level of attainment of proficiency in academic work as evaluated by teachers, or by standardised tests, or by a combination of both.

According to the Dictionary of Education, 'academic achievement means knowledge attained or skills developed in the school subjects, usually designated by test scores or marks assigned by teaches or by both' (*Good,* 1959).

The present study attempts to see whether there is any difference in the achievement of students under the detention and non-detention systems.

3. Percentage of Passes

The term 'pass' refers to the promotion of pupils from one class to the next higher class. The present study aims at making a comparative study of the percentage of passes in the detention and non-detention systems.

4. Rage of Drop-outs

For the purpose of the study the term drop-outs is used to refer to such students who have joined in a class but have not continued their studies in the next class, dropping-out in

---

1 The Headmaster can give 10 per cent condonation for shortage of attendance on medical certificate and merit. The District Educational Officer (DEO) can condone another 20 per cent of absence on medical grounds and merit, based upon his discretion.

the middle of the year or before the beginning of the next higher class. For example a student who has joined in VII class, might have withdrawn from the school during the middle of the year, or he might have completed VI class but failed in the annual examination and discontinued or he might have been promoted to VII class yet he has not constituted his studies.

The number of students who were admitted in a class and the number who have dropped-out before the beginning of the next year was recorded from the registers maintained in the schools to make a comparative study of rate of drop-outs in the detention and non-detention systems.

5. Attitude

Attitude refers to the degree of 'liking' or 'disliking' towards a psychological object and in line with this thinking, *Thurstone* (1946) defined attitude as 'the degree of positive or negative effect associated with some psychological object'.

An attitude is a 'dispositional readiness to respond for certain situations, persons or objects in a constant manner which has been learned and has become one's typical mode of response' (Freeman, 1967).

The attitude of the pupils, teachers and administrators towards the non-detention system was measured by means of an attitude scale developed for the purpose, to make a comparative study of their attitude towards the new system.

6. Level of teaching

In any secondary school setting there are two cadres of teachers—Secondary grade assistants and B.Ed. assistants. The Secondary grade assistants handle classes VI and VII while the B.Ed. assistants handle VIII, IX and X classes. The minimum required qualification for appointment as a Secondary grade teacher is intermediate and secondary grade training, while those who have got atleast a B.A./B.Sc./B.Com. and B.Ed. are appointed as B.Ed. assistants.

Both the categories of teachers were included in the study to see whether there was any significant difference between their attitude towards the non-detention system.

7. Locality

Localities were categorised as urban, semi-urban and rural as explained below:

(a) Urban

A locality was considered as urban if it had (a) a municipality, (b) abundant road and rail connections, (c) educational facilities upto the collegiate level, (d) a large number of government offices (e) good facilities for entertainment like cinema halls, theatres etc. (f) clubs like the Rotary, the Lions, etc. (g) at least medium size industries, (h) a sizeable floating population and (i) business and commercial importance.

(b) Semi-urban

A locality was considered to be semi-urban if it had (a) the headquarters of a taluk, (b) modern means of transport, either road or rail or both with moderate frequency, (c) postal, telegraph and telephone facilities, (d) a few government offices, (e) banks, (f) a hospital and (g) moderate facilities for entertainment.

(c) Rural

A locality was considered as rural if (1) it was not connected by railway lines and did not have frequent motor transport, (b) it did not have adequate communication facilities like telephone and telegraph, (c) it did not have hospital (primary health centre excepted) and government offices, factories etc., (d) it was outside a radius of atleast 15 kilometers from the nearest town and (3) its population was predominantly agricultural.

8. Sex

Students from both the sexes were included in the study to find out whether there was any significant difference between boys and girls with regard to their achievement, percentage of passes, rate of drop-outs and with regard to their attitude towards the non-detention system.

Similarly teaches of both the sexes were included in the study to see whether there was any significant difference between men and women teachers in their attitude towards the non-detention system.

9. Experience of the Teachers

The number of years the individual has worked as a teacher may have an influence on his attitude towards the non-detention system. Hence, the length of service or experience of the teachers was recorded and they were divided into different subgroups on the basis of their experience and the significance of the difference between their attitude was studied.

10. Social Class

In India, the population is divided into 3 major groups depending on the social class to which they belong as (a) forward, (b) backward and (c) scheduled castes/scheduled tribes.

(a) ***Scheduled Castes:*** Scheduled Castes include such castes, races or tribes, or parts of groups within such castes, races or tribes as are deemed under Article 341 (Indian Constitution) to be scheduled castes, and are so declared by the president by public notification after consultation with the concerned Governors of the several states wherein they reside.[2]

(b) ***Scheduled Tribes:*** The Scheduled Tribes and other tribal communities include various tribes and communities which are declared to be such by the president, by the Constitution (Scheduled Tribes)

2 Articles 365 (24)/Article 341-Constitution of India.

order, 1950, and the Constitution (Scheduled Tribes) (Union Territories) order, 1951.[3]

(c) ***Backward Castes:*** Backward Castes are those who are 'socially and educationally backward', and labour under various difficulties and conditions of social, economic or educational backwardness.[4]

(d) ***Forward Castes:*** Forward Castes are those who do not come under the above categories, viz., scheduled castes, scheduled tribes and backward classes and supposed to belong to upper sections of the society.

What is the effect of the non-detention system on pupils belonging to different social classes? To probe into this the information about the social class of the students was recorded from the registers maintained in the Office of the Commissioner for Government Examinations, Hyderabad, and analysis of marks was carried out. For the study of attitude of students, information about their social class was obtained through a carefully worded personal data sheet.

11. Administrators

The Headmasters of secondary schools and supervising authorities like Gazetted Inspectors and District Educational Officers were treated as 'administrators' in this study to examine their attitude towards the non-detention system.

3 Articles 365 (25)/Article 342—Constitution of India.

4 Report of the Backward Classes Commission, I, pp. 39-40.

5

Method of Investigation

The investigation has four aspects—1. comparison of achievement under the detention and non-detention systems, 2. comparison of percentage of passes under the two systems, 3. comparison of rate of drop-outs under the two systems and 4. assessment of attitude of students, teachers and administrators towards the non-detention system.

The method used to carry out the above four aspects of the investigation is described in the following pages:

I. ACHIEVEMENT

As the study is designed to make a comparative study of the achievement of different categories of students under the detention and non-detention system, what was required was to identity representative samples of students who had a sufficiently long period of education under the detention and non-detention systems. The study was essentially of the ex-post-facto type. Thus the marks obtained at the X class public examination by the last batch of students under the detention system and one batch of students under the non-detention system were sought to be collected and analysed.

For this purpose the sample of students was selected by a multistage stratified random sampling procedure. Andhra Pradesh State is divided by the Government into three regions as Circar, Rayalaseema and Telangana for administrative purposes. For the purpose of this investigation, at the outset, one revenue district was selected at random from each region. They were Krishna, Nellore and Nalgonda districts of the three regions respectively. The secondary schools in each of the districts thus selected were divided as urban, semi-urban and rural depending upon the locality in which they were situated. Out of these, those schools which had class before 1969 (at least 3 years before the non-detention system was introduced) were listed and four schools from urban, six from semi-urban and eight from rural areas were selected at random from each district thus giving 54 schools. Unequal number of schools from each locality were selected because the enrolment in urban schools was disproportionately large compared to that in rural schools.

The last batch of students who took the X class public examination under the detention system (i.e., those who appeared for the X class public examination in March 1971) and one batch of students who had their education right from I class to X class under the non-detention system and took the X class public examination from the same schools in March 1983 constituted the sample for the study.

During the year 1980 there was reorganisation of the syllabi and the curriculum was upgraded including several new topics. This new syllabus was introduced at the secondary level, at VIII class during the year 1982. Thus the students who took the X class public examination during the year 1983 with the old curriculum which was followed by the 1971 batch of students were taken for the study. Students who had their education under the detention and non-detention systems from the same schools were taken to avoid differences in the school environment affecting the results. An examination of their history of the schools selected showed that there were no drastic changes in the school environment during the period 1970-1983. A total of 7740 students took the X class public examination from the 54 schools during the selected years. All the students were included in the study. Out of them 2714 belonged to the detention system whereas 5026 belonged to the non-detention system.

The marks obtained at the X class public examination by the sample of subjects thus selected were recorded from the registers maintained in the office of the Commissioner for Government Examinations, Hyderabad. Other information about the students regarding their sex and social class was also recorded from the same registers.

II. PERCENTAGE OF PASSES

The number of students who appeared for the X class public examination from the selected schools during the selected years and the number of those who have passed was recorded from the registers maintained in the respective schools. From the above information the percentage of passes under the two systems was calculated and analysed.

III. RATE OF DROP-OUTS

The phenomenon of drop-outs is one of the most serious problems of Indian education today. One of the contentions of the protagonists of the non-detention system was that it would reduce rate of drop-outs. Thus besides comparison of achievement, the study also aims at the comparison of rate of drop-outs in the two systems.

For this purpose, enrolment in each class during the selected years and the number of students dropping-out by the beginning of the next year under the two systems was recorded from the registers maintained in the schools; from which the rate (percentage) of drop-outs under the two system were calculated and analysed. The size of the sample for this analysis was 37,764.

IV. ATTITUDE TOWARDS THE NON-DETENTION SYSTEM

Before describing the method used for assessing the attitude of the subjects towards the non-detention system, it may not be out of place to discuss the nature and meaning of attitude.

1. Meaning of Attitude

In the Dictionary of Philosophy and Psychology, *Baldwin* (1905) defined attitude as 'readiness for attention or action of a definite sort'.

Allport (1929) prefers to treat attitude as 'a mental and neural state of readiness, organised through experience, exerting a directive or dynamic influence upon the individual's response to all objects and situations with which it is related. This definition stresses that attitude is a generalised pattern in perception or action which is a result of integration of various experiences.

In the words of *Kohler* (1929), from the point of view of Gestalt Psychology a change of attitude involves a definite psychological stress exerted upon a sensory field by a process originating in other parts of the nervous system.

'Attitude is a tendency to act toward or against something in the environment which becomes, thereby, a positive or negative value' (*Bogardus,* 1941).

'Attitudes are literally mental postures, guides for conduct to which each new experience is referred before a response is made' (*Morgan,* 1934).

In *Warren's* (1934) dictionary of psychology, attitude is defined as 'the specific mental disposition towards an incoming (or arising) experience whereby that experience is modified, or a condition of readiness for a certain type of activity.

Guilford (1954), defined attitude as 'personal disposition common to individuals, but possessed to different degrees, which impels them to react to objects, situations or propositions in ways that can be called, favourable or unfavourable'.

'An attitude is a dispositional readiness to respond for certain situations, persons, or objects in a constant manner which has been learned and has become one's typical mode of response' (*Freeman,* 1967).

According to the Advanced Learner's Dictionary of Current English, attitude means 'way of feeling, thinking or believing' (*Hornby, et al.,* 1968).

All the definitions cited above give importance to the degree of liking or disliking towards a psychological object and in the same vein, *Thurstone* (1946) defined attitude as 'the degree of positive or negative affect associated with some psychological object.

2. Different Methods of Measuring Attitude

Attitude can be measured in several ways. One's attitude is revealed in his behaviour. So it can be assessed by direct observation of the overt behaviour of the individual. This has all the defects of observation, in addition to the difficulty of experimentally creating a real situation, wherein the behaviour can be observed.

Projective techniques can also be used to assess an individual's attitude. The basis for the use of projective techniques to measure attitude is that attitude can be inferred by one's unconscious responses to certain stimuli like photographs, cartoons, etc. This method has all the disadvantages of projective techniques like difficulty in administration, scoring, low inter-scorer reliability, etc.

3. Attitude Scales

The most common and popular method of estimating a person's attitude is through an attitude scale, where the individual is asked to express his opinion on several controversial statements about the psychological object under consideration. The logic behind the use of opinion to measure attitude is that there is a positive correlation between what people say about a subject and what they will do about it. To the extent people's actions correlate with their expressed opinion we can predict the former from the later. Any single action, however, will be extremely unreliable from the point of view of measurement. A person's particular actions cannot be predicted with a high degree of accuracy yet, one's position on an attitude continuum can be assessed. No doubt this method of assessing attitude from expressed opinion is also subject to some limitations like faking of responses by the individual, where he tends to give socially acceptable responses, there by, concealing his real attitude. But this could be overcome in several ways, like making the questionnaire anonymous, etc.

4. Construction of the Preliminary Form

Attitude towards any system of evaluation results from many specific attitudes like the effect of the system on (1) the students' interest in studies, (2) discipline in the school (3) teacher's work involvement (4) tuition (5) conduct of tests (6) freedom to the teachers and the students (7) relationship between the teacher and the taught, etc.

Bearing the above important dimensions which may contribute to the positive or negative reactions of the students and teachers towards the non-detention system, as a first step in the development of the attitude scale, a number of statements of opinions of teachers and students about the non-detention system were collected from a number of sources as follows:

30 men and 30 women high school teachers and students were requested to write the merits and demerits of the non-detention system in the light of their experience taking different aspects into consideration. These statements were sorted out and listed. This list of statements was supplemented by a careful study of related literature and informal interviews with high school teachers and headmasters, and a large pool of 75 items was prepared. The pool of items, or universe of items as *Guttman* (1947) calls it, thus collected was refined by observing the following

criteria laid down by different authors like *Likrt* (1932), *Edwards* and *Kilpatric* (1948), Guilford (1954) and others:

(a) The statements must be clear, precise and straight forward;

(b) They should be short and to the point;

(c) 'Double baralled' statements should be removed;

(d) They must be constructed as expressions of desired behaviour, not as statements of fact;

(e) They must be in such a form that the ideas can be accepted or rejected;

(f) Both favourable and unfavourable statements must be included;

(g) Statements that could be endorsed by every one or no one must be avoided;

(h) Positive and negative statements must be approximately equal in number;

(i) Negative and positive statements must be randomised so that any space error or any tendency towards a stereotyped response may be avoided.

The item pool thus refined, was presented to 10 experienced men and women teachers who were requested to:

(a) add other statements that might be relevant to the subject;

(b) point out redundant statements;

(c) mark ambiguous and 'double barelled' items, if any; and

(d) give suggestions for refining the items.

Their suggestions were incorporated and 67 items were selected to be included in the preliminary form *(Appendix B).*

Each of the items was arranged on a five point scale with the following alternatives: strongly agree, agree, doubtful, disagree and strongly disagree. The items were randomised and the pilot form of the scale was prepared. To avoid faking of the responses the instrument was made anonymous.

5. Pilot Study

The pilot study was conducted on 240 secondary school teachers and 240 tenth class students. The sample of teachers and students were selected from 23 schools which were selected by following stratified random sampling procedure from among the schools located in Chittoor District. At the outset the schools in the district were divided based upon the locality in which they were situated and 5, 8 and 10 schools were selected at random from urban, semi-urban and rural localities respectively. 16, 10 and 8 teachers equally distributed between the two sexes and the two levels of teaching, viz., Secondary grade and B.Ed. assistants were selected from each of the schools located in urban, semi-urban and rural localities respectively. Thus giving 240 teachers equally distributed between the three localities, the two sexes and the two levels of teaching. Table 5.1 shows the distribution of the sample of teachers selected for the pilot study.

Table—5.1 Distribution of the Sample of Teachers Selected for the Pilot Study

Urban				Semi-urban				Rural				Total
Men		Women		Men		Women		Men		Women		
B.Ed.	Sec. grade	B.Ed.	Sec. grade	B.Ed.	Sec. grade	B.Ed.	Sec. grade	B.Ed.	Sec. grade	B.Ed.	Sec. grade	
20	20	20	20	20	20	20	20	20	20	20	20	240

The sample of students for the pilot study was also drawn from the same schools selected as mentioned above. 16, 10 and 8 tenth class students equally divided between boys and girls were selected from each of the schools located in urban, semi-urban and rual areas respectively. Table 5.2 shows the sample of students selected for the pilot study.

Table—5.2 Distribution of the Sample of Students Selected for the Pilot Study

Urban		Semi-urban		Rural		Total
Boys	Girls	Boys	Girls	Boys	Girls	
40	40	40	40	40	40	240

The instrument was administered to the teachers individually through personnel contact in their respective schools during leisure hours. Necessary rapport was established with the teaches by explaining the purpose of the investigation. They were also explained how they had to mark their responses. The instrument itself was self-administering.

The maximum number of students selected from any school was only 16. The attitude scale was administered to the sample of students selected in each school in small groups. At first the students were motivated explaining the importance of research in general, and the significance of the present study in particular. They were also explained briefly about the detention system to avoid any ambiguity about the concept of detention system. This was necessary since they had all their education under the non-detention system. The attitude scale forms were then distributed and the instructions were read to the students slowly as they read them for themselves. Doubts if any were clarified and they were asked to mark their responses.

For the purpose of scoring, in line with *Likert* (1932), weights of 5, 4, 3, 2, 1 were assigned to each of the 5 categories of responses, viz., strongly agree, agree, doubtful, disagree, and strongly disagree respectively in the case of positive statements. The scoring procedure was reversed in the case of negative statements. Table 5.3 shows the scoring weights given to the five alternative responses.

Table—5.3 Scoring Weights Given to the Five Alternative Responses

Type of Statement	Strongly agree	Agree	Doubtful	Disagree	Strongly Disagree
Positive	5	4	3	2	1
Negative	1	2	3	4	5

This method of weighting responses is quite sample and highly satisfactory. *Likert* (1932) found that scores based upon this relatively simple assignment of integral weights correlated 0.99 with the scores obtained by the high complicated and time consuming procedure of normal deviate system of weighting.

6. Item Analysis

Item analysis of the responses of the teachers and students, who participated in the pilot study, was carried out separately by the method of criterion of internal consistency suggested by *Likert* (1932). The results obtained by this method of criterion of internal consistency agree very well with the results of the traditional method of item analysis, at the same time this method is far less laborious than the latter, and is advocated by many investigators like *Likert* (1932), *Murphy* and *Likert* (1937), *Edwards* (1969), to mention a few.

This method consists of rank ordering the respondents with respect to their total scores and taking a high group and a low group on the basis of the total score and calculating the internal consistency of each statement using the formula:

Internal consistency of any statement=

Mean score of the high group—mean score of the low group on the statement.

On the basis of the discriminative power of each of the items thus obtained, they can be rank ordered and the required number of items with high discriminative power can be selected for inclusion in the instrument or the discriminative power of each item can be treated for significance using *t* test or any such test and those items which have a significant discriminative power can be selected for inclusion in the final form of the instrument (*Edwards*, 1969).

In the present investigation the highest scoring 27 per cent and the lowest scoring 27 per cent were taken to represent the high and low groups, because with this tail proportions, the coefficient of discrimination is most sensitive (*Kelly*, 1939). Further, instead of taking an arbitrary lower limit for the discriminative power of the items for the purpose of their inclusion in the final form, the discriminative power of each of the items was tested for significance by applying *t* test following *Edwards* (1969).

7. Results of Item Analysis

The results obtained in the item analysis of the responses of the teachers are shown in Table 5.4 along with the *t* values, while the results of item analysis of the responses of the students are shown in Table 5.5.

Table—5.4 Internal Consistency of the Different Items and the Results of the *t* Test (teachers)

Statement number	d	*t*	Statement number	d	*t*
1 *	1.80	8.95	10	1.02	4.64
2.	1.64	8.73	11	1.10	5.84
3	1.28	6.78	12 @	−0.29	−1.31
4	1.93	11.04	13	0.91	3.91
5	1.26	6.33	14	1.18	6.06
6	1.52	9.23	15	1.14	7.34
7	0.73	3.12	16	1.37	8.41
8	1.05	5.20	17 *	0.13	0.75
9	1.20	5.52	18	1.37	8.22

Statement number	d	*t*	Statement number	d	*t*
19	0.67	3.05	43	1.46	8.48
20	1.43	7.66	44	0.94	7.02
21	1.53	7.37	45	1.33	8.53
22	1.20	7.91	46	1.40	9.06
23	0.92	4.60	47 @	–0.15	–0.76
24	1.09	5.14	48 @	0.48	2.01
25	0.97	5.08	49	1.49	8.36
26	0.67	3.94	50	1.39	7.34
27	0.66	2.75	51	1.16	5.77
28	1.81	12.05	52	0.63	2.94
29	0.94	4.19	53	1.30	7.53
30	0.95	4.72	54	0.90	5.16
31	1.69	9.61	55	0.88	4.50
32	1.31	8.18	56	1.44	8.81
33	1.32	8.04	57	0.64	3.07
34	0.73	3.74	58	1.43	8.53
35	1.23	7.49	59	1.76	10.83
36	1.43	9.19	60	1.04	6.66
37	1.22	6.55	61 @	0.25	1.34
38 @	–0.21	–1.33	62	1.59	8.51
39 @	0.49	2.46	63	1.24	8.02
40	1.04	5.01	64 @	0.44	2.02
41	0.86	4.07	65	0.64	3.14
42	0.65	3.06	66	1.27	6.73
			67	0.90	4.49

Note: 1. d = difference between the mean scores (High group-low group).

2. @ = *t* not significant at 0.01 level.

3. * = The statement numbers correspond to the serial numbers of the items in the preliminary form of the attitude scale.

4. The preliminary form of the attitude scale is presented in Appendix—B.

Table—5.5 Internal Consistency of the Different Items and the Results of the *t* Test (Students)

Statement number	d	*t*	Statement number	d	*t*
1 *	1.26	4.50	27	0.42	3.56
2	1.48	5.29	28	1.04	13.68
3	0.63	9.00	29	0.80	12.82
4	0.96	12.80	30	0.93	10.94
5	0.29	3.02	31	1.25	11.43
6	0.36	5.07	32	1.35	12.55
7	0.30	5.56	33	1.49	12.14
8	1.43	11.67	34	1.01	14.72
9	1.73	10.55	35	1.03	10.35
10	0.63	7.50	36	0.46	7.10
11	0.55	7.53	37	0.66	12.00
12 @	0.19	1.04	38 @	0.25	1.28
13	0.39	3.96	39 @	0.21	1.00
14	0.34	12.00	40	0.30	6.45
15	1.08	12.79	41	0.58	7.84
16	1.15	12.35	42	1.11	10.57
17 @	0.29	1.72	43	1.08	9.08
18	0.81	11.74	44	0.52	7.22
19	0.72	9.73	45	0.69	11.62
20	0.78	9.63	46	0.58	12.50
21	0.71	5.46	47 @	0.19	1.02
22	0.32	4.31	48 @	0.22	1.10
23	0.32	4.33	49	0.50	12.20
24	0.47	5.66	50	1.02	15.00
25	0.76	9.10	51	1.91	14.68
26	1.33	11.73	52	1.13	13.42

Statement number	d	*t*	Statement number	d	*t*
53	0.90	15.00	61 @	0.29	1.38
54	1.41	14.41	62	1.08	9.82
55	0.45	7.38	63	0.95	16.41
56	1.29	11.80	64 @	0.02	-0.10
57	1.28	10.48	65	0.68	7.27
58	0.89	13.49	66	0.80	14.04
59	0.65	10.83	67	0.32	5.33
60	0.79	11.53			

Note: See note under Table—5.4.

It may be seen from Table 5.4 that in the case of teachers the *t* values were not significant for items 12, 17, 38, 39, 47, 48, 61 and 64 at 0.01 level. An examination of Table 5.5 shows that for students sample also the *t* value were significant at 0.01 level for all the items for which they were significant in the case of teachers though the strength of significance varied between the two samples. Items 12, 17, 38, 39, 47, 48, 61 and 64 were, therefore, eliminated and 59 statements were selected. Out of the 59 items 22 were positive and 37 were negative.

As a next step the data obtained on the 240 teachers and the 240 students on the attitude scale was separately subjected to factor analysis by Varymax rotation (*Overall* and *Klett,* 1972) with a maximum of 15 factors, to find the structure of the attitude scale. The results of the factor analysis are shown in Table 5.6 for the teacher's sample and in Table 5.7 for the students' sample.

The statement numbers in the two tables correspond to the changed serial order of the items whose discrimination power was not significant. The 59 items, scores on which were subjected to factor analysis are shown in *Appendix—C* for easy reference.

Table—5.6 The Highest Factor Loading of Each of the Items of the Attitude Scale for the Teacher's Sample

Statement number	Factor loading	Statement number	Factor loading
1	0.72	24	0.79
2	0.68	25	0.59
3	0.50	26	0.80
4	0.71	27	0.74
5	0.44	28	0.64
6	0.83	29	0.64
7	0.69	30	0.66
8	0.51	31	0.68
9	0.60	32	0.52
10	0.53	33	0.35
11	0.44	34	0.59
12	0.45	35	0.54
13	0.60	36	0.62
14	0.78	37	0.68
15	0.79	38	0.48
16	0.48	39	0.46
17	0.80	40	0.78
18	0.35	41	0.49
19	0.68	42	0.54
20	0.77	43	0.60
21	0.64	44	0.57
22	0.37	45	0.45
23	0.51	46	0.38

Statement number	Factor loading	Statement number	Factor loading
47	0.57	54	0.36
48	0.48	55	0.74
49	0.39	56	0.48
50	0.77	57	0.71
51	0.44	58	0.55
52	0.53	59	0.62
53	0.60		

Table—5.7 The Highest Factor Loading of Each of the Items of the Attitude Scale for the Student's Sample

Statement number	Factor loading	Statement number	Factor loading
1	0.61	17	0.42
2	0.64	18	0.70
3	0.41	19	0.50
4	0.35	20	0.57
5	0.36	21	0.35
6	0.66	22	0.76
7	0.60	23	0.45
8	0.67	24	0.79
9	0.38	25	0.48
10	0.59	26	0.43
11	0.39	27	0.81
12	0.46	28	0.48
13	0.73	29	0.41
14	0.48	30	0.52
15	0.54	31	0.43
16	0.54	32	0.48

(Contd...)

Table—5.7 (Contd...)

Statement number	Factor loading	Statement number	Factor loading
33	0.45	47	0.42
34	0.50	48	0.47
35	0.36	49	0.41
36	0.73	50	0.61
37	0.35	51	0.36
38	0.42	52	0.35
39	0.41	53	0.56
40	0.54	54	0.54
41	0.67	55	0.67
42	0.71	56	0.58
43	0.71	57	0.72
44	0.45	58	0.71
45	0.48	59	0.61
46	0.48		

Table 5.8 gives the factor-wise distribution of the different items and the number of items in each factor as obtained from the factor analysis of the data from the two sources. It is evident from Table 5.6 that the factor loading of the different items ranged between 0.35 and 0.83 for the sample of teachers. In the case of the students the factor loading of the different items were in the range of 0.35 and 0.81. *Overall* and *Klett* (1972) suggested that those factors defined by 3 or 4 items (variables having factor loading of 0.35 or more were stable and replicalbe. They also stated that 50 per cent to 75 per cent of the total variance was enough to consider for prediction of any psychological or psychiatric domain. Hence, it was decided to consider only those factors that had 3 or more items which had a factor loading of 0.35 or more. Table 5.8 shows the factor-wise distribution of the items. It may be seen that as many as 15 items were grouped under factor I, while most other factors were represented by 3 or 4 items. Only one item (item 24)

Table—5.8 Factor-wise Distribution of the Different Items and the Number of Items in Each Factor

Sl. No.	Factors	Item number in the attitude scale	Total number of items
1	Factor I	3, 19, 26, 32, 33, 38, 39, 40, 41, 42, 44, 48, 50, 54 and 59	15
2	Factor II	13, 25, 28	3
3	Factor III	17, 30, 46, 56, 58	5
4	Factor IV	8, 29, 51	3
5	Factor V	6, 7, 21	3
6	Factor VI	1, 9, 55	3
7	Factor VII	10, 14, 53	3
8	Factor VIII	24	1
9	Factor IX	27, 31, 37	3
10	Factor X	2, 4, 5	3
11	Factor XI	16, 34, 36	3
12	Factor XII	12, 23, 49, 57	4
13	Factor XIII	11, 22, 47, 52	4
14	Factor XIV	15, 18, 20	3
15	Factor XV	35, 43, 45	3
	Total		59

occurred under factor VIII. As such item 24 under factor 8 was eliminated. Similar factor structure was obtained for the teachers sample also, except for variations of the amount of loading of the items in different factors. Thus the final form of the attitude scale containing 58 items, was prepared. The 58 items were grouped under 14 most significant factors. These factors were assigned suitable titles according to the content of the items in each of them.

The ultimate factor structure of the final form is presented in Table 5.8 A.

Table—5.8A Factor-wise Distribution of the Different Items and the Number of Items in Each Factor

Factor Number	Name of the Factor	Item number in the attitude scale (Final Form)	Total number of items
I	Policy Implementation	3, 19, 25, 31, 32, 37, 38, 39, 40, 41, 43, 47, 49, 53 and 58	15
II	Facility	13, 24, 27	3
III	Teaching-learning	17, 29, 45, 55, 57	5
IV	Personality	8, 28, 50	3
V	Discipline	6, 7, 21	3
VI	Incentive for Progress	1, 9, 54	3
VII	Learning Skills	10, 14, 52	3
VIII	Educational Policy	26, 30, 36	3
IX	Freedom for the Teacher	2, 4, 5	3
X	Emotional	16, 33, 35	3
XI	Dullards-Wastage and Stagnation	12, 23, 48, 56	4
XII	Competence	11, 22, 46, 51	4
XIII	Ethical Value	15, 18, 20	3
XIV	Learning in a Natural Setting	34, 42, 44	3
	Total		**58**

The statement numbers in the table correspond to the serial numbers of the items in the final form presented in Appendix—A.

V. VALIDITY AND RELIABILITY

1. Attitude Scale

There are various methods of estimating the validity of

a measuring instrument. The following types of validity were established for the attitude scale that was developed.

(a) *Content Validity*

This type of validity is established by evaluating the relevance of the test items individually and as a whole. Each item should be a sampling of that aspect which the test purports to measure and taken collectively, the items should constitute a representative sample of the variable that is measured.

In the construction of the present instrument items were collected from a large number of high school teachers and students. They were also supplemented by a review of related literature and by interviewing selected teachers and headmasters to make sure that all possible items were included. Thus it can be reasonably assumed that the inventory has content validity.

(b) *Item Validity*

There are numerous procedures by which the item validity can be determined, one of which stresses the number of discriminations of the desired sort that the item is capable of making. It emphasises the extent to which the item predicts segregation of examinees into those with high versus those with low criterion scores. The discriminative power of each of the items was established before including them in the final form. Thus each item of the attitude scale is valid, making the scale valid.

(c) *Intrinsic Validity*

Guilford (1954) defined intrinsic validity as 'the degree to which a test measures what it measures.' This can also be stated in terms of how well the obtained scores measure the test's true score component. This validity is given by the square root of the proportion of true variance *i.e.* square root of its reliability. The intrinsic validity of the present attitude scale was $\sqrt{0.83}$=0.91 for the teachers and $\sqrt{0.95}$ = 0.97 for the students.

(d) Criterion Validity

At the end of the attitude scale a general item: 'The non-detention system is good'— Yes/No, was given to get the overall opinion of the respondents about the system. The sample of teachers were divided into two groups on the basis of their responses to the above item. There were 43 teachers who thought that the system was good, while 197 teachers did not think well about the new system. The mean attitude scores of the two groups of teachers are shown in Table 5.9. The mean score of those who favoured the system was 198.72 while that of those who did not favour it was 145.98. The difference between the two means was highly significant (t = 12.59 significant at 0.001 level for 238 degrees of freedom). This shows that the attitude scale is able to discriminate between those who favoured the system and those who did not.

Table—5.9 Mean Attitude Scores of Teachers Who Favoured and Those Who Did Not Favour the Non-detention System and the Results of *t* Test

	Yes	No	t	r_{bis}
N	43	197		
Mean	198.72	145.98	12.59***	0.58
S.D	25.22	24.88		

Note: *** t significant at 0.001 level for 238 df.

In the same manner, in the case of students, the mean score of those who favoured the system was 176.21, while those who did not favour it obtained a mean score of 149.84 (Table 5.10). The t value for the difference between the two means was 9.88, highly significant at 0.001 level for 238 degrees of freedom.

The Biserial Correlation (r_{bis}) between the type of response to the last item in the attitude scale, viz., 'The non-detention system is good'— Yes/No and the attitude score as measured by the 58 items was calculated for teachers and also for students.

Table—5.10 Mean Attitude Scores of Students Who Favoured and Those Who Did Not Favour the Non-detention System and the Results of *t* Test

	Yes	No	*t*	r_{bis}
N	73	167		
Mean	176.21	149.84	9.88***	0.63
S.D	18.03	23.21		

Note: See note under Table—5.9.

The r_{bis} thus obtained was 0.58 in the case of teachers and 0.63 in the case of students both of which are considerably high.

(e) Factorial Validity

As explained earlier, all the items included in the final form of the scale were having factor loading of 0.35 or more. Each of the 14 factors consisted of 3 or more items. All the factors put together were capable of predicting 94 per cent of the total variance in the domain which was measured. So it could be concluded that the attitude scale is factorially valid.

(f) Cross Validity

The validity of a completed test should always be cross checked on a new sample—*i.e.* one different from that used in the item analysis. This process is called cross validation. The validity of a test, when computed from the 'standardization sample,' will of necessity be exaggerated as the items are so selected as to maximize differences between high and low groups. Further more, the validity coefficient of the test will also be increased by chance factors peculiar to the standardization sample. Thus validity coefficients tend to be spuriously high in the standardization group, making cross validation necessary (*Garrett,* 1985).

The attitude scale was administered to a sample of 120 teachers and 120 students selected from 10 schools. The sample was equally distributed between the two sexes and the three localities. The results obtained are shown in Tables 5.11 and 5.12. It may be seen that the mean score of those who favoured the non-detention system was significantly higher than that of those who did not favour the system showing that the attitude scale was able to discriminate between those who like the system from those who did not. This was true for the teachers and also for the students.

Table—5.11 Mean Attitude Score of Teachers who Favoured and Those who did not Favour the Non-detention System and the Results of *t* Test

	Yes	No	t	r_{bis}
N	27	93		
Mean	179.64	137.22	5.91^{***}	0.75
S.D	34.39	26.89		

Note: *** t significant at 0.001 level for 118 df.

Table—5.12 Mean Attitude Score of Students Who Favoured and Those Who Did Not Favour the Non-detention System and the Results of *t* Test

	Yes	No	t	r_{bis}
N	32	88		
Mean	175.68	152.18	6.00^{***}	0.77
S.D	18.62	19.90		

Note: See note under Table—5.11.

(g) Reliability

The reliability of any instrument can be established by different methods like test-retest method, split-half method, alternate forms method or by Kuder-Richardson formula. The reliability of the attitude scale was estimated by split-half method. The scores on the odd and even items were correlated using Pearson's formula for product moment correlation. This gave the reliability of the half test. The reliability of the half test was 0.71 for the teacher's sample (N = 240) and it was 0.91 for the students' sample (n = 240). This was corrected for the full length of the test by Spearman Brown Prophecy formula. The reliability of the full test thus obtained on the teachers' sample was 0.83 where as it was 0.95 for the students' sample.

The split half reliability was established on the sample of teachers and students who participated in the cross validity. The reliability coefficients thus obtained were 0.81 for teachers and 0.94 for students.

2. Reliability and Validity of the Achievement Scores

In Andhra Pradesh, for the X class public examination the question paper for any subject is first set independently by three experienced teachers. After setting the paper individually, the examiners meet and discuss each question with reference to its relevance to the syllabus, its difficulty level, etc., and evolve one paper agreeable to all the three examiners. Thus the test paper may reasonably be assumed to have content validity.

The answer papers of the students are valued by a team of experienced teachers. The valuation of the papers is done under the direct supervision on a group of Chief Examiners and the Chairman of the Board of Examiners who give guidelines for the valuation of the papers which are required to be strictly followed by the Assistant Examiners. Further, 5 per cent of the papers valued by each Assistant Examiner are checked up for correctness of valuation by the Chief Examiners and necessary instructions are given on the spot to the Assistant Examiners so that they rectify their defects immediately.

The entire valuation of the answer papers is done under a scheme of 'spot valuation' where bundles containing 25 answer scripts are distributed to the examiners at random. The 25 papers are to be valued in 5 hours. To eliminate the possibility of extraneous factors playing their role in the valuation, the answer scripts of students belonging to one zone (consisting 2 or 3 districts) are valued by teachers belonging to a far away zone in the State.

As the valuation was done by taking all the above precautions like, giving common guidelines for valuation, random checking of 5 per cent of the papers valued by each examiner, etc., the scoring of the answer scripts may reasonably be well taken to be objective and reliable.

Further, a panel of experienced subject masters examined the test papers of the two selected years and found that they were comparable with regard to the difficulty level and that they had content validity.

VI. PERSONAL DATA

Information regarding sex, experience, level of teaching of the teachers and sex and social class of the students was obtained from a carefully worded personal data sheet.

VII. SAMPLE

1. Achievement

As mentioned earlier (p. 118 and 119), the sample for the study was selected by a multistage stratified random sampling procedure. At the out set three districts one from each of the three regions Circar, Rayalaseema and Telangana of Andhra Pradesh State were selected at random. Those schools which had X class before 1969 in each of these districts were listed. They were categorised as urban, semi-urban and rural depending upon the locality in which they were situated, and 4 schools from urban, 6 from semi-urban and 8 from rural areas were selected at random from each of the three districts thus giving 54 schools. Unequal number of schools from the different localities were selected because the enrolment in urban areas was disproportionately large compared to that in rural areas. Table 5.13 shows the distribution of the schools selected between the three regions and three localities.

Table—5.13 Distribution of the Schools Selected Between the Three Regions and the Three Localities

District	Urban	Semi-urban	Rural	Total
Krishna	4	6	8	18
Nellore	4	6	8	18
Nalgonda	4	6	8	18
Total				54

The last batch of students under the detention system (*i.e.*) those who appeared for the X class public examination in 1971 and those who took the X class public examination in 1983 from the above 54 schools constituted the sample for the study. All the students who appeared for the above examination in the selected years served at as the sample of subjects for the study for the purpose of analysis of achievement under the detention and non-detention systems.

The system—, and year-wise distribution of the sample of subjects (Ss) whose marks were analysed in the investigation is shown in Table 5.14.

Of the total sample of 7740 students whose marks were analysed 2714 belonged to the detention system, while 5026 had their education under the non-detention system.

Table—5.14 System—, and Year-wise Distribution of the Sample of Subjects

System	Year	Number
Detention	1970-71	2714
Non-detention	1982-83	5026
Total		**7740**

The distribution of the sample of subjects (Ss) in the various sub-groups based upon sex, locality, caste and system is shown in Table 5.15. It may be seen that 5447 students who participated in the study were boys and the remaining 2293 were girls. 1195 Ss belonged to Scheduled Castes/ scheduled tribes (SC/STs) while 6545 were from Other Communities (OCs). 2886 students hailed from urban localities while 2917 belonged to semi-urban localities. The remaining 1937 Ss were from rural areas.

Table—5.15 System—, Sex—, Caste— and Locality-wise Distribution of the Sample of Subjects

System	Sex	Caste	Locality			Total
			Urban	Semi-urban	Rural	
Detention	Boys	SC/ST	70	68	48	186
		OC	724	629	502	1855
	Girls	SC/ST	81	17	7	105
		OC	312	139	117	568
Non-detention	Boys	SC/ST	179	317	156	652
		OC	915	1085	754	2754
	Girls	SC/ST	58	134	60	252
		OC	547	528	293	1368
Total			**2886**	**2917**	**1937**	**7740**

2. Percentage of Passes

The number of students who appeared for the X class public examinations from each of the 54 schools and the number of those who have passed was recorded from the registers maintained in the schools and the percentage of passes under the two systems was calculated. The size of the sample for this analysis was 7740.

3. Rate of Drop-outs

For the purpose of comparison of rate of drop-outs under the detention and non-detention systems the class-wise enrolment and the number of students dropped-out by the beginning of the next year during the years 1970-71 and 1982-83 in the 54 schools, selected as described above, was recorded from the registers maintained in the schools and the drop-out rate was calculated. The total enrolment during the above years was 37,964. The rate of drop-out was calculated based upon this sample. The system—, class—, sex—, and locality-wise distribution of the above sample is shown in Table 5.16.

Table—5.16 Class-wise Enrolment of Students in the Schools Selected for the Study

System	Class	Urban		Semi-urban		Rural		Total
		Boys	Girls	Boys	Girls	Boys	Girls	
Detention	VI	659	353	710	414	674	329	3139
	VII	546	254	553	303	522	192	2370
	VIII	830	271	931	423	704	271	3430
	IX	800	272	749	301	565	158	2845
	X	441	187	667	191	543	144	2173
Non-detention	VI	961	471	946	741	982	451	4552
	VII	949	525	1042	704	830	431	4481
	VIII	1138	594	1676	746	828	397	5379
	IX	1223	742	1296	742	791	369	5163
	X	961	537	1188	588	666	292	4232
Total								37764

4. Attitude

For the purpose of assessing the attitude towards the non-detention system samples of teachers and students were selected from the same 54 schools selected for the purpose of analysis of achievement. The teachers in each of the above 54 schools were categorised as B.Ed. assistants and Secondary grade teachers based upon the classes which they handled as mentioned earlier (p. 114), and 10 B.Eds and 5 secondary grade teachers from each urban school and 6 B.Eds and 4 secondary grade teachers from each semi-urban school were selected by adopting systematic sampling from among the teachers present in the school on the day of the investigation. In the case of rural areas since the number of teachers was rather limited all the B.Ed. and Secondary grade teachers were included in the study by adopting cluster sampling technique. A total of 510 teachers thus selected served as Ss for the study of their attitude towards the non-detention system (Table 5.17).

Table—5.17 Locality—, sex—, and Level of Teaching-wise Distribution of the Sample of Teachers Selected for the Study of Attitude

Urban				Semi-urban				Rural				Total
Men		Women		Men		Women		Men		Women		
B.Ed.	Sec. grade	B.Ed.	Sec. grade	B.Ed.	Sec. grade	B.Ed.	Sec. grade	B.Ed.	Sec. grade	B.Ed.	Sec. grade	
60	30	60	30	60	30	60	30	80	40	20	10	510

From each of the schools located in urban, semi-urban and rural areas respectively 30, 20 and 15 tenth class students were selected by adopting systematic sampling from among the students present in the school on the day of the investigation thus giving a total of 1080 students equally distributed between the two sexes and the three localities. Sex—, and locality-wise distribution of the sample of students selected for the study is shown in Table 5.18.

Table—5.18 Locality—, and Sex-wise Distribution of the Sample of Students Selected for Analysis of Attitude

Urban		Semi-urban		Rural		Total
Boys	Girls	Boys	Girls	Boys	Girls	
180	180	180	180	180	180	1080

The Headmasters of the schools selected for the study, the Gazetted Inspectors and District Educational Officers (DEOs) of the three districts constituted the population of administrators. From this population a random sample of 40 administrators was selected and their attitude towards the new system of evaluation was assessed and analysed.

VIII. DATA COLLECTION AND SCORING

The instrument was administered to the selected teachers individually through personal contact during leisure hours in their respective schools, after establishing adequate rapport and explaining the purpose of the investigation. They were also explained how they had to answer the items as given in the instruction at the beginning of the attitude scale. The instrument itself was self-administering. The time taken by the teachers for completing the attitude scale was about half an hour.

The attitude scale was administered to the sample of students selected from each school in small groups not exceeding 20. At the outset they were well motivated by informing them about the nature and importance of the investigation. They were also explained briefly about the detention system to avoid any ambiguity about the concept of detention system. This was necessary since they had all their education under the non-detention system. The attitude scales were distributed and instructions were read to the students slowly as they read them for themselves. Doubts if any were clarified and they were asked to mark answers. The time taken by the students for completing the attitude scale was about an hour.

For the headmasters of the schools who were included in the sample of administrators the attitude scale was administered individually when the investigator visited the school for the collection of data from the school. For the sample of gazetted inspectors and DEOs, selected for the study the attitude scale was mailed. Since their number was very small, after 2 or 3 reminders all of them returned the filled in attitude scales.

The attitude scale was scored as per the scoring procedure described earlier (p. 126).

IX. ANALYSIS OF DATA

The data thus collected was analysed using relevant statistical techniques like analysis of variance, *t* test etc. The usual levels of significance, *viz.*, 0.05, 0.01 and 0.001 were employed to test the significance of the obtained *F* and *t* values. The obtained numerical results were adumbrated by graphical representation wherever necessary.

6

Results and Discussion

The major hypotheses in the study were concerning the effect of the non-detention system on the achievement of the pupils and on the rate of passes and drop-outs. Another aspects of the study was to find out the attitude of the pupils, teachers and administrators towards the new system.

Hence, the analysis is presented under 4 sections. Section A deals with achievement scores of the pupils under the detention and non-detention systems, which were analysed using analysis of variance. Section B deals with the percentage of passes under the two systems. Similarly Section C contains the analysis of rate of drop-outs under the two systems. The analysis of the attitude scores of pupils, teachers and administrators is presented in Section D.

In the secondary schools of Andhra Pradesh, children take examination in 6 papers at the X class level.

Three of them are languages (as per the 3 language formula*) — the regional language, Hindi and English** and

* India being a large nation which is multiligual and multiracial, people belonging to different regions have their own mother

the remaining three are mathematics, science and social studies.

In the present study therefore, the total marks of the students and also the marks obtained by them in each of the 6 papers were analysed separately to examine the effect of the non-detention system on the achievement of the pupils in each of the different subjects.

Section—A

Achievement in the Two Systems

1. ***Telugu:*** Table 6.1 shows the mean scores and SDs of different sub-groups of *Ss* in Telugu. It could be seen that the mean score of the students who studied under the detention system was 40.45 while that of the students who had their education under the non-detention system was 47.36. This shows that the achievement under the non-detention system was better than that under the detention system.

---

tongue and their own dialect. Though the fathers of the Indian Constitution envisaged that there should be one national language (i.e. Hindi), the constitution was amended to recognise 14 regional languages apart from Hindi (Article 344 (1) — Eighth schedule — The Constitution of India — Twenty First Amendment Act, 1966). To facilitate mobility of the educated within the nation with regard to employment, etc. , and to bring forth some sort of integration and unity within the diversity, the Central Government introduced a formula a called the three language formula. According to this formula child should study a modern Indian language, preferably a South Indian language, in addition to Hindi and English in Hindi speaking states, and Hindi in addition to regional language and English in non-Hindi speaking areas.

** Telugu being the regional language of the students most of the children study Telugu as the I language. In some schools located in the border areas other languages are studied as I language. Those schools were not included in the study. Further, most of the children study Hindi as the II language. In very few schools other North Indian languages are taught. Such students were not included in the study.

Table—6.1 Means and SDs of Different Sub-groups of Ss in Telugu

Group	N	M	S.D.
Detention (DS)	2714	40.45	10.39
Non-detention (NDS)	5026	47.36	14.60
Boys (B)	5447	44.31	13.71
Girls (G)	2293	46.42	13.54
Other Communities (OCs)	6545	45.61	13.55
Scheduled Caste and Scheduled Tribes (SCs/STS)	1195	41.25	13.82
Urban (U)	2886	43.91	14.59
Semi-urban (SU)	2917	44.32	13.70
Rural (R)	1937	47.40	11.83

The mean score of boys was 44.31. Girls obtained a mean score of 46.42. Girls seem to achieve better than boys. When students were classified as urban (U), semi-urban (SU) and rural (R) based upon the locality to which they belonged, it was found that the mean score of students from urban (U) localities was the least, while students from rural (R) localities scored highest . The mean score of urban (U) students was 43.91, while the mean scores of those belonging to semi-urban (SU) and rural (Ŕ) localities were 44.32 and 47.40 respectively.

Considering the social class of the students, the mean score of students belonging to scheduled castes (SCs) and scheduled tribes (STs) (herein after referred as SCs/STs) was 41.25 while that of those belonging to other communities* (hereinafter referred to as OCs) was 45.61. Evidently, the

* Other communities (OCs) include children from forward communities and also backward communities.

The particulars regarding the social class of the students were recorded from the registers maintained in the office of the Commissioner for Government Examinations, Hyderabad, in which the information about SCs/STs and OCs only was available.

achievement of SCs/STs was inferior to that of children belonging to OCs.

To examine whether there was any significant difference between the achievement of students under the detention and non-detention systems and also to analyse the difference between the achievement of students belonging to different localities, social classes etc., the achievement scores of the Ss were further analysed.

Table—6.2 Results of Analysis of Variance (Telugu)

Source	Ss	df	MSS	F
System (D)	1921.18	1	1921.18	8.87**
Sex (S)	1385.26	1	1385.26	6.37**
Caste (C)	1321.76	1	1321.76	6.10**
Locality (L)	2124.42	2	1062.21	4.90*
DxS	1609.36	1	1609.36	7.43**
DxC	1137.47	1	1137.47	5.24*
DxL	2325.48	2	1162.74	5.37*
SxC	803.62	1	803.62	3.71@
SxL	1844.46	2	922.23	4.466*
CxL	1788.73	2	894.37	4.13*
DxSxC	1321.28	1	1321.28	6.10**
DxSxL	1548.64	2	774.32	3.57@
DxCxL	1634.88	2	817.44	3.75@
SxCxL	1624.06	2	812.23	3.75@
DxSxCxL	1927.86	2	963.93	4.45*
Error	1672121.49	7716	216.68	
Total	**1696440.20**	**7739**		

Note: 1. *** significant at 0.001 level.

** significant at 0.01 level.

* significant at 0.05 level.

2. The same notation is used in all the tables that follow.

The sample of students include both boys and girls, children belonging to different localities and caste groups. Achievements of as students is affected by each of these variables as brought about in the section on review of literature. So to avoid contamination of the results pertaining to the effect of the type of system on achievement, analysis of variance of a 2x2x3x2 factorial design (2 systemsx2 sexesx3 localitiesx2 social classes) was used. The results obtained in this analysis (for Telugu) are shown in Table 6.2.

It could be seen from Table 6.2 that the *F* ratio for system (D) was 8.87 which was significant at 0.01 level for 1 and 7716 df. This shows that there was a significant difference between the achievement of students under the detention and non-detention systems.

An examination of the mean scores of the students belonging to the two systems presented in Table 6.1 shows that the mean score of students who studied under the detention system was 40.45 while that of those belonging to the non-detention system was 47.36. This shows that the achievement of students under the non-detention system was significantly better than that under the detention system (*see Fig.6.1 in page 154*).

When the non-detention system was introduced it was contended by many that the system would help students to study under a natural setting, free from fear of examinations and anxiety of detentions, which would facilitate better grasp of the subject matter, leading to better achievement and less wastage and stagnation (*Kabra,* 1971; *Krishna Moorthy,* 1971; *Narasimha Rao,* 1971; *Editorial, Educational India,* 1977). Apart from these opinions the empirical studies conducted by *Keyes* (1911), *Klene* and *Brawn* (1929), *Arthur* (1936), *Coffield* and *Bloomers* (1956), *Kowitz* and *Armstrong* (1961), *Gaite* (1969), and Otto and *Melby* (n.d.) showed that students who were promoted did well in tests than those who were not promoted. Studies by *McCullers* (1978), Gayen and Lyle (1971), *Glucksberg* (1962) and *Dornbush* (1965) have shown that rewards facilitate performance. The results of the present study support the above.

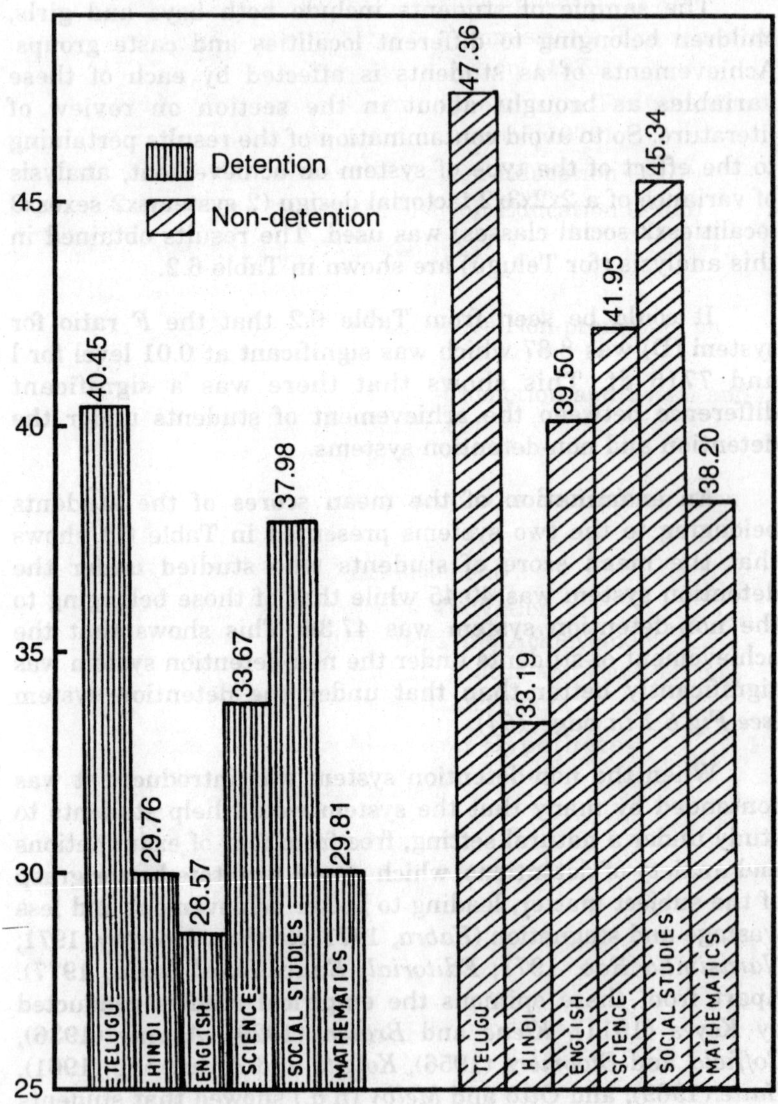

Fig.—6.1 Mean Scores of Students for Different Subjects Under Detention and Non-detention Systems.

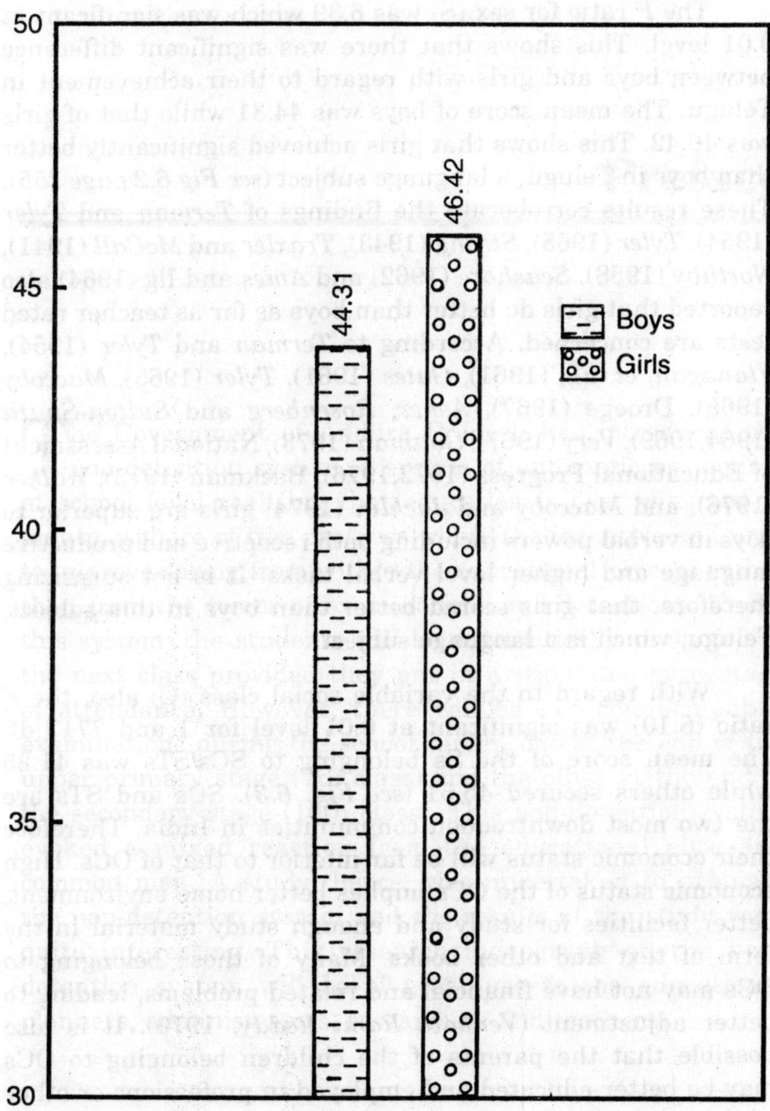

Fig.—6.2 Mean Scores of Boys and Girls (Telugu)

The *F* ratio for sex (S) was 6.39 which was significant at 0.01 level. This shows that there was significant difference between boys and girls with regard to their achievement in Telugu. The mean score of boys was 44.31 while that of girls was 46.42. This shows that girls achieved significantly better than boys in Telugu, a language subject (*see Fig.6.2 page 155*). These results corroborate the findings of *Terman* and *Tyler* (1954). *Tyler* (1965), *Strong* (1943), *Traxler* and *McCall* (1941), *Northby* (1958). *Seashore* (1962) and *Ames* and Ilg (1964) also reported that girls do better than boys as far as teacher rated tests are concerned. According to *Terman* and *Tyler* (1954), *Flanagan, et. al.,* (1961), *Gates* (1961), *Tyler* (1965), *Maccoby* (1965), Droege (1967), *Asher, Rosenberg* and *Sulton-Smith* (1964,1969), *Very* (1967), *Gottman* (1973), National Assessment of Educational Progress (1972,1976), Backman (1972), *Walker* (1976), and *Maccoby* and *Jacklin* (1974) girls are superior to boys in verbal powers including both receptive and productive language and higher level verbal tasks. It is not surprising therefore, that girls scored better than boys in this subject, Telugu, which is a language subject.

With regard to the variable social class (C) also, the *F* ratio (6.10) was significant at 0.01 level for 1 and 7717 df. The mean score of the Ss belonging to SCs/STs was 41.25 while others secured 45.61 (*see Fig. 6.3*). SCs and STs are the two most downtrodden communities in India. Therefore their economic status will be far inferior to that of OCs. High economic status of the OCs implies better home environment, better facilities for study and enough study material in the form of text and other books. Many of those belonging to OCs may not have financial and related problems, leading to better adjustment (*Venkata Rami Reddy,* 1979). It is also possible that the parents of the children belonging to OCs may be better educated and employed in professions or other while collar jobs. Thus these children might be getting better guidance from their parents (*Frankel,* 1960; *Curry,* 1964; *Venkata Rami Reddy,* 1977). All this would naturally help them to achieve better than their counterparts belonging to the Scheduled Castes and Scheduled Tribes which are the

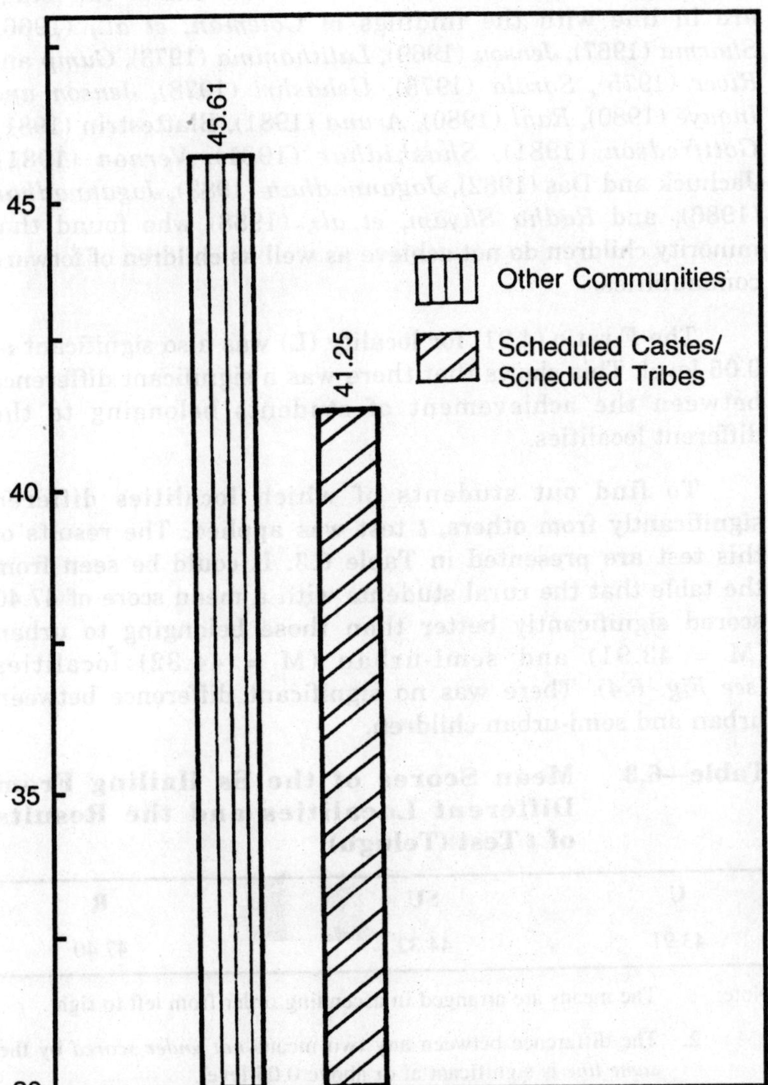

Fig.—6.3 Mean Sscores of Students Belongings to Different Social Classes (Telugu)

poorest of the poor communities. The results of this study are in line with the findings of *Coleman, et al.*, (1966), *Sharma* (1967), *Jenson* (1969), *Lalithamma* (1973), *Gump* and *River* (1975), *Sarala* (1975), *Ushashri* (1978), *Jenson and Inouye* (1980), *Rani* (1980), *Aruna* (1981), Blattestrin (1981), *Gottfredson* (1981), *Shashidhar* (1981), *Vernon* (1981), Jachuck and Das (1982), *Jagannadhan* (1983), *Jagannadhan* (1986), and *Radha Shyam, et al.*, (1988) who found that minority children do not achieve as well as children of forward communities.

The *F* ratio (4.91) for locality (L) was also significant at 0.05 level. This shows that there was a significant difference between the achievement of students belonging to the different localities.

To find out students of which localities differed significantly from others, *t* test was applied. The results of this test are presented in Table 6.3. It could be seen from the table that the rural students with a mean score of 47.40 scored significantly better than those belonging to urban (M = 43.91) and semi-urban (M = 44.32) localities (*see Fig. 6.4*). There was no significant difference between urban and semi-urban children.

Table—6.3 Mean Scores of the Ss Hailing From Different Localities and the Results of *t* Test (Telugu)

U	SU	R
43.91	44.32	47.40

Note: 1. The means are arranged in ascending order from left to right.

2. The difference between any two means *not under scored* by the *same line* is significant at or above 0.05 level.

3. The difference between any two means *under scored* by the *same line* is *not* significant at 0.05 level.

4. The same procedure is followed in all the tables that follow to present the results of *t* test as a continuation of *F* test.

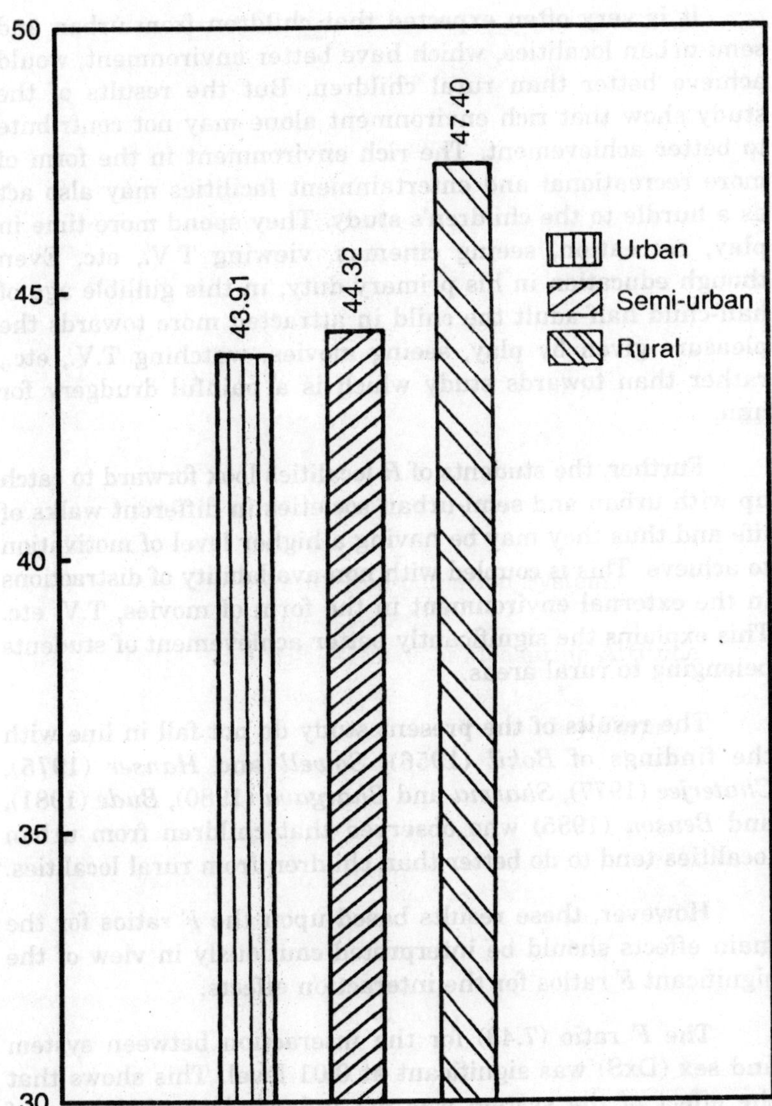

Fig.—6.4 Mean Scores of Students Belonging to Different Localities (Telugu)

It is very often expected that children from urban and semi-urban localities, which have better environment, would achieve better than rural children. But the results of the study show that rich environment alone may not contribute to better achievement. The rich environment in the form of more recreational and entertainment facilities may also act as a hurdle to the children's study. They spend more time in play, recreation, seeing cinemas, viewing T.V., etc. Even though education in his primary duty, in this gullible age of half-child half-adult the child in attracted more towards the pleasure given by play, seeing movies, watching T.V., etc., rather than towards study which is a painful drudgery for him.

Further, the students of *R* localities look forward to catch up with urban and semi-urban societies in different walks of life and thus they may be having a higher level of motivation to achieve. This is coupled with non-availability of distractions in the external environment in the form of movies, T.V. etc. This explains the significantly better achievement of students belonging to rural areas.

The results of the present study do not fall in line with the findings of *Bokil* (1956), *Sowell* and *Hanser* (1975), *Chaterjee* (1977), *Sharma* and *Bhargava* (1980), *Bude* (1981), and *Benson* (1985) who observed that children from urban localities tend to do better than children from rural localities.

However, these results based upon the *F* ratios for the main effects should be interpreted cautiously in view of the significant *F* ratios for the interaction effects.

The *F* ratio (7.43) for the interaction between system and sex (DxS) was significant at 0.01 level. This shows that the effect of the system was not independent of the sex of the students involved and vice versa (*Winer,* 1971, and *Edwards,* 1971).

To probe deep into this, the mean scores of different sub-groups of *Ss* classified according to the two variables—

system and sex were further analysed. It may be seen from Table 6.4a that in the detention system the mean scores of boys and girls were 40.20 and 41.22 respectively. In the non-detention system the mean scores of the two groups were boys: 46.79, girls: 49.91. The differences were significant in both the cases. This shows that achievement of girls was better than that of boys in both the systems. However, the magnitude of the difference was ot of the same order in two systems. In the case of the detention system the difference between the mean scores of boys and girls was only 1.02 points while it was 3.12 points in the non-detention system.

Table—6.4 Mean Scores of Different Sub-groups of *Ss* Classified According to their System and Sex to Explain DxS Interaction (Telugu)

(6.4a) (DxS)			(6.4b) (SxD)		
	B	G		DS	NDS
DS	40.20	41.22	B	40.20	46.79
	B	G		DS	NDS
NDS	46.79	49.91	G	41.22	49.91

Note: See note under Table—6.3.

When the mean scores of the students belonging to the two systems were considered (Table 6.4b) it was found that the achievement in the non-detention system was significantly higher than that in the detention system irrespective of the sex of the students. Here again the direction of difference between the means was same; but the magnitude of the difference in the case of boys was 6.59 while it was 8.69 in the case of girls. This explains the significant *F* ratio for DxS interaction effect.

The *F* ratio of 5.24 for the interaction between the system and caste (DxC) was also significant at 0.05 level, indicating that the effect of the system on achievement was not independent of the caste of *Ss* involved and vice versa.

Table—6.5 Mean Scores of Different Sub-groups of Ss Classified According to their System and Caste to Explain the DxC Interaction (Telugu)

(6.5a) (DxC)			(6.5b) (CxD)		
	SCs/STs	OC		DS	NDS
DS	38.18	40.73	OC	40.73	48.48
	SCs/STs	OC		DS	NDS
NDS	42.24	48.48	SCs/STs	38.18	42.24

Note: See note under Table—6.3.

An examination of the mean scores of students classified according to the two variables (Table 6.5a) shows that in both the detention and non-detention systems, OCs scored significantly higher than SCs/STs. Further from Table 6.5b it may be seen that the achievement was significantly higher in the non-detention system for both OCs and SCs/STs. But the magnitude of improvement from detention to non-detention was far higher in the case of OCs that in the case of SCs/STs. It may also be seen that in the detention system the difference between the achievement of SCs/STs and OCs was only 1.55 points while it was as high as 6.24 points in the non-detention system.

The *F* ratio for the interaction between system and locality (DxL) was also significant at 0.05 level. This shows that the effect of system (D) was not independent of the locality (L) from which the pupils hailed. Or conversely the effect of locality on the achievement of the students was not independent of the system to which they belonged.

An examination of the mean scores of the students classified according to the two variables, system and locality, presented in Table 6.6 explains the situation. It may be seen from Table 6.6a that in the detention system, the mean scores of the students belonging to the three localities U, SU and R were 39.38, 41.17 and 41.45 respectively. In the case of the non-detention system the mean scores of three groups were

45.63, 47.07 and 50.57 respectively. *t* test was applied to see students of which locality differed significantly from the others.

Table—6.6 Mean Scores of Different Sub-groups of *Ss* Classified According to Their System and Locality to Explain the DxL Interaction (Telugu)

(6.6a) DxL				(6.6b) LxD		
	U	SU	R		DS	NDS
DS	39.38	41.17	41.45	U	39.38	47.07
	SU	U	R		DS	NDS
NDS	45.63	47.07	50.57	SU	41.17	45.63
					DS	NDS
				R	41.45	50.57

Note: See note under Table 6.3.

In the case of non-detention system each group differed significantly from every other, rural students scoring the highest and semi-urban children getting the least mean scores. But in the case of the detention system though urban children got the lowest mean and differed significantly from the rural and semi-urban children, there was no significant difference between the latter two groups.

When the mean scores of students belonging to the two systems were considered separately for each locality, it was found that students achieved significantly higher in the non-detention system than in the detention system. This was true for all localities. This shows that the direction of the difference between the two systems was the same irrespective of the locality to which the students belonged. However, here again an examination of the magnitude of the difference between the mean scores obtained in the two systems for different localities shows that in the case of U localities the difference between the mean scores of the students studying under the two systems was 7.69 points, while it was only

4.46 points in the case of SU localities and as much as 9.12 points in the case of R localities. This explains the significant interaction between the two variables, system and locality.

The *F* ratio (3.71) for the interaction effect between sex and caste (SxC) was not significant at 0.05 level. This shows that the difference between the achievement of boys and girls was of the same order for either caste and vice versa.

The *F* ratio for the interaction between sex and locality (SxL) was 4.26, significant at 0.05 level.

Table—6.7 Mean Scores of Different Sub-groups of *Ss* Classified According to their Sex and Locality to Explain the SxL Interaction (Telugu)

(6.7a) SxL				(6.7b) LxS		
	U	SU	R		B	G
B	42.63	43.97	46.99	U	42.63	46.33
	SU	U	R		B	G
G	45.22	46.33	48.66	SU	43.97	45.22
					B	G
				R	46.99	48.66

Note: See note under Table—6.3.

An examination of the mean scores of the students classified according to these two variables presented in Table 6.7 shows that in the case of both boys as well as girls children from each locality differed significantly from others. But in the case of boys, rural children scored highest while urban children got the lowest mean score, SU children falling in between . But in the case of girls, though children from *R* localities scored highest, those from *SU* localities scored least, urban children falling in between.

The *F* ratio for the interaction between locality and caste (4.13) was also significant at 0.05 level. The mean score of students classified according to the two variables locality and caste, presented in Table 6.8 show that in the case of SCs/STs those belonging to rural areas scored significantly better marks than the other two groups. This was true in the case of OCs also . But the difference between U and SU children was significant in the case of SCs/STs but not in the case of OCs.

Table—6.8 Mean Scores of Different Sub-groups of *Ss* Classified According to their Social Class and Locality to Explain the CxL Interaction (Telugu)

(6.8a) CxL					(6.8b) LxC	
	U	SU	R		SCs/STs	OC
SCs/STs	38.67	41.16	45.14	U	38.67	44.72
	U	SU	R		SCs/STs	OC
OC	44.72	45.04	47.77	SU	41.16	45.04
					SCs/STs	OC
				R	45.14	47.77

Note: See note under Table—6.3.

The 3 factor interaction SxCxL) (between sex, social class and locality) was also significant indicating that the interaction between any two of the above variables taken at a time was not independent of the level of the third variable. The DxSxC, DxSxL and DxCxL interactions were not significant. The four factor interaction DxSxCxL was, however, significant indicating that the interaction between any three of the variables taken at a time was not independent of the level of the fourth variable.

2. Hindi and English

The mean scores and SDs of different sub-groups of students in Hindi and English are presented in Table 6.9 and 6.10 respectively. It could be seen from Table 6.9 that in Hindi the mean score of students under the detention system was 29.76 while under the non-detention system the mean score was 33.19. This shows that the students achieved better in the non-detention system than in the detention system. In the case of English the mean scores of the two groups were 28.57 and 39.50 respectively. In this subject also students achieved better in the non-detention system (*see Fig. 6.1*).

Table—6.9 Mean and SDs of Different Sub-groups of *Ss* in Hindi.

Group	N	M	S.D.
DS	2714	29.76	11.13
NDS	5026	33.19	14.05
B	5447	31.13	13.41
G	2293	33.15	14.71
OCs	6545	32.54	13.93
SCs/STs	1195	27.29	12.37
U	2886	31.03	14.20
SU	2917	31.64	13.89
R	1937	32.89	13.10

Table—6.10 Means and SDs of Different Sub-groups of *Ss* in English

Group	N	M	S.D.
DS	2714	28.57	13.58
NDS	5026	39.50	15.48
B	5447	35.07	15.68
G	2293	37.08	15.75
OCs	6545	36.41	15.92
SCs/STs	1195	31.59	13.97
U	2886	34.66	16.08
SU	2917	35.20	16.58
R	1937	38.04	13.99

An examination of the mean scores of boys and girls shows that girls scored better than boys in both the subjects.

Considering the mean scores of students belonging to the two social classes it could be seen from the tables that OCs achieved better than SCs/STs in both the subjects.

The mean scores of students belonging to urban, semi-urban and rural localities were 31.03, 31.64 and 32.89 respectively in the case of Hindi. In the case of English the mean scores were 34.66, 35.20 and 38.04 respectively for the three groups.

To examine whether these differences between the different sub-groups were significant, the achievement scores were analysed by analysis of variance of a 2x2x2x3 factorial design as in the case of Telugu. The results obtained are shown in Tables 6.11 and 6.12 for Hindi and English respectively.

Table—6.11 Results of Analysis of Variance (Hindi)

Source	SS	df	MSS	*F*
System (D)	989.54	1	989.54	5.34*
Sex (S)	544.18	1	544.18	2.94@
Caste (C)	968.43	1	968.43	5.22*
Locality (L)	1804.46	2	902.23	4.87*
DxS	737.43	1	737.43	3.98*
DxC	218.23	1	218.23	1.18@
DxL	854.26	2	427.23	2.30@
SxC	283.76	1	283.76	1.53@
SxL	624.64	2	312.32	1.68@
CxL	698.46	2	349.23	1.88@
DxSxC	394.46	1	394.46	2.13@
DxSxL	784.23	2	392.12	2.12@
DxCxL	698.46	2	349.23	1.89@
SxCxL	594.23	2	297.12	1.60@
DxSxCxL	721.36	2	360.68	1.95@
Error	1430690.30	7716	185.39	
Total	**1441606.40**	**7739**		

Note: See note under Table 6.2.

Table—6.12 Results of Analysis of Variance (English)

Source		SS	Df	MSs	F
System	(D)	1352.01	1	1352.01	5.61*
Sex	(S)	895.37	1	895.37	3.71@
Caste	(C)	1344.86	1	1344.86	5.58*
Locality	(L)	2165.48	2	1082.74	4.49*
DxS		384.31	1	384.31	1.59@
DxC		887.36	1	887.36	3.68@
DxL		736.46	2	368.23	1.53@
SxC		992.23	1	992.23	4.12*
SxL		998.46	2	499.23	2.07@
CxL		632.84	2	316.42	1.31@
DxSxC		528.46	1	528.46	2.19@
DxSxL		485.23	2	242.61	1.01@
DxCxL		956.84	2	478.42	1.98@
SxCxL		764.83	2	382.42	1.59@
DxSxCxL		532.23	2	266.12	1.10@
Error		1860439.13	7716	241.08	
Total		**1874096.10**	**7739**		

Note: See note under Table 6.2.

It could be seen from Table 6.2 that the *F* ratio for system was 5.34 which is significant at 0.05 level for 1 and 7716 df. An examination of the mean scores presented in Table 6.9 shows that the achievement in the non-detention system (M=33.19) was significantly better than that in the detention system (M= 29.76) . Similar results were obtained in the case of the subjects English also.

As mentioned earlier (p.153) learning would be better if imparted under a natural setting free from fear, stress and anxiety caused by examinations coupled with detentions. The results obtained in these two subjects as in the case of Telugu corroborate the above point of view.

The *F* ratios for sex, 2.94 and 3.71 respectively for Hindi and English were not significant at 0.05 level. The insignificant *F* ratios indicate no difference between the achievement of boys and girls in these two subjects. However, these results based upon the insignificant *F* ratio for sex should be interpreted cautiously, in view of the significant *F* ratios for DxS interaction (in Hindi) and SxC interaction (in English).

The *F* ratio 5.22 for social class variable (in Hindi) was significant at 0.05 level. The mean score of OCs was 32.54 while it was 27.29 for the SCs/STs showing that the former achieved better than the latter. In the case of English the means of the two groups were 36.41 and 31.59 respectively and the difference between the two was significant (*F*= 5.58, significant at 0.05 level for 1 and 7716 df). Thus in both the subjects OCs scored significantly higher than SCs/STs (see Figs. 6.5 and 6.6). As mentioned earlier this must be because of the difference in economic conditions of the two groups , which result in better living conditions, enough study materials and less financial worries.

The *F* ratio for locality was 4.87 for Hindi while it was 4.49 for English, both significant at 0.05 level for 2 and 7716df. This shows that there was significant difference between the achievement of students belonging to different localities in both the subjects.

To find out which group differed significantly from others, *t* test was applied. The results of this analysis are presented in Table 6.13 and 6.14 respectively for Hindi and English. It could be seen from the tables that in the case of Hindi the mean scores of the *Ss* belonging to U, SU and R localities were 31.03, 31.64 and 32.89 respectively while they were 34.66, 35.20 and 38.04 respectively for English. Rural *Ss* scored significantly better than U and SU children. There

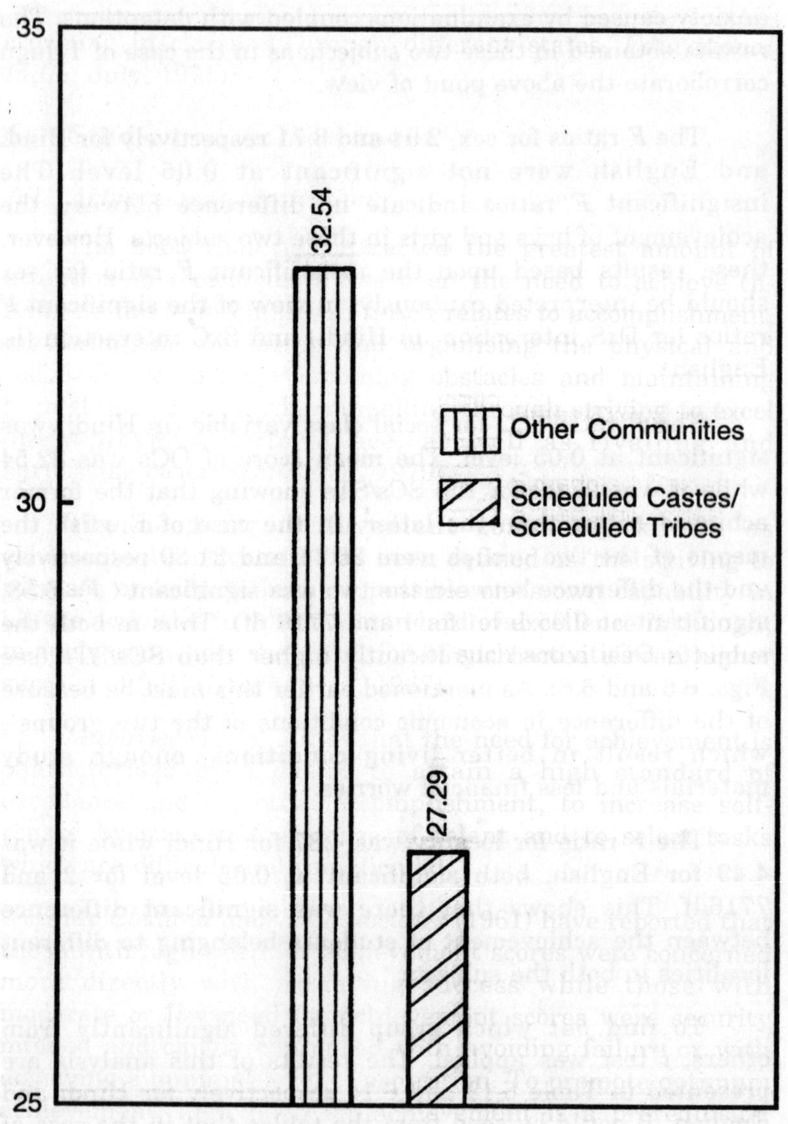

Fig.—6.5 Mean Scores of Students Belonging to Different Social Classes (Hindi).

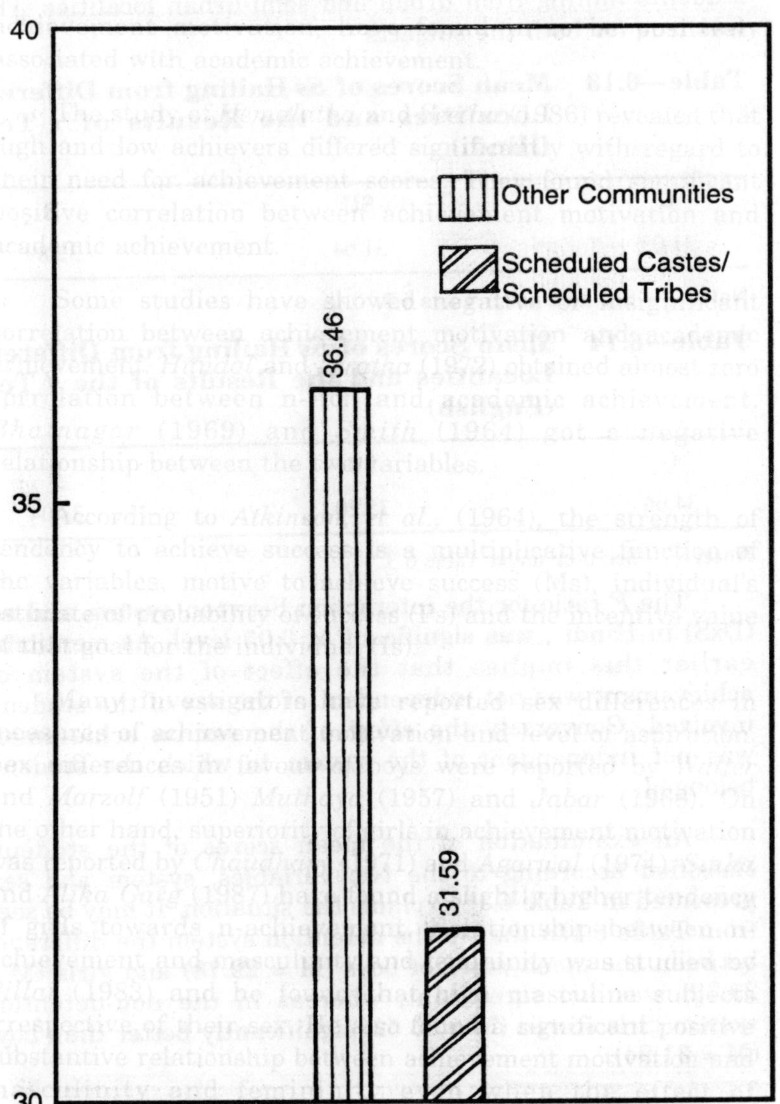

Fig.—6.6 Mean Scores of Students Belonging to Different Social Classes (English).

was no significant difference between the mean scores of students hailing from urban and semi-urban localities. This was true for both the subjects.

Table—6.13 Mean Scores of *Ss* Hailing from Different Localities and the Results of *t* Test (Hindi)

U	SU	R
31.03	31.64	32.89

Note: See note under Table 6.3.

Table—6.14 Mean Scores of *Ss* Hailing from Different Localities and the Results of the *t* Test (English)

U	SU	R
34.66	35.20	38.04

Note: See note under Table 6.3.

The *F* ratio for the interaction between system and sex (DxS) in Hindi , was significant at 0.05 level. As mentioned earlier this implies that the effect of the system on achievement was not independent of the sex of the students involved. Conversely the effect of the sex on achievement was not independent of the system to which the students belonged.

An examination of the mean scores of the students classified according to the two variables, system and sex, presented in Table 6.15 explains the situation. It may be seen from Table 6.15a that in the detention system the difference between the mean score of boys (M = 29.78) and girls (M = 29.72) was not significant, whereas in the non-detention system girls scored (M = 35.52) significantly better than boys (M = 31.94).

It may be seen from Table 6.15b that both boys and girls achieved significantly better in the non-detention system. But the increase in achievement in the case of boys was only 2.16 points while it was 5.80 points for girls. This difference, in the magnitude of the difference between the mean scores, explains the significant interaction between sex and system.

Table—6.15 Mean Scores of Different Sub-groups of *Ss* Classified According to Their System and Sex to Explain DxS Interaction (Hindi)

(6.15a) DxS			(6.15b) SxD		
	G	B		DS	NDS
DS	29.72	29.78	B	29.78	31.94
	B	G		DS	NDS
NDS	31.94	35.52	G	29.72	35.52

Note: See note under Table 6.3.

The *F* ratio (4.12) for the interaction between sex and caste was significant in the case of English . An examination of the mean scores of the *Ss* classified according to the two variables (Table 6.16) shows that irrespective of sex, OCs scored better than SCs/STs. When the mean scores of boys and girls were compared, it was found that there was no significant difference between the two sexes in the case of SCs/STs while in the case of OCs girls scored significantly better than boys.

Table—6.16 Mean Scores of Different Sub-groups of *Ss* Classified According to Their Sex and Social Class to Explain SxC Interaction Effect (English)

(6.16a) SxC			(6.16b) CxS		
	SCs/STs	OC		B	G
B	31.24	35.76	SCs/STs	31.24	32.43
	SCs/STs	OC		B	G
G	32.43	37.94	OC	35.76	37.94

Note: See note under Table 6.3.

None of the *F* ratios for other interaction effects was significant at 0.05 level.

3. Science and Social Studies

The mean scores and SDs of different sub-groups of Ss in science and social studies are shows in Tables 6.17 and 6.18 respectively. It could be seen from the tables that in both these subjects as in the case of the other subjects discussed earlier, those who studied under the non-detention system scored better marks than those who studied under the detention system. Similarly girls scored better than boys in both the subjects, while OCs surpassed SCs and STs. Rural children excelled their counterparts fro urban and semi-urban localities.

Table—6.17 Mean and SDs of Different Sub-groups of *Ss* in Science

Group	N	M	S.D.
DS	2714	33.67	12.18
NDS	5026	41.95	17.50
B	5447	38.27	21.03
G	2293	40.91	16.16
OCs	6545	39.74	16.42
SCs/STs	1195	35.28	15.25
U	2886	37.23	16.58
SU	2917	38.97	15.89
R	1937	41.54	17.25

Table—6.18 Mean and SDs of Different Sub-groups of *Ss* in Social Studies

Group	N	M	S.D.
DS	2714	37.98	11.47
NDS	5026	45.34	14.69
B	5447	42.53	14.20
G	2293	43.32	13.81
OCs	6545	43.22	14.10
SCs/STs	1195	40.24	13.78
U	2886	41.18	13.11
SU	2917	42.58	14.07
R	1937	45.51	12.94

The achievement scores of the *Ss* were further analysed by analysis of variance of 2x2x2x3 factorial design as in the earlier cases. The results of this analysis are presented in Tables 6.19 and 6.20 for science and social studies respectively.

Table—6.19 Results of Analysis of Variance (Science)

Source		SS	df	MSS	*F*
System	(D)	1604.24	1	1604.24	6.36**
Sex	(S)	1055.76	1	1055.76	4.19*
Caste	(C)	1236.46	1	1236.46	4.90*
Locality	(L)	2124.22	2	1062.11	4.21*
DxS		452.26	1	452.26	1.79@
DxC		423.36	1	423.36	1.68@
DxL		858.12	2	429.06	1.70@
SxC		534.23	1	534.23	2.12@
SxL		718.46	2	359.23	1.42@
CxL		912.62	2	456.31	1.81@
DxSxC		448.46	1	448.46	1.78@
DxSxL		1211.23	2	560.61	2.22@
DxCxL		1608.46	2	804.23	2.00@
SxCxL		882.46	2	441.23	1.75*
DxSxCxL		488.46	2	244.23	0.97@
Error		1945462.40	7716	252.10	
Total		**1960021.20**	**7739**		

Note: See note under Table 6.2.

It could be seen from these tables that the *F* ratios for system were 6.36 and 5.38 respectively for science and social studies. Both the *F* ratios were significant at or above 0.05 level. These results along with the mean scores of the students belonging to the two systems presented in Tables 6.17 and 6.18 show that the non-detention system was more conducive for better achievement. These results are in line with the results obtained in other subjects discussed so far.

Table—6.20 Results of Analysis of Variance (Social Studies)

Source	SS	df	MSS	*F*
System (D)	835.44	1	835.44	5.38*
Sex (S)	704.26	1	704.26	4.54*
Caste (C)	744.46	1	744.46	4.80*
Locality (L)	1324.82	2	662.41	4.27*
DxS	214.41	1	214.41	1.38@
DxC	421.64	1	421.64	2.72@
DxL	638.06	2	319.03	2.06@
SxC	198.46	1	198.46	1.23@
SxL	584.42	2	292.21	1.88@
CxL	624.32	2	312.16	2.02@
DxSxC	486.46	1	486.46	3.13@
DxSxL	558.34	2	279.17	1.80@
DxCxL	644.81	2	322.41	2.08@
CxSxL	597.86	2	298.93	1.93@
DxSxCxL	614.46	2	307.23	1.98@
Error	1198016.73	7716	155.24	
Total	**1207953.40**	**7739**		

Note: See note under Table 20.

In the case of sex, the *f* ratios 4.19 for science and 4.54 for social studies were also significant at 0.05 level for 1 and 7717 df. In the case of science the mean scores of boys and girls were 38.27 and 40.91 respectively (see Fig. 6.7) . While

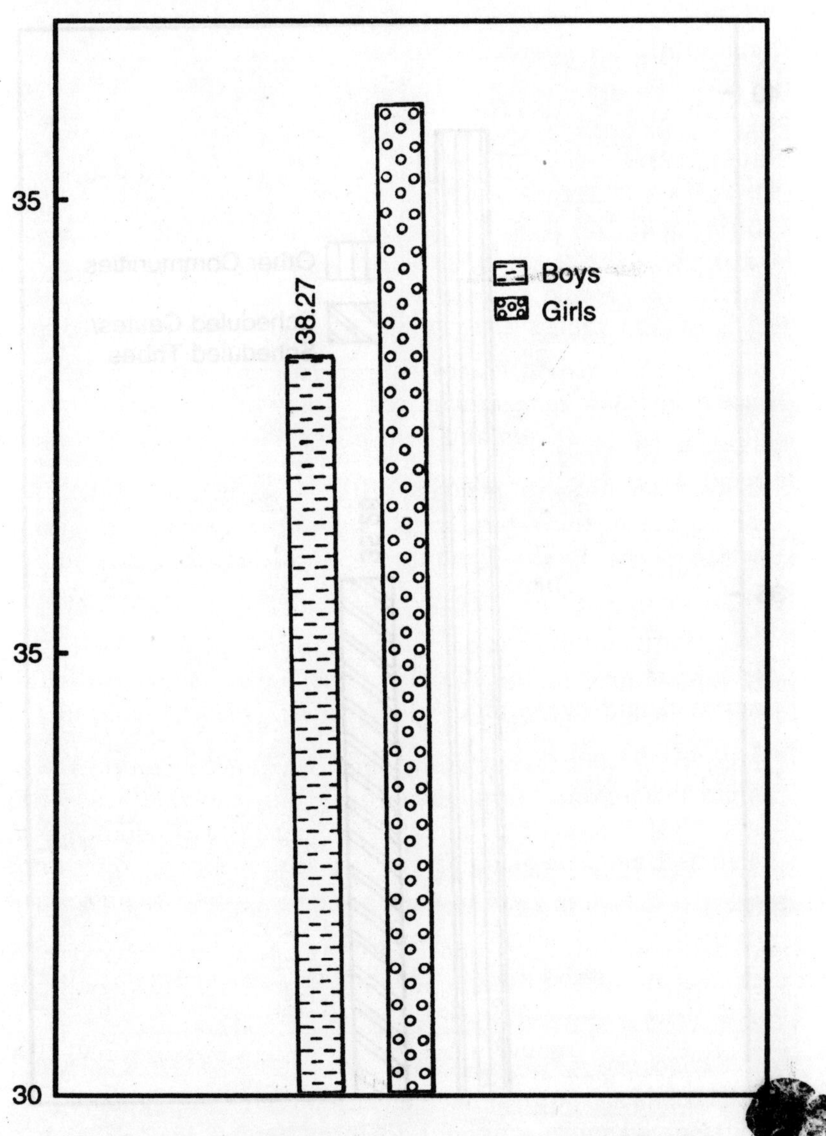

Fig.—6.7 Mean Scores of Boys and Girls (Science)

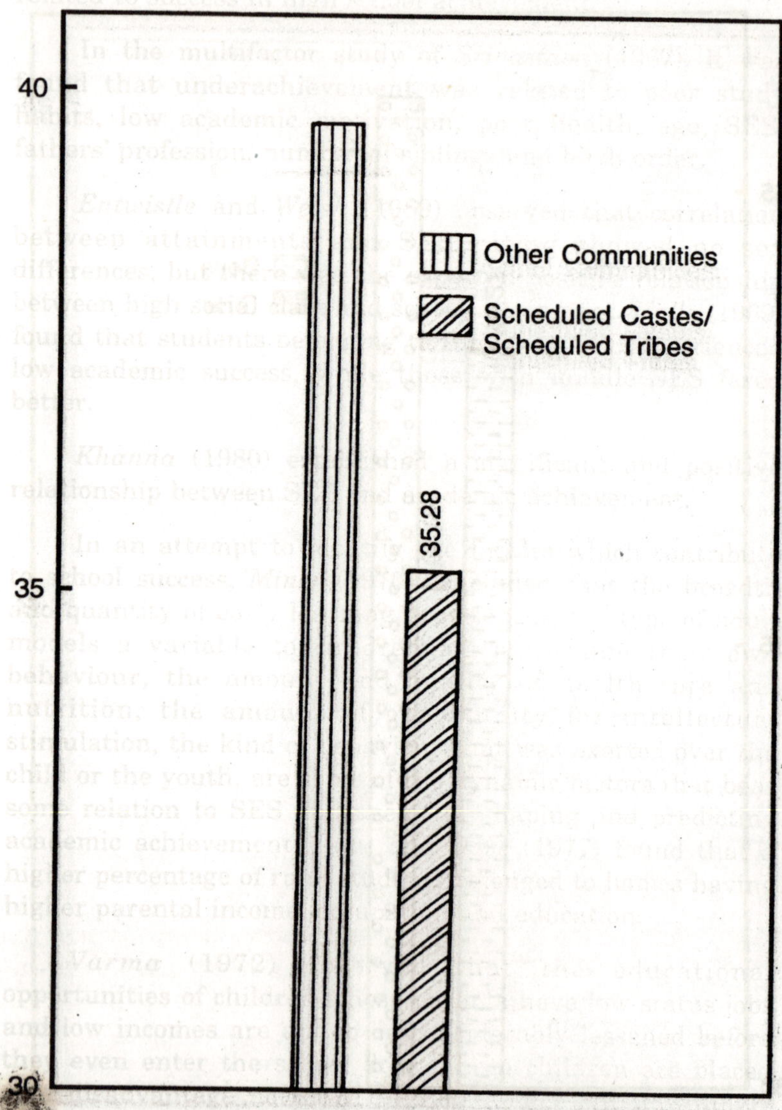

Fig.—6.8 Mean Scores of Students Belonging to Different Social Classes (Science)

in the case of social studies the mean scores were, boys: 42.53 and girls: 43.32 . This shows that girls achieved significantly better than boys in these two subjects also in the case of other subjects viz., Telugu, Hindi and English discussed earlier.

The *F* ratio for caste was 4.90 in the case of science while it was 4.80 for social studies. Both these *F* ratios were also significant at 0.05 level. In science the mean score of OCs was 39.74 while that of SCs/STs was 35.28 (*see Fig. 6.8 in page 178*) . In the case of social studies the mean of the two groups were, OCs: 43.22 and SCs/STs: 40.24 (*see Fig. 6.10 in page 183*). These results show that in both the subjects students belonging to OCs scored significantly better than those belonging to SCs/STs. Here also, the results are in general similar to the results obtained in other subjects.

The *F* ratios for locality were also significant at 0.05 level for 2 and 7716 df for both the subjects. To find out students of which locality differed significantly from others, *t* test was applied as in the earlier cases. The results of this analysis are presented in Tables 6.21 and 6.22.

Table—6.21 Mean Scores of *Ss* Hailing From Different Localities and Results of the *t* Test (Science)

U	SU	R
41.18	42.58	45.51

Note: See note under Table 6.3.

Table—6.22 Mean Scores of *Ss* Hailing from Different Localities and Results of the *t* Test (Social Studies)

U	SU	R
41.18	42.58	45.51

Note: See note under Table 6.3.

It may be seen from the tables that the *Ss* from each locality differed significantly from the others in both the subjects. Rural children achieved the highest mean score, while urban children obtained the lowest mean, semi-urban children falling in between (*see Figs. 6.9 and 6.11*).

None of the *F* ratios either for the 2 factor 3 factor or 4 factor interactions were significant at 0.05 level for both the subjects.

4. Mathematics

The mean scores and SDs of the different sub-groups of *Ss* in mathematics are shown in Table 6.23. The mean score of the Ss who studied under the detention system was 29.81 while it was 38.20 in the non-detention system. This shows that there was better achievement under the non-detention system than in the detention system.

Table—6.23 Means and SDs of Different Sub-groups of Students in Mathematics

Group	N	M	S.D
DS	2714	29.81	13.92
NDS	5026	38.20	20.40
B	5447	34.58	18.29
G	2293	36.88	19.94
OCs	6545	36.30	19.54
SCs/STs	1195	29.52	12.80
U	2886	32.94	18.49
SU	2917	34.60	18.49
R	1937	40.21	19.67

Girls (M = 36.88) achieved better than the boys (M = 34.58) With regard to the social class Variable, the mean score of OCs was 36.30 while it was 29.52 for SCs/STs indicating OCs achieved better than SCs/STs.

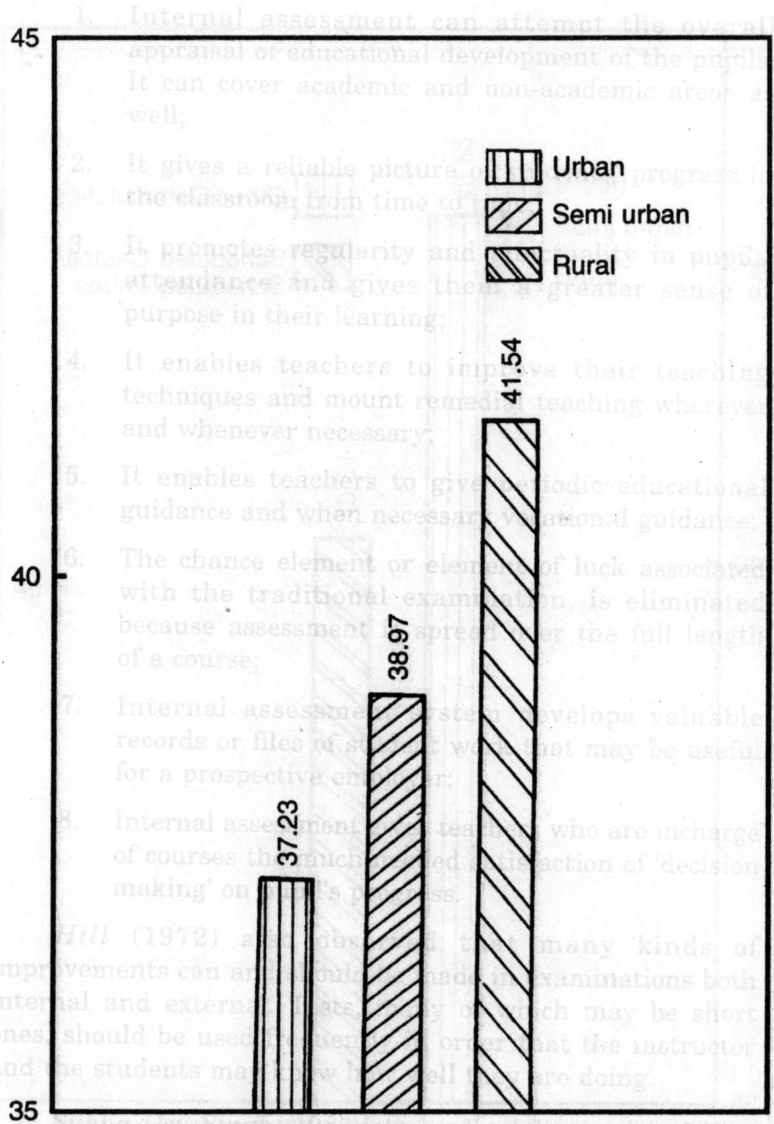

Fig.—6.9 Mean Scores of Students Belonging to Different Localities (Science)

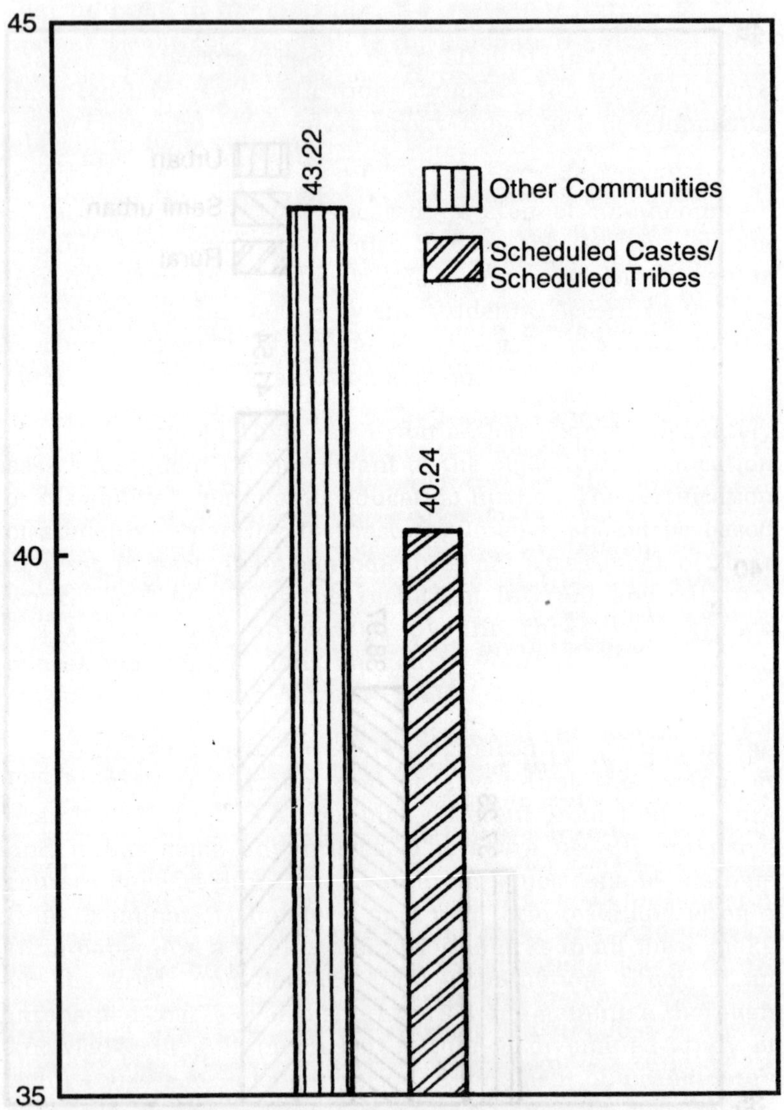

Fig.—6.10 Mean Scores of Students Belonging to Different Social Classes (Social Studies)

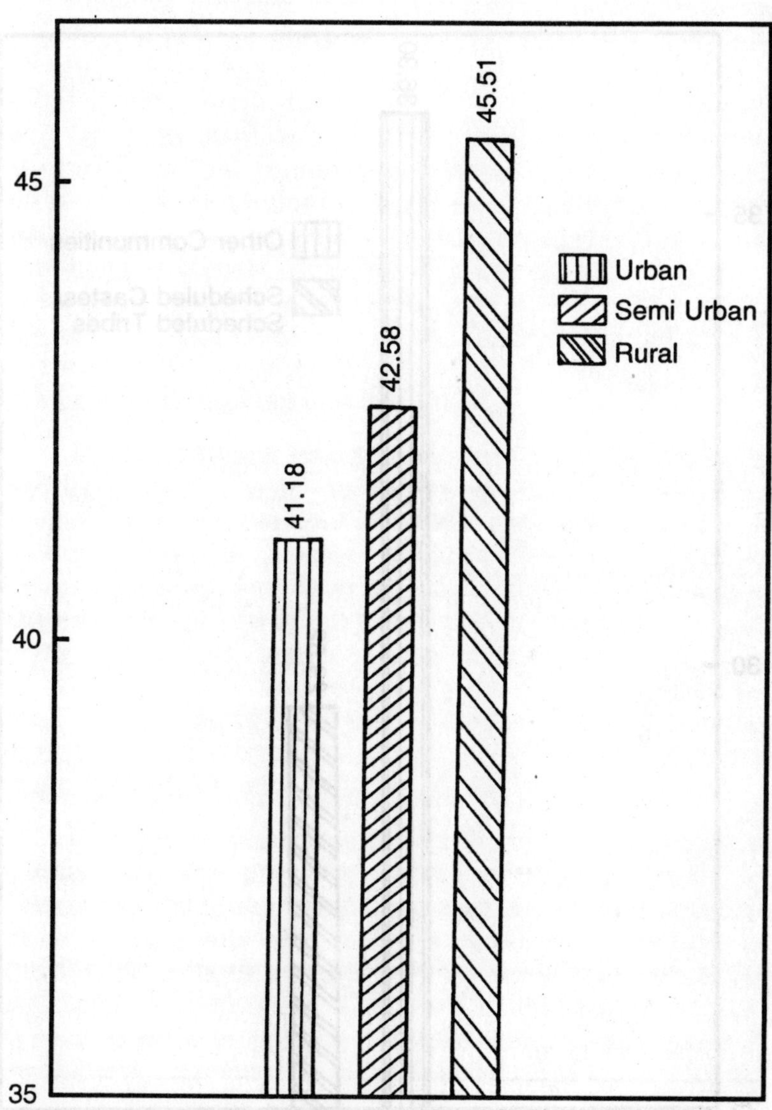

Fig.—6.11 Mean Scores of Students Belonging to Different Localities (Social Studies)

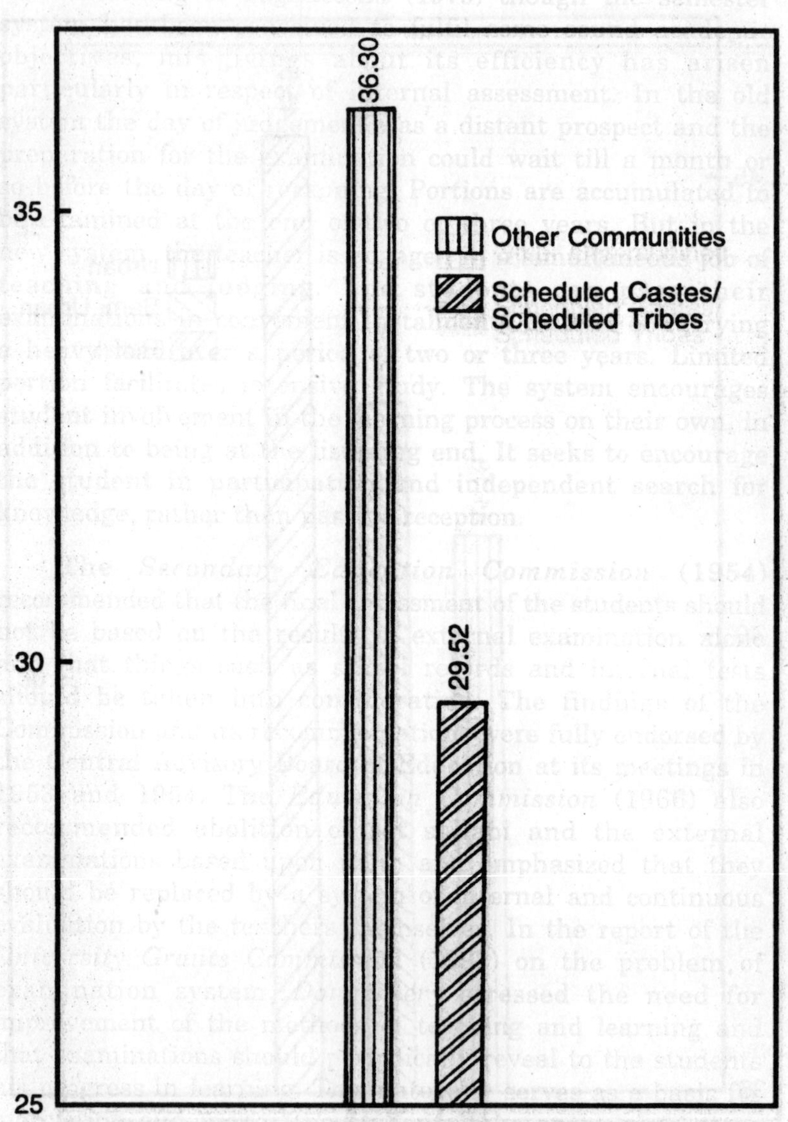

Fig.—6.12 Mean Scores of Students Belonging to Different Social Classes (Mathamatics)

When the students were classified as urban, semi-urban and rural based upon the locality to which they belonged, it was found that those from rural localities scored far better than those of the other two localities. The mean scores of the three groups U, SU and R, were 32.94, 34.60 and 40.21 respectively.

As in the earlier cases the achievement scores were further analysed by ANOVA. The results obtained in this analysis are shown in Table 6.24.

Table—6.24 Results of Analysis of Variance (Mathematics)

Source	SS	df	MSS	F
System (D)	1754.14	1	1754.14	5.37*
Sex (S)	1348.18	1	1348.18	4.13*
Caste (C)	1814.26	1	18.14.26	5.55*
Locality (L)	3352.68	2	1676.34	5.13*
DxS	15.33.16	1	1533.16	4.69*
DxC	2306.73	1	2306.73	7.06**
DxL	2634.48	2	1317.24	4.03*
SxC	1813.23	1	1813.23	5.55*
SxL	2848.06	2	1424.03	4.35*
CxL	2324.12	2	1162.24	3.56@
DxSxC	1654.76	1	1654.76	5.07*
DxSxL	2836.70	2	1418.35	4.34*
DxCxL	2586.46	2	1293.23	3.95*
SxCxL	2634.23	2	1317.12	4.03*
DxSxCxL	2428.78	2	1214.39	3.72@
Error	252066.17	7716		
Total	**285936.14**	**7739**		

Note: See note under Table 6.2.

It could be seen from the table that the *F* ratio for system was 5.37 which is significant at 0.05 level for 1 and 7716 df indicating a significant difference between the achievement of *Ss* under the detention and non-detention systems. An examination of the mean scores of the students studying under the two systems presented in Table 6.23 shows that the mean score of students belonging to the detention system was 29.81, while it was 38.20 in the non-detention system (*see Fig. 6.1*). Evidently the achievement under the non-detention system was significantly better than that in the detention system.

Tension-free and anxiety-free atmosphere is essential for grasping of the concepts and principles underlying the different problems in mathematics, which is provided by the non-detention system. The results of the study belie the contention of the opponents of the system that it would tell upon the standards of education. Contrary to their expectations the non-detention system seems to reflect proper assessment of realities and wisdom on the part of the government in abolishing detentions.

The *F* ratio for sex was 4.13 which is significant at 0.05 level. This shows that there was a significant difference between the achievement of the two sexes. The mean score of boys was 34.58 while it was 36.88 for girls. This shows that girls scored significantly better than boys.

With regard to the variable social class, the *F* ratio was 5.55 which is significant at 0.05 level for 1 and 7716 df. The mean score of SCs/STs was 29.52 while it was 36.30 for the other castes (*see Fig. 6.12 in page 184*). This shows that students belonging to OCs achieved significantly better than SCs/STs.

The *F* ratio for locality was 5.13 which is also significant at 0.05 level for 2 and 7717 df. This shows that there was a significant difference between the achievement of students belonging to the different localities.

To find out which group differed significantly from the other, *t* test was applied. The results of this analysis are presented in Table 6.25. It may be seen from the table that each group differed significantly from the others. The mean scores of urban, semi-urban and rural *Ss* were 32.94, 34.60 and 40.21 respectively, showing that rural *Ss* achieved the highest while urban *Ss* scored the least (*see Fig. 6.13*).

Table—6.25 Mean Scores of Ss Hailing from Different Localities and the Results of the *t* Test (Mathematics)

U	SU	R
32.94	34.60	40.21

Note: See note under Table—6.3.

The *F* ratio of 4.69 for the interaction between system and sex was significant at 0.05 level. To make a deeper probe into this, the mean scores of the *Ss* were classified according to the two variables and *t* test was applied. The results of this analysis are shown in Table 6.26.

Table—6.26 Mean Scores in Mathematics of Different Sub-groups of *Ss* Classified According to the System and Sex Variables to Explain the DxS Interaction Effect.

	(6.26a) DxS			(6.26b) SxD	
DS	B 29.74	G 30.02	B	DS 29.74	NDS 37.47
NDS	B 37.47	G 40.81	G	DS 30.02	NDS 40.81

Note: See note under Table—6.3.

It may be seen from Table 6.26a that in the case of detention system the mean scores of boys and girls were 29.74 and 30.02 respectively while they were 37.47 and 40.81 respectively under the non-detention system. In both the

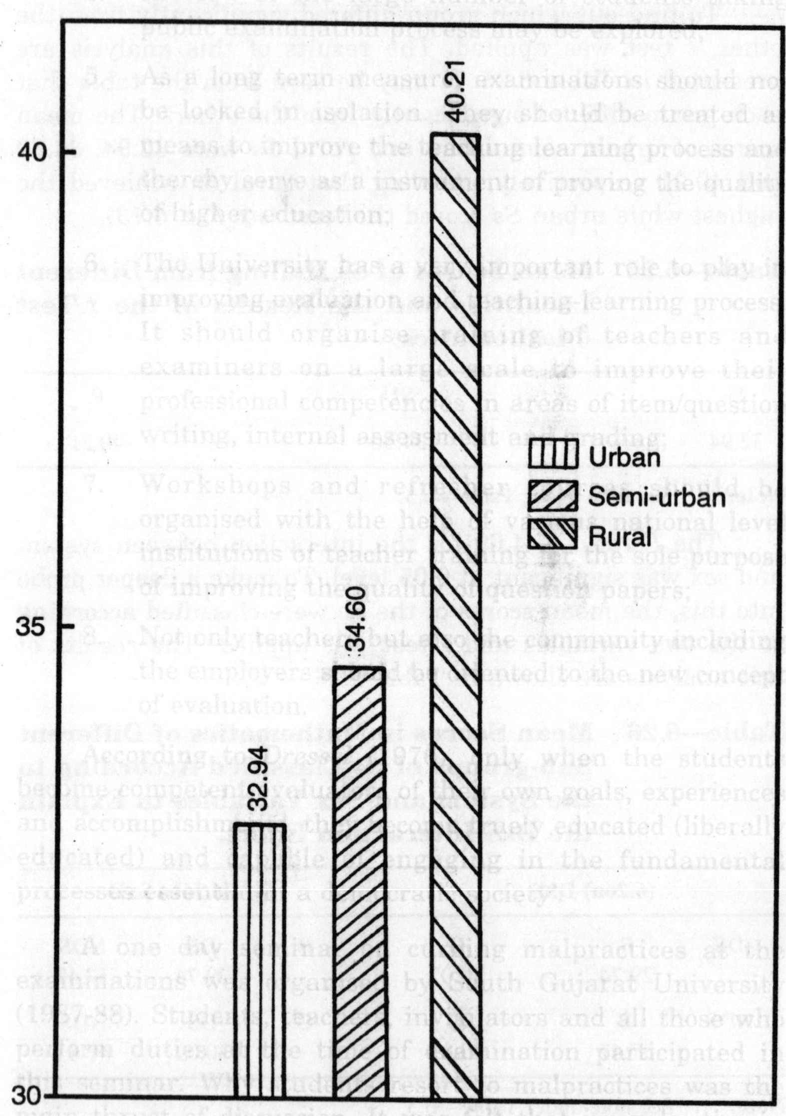

Fig.—6.13 Mean Scores of Students Belonging to Different Localities (Mathamatics)

systems girls achieved better than boys. But in the detention system the difference between the mean scores of boys and girls was not significant, however, it was significant in the case of the non-detention system.

The *F* ratio (7.06) for the interaction between system and caste was significant at 0.01 level for 1 and 7716 df. An examination of the mean scores of the students classified according to the two variables (Table 6.26a) shows that in both detention and non-detention systems OCs scored significantly better than SCs/STs.

Further, performance under the non-detention system was better than that in the detention system. This was true for both the communities (Table 6.27b). However, a deeper probe into the magnitude of the difference between the mean scores of the *Ss* belonging to the two social classes under the two systems shows that in the case of SCs/STs the difference in the mean score was only 4.40 points while it was 9.15 points in the case of OCs explaining the significant DxC interaction.

The *F* ratio (4.03) for the interaction between system and locality was also significant at 0.05 level. An examination of the mean scores of the students classified according to the two variables, presented in Table 6.26a shows that in the detention system *Ss* from R localities got the highest score and differed significantly from those belonging to U localities. There was no significant difference between U and SU localities or between SU and R localities. But in the case of the non-detention system R children differed significantly from those belonging to U and SU localities.

When the mean scores of students belonging to the two systems were considered separately for each locality (Table 6.28b), it was found that the achievement in the non-detention system was significantly higher than that in the detention system in all the three localities. This shows that the direction of the difference between the two system was the same irrespective of the locality to which the students belonged. But the difference between the mean scores under the two systems was very high in the case of *R* localities compared to that in the case of *U* and *SU* localities.

Table—6.27, 6.28, 6.29, 6.30: Mean scores of Different Sub-groups of Ss Classified According to Different Variables to Explain the Corresponding Interaction Effects (Mathematics)

(6.27a) (DxC)

	SCs/STs	OCs
DS	25.88	30.69
NDS	30.28	39.84

(6.27b) (CxD)

	DS	NDS
SCs/STs	25.88	30.28
OCs	30.69	39.84

(6.28a) (DxL)

	U	SU	R
DS	*28.99*	*29.94*	*31.10*
NDS	*35.70*	*36.53*	45.08

(6.28b) (LxD)

	DS	NDS
U	28.99	35.70
SU	29.94	36.53
R	31.10	45.08

(6.29a) (SxC)

	SCs/STs	OCs
B	28.70	35.64
G	31.44	37.88

(6.29b) (CxS)

	B	G
SCs/STs	28.70	31.44
OC	35.64	37.88

(6.30a) (SxL)

	U	SU	R
B	32.15	34.00	38.55
G	34.43	36.15	45.34

(6.30b) (LxS)

	B	G
U	32.15	34.43
SU	34.00	36.15
R	38.55	45.34

Note: See note under Table—6.3.

The *F* ratio (4.35) for the interaction between sex and caste was also significant. An examination of the mean scores of the *Ss* classified according to the two variables shows that in both the sexes OCs scored significantly higher marks than SCs/STs (Table 6.29a). When the mean scores of boys and girls were compared separately for OCs and SCs/STs (Table 6.29b), it was found that in both the social classes girls achieved significantly better than boys. However, the variations in the magnitude of the differences between the mean scores resulted in the significant interaction effect.

Considering the sex and locality variables, the *F* ratio (4.35) for the interaction between sex and locality (SxL) was significant at 0.05 level. An examination of the mean scores of the students classified according to the two variables presented in Tables 6.30a and 6.30b shows that children from R localities scored the highest. Those belonging to *U* localities got the lowest mean scores, *Ss* from *SU* localities falling in between. This was true for both the sexes. Similarly, girls scored better than boys in all the localities. However, the magnitude of the difference between mean scores of certain groups was quite larger compared to that in some other groups resulting in a significant *F* ratio for the interaction between the two variables.

The *F* ratio for the interaction between caste and locality (CxL) was not significant. This shows that the effect of caste was independent of the locality from which the students hailed and vice versa.

All the three factor interactions DSC, DSL, and SCL were significant showing that the interaction between any two variables taken at a time was not independent of the level of the third variable. The four factor interaction was not significant.

5. Total Score

Generally, a pupil's performance is judged on the basis of the total marks obtained in all the papers/subjects. Thus an attempt was made to analyse and examine the overall performance of the *Ss* under the two systems.

Table 6.31 shows the mean scores and SDs of different sub-groups of Ss on the total marks obtained in all the six subjects. It could be seen from the table that the mean score of the students who had their education under the detention system was 202.13 while that of those who had their education under the non-detention system was 245.78 (*see Fig. 6.14*). These mean scores coupled with the results of ANOVA presented in Table 6.32 in page 195 show that performance under the non-detention system was significantly better than that in the detention system ($F = 4.57$, significant at 0.05 level). With regard to sex variable, boys obtained a mean score of 226.85 while that of girls was 239.06 (*See Fig. 6.15 in page 194*). The difference between the two means was significant at 0.05 level ($F = 4.26$) showing that girls achieved significantly better than boys.

Table—6.31 Means and SDs of Different Sub-groups of *Ss* (Total Scores)

Group	N	M	S.D.
DS	2714	202.13	48.65
NDS	5026	245.78	81.40
B	5447	226.85	72.21
G	2293	239.06	79.35
OCs	6545	235.01	74.59
SCs/STs	1195	205.55	69.76
U	2886	223.58	74.74
SU	2917	227.11	73.07
R	1937	245.80	74.55

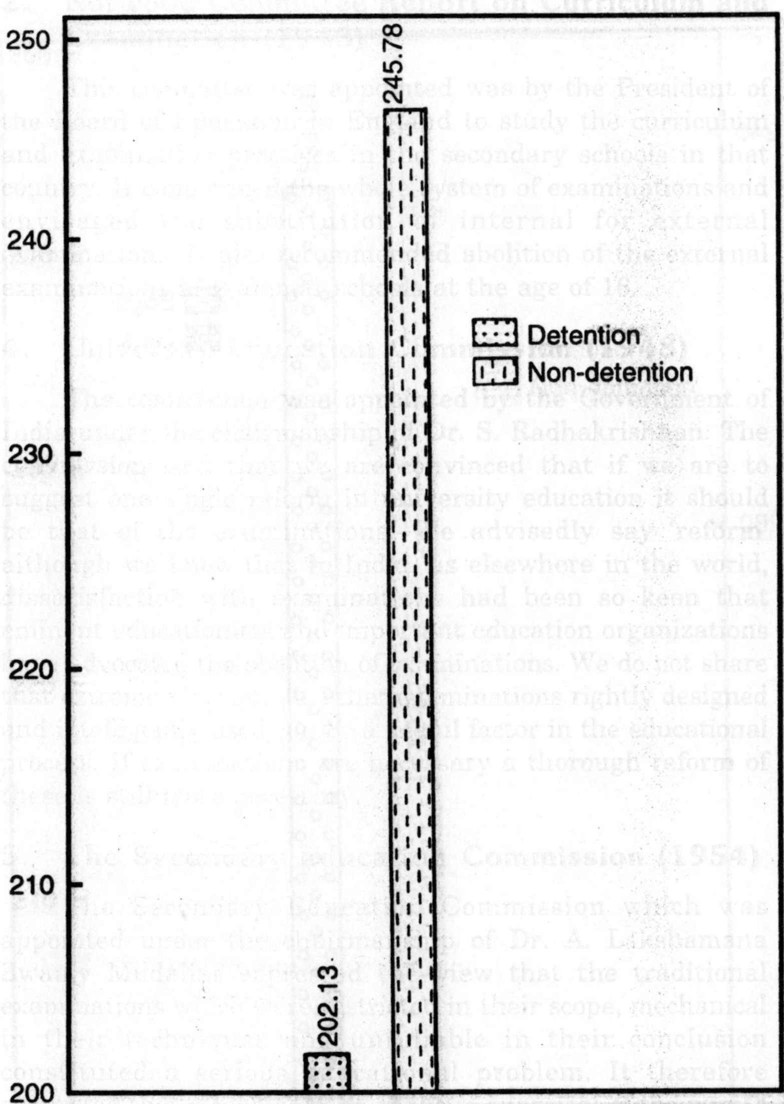

Fig.—6.14 Mean Scores of Students Under Detention and Non-detention System (Total Score)

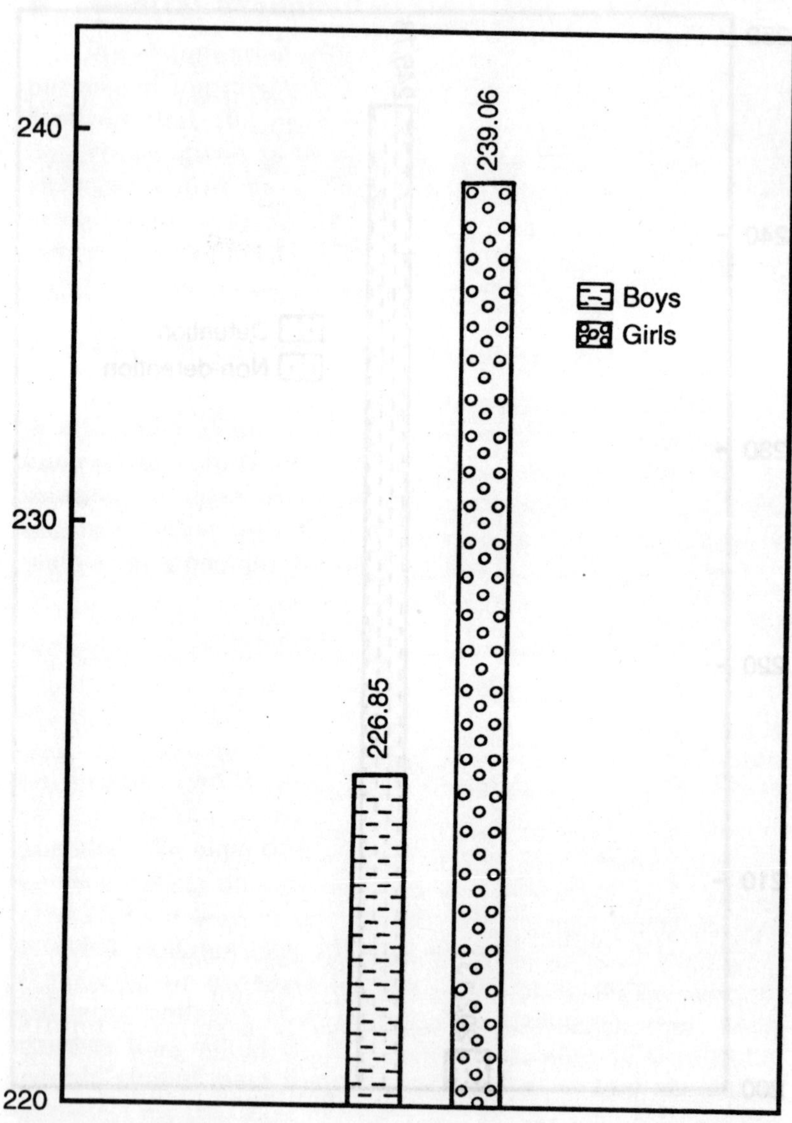

Fig.—6.15 Mean Scores of Boys and Girls (Total Scores)

Table—6.32 Results of Analysis of Variance (Total Scores)

Source		SS	df	MSS	*F*
System	(D)	15282.64	1	15282.64	4.57*
Sex	(S)	14248.06	1	14248.06	4.26*
Caste	(C)	16984.56	1	16984.56	5.08*
Locality	(L)	42224.64	2	21112.32	6.32**
DxS		12985.19	1	12985.19	3.88*
DxC		14975.33	1	14975.33	4.48*
DxL		28734.46	2	14367.23	4.29*
SxC		16387.16	1	16387.16	4.90*
SxL		31384.16	2	15692.08	4.69*
CxL		27646.06	2	13823.03	4.14*
DxSxC		17161.86	1	17161.86	5.13*
DxSxL		24565.58	2	12282.79	3.67*
DxCxL		23214.86	2	11607.43	3.47@
SxCxL		24816.62	2	12408.31	3.71@
DxSxCxL		25924.26	2	12962.13	3.88*
Error		25796306.46	7716	3342.79	
Total		**26132841.46**	**7739**		

Note: See note under Table—6.2.

Considering the caste variable, OCs (M = 235.01) scored significantly better than SCs/STs (M = 205.55) (*F* significant at 0.05 level) (*See Fig. 6.16*). When the students were classified as urban, semi-urban and rural based upon the locality to which they belonged, the mean scores of U, SU and R children were 223.58, 227.11 and 245.80 respectively (*See Fig. 6.17*). The difference between the means was significant at 0.01 level (*F* = 6.32). Further analysis by *t* test

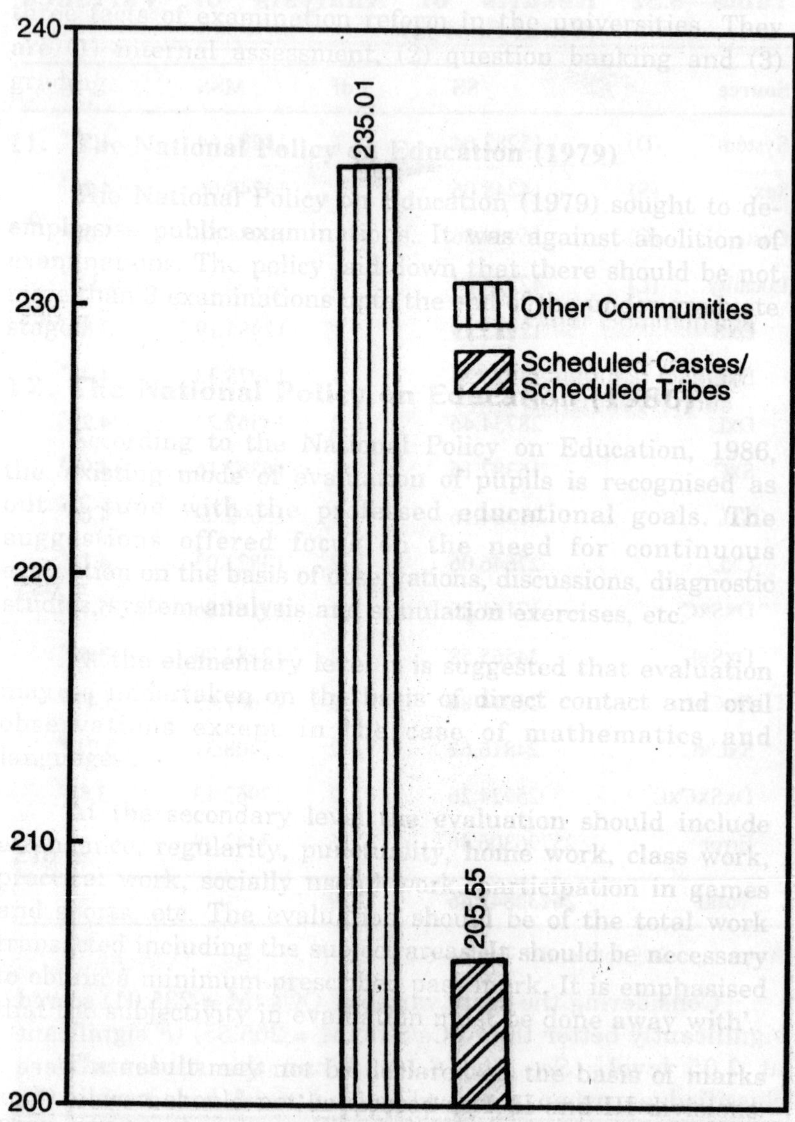

Fig.—6.16 Mean Scores of Students Belonging to Different Social Classes (Total Score)

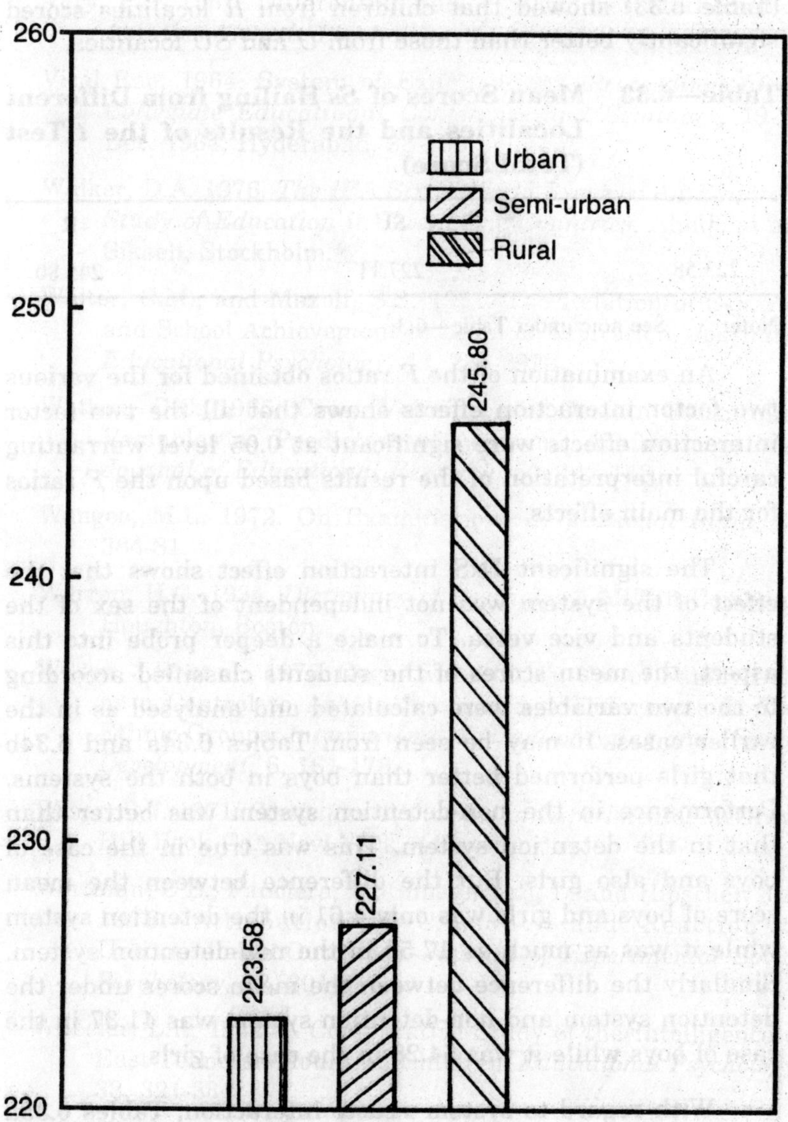

Fig.—6.17 Mean Scores of Students Belonging to Different Localities (Total Score)

(Table 6.33) showed that children from *R* localities scored significantly better than those from *U* and *SU* localities.

Table—6.33 Mean Scores of *Ss* Hailing from Different Localities and the Results of the *t* Test (Total Score)

U	SU	R
223.58	227.11	245.80

Note: See note under Table—6.3.

An examination of the *F* ratios obtained for the various two factor interaction effects shows that all the two factor interaction effects were significant at 0.05 level warranting careful interpretation of the results based upon the *F* ratios for the main effects.

The significant DxS interaction effect shows that the effect of the system was not independent of the sex of the students and vice versa. To make a deeper probe into this aspect, the mean scores of the students classified according to the two variables were calculated and analysed as in the earlier cases. It may be seen from Tables 6.34a and 6.34b that girls performed better than boys in both the systems. Performance in the non-detention system was better than that in the detention system. This was true in the case of boys and also girls. But the difference between the mean score of boys and girls was only 4.61 in the detention system while it was as much as 17.52 in the non-detention system. Similarly the difference between the mean scores under the detention system and non-detention system was 41.37 in the case of boys while it was 54.28 in the case of girls.

With regard to system x caste interaction, Tables 6.35a and 6.35b show that OCs scored better than SCs/STs in both the systems. Performance in the non-detention system was better for both the social classes. But there were large variations in the magnitude of the difference between means.

Tables—6.34, 6.35 6.36: Mean Scores of Different Sub-groups of *Ss* Classified According to Different Variables to Explain the Corresponding Interaction Effect (Total Score)

(6.34a) (DxS)				**(6.34b) (SxD)**	
	B	G		DS	NDS
DS	200.98	205.59	B	200.98	242.35
	B	G		DS	NDS
NDS	242.35	259.87	G	205.59	259.87

(6.35a) (DxC)				**(6.35b) (CxD)**	
	SCs/STs	OCs		DS	NDS
DS	184.19	204.19	SCs/STs	184.91	212.20
	SCs/STs	OCs		DS	NDS
NDS	212.20	253.14	OC	204.19	253.14

(6.36a) (DxL)					**(6.36b) (LxD)**	
	U	SU	R		DS	NDS
DS	199.63	202.80	205.66	U	199.63	240.30
	SU	U	R		DS	NDS
NDS	237.16	240.30	267.22	SU	202.80	237.16
					DS	NDS
				R	205.66	267.22

Note: See note under Table—6.3.

The system x locality (DxL) interaction was also significant at 0.05 level. Table 6.36a shows that *R* children scored highest in both the systems. Children from *U* localities got the lowest mean score in the case of detention system while in the case of non-detention system children from *SU* localities scored least. The mean score of the *R* children was significantly higher than that of those from both *U* and *SU* localities, in the case of the non-detention system, while in the detention system the mean score of *R* localities was significantly higher than that of *U* localities only. This shows that there were variations in the effect of the localities in the two systems.

Tables—6.37, 6.38, 6.39: Mean Scores of Different Sub-groups of *Ss* Classified According to Different Variables to Explain the Corresponding Interaction Effect (Total Scores)

	(6.37a) (SxC)				(6.37b) (CxS)	
	SCs/STs	OCs			B	G
B	203.68	231.07		SCs/STs	203.68	209.95
	SCs/STs	OCs			B	G
G	209.95	244.43		OCs	231.07	244.43
	(6.38a) (SxL)				(6.38b) (LxS)	
	U	SU	R		B	G
B	217.37	225.36	241.26	U	217.37	235.31
	SU	U	R		B	G
G	231.60	235.31	259.70	SU	225.36	231.60
					B	G
				R	241.26	259.70
	(6.39a) (CxL)				(6.39b) (LxC)	
	U	SU	R		SCs/STs	OCs
SCs/STs	191.63	201.62	233.26	U	191.63	228.54
	U	SU	R		SCs/STs	OCs
OCs	228.54	232.85	236.21	SU	201.62	232.85
					SCs/STs	OCs
				R	233.26	236.21

Note: See note under Table—6.3.

The results presented in Tables 6.37, 6.38 and 6.39 explain the significant sex x caste, sex locality and caste x locality interaction effects.

The 3 factor interaction DxSxC (between system, sex and caste) was also significant indicating that the interaction between any two of the above variables taken at a time was not independent of the level of the third variable. The DxLxS, DxLxC, LxSxC interactions were not significant. The 4 factor interaction DxLxSxC was, however, significant indicating that the interaction between any three of the variables taken at a time was not independent of the level of the fourth variable.

Conclusions

From the above result the following conclusions may be drawn:

1. Students achieved significantly better in the non-detention system than in the detention system in all subjects irrespective of their sex, social class or locality to which they belonged;
2. Girls out performed boys in all subjects;
3. The performance of SCs/STs was significantly inferior to that of children belonging to other communities. This was also true for all subjects without any exception;
4. In general, students hailing from *R* localities achieved better than those belonging to *U* and *SU* localities. This was also true for all subjects.

Section B

Percentage of Passes in the Two Systems

When the non-detention system was introduced it was contended by many that there will be a steep rise in the percentage of failures at the X class public examinations. It was felt that since the pupils were not trained all the while to face serious examinations of any kind, they will find these external examinations at the X class level insurmountable barriers in their educational march. They will be overwhelmed, confused and perplexed, the effort required being entirely new to them, resulting in stagnation of unprecedented dimensions (*Editorial, Educational India*, 1977; *Venkata Rao*, 1971).

To probe into this aspect the number of students who appeared and the number of those who have passed the X class public examination under the two systems from the schools selected for the study was recorded from the school records* selected for the study and the percentage of passes under the two systems was calculated.

Table 6.40 *(in page 204)* shows the results of this analysis for different sub-groups of *Ss*. It could be seen from the table that under the detention system 2714 students appeared for the X class public examination from the sample of schools selected for the study. Among them 935 have passed. This amounted to a pass percentage of 34.45. From the same schools the total number of students who appeared for X class public examination under the non-detention system was 5026. Among them 2958, or 58.85 per cent passed the examination. It could be seen that under the non-detention system the percentage of passes was very high (*see Fig. 6.18*).

The difference between the two percentage was highly significant ($t = 20.48$).

When the *Ss* were classified as boys and girls the pass percentage of boys under the detention system was 33.56, while it was as high as 56.81 per cent in the non-detention system. In the case of girls the percentages of passes were 37.15 and 63.64 in the detention and non-detention systems respectively. This shows that in the case of boys as well as girls the percentage of passes was higher in the non-detention system than that under the detection system. Similar results were obtained when the *Ss* were classified as urban, semi-urban and rural depending upon the locality to which they belonged.

---

* Since pass/fail information was destroyed in some records maintained by the Office of the Commissioner for Government Examinations, Hyderabad, it was recorded from the school records.

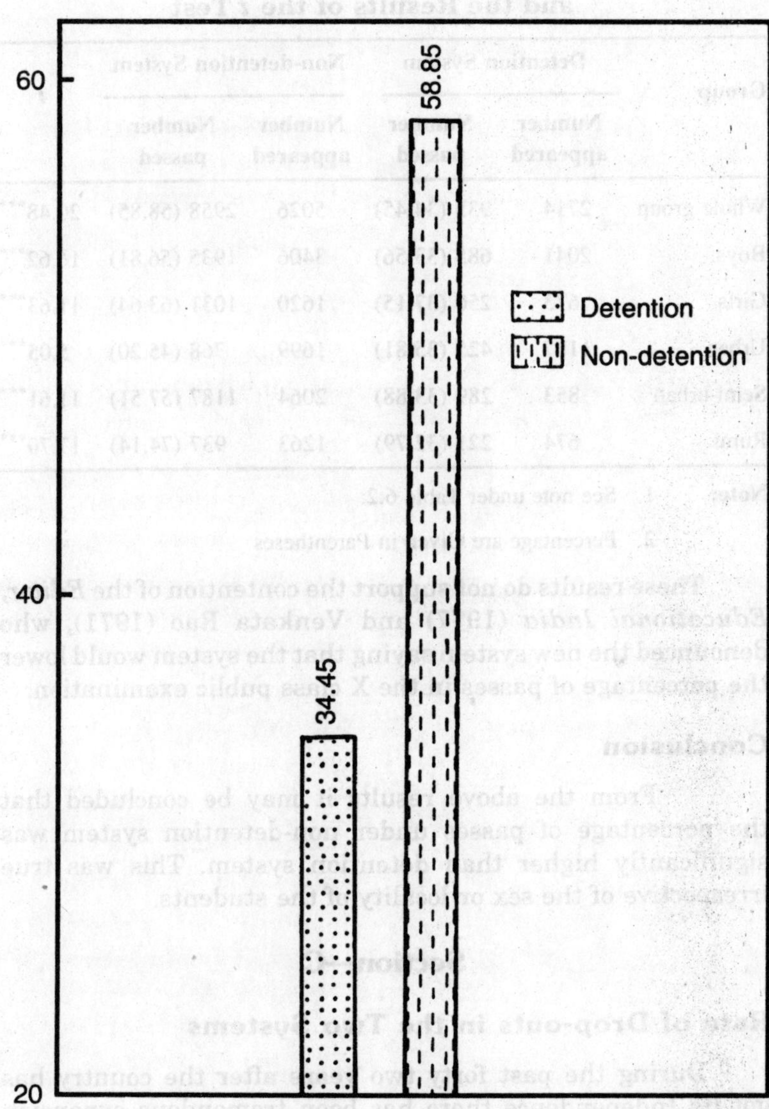

Fig.—6.18 Percentage of Passes Under Detention and Non-detention Systems

Table—6.40 Percentage of Passes in the Two System and the Results of the *t* Test

Group	Detention System		Non-detention System		*t*
	Number appeared	Number passed	Number appeared	Number passed	
Whole group	2714	935 (34.45)	5026	2958 (58.85)	20.48***
Boys	2041	685 (33.56)	3406	1935 (56.81)	16.62***
Girls	673	250 (37.15)	1620	1031 (63.64)	11.63***
Urban	1187	425 (35.81)	1699	768 (45.20)	5.05***
Semi-urban	853	289 (33.88)	2064	1187 (57.51)	11.61***
Rural	674	221 (32.79)	1263	937 (74.14)	17.70***

Note: 1. See note under Table 6.2.

2. Percentage are Given in Parentheses

These results do not support the contention of the *Editor, Educational India* (1977) and Venkata Rao (1971), who denounced the new system saying that the system would lower the percentage of passes in the X class public examination.

Conclusion

From the above results it may be concluded that the percentage of passes under non-detention system was significantly higher than detention system. This was true irrespective of the sex or locality of the students.

Section—C

Rate of Drop-outs in the Two Systems

During the past forty two years after the country has got its Independence there has been tremendous expansion in the field of education in India. Curriculum has been broadened and enriched, qualified staff has been appointed and there has been a great quantitative expansion of educational institutions with increase in enrolment right from the primary to the collegiate level. Education has occupied a priority area and is given a place next only to defence in the national budget. Despite all these efforts, a perennial and menacing problem remains. It is the problem of drop-outs.

India is wedded to democratic political ideology which demands educated citizens. The Constitution of India under the 'Directive Principles of State Policy' envisages free and compulsory education to all the children of the age group 6-14 years. But it has not been possible to achieve this goal. The alarming rate of drop-outs is the striking feature of our education system. All the students who enter primary school do not complete school education. Many drop-out somewhere in the middle. This is an undesirable phenomenon both for the individual, the society and the government. The money spent by the state does not yield significant results. Dropping-out of school has been viewed as a serious educational and social problem. Efforts are made by both the Central and State Governments to arrest it.

One of the major measures taken up by the Government of Andhra Pradesh state in this direction is the introduction of the non-detention system. According to *Kabra* (1971), *Narasimha Rao* (1971), *Sarabachari* (1971) and *Satyanarayana* (1971) the new system would reduce the problem of drop-outs.

To what extent the new system has really reduced the rate of drop-outs is not known. Hence, an attempt is made to assess and to compare the rate of drop-outs under the detention and non-detention systems. This section deals with this analysis.

From the schools* selected for the study, the number of students enrolled in each class in the beginning of the year and the number dropped-out by the beginning of the next year was recorded for both the systems. The percentage of

* Because of various reasons some of the records were destroyed in some schools. Hence, the data from such schools was incomplete.

drop-outs in each class under either system was calculated. These percentages were analysed by applying *t* test to see whether there was any significant difference between the rate of drop-outs under the two systems.

Table—6.41 Number of Students Enrolled and the Number and Percentage (Given in Parantheses) Dropped-out Under the two Systems and the Results of the *t* Test (Class VI)

Group	Detention System		Non-detention System		*t*
	Number enrolled	Number dropped-out	Number enrolled	Number dropped-out	
Whole group	3139	300 (9.56)	4552	171 (3.76	10.43***
Boys	2043	184 (9.01)	2889	120 (4.15)	6.98***
Girls	1096	116 (10.58)	1663	51 (3.07)	8.10***
Urban	1012	111 (10.97)	1432	61 (4.26)	6.39***
Semi-urban	1124	81 (7.21)	1687	67 (3.97)	3.76***
Rural	1003	108 (10.77)	1433	43 (3.00)	7.82***

Note: See note under Table—6.2.

Table 6.41 shows the number of students enrolled in class VI and the number dropped-out by the beginning of the next year under the two systems. It could be seen from the table that 3139 students were enrolled in class VI under detention system. Out of them 300 or 9.50 per cent dropped-out. In the non-detention system the total number of students who were admitted into the VI class in the sample of schools was 4552, out of them 171 students dropped-out. The percentage of drop-outs under the non-detention system was 3.76. From this it could be seen that the drop-out rate was lower in the non-detention system. The *t* value for the significance of the difference between the two percentage was 10.43, which is highly significant even at 0.001 level. Thus it could be said that the drop-out rate was significantly reduced in the non-detention system.

When the *Ss* were classified as boys and girls, out of 2043 boys 184 (9.01%) dropped-out in the detention system, while it was 120 out of 2889 (4.15%) in the non-detention system. The *t* value of 6.98 for the significance of the difference between the percentages reveals that the rate of drop-out was significantly low in the non-detention system in the case of boys. Similarly, in the case of girls the rate of drop-outs was 10.58 per cent in the detention system and 3.07 per cent in the non-detention system. The difference between the two percentages was highly significant even at 0.001 level ($t = 8.10$).

Similar results were obtained when the students were classified as urban, semi-urban and rural based upon the locality to which they belonged. Thus it could be concluded that the rate of drop-outs in class VI was significantly low in the non-detention system compared to that in the detention system. This was true irrespective of the sex or locality of the students involved. (*see Fig. 6.19 in page 208*).

Tables 6.42, 6.43, 6.44 and 6.45 show the results of similar analysis carried out for classes VII, VIII, IX and X respectively.

Table—6.42 Number of Students Enrolled and the Number and Percentage (Given in Parantheses) of Students Dropped-out Under the Two Systems and the Results of the *t* Test (Class VII)

Group	Detention System		Non-detention System		*t*
	Number enrolled	Number dropped-out	Number enrolled	Number dropped-out	
Whole group	2370	193 (8.14)	4481	245 (5.47)	4.31***
Boys	1621	120 (7.40)	2821	144 (5.10)	3.12**
Girls	749	73 (9.75)	1660	101 (6.08)	3.21**
Urban	800	94 (11.75)	1474	130 (8.81)	2.24*
Semi-urban	856	42 (4.91)	1746	58 (3.32)	1.98*
Rural	714	57 (7.98)	1261	57 (4.52)	3.17**

Note: See note under Table—6.2.

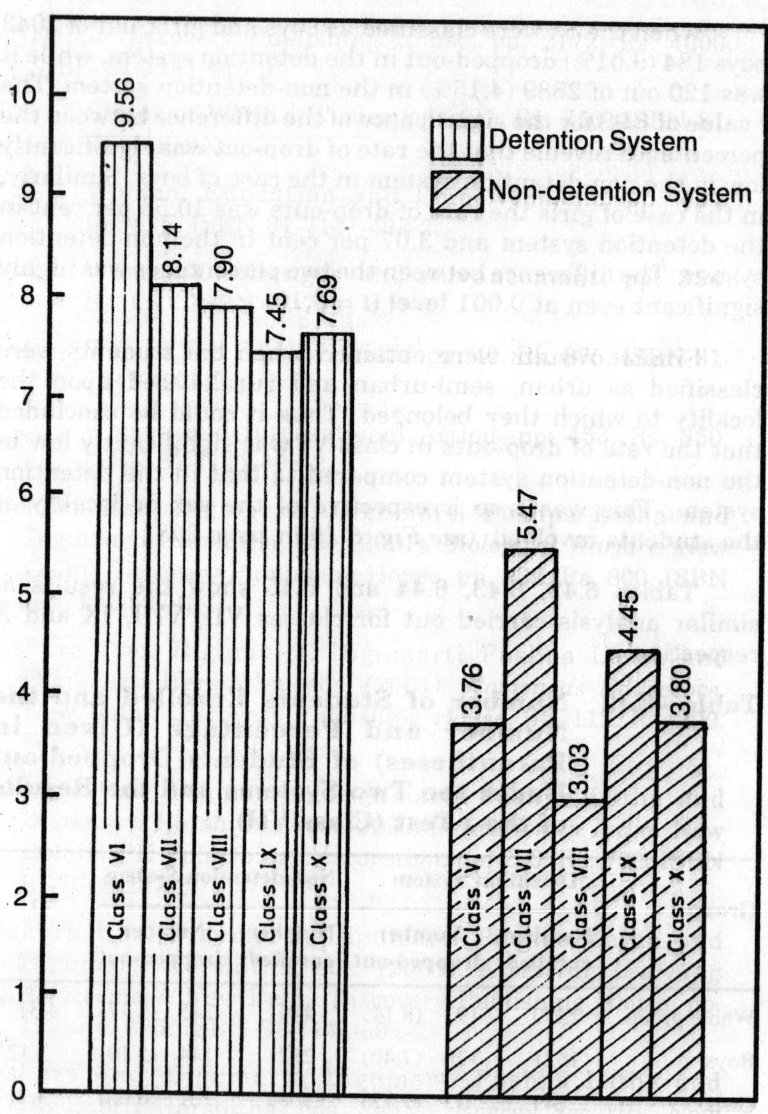

Fig.—6.19 Class-wise Rate of Drop-outs Under Detention and Non-detention Systems

Table—6.43 Number of Students Enrolled and the Number and Percentage (Given in Parantheses) of Students Dropped-out Under the Two Systems and the Results of *t* Test (Class VIII)

Group	Detention System		Non-detention System		*t*
	Number enrolled	Number dropped-out	Number enrolled	Number dropped-out	
Whole group	3430	271 (7.90)	5379	163 (3.03)	10.30***
Boys	2465	184 (7.46)	3642	110 (3.02)	7.96***
Girls	965	87 (9.02)	1737	53 (3.05)	6.90***
Urban	1101	149 (4.45)	1732	53 (3.06)	10.56***
Semi-urban	1354	74 (5.47)	2422	70 (2.89)	3.96***
Rural	975	48 (4.92)	1255	40 (3.19)	2.09*

Note: See note under Table 6.2.

Table—6.44 Number of Students Enrolled and the Number and Percentage (Given in Parantheses) of Students Gropped-out Under the Two Systems and the Results of *t* Test (Class IX)

Group	Detention System		Non-detention System		*t*
	Number enrolled	Number dropped-out	Number enrolled	Number dropped-out	
Whole group	2845	212 (7.15)	5163	230 (4.45)	5.62***
Boys	2114	124 (5.87)	3310	154 (1.63)	1.98*
Girls	731	88 (12.04)	1853	76 (4.10)	7.45***
Urban	1072	85 (7.93)	1965	98 (4.99)	3.26**
Semi-urban	1050	61 (5.81)	2038	85 (4.17)	2.03*
Rural	723	66 (9.13)	1160	47 (4.05)	4.51***

Note: See note under Table—6.2.

Table—6.45 Number of Students Enrolled and the Number and Percentage (Given in Parantheses) of Students Dropped-out Under the Two Systems and the Results of the t Test (Class X)*

Group	Detention System		Non-detention System		t
	Number enrolled	Number dropped-out	Number enrolled	Number dropped-out	
Whole group	2173	167 (7.69)	4232	161 (3.80)	6.67***
Boys	1651	98 (5.94)	2815	124 (4.40)	2.27*
Girls	522	69 (13.22)	1417	37 (2.61)	9.11***
Urban	633	56 (9.32)	1498	39 (2.60)	6.76***
Semi-urban	853	67 (7.85)	1776	86 (4.84)	3.09**
Rural	687	41 (5.97)	958	36 (3.76)	2.09*

Note: See note under Table 6.2.

It may be seen that similar results on those obtained in the case of VI class were got in all the classes—VII, VIII, IX and X. Thus the rate of drop-outs was significantly less in the non-detention system that in the detention system. This was true irrespective of the sex or locality of the *Ss*.

As mentioned earlier, when the non-detention system was introduced it was contended by the protagonists of the system, like *Kabra* (1971), *Narasimha Rao* (1971), *Sarabhachari* (1971) and *Satyanarayana* (1971), that the new system would reduce wastage and stagnation. The results of the present study support the opinion expressed by the above authors with regard to wastage.

* Only those who have dropped-out in the middle of the year were taken in the case of X class as it is the terminal class of Secondary Education and the schools do not have information about the continuation of education of the students after X class.

Conclusions

From the above results it may be concluded that the rate of drop-outs was significantly less in the non-detention system than that in the detention system in all classes from VI to X. This was true irrespective of the sex or locality of the *Ss*.

Section-D

Attitude of Students, Teachers and Administrators Towards the Non-detention System

This section deals with the attitude of students, teachers and administrators towards the non-detention system. Part I of this section deals with the results of the analysis of the attitude of students towards the non-detention system, while Part II deals with teachers' attitude towards the new system. In part III results of analysis of the attitude of administrators is presented, while a comparative analysis of the attitude of the three groups of *Ss* is presented in Part IV.

As described in Chapter V, an attitude scale was developed to measure the attitude of the students, teachers and administrators towards the non-detention system. The attitude scale was factor analysed to identify the most significant factors contributing to the attitude and 14 factors were obtained. The overall attitude score and also the factor-wise scores of the *Ss* were analysed applying analysis of variance to examine the effect of different variables on the attitude.

PART I

Attitude of Students Towards the Non-detention System

1. Overall Score

The attitude scale consists of 58 items with the score on any item ranging between 1 and 5. Hence the score on the scale could range between 58 and 290 with a neutral point of 174 (*Shaw* and *Wright,* 1967).

It may not be out of place to mention a few points about neutral point in this context.

According to *Krech, et al.,* (1962), *McGrath* (1964) and *New Comb, Turner* and *Converse* (1965) attitude may be construed as varying in quality and intensity (or strength) on a continum from positive through neutral to negative. The strength or intensity of an attitude, positive or negative, is represented by the extremity of the position occupied by it on the continum, becoming stronger as it goes outward from a neutral position. But the neutral point of the attitude continum poses a problem with regard to its meaning and interpretation, to which several alternative solutions have been proposed.

First, one may consider the statement, that an attitude is neutral to be self-contradictory, indicating the presence of a response predisposition on the hand and the lack of a predisposition on the other. From this point of view, the neutral position on the attitude continum represents no attitude towards the object in question (*Shaw* and *Wright,* 1967). This interpretation supports the idea of *Krech* and *Crutchfield* (1948) that attitudes always have either a positive or negative sign; if they have no sign (*i.e.,* neutral or at the zero point), they cannot be called attitudes at all.

The second alternative interpretation suggested by *Shaw* and *Wright* (1967) is that it represents the point of balance in the positive-negative evaluative conflict, thereby reflecting an ambivalent attitude, where ambivalance is used to indicate the existence of two or more attitudes towards the same referent or several referents possessing some degree of similarity of stimulus value and being grouped as a referent class.

The second interpretation suggested by *Shaw* and *Wright* seems to be more reasonable and has been adopted by investigators like *Venkatarami Reddy* (1978a, 1978b, 1979, 1980), *Venkatarami Reddy* and *Ramakrishnaiah* (1981) and *Venkatarami Reddy* (1984).

A mean score above the neutral point indicates positive attitude towards the non-detention system while a mean score below the neutral point shows a negative attitude towards the system. It is needless to mention, however, that a mean score of one or two points above or below the neutral point does not given any definite idea about the nature of the attitude, since this very little difference may be due to error variance, that is bound to occur in any investigation, more so in investigations in educational and psychological research. Hence, *t* test was applied to see whether the mean scores of different sub-groups of *Ss* differed significantly from the neutral point.

Table 6.46 shows the mean overall attitude scores and SDs of the whole group ass well as different sub-groups of *Ss* towards the new system. It could be seen from the table that the mean score of the whole group was 156.36 which is far below the neutral point (174) indicating a negative attitude of the students towards the system. The difference between the mean score and the neutral point was highly significant even at 0.001 level (t= 39.38). (*see Fig. 6.20*).

Table—6.46 Means, SDs and *t* Values of Different Sub-groups of Students (Overall Attitude)

Group	N	M	S.D	*t*
Whole group	1080	156.36	14.72	39.38***
Boys	540	158.31	14.49	25.16***
Girls	540	154.31	18.56	24.65***
Urban	360	154.95	14.43	25.73***
Semi-urban	360	158.17	15.08	19.91***
Rural	360	155.96	14.48	23.65***
FCs	508	155.60	13.94	29.75***
BCs	400	157.04	15.47	21.92***
SCs/STs	172	157.01	15.01	14.76***

Note: See note under Table—6.2.

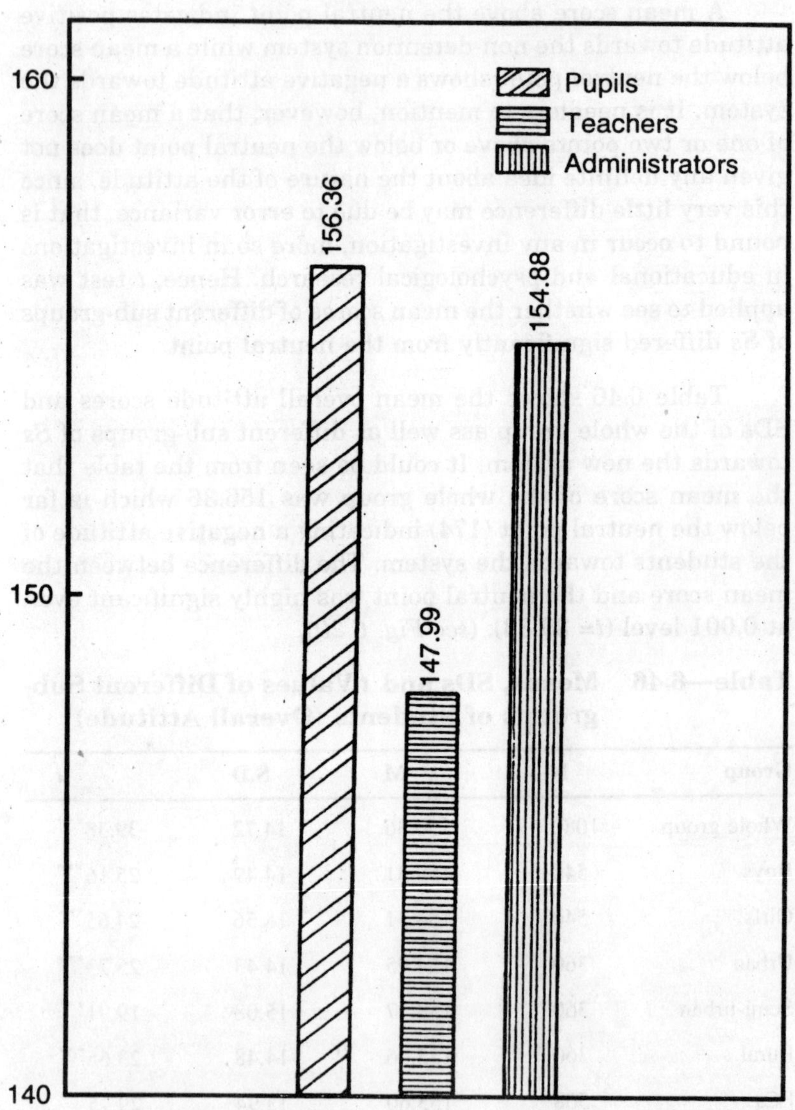

Fig.—6.20 Overall Mean Attitude Scores of Pupils, Teachers and Administrators Towards Non-detention System

Considering the sex of the students the mean score of boys was 158.31 while it was 154.31 for girls. Both the means were significantly below the neutral point, indicating that both the sexes were against the non-detention system. (*see Fig. 6.21 in page 216*).

Similarly, when the students were classified as urban, semi-urban and rural depending upon the locality to which they belonged, all the three groups of *Ss* exhibited a significantly negative attitude towards the new system. (*see Fig. 6.22 in page 217*).

As mentioned earlier, it was contended by some who opposed the new system, that the students belonging to the downtrodden communities will be the worst affected by the new system. Hence, to examine the attitude of students belonging to such communities in relation to that of students belonging to other communities information regarding the social class to which they belonged was obtained from the personal data sheet. On the basis of the above information the students were classified as those belonging to: (i) Forward Castes (FCs), (ii) Backward Castes (BCs) and (iii) Scheduled Castes/Scheduled Tribes (SCs/STs), and their attitude towards the new system was analysed.

It may be seen from the table that the mean attitude score of FCs was 155.60 while that of BCs was 157.04. SCs/STs obtained a mean score of 157.01. All the three means were significantly below the neutral point (*see Fig. 6.23 in page 218*).

To examine whether there was any significant difference in the attitude of the students belonging to different sexes, different localities and castes and the interaction between different variables, the attitude scores of the *Ss* were further analysed by analysis of variance of 2x2x3 factorial design (2 sexes x 3 localities x 3 castes). The results of this analysis are shown in Table 6.47.

It could be seen from the table that the *F* ratio for sex was 17.26 which was significant at 0.001 level for 1 and 1062 df. This shows that there was a significant difference between

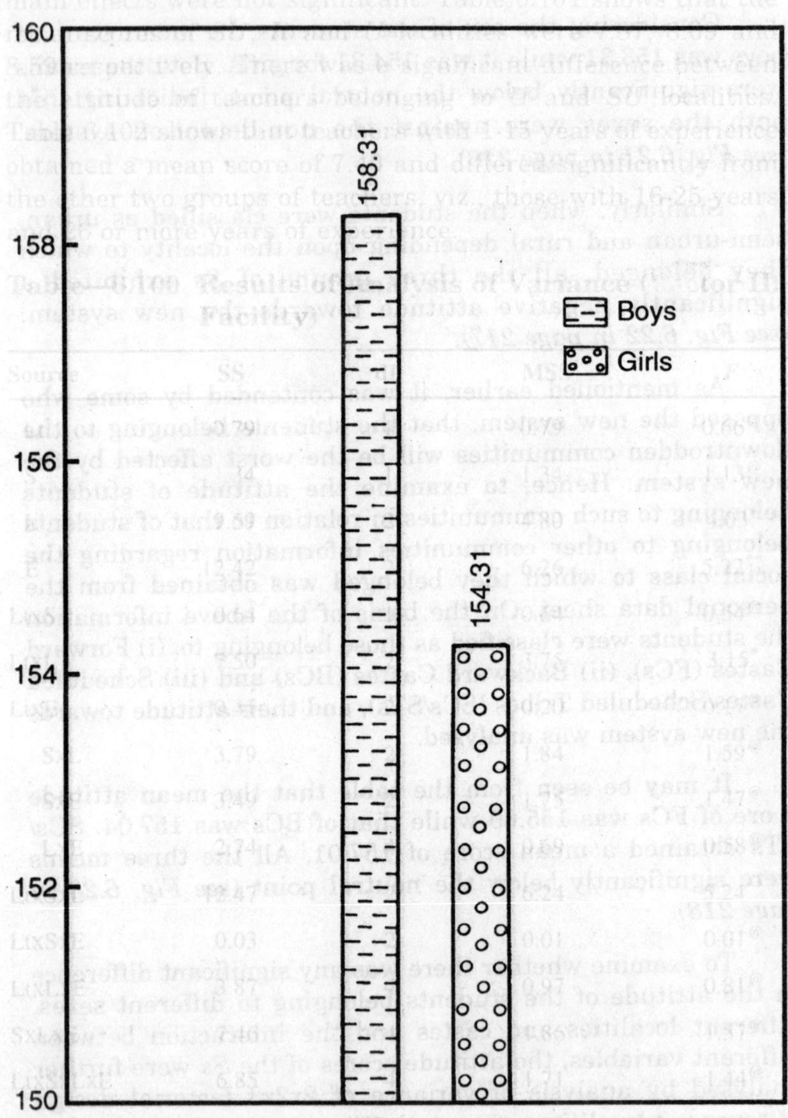

Fig.—6.21 Mean Attitude Scores Boys and Girls Towards Non-detention Systems

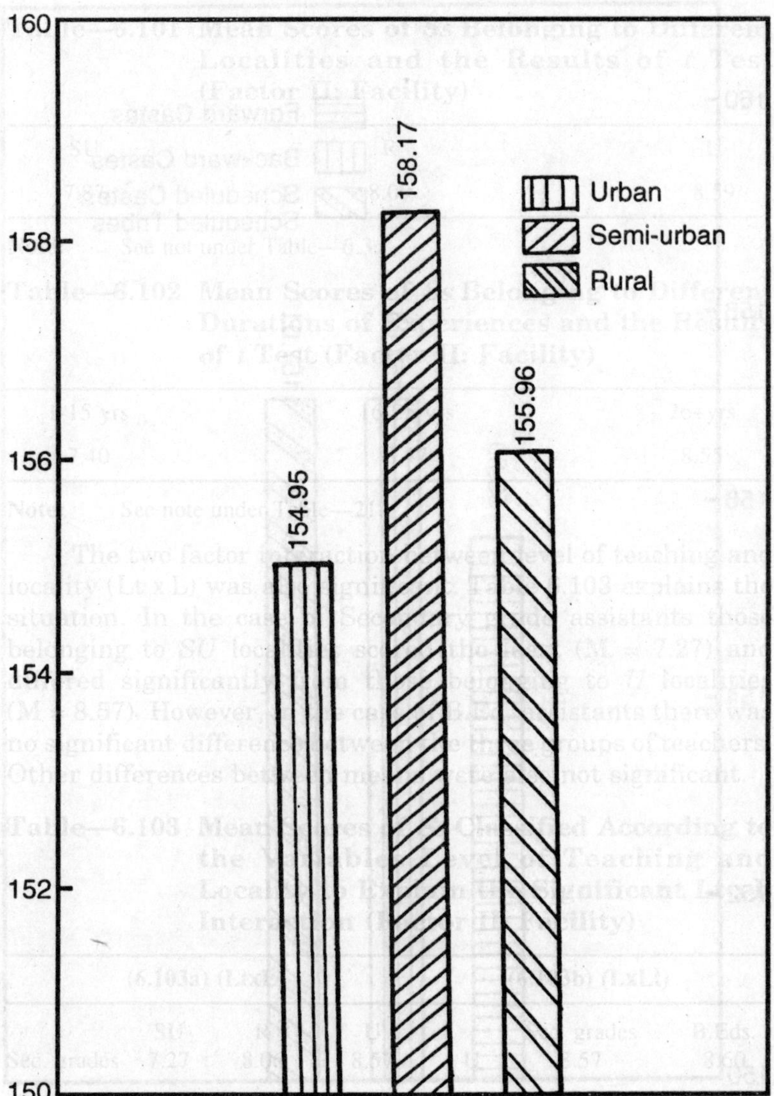

Fig.—6.22 Mean Attitude Scores of Students Belonging to Different Localities Towards Non-detention Systems

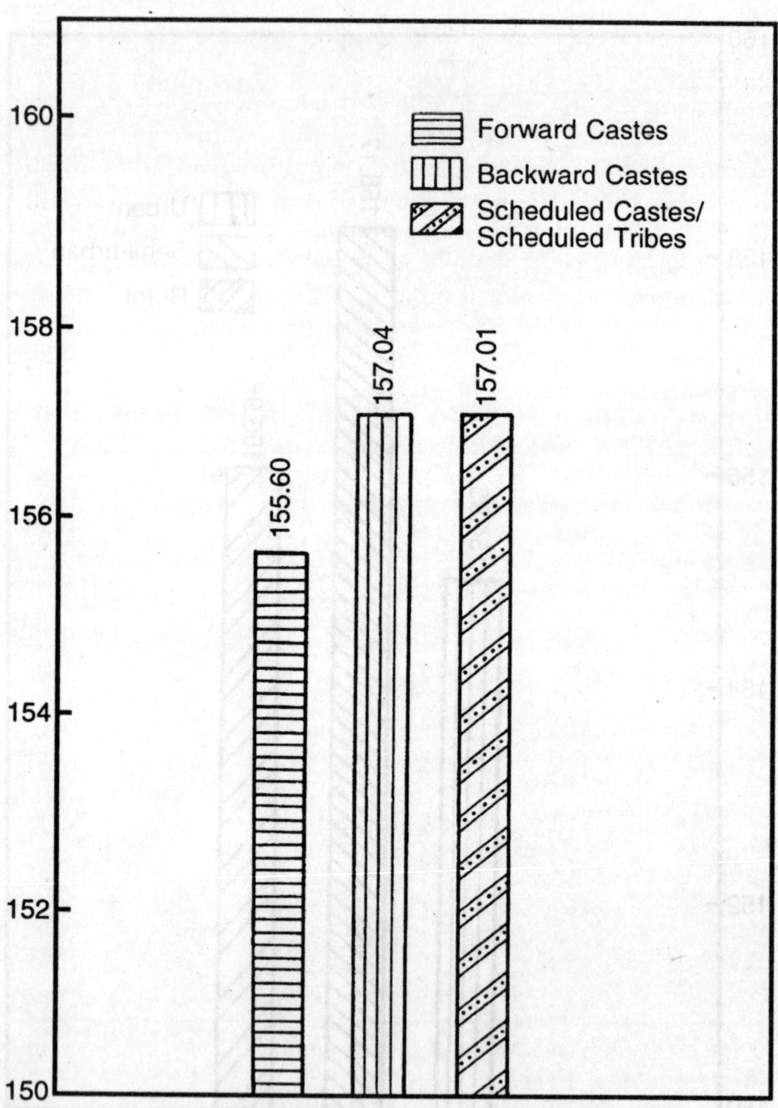

Fig.—6.23 Mean Attitude Score of Students Belonging to Different Social Classes Towards Non-detention System

boys and girls with regard to their attitude towards the system. The mean score of boys was 158.31 while it was 154.31 for girls. Though both the sexes had a negative attitude, girls had a far more negative attitude than boys.

Table—6.47 Results of Analysis of Variance

Source		SS	df	MSS	*F*
Sex	(S)	85.88	1	85.88	17.26***
Locality	(L)	54.50	2	27.25	5.48**
Caste	(C)	2.06	2	1.03	0.21@
SxL		12.69	2	6.34	1.28@
SxC		3.81	2	1.91	0.38@
LxC		19.44	4	4.86	0.98@
SxLxC		10.44	4	2.61	0.53@
Error		5288.76	1062	4.98	
Total		**5477.58**			

Note: 1. See note under Table 6.2.

2. As the number of observations in the different cells were different, the method suggested by *Edwards* (1971) and *Winer* (1971) was used for the purpose of analysis of variance which was carried out without the assistance of computer.

The *F* ratio for locality was 5.48 which was also significant at 0.01 level for 2 and 1062 df. This shows that there was a significant difference between the attitude of students belonging to different localities.

To find out which group differed significantly from the others, *t* test was applied as in the earlier cases. The results of the *t* test are presented in Table 6.48. The mean scores of the Ss belonging to *U, R* and *SU* localities were 154.95, 155.96 and 158.17 respectively. The mean scores of the *Ss* belonging to *U* and *R* localities were significantly lower than that of those from *SU* localities. The difference between the mean scores of *U* and *R* localities was not significant.

Table—6.49 Mean Scores of *Ss* Belonging to Different Localities and the Results of the *t* Test (Overall Score)

U	R	SU
154.95	155.96	158.17

Note: See under Table—21.

The *F* ratio for caste (0.21) which was not significant at 0.05 level, shows that there was no significant difference between the Ss belonging to different social classes with regard to their attitude towards the non-detention system.

None of the *F* ratios for interaction effects were significant at 0.05 level. This shows that the effect of each variable on the attitude was independent of the level of the other variables involved.

2. Factor-wise Analysis

A similar analysis was carried out on the attitude scores of different sub-groups of *Ss* on each of the 14 factors to see the effect of different variables on the factor-wise scores. The results of this analysis are presented hereunder;

(a) Factor I: Policy Implementation

Table 6.49 shows the mean attitude scores of different sub-groups of *Ss* on factor I. This factor contained 15 items. Hence, the neutral point on this factor was 45. From Table 6.49 it could be seen that the mean score of the whole group was 31.31, which is significantly below the neutral point. Indicating a negative attitude towards the system as measured by this factor. It may also be seen from the table that all the sub-groups irrespective of sex, locality or caste had a significantly negative attitude towards the system.

The basic philosophy of the non-detention system was that education can be best imparted under a natural set up, free from fear of examinations and annual detentions. It was also hoped that the teacher becomes trusted and honoured as a philosopher, friend and guide to his pupil. It was expected that this reform could yield true fruits of education.

Table—6.49 Means, SDs and *t* Values of Different Sub-groups of *Ss* (Factor I: Policy Implication)

Group	N	M	S.D	*t*
Whole group	1080	31.31	7.00	64.27***
Boys	540	32.33	6.90	42.70***
Girls	540	30.29	6.97	49.04***
Urban	360	31.13	7.13	36.91***
Semi-urban	360	31.58	7.31	34.85***
Rural	360	31.22	6.55	39.90***
FCs	508	31.26	6.64	46.64***
BCs	400	31.30	7.15	38.30***
SCs/STs	172	31.49	7.71	22.99***

Note: See note under Table—6.2.

But the results of the analysis of the attitude of the students towards the system did not corroborate the contention of the protagonists of this system. Students seem to have realised the ill-effects of this system in which every one could get promoted irrespective of his learning if he puts in the required percentage of attendance. As such, students do not work hard. Some of them go to school only for the sake of attendance and one need not be surprised if some left the school immediately after giving attendance and indulged in unworthy activities. Some students may not even buy their text books. They do not evince interest in taking the periodical tests seriously, on the other hand some of them may not even hesitate to give blank answer scripts during the tests and examinations (Through different states, *Educational India*, 1972) with the result even sincere students lose interest in their studies. These facts, explain the negative attitude of the *Ss* towards the new system as measured by this factor.

The scores of the *Ss* were further analysed by ANOVA to examine the effect of the different variables on the attitude of the students towards the new system as measured by this factor. The results of the analysis are presented in Table 6.50.

Table—6.50 Results of Analysis of Variance (Factor I: Policy Implementation)

Source	SS	df	MSS	*F*
Sex	26.05	1	26.05	23.09***
Locality	1.93	2	0.97	0.86@
Caste	1.23	2	0.61	0.54@
SxL	6.39	2	3.20	2.83@
SxC	5.19	2	2.60	2.30@
LxC	4.48	4	1.12	0.99@
SxLxC	0.20	4	0.05	0.05@
Error	1200.06	1062	1.13	
Total	**1245.53**			

Note: See note under Table—6.2.

It could be seen from the table that the *F* ratio (23.09) for sex was significant at 0.001 level for 1 and 1062 df. From Table 6.49 we find that the mean score of boys was 32.33 while that of girls was 30.29. Both the means were below the neutral point. Girls seem to the more averse than boys towards the system as measured by this factor. This may be because of sharper reaction of girls compared to that of boys for some of the items in the factor like: The system encourages students to spend their time wastefully, attending school for attendance sake, leaving the school immediately after giving attendance, etc.

The *F* ratio of 0.36 for locality was not significant at 0.05 level. This shows that the reaction of the students belonging to different localities towards the new system of evaluation as measured by this factor was more or less similar. Similarly, there was no significant difference in the attitude of FCs, BCs and SCs/STs towards the non-detention system as indicated by the *F* ratio of 0.54 which was not significant.

None of the *F* ratios for interaction effects were significant which shows that the effect of each of the different variables (ses, locality or caste) on the attitude of the students towards the non-detention system was independent of the level of the other variables involved.

(b) Factor II: (Facility)

Table 6.51 shows the mean scores of different sub-groups of Ss on this factor. As there were 3 items in this factor the neutral point was 9.

Table—6.51 Means, SDs and *t* Values of Different Sub-groups of *Ss* (Factor II: Facility)

Group	N	M	S.D	*t*
Whole group	1080	9.37	2.70	4.50***
Boys	540	9.26	2.67	2.23**
Girls	540	9.48	2.72	4.10***
Urban	360	9.54	2.61	3.93***
Semi-urban	360	9.59	2.62	4.30***
Rural	360	8.97	2.82	0.19@
FCs	508	9.33	2.77	2.69**
BCs	400	9.46	2.63	3.49***
SCs/STs	172	9.26	2.62	1.28@

Note: See note under Table—6.2.

The mean score of the whole group of *Ss* on this factor was 9.37 which was above the neutral point. It may be seen from the table that the mean scores of most of the sub-groups except rural were above the neutral point. The difference between the mean score and the neutral point was significant at or above 0.05 level for the whole group as well as all sub-groups except rural and SCs/STs.

It may be concluded that considering the whole group, the *Ss* had a positive attitude towards the new system of evaluation as measured by this factor.

Against the baneful effects of the traditional system of examinations the Government of Andhra Pradesh abolished detentions stressing the fact that examinations are only a means to an end but not an end in itself and that education can be best imparted in an atmosphere of free progress when the incentive and urge to improve springs from within the educational process rather than from the fear of detentions *Narasimha Rao,* 1971). The sample of students seem to endorse this aspect as revealed by their scores on this factor.

The mean scores of boys and girls were 9.26 and 9.48 respectively, showing that there was not much difference between them with regard to their attitude as measured by this factor. The mean scores of urban, semi-urban and rural students were 9.54, 9.59 and 8.97 respectively. Social class-wise, there does not seem to be much difference between the attitude of the 3 groups, FCs, BCs and SCs/STs. The mean scores of the three groups were: 9.36, 9.46 and 9.26 respectively.

However, to examine whether there was any significant difference between the mean scores of different sub-groups of *Ss,* ANOVA was applied as in the earlier cases. The results obtained in this analysis are shown in Table 6.52.

It could be seen from the table that the *F* ratios for sex and caste were not significant at 0.05 level. However, the *F* ratio for locality was significant at 0.05 level indicating a significant difference between the attitude of the *Ss* belonging to different localities.

Table—6.52 Results of Analysis Variance (Factor II: Facility)

Source	SS	df	MSS	*F*
Sex	0.06	1	0.06	0.37@
Locality	1.39	2	0.70	4.09*
Caste	0.04	2	0.02	0.11@
SxL	0.06	2	0.03	0.19@
SxC	0.14	2	0.07	0.41@
LxC	0.40	4	0.10	0.59@
SxLxC	0.59	4	0.15	0.87@
Error	180.54	1062	0.17	
Total	**183.22**			

Note: See note under Table—6.2.

To find out *Ss* of which locality differed significantly form others, *t* test was applied. Table 6.53 shows the results of the *t* test. From the table it could be seen that the mean score of the *Ss* belonging to *R* localities was the least and differed significantly from the mean scores of the other two localities. Rural *Ss* had a neutral attitude on this factor while the *Ss* from *U* and *SU* localities had a positively attitude.

Table—6.53 Mean Scores of *Ss* Hailing from Different Localities and the Results of the *t* Test (Factor II: Facility)

R	U	SU
8.97	9.54	9.59

Note: See note under Table—6.23.

None of the 2 factor or 3 factor interaction effects was significant, showing that the effect of each variable was independent of the level of the others.

(c) Factor III: Teaching-learning

The mean scores, SDs and *t* values of different sub-groups of *Ss* on this factor are presented in Table 6.54. It could be seen from the table that the whole group of *Ss* as well as all the sub-groups scored significantly less than the neutral point.

Table—6.54 Means, SDs and *t* Values of Different Sub-groups (Factor III: Teaching-learning)

Group	N	M	S.D	*t*
Whole group	1080	14.18	2.93	9.20***
Boys	540	14.15	3.05	6.48***
Girls	540	14.20	2.80	6.64***
Urban	360	14.29	2.89	4.66***
Semi-urban	360	14.29	3.05	4.39***
Rural	360	13.94	2.82	7.11***
FCs	508	14.21	2.97	6.00***
BCs	400	14.15	2.97	5.76***
SCs/STs	172	14.15	2.70	4.15***

Note: See note under Table—6.2.

Though the students realise the merit of the system because it could facilitate more number of students to go freely without getting detained or dropped-out, upto X class, there by raising the percentage of literacy, they tend to denounce the system because many students do not show the desired interest in the examinations since the marks in the examinations were not going to counter for their promotion. Further, when the students do not take their studies and examinations seriously there was no opportunity for the parents to know the skills and abilities of their children. This is what has been found from an examination of the responses of a sample of 100 students.

Table—6.55 Results of Analysis of Variance (Factor III: Teaching-learning)

Source	SS	df	MSS	*F*
Sex	0.00	1	0.00	0.00@
Locality	0.84	2	0.42	2.07@
Caste	0.03	2	0.02	0.07@
SxL	0.15	2	0.07	0.36@
SxC	0.15	2	0.07	0.37@
LxC	0.19	4	0.05	0.23@
SxLxC	1.31	4	0.33	1.62@
Error	212.40	1062	0.20	
Total	**215.07**			

Note: See note under Table—6.2.

It could be seen from Table 6.55 that none of the *F* ratios either for the main effects or interaction effects were significant, which shows that all students irrespective of their sex, locality or caste hold a similar view about the system as measured by this factor.

(d) Factor IV: Personality

Table 6.56 shows the mean scores of different sub-groups of *Ss* on factor IV which had 3 items with a neutral point of 9. From the table it could be seen that all the sub-groups of *Ss* without any exception had a significant positive attitude towards the system as measured by this factor.

In this system the role of examinations is minimised and a student's promotion is not linked with his performance in the examinations. Hence, students need not indulge in malpractices and parents too need not resort to unworthy practices like getting external pressures, etc., on the teachers and headmasters for the promotion of their wards. This naturally reduces the scope for corruption in schools to a large extent. Moreover students feel that in this system there is ample opportunity for the teacher to develop the personality of the pupils. Students seem to favour the new system on these points.

Table—6.56 Means, SDs and *t* Values of Different Sub-groups (Factor IV: Personality)

Group	N	M	S.D	t
Whole group	1080	9.83	2.29	11.91***
Boys	540	9.78	2.24	8.11***
Girls	540	9.89	2.34	8.84***
Urban	360	9.98	2.37	7.85***
Semi-urban	360	9.60	2.29	4.98***
Rural	360	9.92	2.19	7.93***
FCs	508	9.92	2.33	8.90***
BCs	400	9.72	2.39	6.01***
SCs/STs	172	9.85	1.92	5.84***

Note: See note under Table—6.2.

Table 6.57 *(in page 229)* shows the results of ANOVA for this factor. From the table it could be seen that none of the *F* ratios were significant indicating that there was no significant difference between the different sub-groups in their reaction towards the non-detention system as assessed by this factor.

(e) Factor V: Discipline

Table 6.58 shows the mean scores of different sub-groups of *Ss* on factor V. The mean score of the whole group was

9.67 which was significantly above the neutral point 9 indicating that the *Ss* on the whole had a positive attitude towards the system as measured by this factor also.

Table—6.57 Results of Analysis of Variance (Factor IV: Personality)

Source	SS	df	MSS	*F*
Sex	0.03	1	0.03	0.23@
Locality	0.42	2	0.21	0.70@
Caste	0.08	2	0.04	0.33@
SxL	0.23	2	0.12	0.95@
SxC	0.04	2	0.02	0.16@
LxC	0.12	4	0.03	0.24@
SxLxC	0.58	4	0.15	1.18@
Error	127.44	1062	0.12	
Total	**128.94**			

Note: See note under Table—6.2.

Table—6.58 Means, SDs and *t* Values of Different Sub-groups of *Ss* (Factor V: Discipline)

Group	N	M	S.D	*t*
Whole group	1080	9.67	2.42	9.10***
Boys	540	9.75	2.42	7.19***
Girls	540	9.59	2.41	5.69***
Urban	360	9.23	2.61	1.67@
Semi-urban	360	9.92	2.31	7.52***
Rural	360	9.86	2.25	7.21***
FCs	508	9.59	2.45	5.43***
BCs	400	9.88	2.46	7.16***
SCs/STs	172	9.40	2.14	2.46*

Note: See note under Table—6.2.

With regard to the sex variable the mean score of boys was 9.75 while the mean score of girls was 9.59. The mean scores of students belonging to *U, SU* and *R localities* were 9.23, 9.92, and 9.86 respectively. The mean scores of FCs, BCs and SCs/STs were 9.59, 9.88 and 9.40 respectively. The mean scores of all sub-groups of Ss except those belonging to *U* localities were significantly above the neutral point.

Traditionally, failing, or the threat of failure has been considered to act as a spur for learning. Apparently, the reverse is more often true. The adage 'nothing succeeds like success' is demonstrated in learning activities. Failure especially repeated failure, is likely to kill the pupil's incentive and enthusiasm to learn. It develops an aversion to the school and the whole system of education as such. Further, pupils who are encouraged and whose work is praised achieve more than those who are warned that they will fail unless they keep their work up to a standard (*Otto* and *Melby,* n.d.). According to *Schunk* (1983) as children observe their progress they develop a heightened sense of efficacy, which would help sustain task involvement and lead to greater skill development. The studies of McCullers (1978), *McGraws* (1978), *Gayen* and *Lyle* (19710, *Glucksberg* (1962), and *Dornbush* (1965) have also shown that rewards facilitate performance.

Further in the new system of evaluation teachers were made free from the clutches of the external pressures (*Sarabachari,* 1971; *Satyanarayana,* 1971) with regard to the promotion of the students to the higher classes. These points seem to be realised by the students as reflected in their positive attitude towards the new system as measured by this factor. At the same time the students do endorse that his system has affected the discipline in the schools. The positive aspects mentioned earlier, however, seem to out weigh this negative aspect of the system.

The results of ANOVA (Table 6.59) show that the *F* ratio for locality was significant indicating a significant difference between the attitude of students belonging to different localities. From Table 6.60 it could be seen that the students belonging to *U* localities obtained the lowest mean and differed significantly from the others.

The *F* ratio (2.45) for the 2 factor interaction LxC was also significant at 0.05 level which warrants cautious interpretation of the main effects of locality and caste as mentioned earlier.

Table—6.59 Results of Analysis of Variance (Factor V: Discipline)

Source	SS	df	MSS	*F*
Sex	0.07	1	0.07	0.52@
Locality	2.04	2	1.02	7.65***
Caste	0.67	2	0.35	2.62@
SxL	0.09	2	0.05	0.34@
SxC	0.47	2	0.24	1.77@
LxC	1.31	4	0.33	2.45*
SxLxC	0.79	4	0.20	1.48@
Error	138.06	1062	0.13	
Total	**143.50**			

Note: See note under Table—6.2.

Table—6.60 Mean Scores of *Ss* Hailing from Different Localities and the Results of the *t* Test (Factor V: Discipline)

U	R	SU
9.23	9.86	9.92

Note: See not under table 6.2.

An examination of the mean scores of the student classified according to the two variables locality and caste (Table 6.61a) shows that in the case of BCs the mean score of students belonging to *R* localities was the highest, while among SCs/STs, children belonging to SU localities obtained the highest mean. In the case of rural children the mean scores of BCs and FCs were significantly higher than that of SCs/STs, while in the SU localities, the mean score of SCs/STs was significantly higher than that of BCs. This shows that the effect of locality differences on the attitude of the *Ss* was not independent of the social class of the students and vice versa.

Table—6.61 Mean Scores of Different Sub-groups of *Ss* Classified According to Different Variables to Explain the LxC Interaction Effect (Factor V: Discipline).

	6.61a (CxL)				6.1b (LxC)		
	U	SU	R	U	SCs/STs	FCs	BCs
FCs	9.24	9.65	10.06		8.97	9.24	9.30
	U	SU	R	SU	BCs	FCs	SCs/STs
BCs	9.30	9.39	10.11		9.39	9.65	10.14
	U	R	SU	R	SCs/STs	FCs	BCs
SCs/STs	8.97	9.00	10.14		9.00	10.06	10.11

Note: See note under Table—6.3.

(f) Factor VI: Incentive for Progress

Table 6.62 shows the mean scores of different sub-groups of *Ss* on this factor which also had 3 items. From the table it could be observed that the group as a whole and also all the sub-groups without any exception had a significantly positive attitude towards the new system.

Students seem to endorse that the defects and ill effects of the examination system are reduced in the non-detention system; and that in the new system incentive to work is within the system itself rather than from the threat of detentions.

Table 6.63 shows the results of analysis of variance of the scores of this factor. From the table it could be observed

that none of the *F* ratios, except that for the interaction between locality and caste were significant.

Table—6.62 Means, SDs and *t* Values of Different Sub-groups of *Ss* (Factor VI: Incentive for Progress)

Group	N	M	S.D	*t*
Whole group	1080	10.60	2.49	21.11***
Boys	540	10.69	2.39	16.48***
Girls	540	10.51	2.59	13.55***
Urban	360	10.60	2.57	11.81***
Semi-urban	360	10.58	2.53	11.87***
Rural	360	10.62	2.37	12.98***
FCs	508	10.61	2.43	14.93***
BCs	400	10.72	2.57	13.36***
SCs/STs	172	10.31	2.46	7.00***

Note: See note under Table—6.2.

Table—6.63 Results of Analysis of Variance (Factor VI)

Source	SS	df	MSS	*F*
Sex	0.08	1	0.08	0.54@
Locality	0.14	2	0.07	0.49@
Caste	0.64	2	0.32	2.26@
SxL	0.77	2	0.38	2.68@
SxC	0.61	2	0.31	2.15@
LxC	1.93	4	0.48	3.39**
SxLxC	1.19	4	0.30	2.09**
Error	148.68	1062	0.14	
Total	**154.04**			

Note: See note under Table—6.2.

Table 6.64 explains the significant LxC interaction. From the table it could be seen that in the case of FCs, SU children scored the highest (M = 10.94) and differed significantly from the children of U localities who scored the least (M= 10.38), whereas in the case of BCs, U children scored significantly higher (M = 34.58) than SU and R children. In the case of SCs/STs, there was no significant difference between the three groups of children. Further, considering the differences between different caste groups in the case of urban areas, children belonging to BCs obtained a significantly higher mean score than the other two groups, and there was no significant difference between the attitude of students belonging to FCs and SCs/STs. On the other hand, in the case of SU localities FCs obtained the highest mean score and differed significantly from SCs/STs. This explains the significant LxC interaction.

Table—6.64 Mean Scores of Different Sub-groups of *Ss* Classified According to Different Variables to Explain LxC Interaction Effect (Factor VI)

	6.64a (LxC)			6.64b (CxL)			
	SCs/STs	FCs	BCs	FCs	U	R	SU
U	9.89	10.38	11.19		10.38	10.76	10.94
	SCs/STs	BCs	FCs	BCs	R	SU	U
SU	10.15	10.56	10.94		10.42	10.56	11.19
	SCs/STs	BCs	FCs	SCs/STs	U	SU	R
R	10.34	10.42	10.76		9.89	10.15	10.34

Note: See note under Table—6.3.

(g) *Factor VII: Learning Skills*

Table 6.65 shows the mean scores of different sub-groups of *Ss* on factor VII, while Table 6.66 shows the results of ANOVA of the scores on this factor. As there were three items in the factor the neutral point was 9.

The mean score of the while group was 7.63 which was below the neutral point. The mean scores of different sub-groups of *Ss* also were below the neutral point indicating that all the *Ss* irrespective of their sex, locality or caste had a significantly negative attitude.

Table—6.65 Means, SDs and *t* Values of *Ss* of Different Sub-groups (Factor VII: Learning Skills)

Group	N	M	S.D	*t*
Whole group	1080	7.63	2.57	17.52***
Boys	540	7.82	2.67	10.32***
Girls	540	7.45	2.46	14.64***
Urban	360	7.54	2.54	10.91***
Semi-urban	360	7.75	2.51	9.46***
Rural	360	7.60	2.66	9.95***
FCs	508	7.54	2.48	13.27***
BCs	400	7.62	2.63	10.53***
SCs/STs	172	7.95	2.68	5.11***

Note: See note under Table—6.2.

Table—6.66 Results of Analysis of Variance (Factor VII: Learning Skills)

Source	SS	df	MSS	*F*
Sex	0.79	1	0.79	5.15*
Locality	0.46	2	0.23	1.48@
Caste	0.18	2	0.09	0.56@
SxL	0.47	2	0.24	1.54@
SxC	0.15	2	0.07	0.48@
LxC	0.56	4	0.14	0.91@
SxLxC	0.84	4	0.21	1.37@
Error	159.30	1062	0.15	
Total	**162.75**			

Note: See note under Table—6.2.

Since the role of examination is minimised, and students do not show real interest in them, many students seem to feel that there is no scope to show their real capacities. Further, as there are no detentions, in the new system students can go upto VII class, if not upto X class, without adequate knowledge of basic skills. This is what is observed from an analysis of the responses of a sample of 100 students. A majority of the students do not seem to agree, however, with the statement 'detentions do not help learning.'

It could be seen from Table 6.66 that only the *F* ratio (5.15) for the main effect of sex was significant at 0.05 level for 1 and 1062 df. The mean score of boys was 7.82 while that of girls was 7.45. Both the mean scores indicate a negative attitude. However, girls were more averse than boys towards the new system.

(h) Factor VII: Educational Policy

Table 6.67 shows the mean scores of different sub-groups of *Ss* of factor VIII. There were only three items in this factor also. Hence, the neutral point was 9. The mean score of the whole group of *Ss* on this factor was 7.95 which is far below the neutral point, indicating that the students had a strong negative attitude towards the system as measured by the items in this factor. This was true irrespective of the sex, locality or caste of the *Ss*.

Though it is opined by many that the non-detention system is helpful in implementing free and compulsory primary education, many teachers and parents feel that the government would not have abolished detentions had it followed correct educational principles (The *Editor, The Educational Review,* 1971). Students also seem to endorse this point. It was also felt by many of the students that the backward class children whose aptitude for education was already low would be more adversely affected by this new system as there was no immediate incentive to learn in the form of passing examinations, resulting in a negative attitude towards the system as measured by this factor.

Table—6.67 Means, SDs and *t* Values of Different Sub-groups of *Ss* (Factor VIII: Educational Policy)

Group	N	M	S.D	*t*
Whole group	1080	7.95	2.41	14.32***
Boys	540	7.91	2.44	10.40***
Girls	540	7.98	2.39	9.92***
Urban	360	7.89	2.43	8.67***
Semi-urban	360	8.19	2.37	6.47***
Rural	360	7.76	2.42	9.74***
FCs	508	8.08	2.45	8.46***
BCs	400	7.83	2.40	9.76***
SCs/STs	172	7.83	2.34	6.60***

Note: See note under Table—6.2.

From Table 6.68 in which the results of ANOVA are presented it could be seen that the *F* ratio for locality was

Table—6.68 Results of Analysis of Variance (Factor VIII: Educational Policy)

Source	SS	df	MSS	*F*
Sex	0.02	1	0.02	0.15@
Locality	1.04	2	0.52	3.81*
Caste	0.30	2	0.15	1.09@
SxL	0.59	2	0.29	2.16@
SxC	0.15	2	0.07	0.54@
LxC	0.42	4	0.11	0.77@
SxLxC	0.18	4	0.05	0.33@
Error	148.68	1062	0.14	
Total	**151.38**			

Note: See note under Table—6.2.

significant. To see which locality differed significantly from the others, *t* test was applied. Table 6.69 in which the results of *t* test are presented shows that the *Ss* belonging to SU localities got the highest mean score and differed significantly from those belonging to *R* localities. The children from R localities had a more unfavourable attitude than those from SU localities.

Table—6.69 Mean Scores of *Ss* Hailing from Different Localities and the Results of the *t* Test (Factor VIII: Educational Policy)

R	U	SU
7.76	7.89	8.19

Note: See note under Table—21.

(i) Factor IX: Freedom for the teacher

Table 6.70 shows the mean attitude scores of different sub-groups of *Ss* on factor IX. This factor had 3 items, hence the neutral point was 9. From the table it could be seen that all the sub-groups without any exception had a highly significant positive attitude towards the system as measured by this factor.

Table—6.70 Means, SDs and *t* Values of Different Sub-groups of *Ss* (Factor IX: Freedom for the Teachers)

Group	N	M	S.D	*t*
Whole group	1080	9.76	2.76	9.05***
Boys	540	9.85	2.70	7.35***
Girls	540	9.65	2.82	5.36***
Urban	360	9.75	2.51	5.67***
Semi-urban	360	10.02	2.86	6.76***
Rural	360	9.51	2.89	3.36***
FCs	508	9.66	2.60	5.72***
BCs	400	9.83	2.96	5.58***
SCs/STs	172	9.89	2.76	4.23***

Note: See note under Table 6.2.

Though it is felt by some that the system may adversely affect the academic career of the students, many of the *Ss* seem to feel that this system provides ample time and opportunity for the teacher to experiment with new methods of teaching and testing. They are also of the opinion that teachers would have time and scope to develop the desired intellectual skills among the students.

It could be observed from Table 6.71 in which the results of ANOVA are presented that the *F* ratio (6.38) for SxL interaction alone was significant. Table 6.72 explains the significant interaction between the two factors. It could be seen from the table that in the case of boys, children from *R* localities scored the least (M=9.16) and differed significantly from those belonging to U and *SU* localities, whereas in the case of girls, children from *R* localities scored the highest (M=9.86) and differed significantly from *U* children, who scored the least (M=9.56).

Table—6.71 Results of Analysis of Variance (Factor IX: Freedom for the Teachers)

Source	SS	df	MSS	*F*
Sex	0.01	1	0.01	0.04@
Localatiy	0.49	2	0.24	1.40@
Caste	0.72	2	0.36	2.05@
SxL	2.23	2	1.12	6.38@
Sxc	0.60	2	0.30	1.71@
LxC	1.17	4	0.30	1.68@
SxLxC	1.25	4	0.31	1.78@
Error	191.16	1062	0.18	
Total	**197.63**			

Note: See note under Table—6.2.

Comparing boys and girls, it may be seen that the mean score of boys was higher than that of girls in *SU* localities, while the reverse was true in the case of *R* localities. This explains the significant locality x sex interaction effect.

Table—6.72 Mean Scores of Different Sub-groups of *Ss* Classified According to Different Variable to Explain SxL Interaction Effect (Factor IX: Freedom for the Teacher)

(6.72a) (SxL)

B	R 9.16	U 9.94	SU 10.46
G	U 9.56	SU 9.58	R 9.86

(6.72b) (LxS)

U	G 9.56	B 9.94
SU	G 9.58	B 10.46
R	B 9.16	G 9.86

Note: See note under Table—6.3.

(j) *Factor X: Emotional*

The mean scores of the different sub-groups of *Ss* on this factor were significantly below the neutral point (Table 6.73). The *Ss* feel that since in the non-detention system the students do not take the tests and examinations seriously and tend to view the entire study in a casual way, they would naturally find it difficult to face the competitive examinations boldly. Students seem to agree that they would study well if there is the fear of detention contrary to the belief of the protagonists of the new system.

Table—6.73 Means, SDs and *t* Values of Different Sub-groups of *Ss* (Factor X: Emotional)

Group	N	M	S.D	*t*
Whole group	1080	8.34	2.35	9.22^{***}
Boys	540	8.53	2.46	4.44^{***}
Girls	540	8.16	2.23	8.78^{***}
Urban	360	8.27	2.43	5.70^{***}
Semi-urban	360	8.50	2.33	4.05^{***}
Rural	360	8.25	2.29	6.18^{***}
FCs	508	8.11	2.18	9.20^{***}
BCs	400	8.54	2.52	3.67^{***}
SCs/STs	172	8.59	2.40	2.22^{*}

Note: See note under Table—6.2.

The significant *F* ratio (3.69) for caste (Table 92) shows that there was a significant difference between different castes with regard to their attitude as measured by this factor. Though children belonging to all social classes (FCs, BCs, SCs/STs) obtained mean scores below the neutral point, the mean score of FCs was significantly lower than that of those belonging to the other two social classes, viz., BCs and SCs/STs (Table 93).

However, the significant *F* ratio for the interactic between sex and caste warrants caution in interpreting the above result based upon the main effect for caste.

Table—6.74 Results of Analysis of Variance (Factor X: Emotional)

Source	SS	df	MSS	*F*
Sex	0.06	1	0.06	0.48@
Locality	0.14	2	0.07	0.54@
Caste	0.94	2	0.47	3.69*
SxL	0.50	2	0.25	1.94@
SxC	1.21	2	0.60	4.73**
LxC	0.30	4	0.08	0.60@
SxLxC	1.09	4	0.27	2.13@
Error	138.06	1062	0.13	
Total	**142.30**			

Note: See note under Table—6.2.

Table—6.75 Mean Scores of *Ss* Belonging to Different Social Classes and the Results of *t* Test (Factor X: Emotional)

FCs	BCs	SCs/STs
8.11	8.54	8.59

Note: See note under Table—6.3.

An examination of the mean scores of students classified according to the two variables sex and caste presented in Table 6.76 explains the situation. From Table 6.76a it could be said that boys of Forward Castes differed significantly from boys of Backward Castes. The difference between the other two groups was not significant. In the case of girls the mean score of SCs/STs was higher than that of FCs and BCs.

Further, from Table 6.76b it could be seen that with in the social class of FCs the difference in the mean scores of boys and girls was not significant. But in the case of BCs and SCs/STs the difference between the two sexes was significant. Further, the mean score of girls was higher than that of boys in the case of SCs/STs while among BCs the mean of boys was higher than that of girls indicating that the effect of sex was not the same for all the social classes.

Table—6.76 Mean Scores of Different Sub-groups of *Ss* Classified According to Different Variables to Explain (SxC) Interaction Effect (Fractor X: Emotional).

(6.76a) (SxC)				(6.76b) (CxS)		
	FCs	SCs/STs	BCs	FCs	G	B
B	8.26	8.39	8.87		7.99	8.26
	FCs	BCs	SCs/STs	BCs	G	B
G	7.99	8.15	8.94		8.15	8.87
					B	G
				SCs/STs	8.39	8.94

Note: See note under Table—6.3.

(k) Factor XI: Dullards-Wastage and Stagnation

The mean scores of the different sub-groups of *Ss* presented in Table 6.77 show that the whole group as well as all the sub-groups had a significantly negative attitude towards the new system of evaluation as measured by this factor as in the case of factor X: Emotional.

Though it is agreed that this system reduced wastage and stagnation, a majority of the *Ss* are of the opinion that those who are dull can improve their learning during the repeated years if detained in the same class. The system seems to have a negative effect on the attitude of parents towards the education of their wards. Since there are examinations coupled with detentions only at the VII and X classes, they tend to take serious interest in their wards' education at this stage and pressurise the teachers to take their children for tutions in theses classes. Tutions have become a common feature for most of the students in these two classes.

Table—6.77 Means, SDs and *t* Values of Different Sub-groups of *Ss* (Factor XI: Dullards-Wastage and Stagnation)

Group	N	M	S.D	*t*
Whole group	1080	10.61	2.60	17.57***
Boys	540	10.77	2.64	10.86***
Girls	540	10.45	2.56	14.07***
Urban	360	10.34	2.48	12.70***
Semi-urban	360	10.50	2.74	10.41***
Rural	360	10.98	2.55	7.57***
FCs	508	10.58	2.54	12.60***
BCs	400	10.67	2.64	10.07***
SCs/STs	172	10.55	2.70	7.07***

Note: See note under Table—6.2.

When analysis of variance was carried out it was found that the effects of sex and locality and that of sex x locality were significant (Table 6.78).

It may be seen from Table 6.77 though both boys and girls obtained scores lower than the neutral point the mean score (10.45) of girls was significantly less than that (10.77) of boys. This shows that girls were more averse to the new system as measured by this factor.

Table—6.78 Results of Analysis of Variance (Factor XI: Dullards-Wastage and Stagnation)

Source	SS	df	MSS	*F*
Sex	0.67	1	0.67	4.32*
Locality	1.52	2	0.76	4.86**
Caste	0.29	2	0.15	0.93@
SxL	1.18	2	0.59	3.77*
SxC	0.16	2	0.08	0.53@
LxC	0.69	4	0.17	1.10@
SxLxC	0.33	4	0.08	0.53@
Error	169.92	1062	0.16	
Total	**174.76**			

Note: See note under Table—6.2.

The significant *F* ratio for locality warrants further analysis and the results of *t* test presented in Table 6.79, show that children from *U* and *SU* localities obtained significantly lower mean scores than those from *R* localities.

Table—6.79 Means scores of *Ss*Hailing from Different Localities and the Results of the *t* Test (Factor XI: Dullards-Wastage and Stagnation)

U	SU	R
10.34	10.50	10.98

Note: See note under Table—6.3.

These results however, should be interpreted cautiously in view of the significant *F* ratio for sex x locality. Table 6.80 shows that in the case of boys *SU* children obtained a higher mean score than *U* children, while in the case of girls *SU* children obtained the lowest mean score and differed significantly from *U* and *R* children. The mean scores of boys and girls were significantly different only in the case of *SU* localities but not in the case of the other two localities.

Table—6.80 Mean Scores of Different Sub-groups of *Ss* Classified According to Different Variables to Explain SxL Interaction Effect (Factor XI: Dullards-Wastage and Stagnation)

	(6.80a) (SxL)				(6.80b) (LxS)	
	U	R	SU		G	B
B	10.38	10.86	11.06	U	10.31	10.38
	SU	U	R		G	B
G	9.34	10.31	11.11	SU	9.34	11.06
					B	G
				R	10.86	11.11

Note: See note under Table—6.3.

This shows how the sex effect was not independent of the locality of the students and vice versa and explains the significant sex x locality interaction effect.

(l) Factor XII: Competence

Table 6.81 shows the mean scores of different sub-groups of *Ss* on factor XII. The mean scores of all the sub-groups were significantly below the neutral point on this factor also.

Table—6.81 Means, SDs and *t* Values of *Ss* of Different Sub-groups (Factor XII: Competence)

Group	N	M	S.D	*t*
Whole group	1080	9.82	3.17	22.60***
Boys	540	10.14	3.24	13.34***
Girls	540	9.50	3.06	18.98***
Urban	360	9.44	3.19	15.22***
Semi-urban	360	10.16	3.27	10.70***
Rural	360	9.86	3.00	13.52***
FCs	508	9.50	3.01	18.72***
BCs	400	10.02	3.26	12.67***
SCs/STs	172	10.28	3.31	6.83***

Note: See note under Table—6.2.

The students seem to be of the opinion that since examinations were not taken seriously, it was but natural that in this system there was no scope for differentiation between the capable and incapable. As education was not a serious endeavour because of lack of threat of detentions students tend to spend their time wastefully, without any seriousness towards their work, with the result, one tends to think that they may not become useful citizens later.

From Table 6.82 it may be seen that the *F* ratio for sex and locality were significant. From Table 6.81 it may be seen that the mean score of girls was less than that of boys. When the students were classified according to the locality to which they belonged the *Ss* from *U* localities scored significantly less than those from *SU* localities (Table 6.83).

Table—6.82 Results of Analysis of Variance (Factor XII: Competence)

Source	SS	df	MSS	*F*
Sex	2.38	1	2.38	10.29**
Locality	1.74	2	0.87	3.76*
Caste	1.06	2	0.53	2.29@
SxL	0.47	2	0.23	1.01@
SxC	0.40	2	0.20	0.86@
LxC	1.27	4	0.32	1.37@
SxLxC	0.31	4	0.08	0.34@
Error	244.26	1062	0.23	
Total	**251.89**			

Note: See note under Table—6.2.

Table—6.83 Mean Scores of *Ss* Hailing from Different Localities and the Results of *t* Test (Factor XII: Competence)

U	R	SU
9.44	9.86	10.16

Note: See note under Table—6.3.

(m) Factor XIII: Ethical Value

This factor had 3 items with a neutral point of 9. It could be seen from Table 6.84 that the mean score of the whole group as well as those of different sub-groups were far below the neutral point indicating a negative attitude towards the system as measured by this factor also.

Table—6.84 Means, SDs and *t* Values of Different Sub-Groups of *Ss* (Factor XIII: Ethical Value)

Group	N	M	S.D	*t*
Whole group	1080	6.43	2.88	29.33***
Boys	540	6.58	2.84	19.79***
Girls	540	6.28	2.91	21.72***
Urban	360	6.10	2.57	21.41***
Semi-urban	360	6.76	3.13	13.59***
Rural	360	6.43	2.88	16.94***
OCs	508	6.28	2.83	21.66***
BCs	400	6.56	2.86	17.08***
SCs/STs	172	6.57	3.05	10.46***

Note: See note under Table—6.2.

Since there are no detentions in this system, the intermediary goals, viz., passing of examinations, are removed. As such the students do not take real interest in studies and examinations. Teachers also tend to take things easy since in this system there is no possibility for evaluating their efficiency of teaching in terms of percentage of passes. Most of the *Ss* endorsed these points as reflected in their negative attitude towards the system as measured by this factor.

From the results of ANOVA (Table 6.85) and the results of *t* test (Table 6.86) it may be seen that students belonging to *U* localities obtained a significantly lower mean score than those belonging to *SU* localities. No other differences between the sub-groups was significant.

Table—6.85 Results of Analysis of Variance (Factor XIII: Ethical Value)

Source	SS	df	MSS	*F*
Sex	0.43	1	0.43	2.21@
Locality	2.15	2	1.08	5.60**
Caste	0.10	2	0.05	0.26@
SxL	0.24	2	0.12	0.63@
SxC	0.21	2	0.11	0.55@
LxC	1.80	4	0.45	2.35@
SxLxC	0.16	4	0.04	0.21@
Error	201.78	1062	0.19	
Total	**206.87**			

Note: See note under Table—6.2.

Table—6.86 Mean Scores of *Ss* Hailing from Different Localities and the Results of the *t* Test (Factor XIII: Ethical Value)

U	R	SU
6.10	6.43	6.76

Note: See note under Table—6.3.

(n) Factor XIV: Natural Setting

Table 6.87 shows the mean scores of different sub-groups of *Ss* on this factor which had 3 items with a neutral point of 9. From the table it could be seen that all the mean scores of the different sub-groups of *Ss* without any exception were significantly above the neutral point, indicating a positive attitude towards the system as measured by the items in this factor.

Table—6.87 Means, SDs and *t* Values of Different Sub-Groups of *Ss* (Factor XIV: Natural Setting)

Group	N	M	S.D	*t*
Whole group	1080	10.87	2.59	23.73***
Boys	540	10.77	2.65	15.47***
Girls	540	10.97	2.52	18.17***
Urban	360	10.85	2.62	13.40***
Semi-urban	360	10.73	2.62	12.50***
Rural	360	11.03	2.52	15.32***
FCs	508	10.94	2.60	16.82***
BCs	400	10.77	2.64	13.37***
SCs/STs	172	10.90	2.44	10.19***

Note: See note under Table—6.2.

Since there are automatic promotions to the next higher classes, the students in any class would be mostly a homogeneous group with regard to age. This would make the work of the teacher easier. Further, in the new system there is scope for one to learn in a natural setting free from fear of detentions. Students seem to endorse these aspects as reflected in their positive attitude towards this system as measured by this factor.

The results of ANOVA presented in Table 6.88 show that the *F* ratio (5.06) for SxL interaction alone was significant. Table 6.89 explains the situation. It could be observed from the table that in the case of boys, *U* children scored the least (M = 10.49) while *R* children scored the highest (M = 11.31) and differed significantly from *U* and *SU* children. In the case of girls on the other hand, *R* children scored the least (M = 10.76), whereas the *U* children scored the highest (M = 11.19) and differed significantly from *R* and *SU* children. This shows how the differences between children belonging to different localities was not independent of their sex, resulting in a significant *F* ratio for the sexxlocality interaction.

Table—6.88 Results of Analysis of Variance (Factor XIV: Natural Setting)

Source	SS	df	MSS	*F*
Sex	0.01	1	0.01	$0.03^{@}$
Locality	0.18	2	0.09	$0.58^{@}$
Caste	0.17	2	0.08	$0.53^{@}$
SxL	1.57	2	0.78	5.06^{**}
SxC	0.92	2	0.46	$2.98^{@}$
LxC	0.65	4	0.16	$1.05^{@}$
SxLxC	0.23	4	0.05	$0.35^{@}$
Error	169.92	1062	0.16	
Total	**173.65**			

Note: See note under Table—6.2.

Table—6.89 Mean Scores of Different Sub-groups of *Ss* Classified According to Different Variables to Explain SxL Interaction Effect (Factor XIV: Natural Setting)

(6.89a) (SxL)				(6.89b) (LxS)		
B	U 10.49	SU 10.50	R 11.31	U	B 10.49	G 11.19
G	R 10.76	SU 10.96	U 11.19	SU	B 10.50	G 10.96
				R	G 10.76	B 11.31

Note: See note under Table—6.3.

PART II

Attitude of Teachers Towards the Non-detention System

1. Overall Score

The burden of implementing the non-detention system in right earnest, and converting the essence and spirit of the new system into practice rests on the shoulders of the teachers. Hence, an analysis of their reactions towards different aspects of the system may be of real interest to the educational administrators and reformers. As mentioned earlier, the attitude scale was administered to 510 men and women teachers drawn from the three localities. The attitude scores of these teachers were analysed employing analysis of variance of a 2x2x3x3 (2 levels of teaching x 2 sexes x 3 localities x 3 levels of experience) factorial design. This section deals with this analysis.

The mean overall attitude scores and SDs of different sub-groups of teacher towards the non-detention system are shown in Table 6.90.

Table—6.90 Means, SDs and *t* Values of Different Sub-groups of Teachers (Overall Score)

Group	N	M	S.D	*t*
Whole group	510	147.99	18.87	31.13***
Secondary grades (Sec. gr.)	170	146.31	17.81	20.27***
B.Eds.	340	148.83	19.35	23.99***
Men (M)	300	149.62	18.56	23.04***
Women (W)	210	146.09	19.20	21.07***
Urban (U)	180	151.41	19.00	15.95***
Semi-urban (SU)	180	145.94	19.61	19.25***
Rural (R)	150	146.34	17.27	19.55***
1-15 Years	157	142.34	15.82	24.88***
16-25 Years	232	149.53	19.61	19.61***
26+Years	121	152.05	20.74	11.64***

Note: See note under Table—6.2.

The mean score of the whole group was 147.99 which is far below the neutral point (174). The difference between the mean score and the neutral point was highly significant even at 0.001 level (t = 31.13). This shows a significantly negative attitude of the teachers towards the non-detention system (See Fig. 6.20).

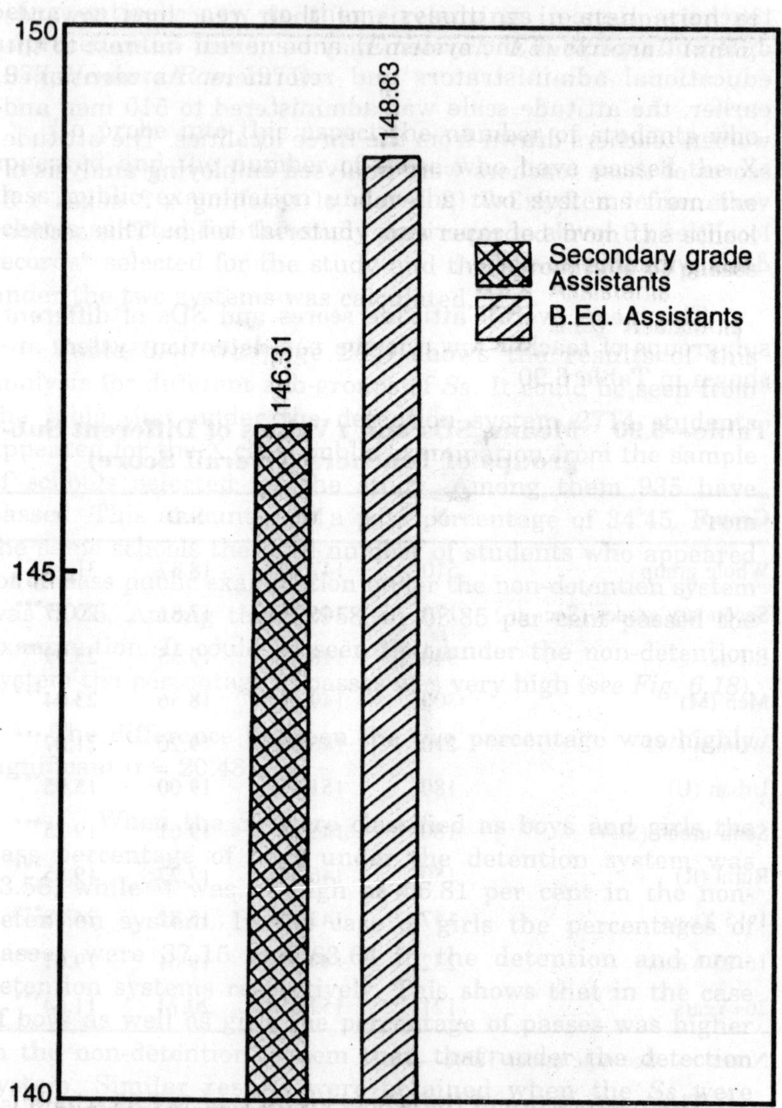

Fig.—6.24 Mean Attitude Scores of Secondary Grade and B.Ed. Assistants Towards Non-detention System.

When the teachers were classified as per their level of teaching, the mean score of the Secondary Grade Assistants was 146.31 while it was 148.83 for the B. Ed. Assistants (*see Fig. 6.24*). Both the means were significantly below the neutral point, indicating that Secondary Grades as well as B.Eds. were against the non-detention system.

Sex-wise classification of the teachers shows that the mean score of men teachers was 149.62 while that of women teachers was 146.09. These means also were significantly below the neutral point, indicating that men teachers as well as women teachers had a negative attitude towards the new system of evaluation.

When the teachers were categorised as urban, semi-urban and rural depending upon the locality to which they belonged all the three sub-groups exhibited a significantly negative attitude towards the new system. This was true when teachers were classified according to their experience also.

To examine whether there was any significant difference in the attitude of the teachers belonging to different levels of teaching, different sexes, different localities and different spans of experience, the attitude scores of the *Ss* were further analysed by analysis of variance of a 2x2x3x3 factorial design (2 levels of teaching x 2 sexes x 3 localities x 3 lengths of experience). The results of this analysis are shown in Table 6.91.

It could be seen from the table that the *F* ratio for level of teaching (1.05) was not significant at 0.05 level. This shows that there was no significant difference between B.Ed. assistants and Secondary grade assistants with regard to their attitude towards this system.

The *F* ratio for sex (7.70) which was significant at 0.01 level indicates that men and women teachers differed significantly with regard to their attitude towards this system. The mean score of men teachers was 149.62 while that of women teachers was 146.09. Though both the groups had a negative attitude, women teachers had a far more negative attitude than men teachers (*see Fig. 6.25*).

Table—6.91 Results of Analysis of Variance (Overall Score)

Source	SS	df	MSS	F
Level of teaching (Lt)	53.50	1	53.50	1.05@
Sex (S)	391.69	1	391.69	7.70**
Locality (L)	902.81	2	451.41	8.88***
Experience (E)	725.06	2	362.53	7.13***
LtxS	1.50	1	1.50	0.03@
LtxL	314.13	2	157.06	3.09*
LtxE	83.31	2	41.66	0.82@
SxL	210.38	2	105.19	2.07@
SxE	289.25	2	144.63	2.85@
LxE	389.75	4	97.44	1.92@
LtxSxL	428.13	2	214.06	4.25*
LtxSxE	220.75	2	110.38	2.17@
LtxLxE	65.44	4	16.36	0.32@
SxLxE	265.38	4	66.34	1.31@
LtxSxLxE	777.06	4	194.27	3.82**
Error	24099.30	474	50.84	
Total	**29217.42**	**509**		

Note: See note under Table—6.2.

The *F* ratio for locality was 8.88, which was also significant at 0.01 level for 2 and 474 df. This shows that there was a significant difference between the attitude of teachers belonging to different localities.

To find out teachers of which locality differed significantly from the others, *t* test was applied as in the earlier cases. The results of the *t* test are presented in Table 6.92. The mean scores of the *Ss* belonging *SU, R* and *U*

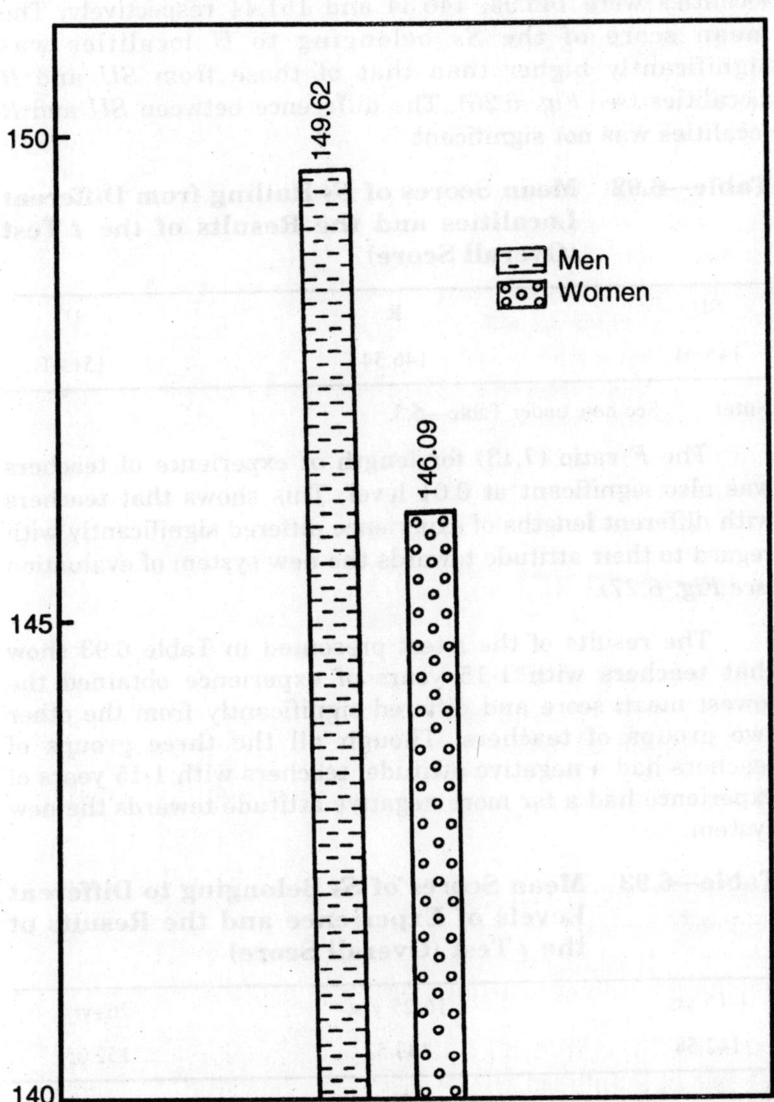

Fig.—6.25 Mean Attitude Scores of Men and Women Teachers Towards Non-detention System.

localities were 145.94, 146.34 and 151.41 respectively. The mean score of the *Ss* belonging to *U* localities was significantly higher than that of those from *SU* and *R* Localities (*see Fig. 6.26*). The difference between *SU* and *R* localities was not significant.

Table—6.92 Mean Scores of *Ss* Hailing from Different Localities and the Results of the *t* Test (Overall Score)

SU	R	U
145.94	146.34	151.41

Note: See note under Table—6.3.

The *F* ratio (7.13) for length of experience of teachers was also significant at 0.01 level. This shows that teachers with different lengths of experience differed significantly with regard to their attitude towards the new system of evaluation (*see Fig. 6.27*).

The results of the *t* test presented in Table 6.93 show that teachers with 1-15 years of experience obtained the lowest mean score and differed significantly from the other two groups of teachers. Though all the three groups of teachers had a negative attitude, teachers with 1-15 years of experience had a far more negative attitude towards the new system.

Table—6.93 Mean Scores of *Ss* Belonging to Different Levels of Experience and the Results of the *t* Test (Overall Score)

1-15 yrs	16-25 yrs.	26+yrs
142.58	149.53	152.05

Note: See note under Table—6.2.

The *F* ratio for Lt x L (Level of teaching x locality) interaction was significant indicating that the effect of level of teaching was not independent of the locality of the *Ss* involved and vice versa.

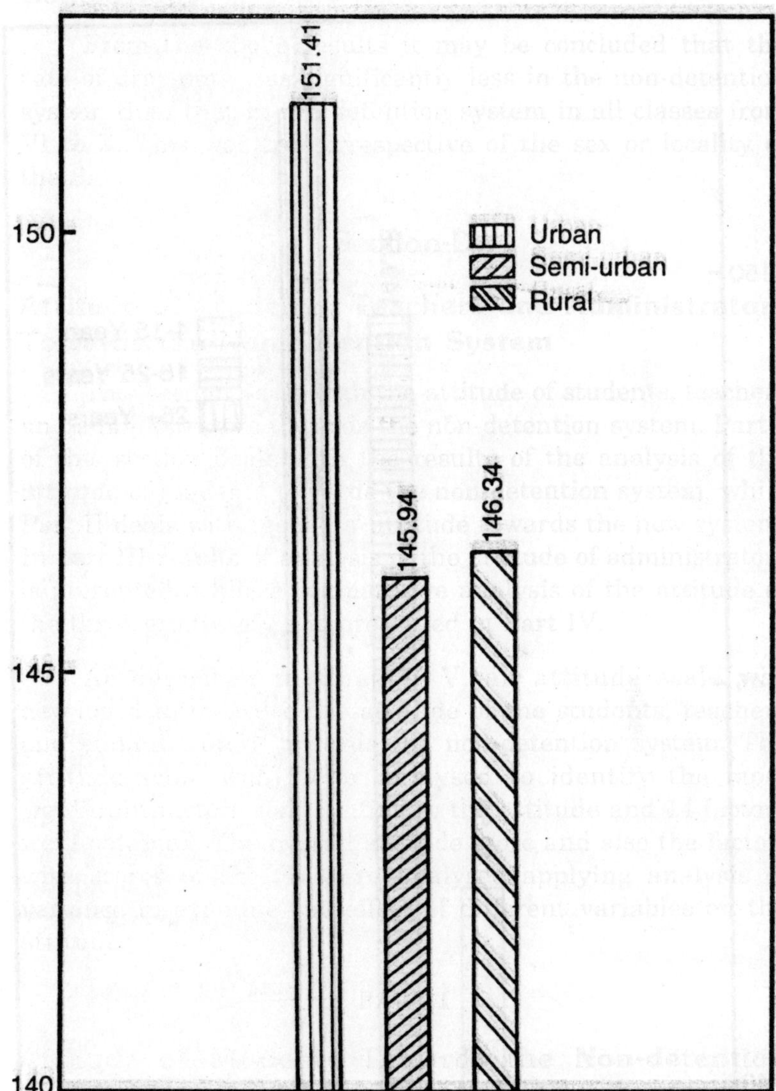

Fig.—6.26 Mean Attitude Scores of Teachers Belonging to Different Localities Towards Non-detention System.

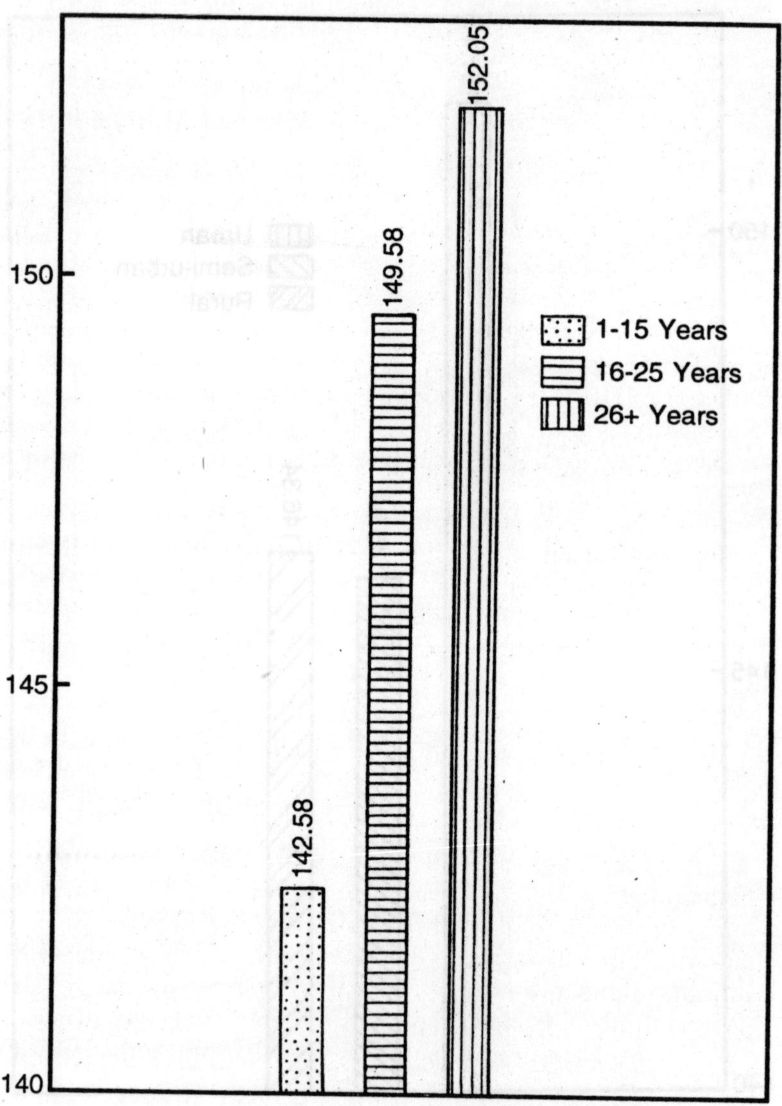

Fig.—6.27 Mean Attitude Scores of Men Women Teachers Towards Non-detention System.

An examination of the mean scores of the teachers classified according to the two variables, level of teaching and locality, presented in Table 6.94 shows that in the case of Secondary grade assistants the mean score of teachers from *SU* localities was the least while that of those from *U* localities was the highest, whereas in the case of B.Ed. assistants the mean score of teachers working in *R* localities was the least and that of those working in *U* localities was the highest. Considering the differences between B.Eds. and Secondary grades, in the case of *SU* localities B.Ed. teachers scored higher than secondary grade assistants, while with regard to *U* and *R* localities the difference between the two categories of teachers was not significant. This explains the Lt x L interaction.

Table—6.94 Mean Scores of Different Sub-groups of *Ss* Classified According to Level of Teaching and Locality Variables to Explain the Lt x L Interaction Effect (Overall Score)

	(6.94a) (LtxL)				(6.94b) (LxLt)	
	SU	R	U		Sec. grade	
Sec. grade	140.83	146.90	151.30	U	151.30	151.47
	R	SU	U	SU	Sec. grade	B. Eds.
B.Eds.	146.06	148.47	151.47		140.83	148.47
					B.Eds.	Sec. grade
				R	146.06	146.90

Note: See note under Table—6.3.

None of the remaining two factor interactions were significant, indicating that the effect of one variable was independent of the level of the other variable involved and vice versa.

The *F* ratio (4.25) for the three factor interaction, Lt x S x L was significant indicating that the effect of any two variables taken at a time was not independent of the level of the third variable involved. The other three factor interactions were not significant. However, the four factor interaction was significant (F = 3.82) indicating that the interaction between any three of the variables taken at a time was not independent of the level of the fourth variable.

2. Factor-wise Analysis

A similar analysis was carried out on the scores of different sub-groups of *Ss* on each of the 14 factors to see the effect of different variables on the factor-wise scores. The results of this analysis are presented hereunder:

(a) Factor I: Policy Implementation

This factor contained 15 items, hence the neutral point was 45. Table 6.95 shows the mean scores of different sub-groups of *Ss* and the results of the t test on this factor. It may be seen that the group as a whole and all the sub-groups without any exception had a highly negative attitude towards the new system as measured by this factor.

Table—6.95 Means, SDs and *t* Values of Different Sub-groups of Teachers (Factor I: Policy Implementation)

Group	N	M	S.D	t
Whole group	510	31.56	6.92	43.92***
Sec. grades	170	31.63	6.35	27.46***
B.Eds.	340	31.53	7.19	34.53***
M	300	31.88	6.69	33.97***
W	210	31.11	7.22	27.88***
U	180	32.19	7.46	23.03***
SU	180	31.56	7.07	25.57***
R	150	30.81	5.94	29.15***
1-15	157	30.54	6.14	29.50***
16-25	232	31.77	6.94	29.06***
26+	121	32.50	7.68	17.91***

Note: See note under Table—6.2.

Table 6.96 shows the results of analysis of variance of the scores of different sub-groups of *Ss* on this factor. From the Table it could be observed that the *F* ratio for the main effect of experience was significant. Table 6.97 shows that the teachers with 1-15 years of experience obtained the least score (M = 30.54) and differed significantly from teachers with 26 or more years of experience, who obtained the highest mean score (M = 32.50).

Table—6.96 Results of Analysis of Variance (Factor I: Policy Implementation)

Source	SS	df	MSS	*F*
Lt	2.16	1	2.16	0.30@
S	15.13	1	15.13	2.12@
L	27.11	2	13.55	1.90@
E	49.71	2	24.85	3.48*
LtxS	10.55	1	10.55	1.48@
LtxL	19.80	2	9.90	1.39@
LtxE	6.54	2	3.27	0.46@
SxL	52.42	2	26.21	3.67*
SxE	0.27	2	0.13	0.02@
LxE	22.61	4	5.65	0.79@
LtxSxL	4.44	2	2.22	0.31@
LtxSxE	28.98	2	14.49	2.03@
LtxLxE	5.34	4	1.34	0.19@
SxLxE	88.40	4	22.10	3.09*
LtxSxLxE	65.87	4	16.47	2.30@
Error		474	7.15	
Total	**399.32**	**509**		

Note: See note under Table—6.2.

Table—6.97 Mean Scores of *Ss* Having Different Years of Experiences and the Results of *t* Test (Factor I: Policy Implementation)

1-15 yrs	16-25 yrs	26+yrs
30.54	31.77	32.50

Note: See note under Table—6.3.

The two factor interaction between sex and locality was significant ($F = 3.67$). Table 6.98 explains this interaction. From the Table it could be seen that in the case of men teachers those from *R* localities scored the least (M = 30.90) and differed significantly from those belonging to U localities who scored the highest (M = 32.50). In the case of women teachers there was no significant difference between the teachers belonging to the different localities. This explains the significant SxL interaction effect.

Table—6.98 Mean Scores of Different Sub-groups of *Ss* Classified According to the Two Variables Sex and Locality to Explain S x L Interaction Effect (Factor I: Policy Implementation)

(6.98a) (SxL)				(9.98b) (LxS)		
	R	SU	U		W	M
M	30.93	32.48	32.84	U	31.53	32.84
	SU	R	U		W	M
W	30.62	31.33	31.53	SU	30.62	32.48
					M	W
				R	30.93	31.33

Note: See note under Table—6.3.

The SxLxE interaction was also significant indicating that the interaction between any two variables taken at a time was not independent of the level of the third variable.

(b) *Factor II: Facility*

From Table 6.99 it could be said that all the sub-groups of *Ss* irrespective of their level of teaching or sex or locality or experience (except those with 26 or more years of experience) had a significantly negative attitude towards the non-detention system as measured by this factor.

Table—6.99 Means, SDs and *t* Values of Different Sub-groups of Teachers (Factor II: Facility)

Group	N	M	S.D	*t*
Whole group	510	8.19	2.81	6.53***
Sec. grades	170	7.96	2.84	4.77***
B. Eds.	340	8.30	2.79	4.61***
M	300	8.29	2.79	4.40***
W	210	8.04	2.84	4.89***
U	180	8.59	2.63	2.10*
SU	180	7.87	3.04	5.01***
R	150	8.09	2.69	4.11***
1-15	157	7.49	2.71	6.98***
16-25	232	8.47	2.72	2.97**
26+	121	8.55	2.97	1.66@

Note: See note under Table—6.2.

When the non-detention system was introduced it was thought that under the new system students can learn in a free atmosphere and examinations become only a means to an end but not an end in themselves. Teachers do not seem to feel that this is what occurs in reality.

Table 6.100 shows the results of analysis of variance of the scores on this factor. It could be seen from the table that the *F* ratios for the main effects of locality (F = 4.03) and experience (F = 5.22) were significant, while the other two main effects were not significant. Table 6.101 shows that the mean scores of *SU*, *R* and *U* localities were 7.87, 8.09 and 8.59 respectively. There was a significant difference between the attitude of teachers belonging to *U* and *SU* localities. Table 6.102 shows that teachers with 1-15 years of experience obtained a mean score of 7.40 and differed significantly from the other two groups of teachers, viz., those with 16-25 years and 26 or more years of experience.

Table—6.100 Results of Analysis of Variance (Factor II: Facility)

Source	SS	df	MSS	*F*
Lt	0.79	1	0.79	0.66@
S	1.34	1	1.34	1.13@
L	9.59	2	4.80	4.03*
E	12.42	2	6.26	5.22**
LtxS	0.64	1	0.64	0.54@
LtxL	7.50	2	3.75	3.15*
LtxE	0.41	2	0.20	0.17@
SxL	3.79	2	1.84	1.59@
SxE	3.49	2	1.75	1.47@
LxE	2.74	4	0.69	0.58@
LtxSxL	12.47	2	6.24	5.24**
LtxSxE	0.03	2	0.01	0.01@
LtxLxE	3.87	4	0.97	0.81@
SxLxE	7.46	4	1.86	1.57@
LtxSxLxE	6.85	4	1.71	1.44@
Error	564.01	474	1.19	
Total	**704.10**	**509**		

Note: See note under Table—6.2.

Table—6.101 Mean Scores of *Ss* Belonging to Different Localities and the Results of *t* Test (Factor II: Facility)

SU	R	U
7.87	8.09	8.59

Note: See not under Table—6.3.

Table—6.102 Mean Scores of *Ss* Belonging to Different Durations of Experiences and the Results of *t* Test (Factor II: Facility)

1-15 yrs	16-25 yrs	26+yrs
7.40	8.47	8.55

Note: See note under Table—21.

The two factor interaction between level of teaching and locality (Lt x L) was also significant. Table 6.103 explains the situation. In the case of Secondary grade assistants those belonging to *SU* localities scored the least (M = 7.27) and differed significantly from those belonging to *U* localities (M = 8.57). However, in the case of B.Ed. assistants there was no significant difference between the three groups of teachers. Other differences between means were also not significant.

Table—6.103 Mean Scores of *Ss* Classified According to the Variables Level of Teaching and Locality to Explain the Significant Lt x L Interaction (Factor II: Facility)

(6.103a) (LtxL)				(6.103b) (LxLt)		
	SU	R	U		Sec. grades	B.Eds.
Sec. grades	7.27	8.06	8.57	U	8.57	8.60
	R	SU	U		Sec. grades	B.Eds.
B.Eds.	8.11	8.17	8.60	SU	7.27	8.17
				R	Sec. grades	B.Eds.
					8.06	8.11

Note: See note under Table—6.3.

(c) Factor III: Teaching-Learning

This factor had 5 items and hence the neutral point was 15. The mean scores of the different sub-groups of *Ss* on this factor are presented in Table 6.104. The mean score of the whole group as well as those of all the sub-groups were significantly below the neutral point. This indicates that the teachers as a whole irrespective of their level of teaching, or sex, or locality, or experience, had a negative attitude towards the non-detention system as measured by the items in this factor.

Table—6.104 Means, SDs and *t* Values of Different Sub-groups of Teachers (Factor III: Teaching-learning)

Group	N	M	S.D	*t*
Whole group	510	14.12	2.58	7.72***
Sec. grades	170	14.15	2.66	4.14***
B.Eds.	340	14.11	2.53	6.51***
M	300	14.30	2.54	4.77***
W	210	13.87	2.61	6.30***
U	180	14.39	2.78	2.93**
SU	180	13.71	2.36	7.34***
R	150	14.29	2.53	3.43***
1-15	157	14.05	2.58	4.65***
16-25	232	14.11	2.51	5.34***
26+	121	14.22	2.71	3.15**

Note: See note under Table—6.2.

As mentioned earlier, in this system, students do not evince interest in the examinations since the marks obtained in them have no consequence for them. Further, since the tests are not taken seriously the relation between teaching, learning and evaluation is hampered, though in a good system of education these three should go hand in hand each contributing to the other. Since students do not show much interest in examinations, parents have lost the means of knowing the progress of their wards in education. It is but natural that teachers were averse to this system as measured by this factor.

Table 6.105 shows the results of analysis of variance. It may be seen that none of the *F* ratios was significant. This shows that there was no significant difference between the attitude of different sub-groups of teachers with regard to their attitude as measured by this factor.

Table—6.105 Results of Analysis of Variance (Factor III: Teaching-learning)

Source	SS	df	MSS	*F*
Lt	0.50	1	0.50	0.48@
S	0.34	1	0.34	0.33@
L	4.59	2	2.30	2.24@
E	0.85	2	0.43	0.41@
LtxS	0.12	1	0.12	0.12@
LtxL	1.99	2	0.99	0.97@
LtxE	2.56	2	1.28	1.25@
SxL	2.78	2	1.39	1.36@
SxE	1.09	2	0.54	0.53@
LxE	2.08	4	0.52	0.51@
LtxSxL	0.45	2	0.22	0.22@
LtxSxE	0.82	2	0.41	0.40@
LtxLxE	3.30	4	0.82	0.80@
SxLxE	2.05	4	0.51	0.50@
LtxSxLxE	2.45	4	0.61	0.60@
Error	485.76	474	1.03	
Total	**511.72**	**509**		

Note: See note under Table—6.2.

(d) Factor IV: Personality

Table 6.106 shows the mean scores of different sub-groups of *Ss* on factor IV. It could be observed that the mean scores of all the sub-groups were significantly above the neutral point indicating a positive attitude towards the new system as far as the items of this factor were concerned. This was true irrespective of the level of teaching, or sex or locality or experience of the teachers.

Table—6.106 Means, SDs and *t* Values of Different Sub-groups of Teachers (Factor IV: Personality)

Group	N	M	S.D	*t*
Whole group	510	10.77	1.91	20.92***
Sec. grades	170	10.66	1.91	11.35***
B.Eds.	340	10.81	1.91	17.56***
M	300	10.82	1.90	16.60***
W	210	10.70	1.93	12.72***
U	180	10.66	2.01	11.11***
SU	180	10.99	1.82	14.68***
R	150	10.62	1.87	10.54***
1-15	157	10.59	1.96	10.13***
16-25	232	10.76	2.00	13.11***
26+	121	11.00	1.62	13.60***

Note: See note under Table—6.2.

Since a student's promotion was not linked with his performance in tests in this system, students need not indulge in malpractices and parents also need not resort to unholy practices like getting different types of pressures on the teachers and headmasters for the promotion of their children. Thus the non-detention system has reduced the scope for corruption in schools. Further, since the teacher is free from the cluthces of external examinations and detentions, he has scope to develop the desired personality traits among the students. On these scores teachers do favour the new system as assessed by this factor.

From Table 6.107 where the results of analysis of variance are presented, it may be seen that none of the *F* ratios were significant at 0.05 level.

Table—6.107 Results of Analysis of Variance (Factor IV: Personality)

Source	SS	df	MSS	*F*
Lt	0.40	1	0.40	0.69@
S	1.73	1	1.73	3.00@
L	1.85	2	0.93	1.61@
E	1.05	2	0.53	0.92@
LtxS	1.57	1	1.57	2.73@
LtxL	0.45	2	0.23	0.39@
LtxE	0.07	2	0.04	0.06@
SxL	0.59	2	0.30	0.52@
SxE	1.09	2	0.54	0.94@
LxE	1.03	4	0.26	0.45@
LtxSxL	0.44	2	0.22	0.38@
LtxSxE	1.41	2	0.71	1.22@
LtxLxE	2.50	4	0.63	1.09@
SxLxE	0.52	4	0.13	0.23@
LtxSxLxE	1.36	4	0.34	0.59@
Error	273.12	474	0.58	
Total	**289.20**	**509**		

Note: See note under Table—6.2.

(e) *Factor V: Discipline*

Table 6.108 shows the mean scores of different sub-groups of *Ss* on this factor. The mean score of the whole group was 9.09. The difference between the mean score of the whole group and the neutral point was not significant (t = 0.91). This shows that the group as a whole had a neutral attitude towards the new system as measured by this factor. Similar results were obtained on all sub-groups except urban teachers and teachers with 26 or more years of experience, whose attitude score was significantly above the neutral point.

Table—6.108 Mean, SDs and *t* Values of Different Sub-groups of Teachers (Factor V: Discipline)

Group	N	M	S.D	*t*
Whole group	510	9.09	2.23	0.91@
Sec. grades	170	9.14	1.95	0.91@
B.Eds.	340	9.07	2.36	0.55@
M	300	9.16	2.17	1.25@
W	210	9.00	2.31	0.00@
U	180	9.38	2.29	2.21*
SU	180	8.87	2.16	0.79@
R	150	9.01	2.21	0.07@
1-15	157	8.86	1.98	0.89@
16-25	232	9.03	2.40	0.19@
26+	121	9.51	2.14	2.63**

Note: See note under Table—6.2.

Teachers with more than 26 years of experience have naturally a wider experience with the ill effects of the detention system. Further, external pressures on teachers with regard to promotion of students are usually more in U localities. Hence, urban teachers did not favour the detention system and had a positive attitude towards the new system as measured by this factor.

From Table 6.109 it could be seen that the *F* ratios for the main effects of sex and locality were significant. The mean score of men (9.16) was a little above the neutral point, while that of women (9.00) was neutral.

The *F* ratio 4.77 for locality was also significant. An examination of the mean scores presented in Table 6.110 shows that the mean scores of *SU, R* and *U* localities were 8.87, 9.01 and 9.38 respectively. Teachers from *U* localities (whose attitude score was significantly above the neutral point) differed significantly from those from *SU* localities.

Table—6.109 Results of Analysis of Variance (Factor V: Discipline)

Source	SS	df	MSS	F
Lt	2.82	1	2.82	3.73@
S	4.52	1	4.52	5.99*
L	7.20	2	3.60	4.77**
E	2.16	2	1.08	1.43@
LtxS	0.01	1	0.01	0.01@
LtxL	2.25	2	1.13	1.49@
LtxE	1.16	2	0.58	0.77@
SxL	0.46	2	0.23	0.30@
SxE	7.17	2	3.59	4.75**
LxE	9.16	4	2.29	3.03*
LtxSxL	3.54	2	1.77	2.34@
LtxSxE	2.00	2	1.00	1.33@
LtxLxE	3.45	4	0.86	1.14@
SxLxE	1.21	4	0.30	0.40@
LtxSxLxE	9.83	4	2.46	3.25*
Error	358.15	474	0.76	
Total	**415.11**	**509**		

Note: See note under Table—6.2.

Table—6.110 Mean Scores of *Ss* Hailing from Different Localities and the Results of *t* Test (Factor V: Discipline)

SU	R	U
8.87	9.01	9.38

Note: See note under Table—6.3.

The interaction effects between sex and experience, and locality and experience were significant. An examination of the mean scores presented in Tables 6.111 and 6.112 explains these interaction effects.

Table—6.111 Mean Scores of Different Sub-groups of *Ss* Classified According to Sex and Length of Experience of Teachers to Explain the SxE Interaction Effect (Factor V: Discipline)

	(6.111a) (SxE)				(6.111b) (ExS)	
	16-25 Yrs	1-15 Yrs	26+Yrs		W	M
M	8.93	9.00	9.73	1-15 Yrs	8.65	9.00
	1-15 Yrs	26+Yrs	16-25 Yrs		M	W
W	8.65	9.14	9.16	16-25 Yrs	8.93	9.16
					W	M
				26+Yrs	9.14	9.73

Note: See note under Table—6.3.

(f) Factor VI: Incentive for Progress

This factor also had three items, hence the neutral point was 9. From Table 6.113 it could be observed that the group as a whole (M = 9.60) had a significantly positive attitude towards the non-detention system as measured by this factor. Though the mean scores of all the sub-groups were above 9.00, some of them were not significantly different from the neutral point.

Table—6.112 Mean Scores of Different Sub-groups of *Ss* Classified According to Locality and Length of Experience to Explain the LxE Interaction Effect (Factor V: Discipline)

(6.112a) (LxE)				(6.112b) (ExL)			
	1-15 yrs	16-25 yrs	26+ yrs		R	SU	U
U	9.08	9.14	9.95	1-15 yrs	8.72	8.78	9.08
	1-15 yrs	16-25 yrs	26+ yrs		R	SU	U
SU	8.78	8.87	9.00	16-25 yrs	7.79	8.87	9.14
	16-25 Yrs	1-15 yrs	26+ yrs		SU	R	U
R	7.79	8.72	9.35	26+ yrs	9.00	9.35	9.95

Note: See note under Table—6.3.

Table—6.113 Mean, SDs and *t* Values of Different Sub-groups of Teachers (Factor VI: Incentive for Progress)

Group	N	M	S.D	*t*
Whole group	510	9.60	2.64	5.13***
Sec. grades	170	9.28	2.64	1.40@
B.Eds.	340	9.76	2.62	5.31***
M	300	9.66	2.63	4.35***
W	210	9.51	2.65	2.79**
U	180	10.14	2.56	6.00***
SU	180	9.32	2.63	1.63@
R	150	9.28	2.64	1.27@
1-15	157	9.26	2.75	1.16@
16-25	232	9.60	2.55	3.58***
26+	121	10.04	2.61	4.39***

Note: See note under Table—6.2.

From Table 6.114 it could be seen that the *F* ratio (3.81) for locality was significant at 0.05 level. It may be seen from Table 6.115 that the teachers from *U* localities obtained a higher mean score and differed significantly from the teachers of *R* and *SU* localities. This may be because in urban areas schools are over-crowded and students and their friends indulge in many kinds of undisciplined and unworthy activities during the examinations.

When the role of examination coupled with detentions was reduced to a minimum in the new system probably the teachers feel relieved from the atrocities being committed during examinations resulting in a favourable attitude towards the non-detention system as measured by this factor.

Table—6.114 Results of Analysis of Variance (Factor VI: Incentive for Progress)

Source	SS	df	MSS	*F*
Lt	0.01	1	0.01	0.01@
S	1.19	1	1.19	1.17@
L	7.70	2	3.85	3.80*
E	0.90	2	0.45	0.44@
LtxS	1.60	1	1.60	1.57@
LtxL	0.53	2	0.26	0.26@
LtxE	4.62	2	2.31	2.28@
SxL	1.16	2	0.58	0.58@
SxE	10.31	2	5.15	5.09*
LxE	4.20	4	1.05	1.04@
LtxSxL	2.57	2	1.28	1.27@
LtxSxE	0.17	2	0.08	0.08@
LtxLxE	5.07	4	1.27	1.25@
SxLxE	2.58	4	0.64	0.64@
LtxSxLxE	1.36	4	0.34	0.34@
Error	479.64	474	1.01	
Total	**525.20**	**509**		

Note: See note under Table—6.2.

Among the interactions, SxE interaction effect alone was significant. None of the three factor or the four factor interactions were significant. The significant *F* ratio (5.09) for the interaction between sex and experience (SxE) shows that the effect of the sex of the teachers on their attitude was not independent of their experience and vice versa.

Table—6.115 Mean Scores of *Ss* Hailing from Different Localities and the Results of *t* Test (Factor VI: Incentive for Progress)

R	SU	U
9.28	9.32	10.14

Note: See note under Table—6.3.

Table—6.116 Mean Scores of *Ss* Classified According to the Variables Sex and Length of Experience to Explain SxE Interaction Effect (Factor VI: Incentive for Progress)

	(6.116a) (SxE)			(6.116b) (ExS)		
	1-15 yrs	16-25 yrs	26+yrs		M	W
M	8.89	9.78	10.40	1-15 yrs	8.89	9.79
	16-25 yrs	26+ yrs	1-15 yrs		W	M
W	9.38	9.41	9.79	16-25 yrs	9.38	9.78
					W	M
				26+ yrs	9.41	10.40

Note: See note under Table—6.3.

From Table 6.116 it could be seen that in the case of men, teachers with 1-15 years of experience scored the least and differed significantly from the other two sub-groups of *Ss* while in the case of women there was no significant difference between the three groups of teachers. Examining the difference between men and women teachers it may be seen from Table 6.116b that in the case of teachers with

1-15 years of experience men teachers who had a negative attitude scored significantly less than the women teachers who had a positive attitude, whereas in the case of the other two categories of teachers the differences between men and women teachers were not significant.

(g) Factor VII: Learning Skills

Table 6.117 shows the mean scores of different sub-groups of *Ss* and the results of *t* test. It could be seen from the table that all the sub-groups without any exception had a highly negative attitude towards the new system as measured by this factor.

Table—6.117 Means, SDs and *t* Values of Different Sub-groups of Teachers with *t* Value for the Neutral Point (Factor VII: Learning Skills)

Group	N	M	S.D	*t*
Whole group	510	6.40	2.73	21.67***
Sec. grades	170	6.21	2.53	14.35***
B.Eds.	340	6.50	2.78	16.57***
M	300	6.37	2.62	17.37***
W	210	6.45	2.82	13.09***
U	180	6.59	2.72	11.85***
SU	180	6.45	2.73	12.39***
R	150	6.12	2.64	13.30***
1-15	157	5.78	2.17	18.74***
16-25	232	6.62	8.81	12.94***
26+	121	6.84	2.98	7.98***

Note: See note under Table—6.2.

Teachers seem to feel that the system does not provide for intelligent students to exhibit their talents. Sometimes even dullards who do not have adequate knowledge even in basic skills go up the educational ladder.

Table 6.118 shows the results of ANOVA. From the table, it could be observed that the *F* ratios for the main effects of locality and experience were significant. Table 6.119 shows that teachers from *U* localities obtained the highest means score while those from *R* localities scored least. The difference between the means however, was not significant. Table 6.120 shows that the teachers with 1-15 years of experience obtained the lowest attitude score and differed significantly from the other two categories of teachers.

Table—6.118 Results of Analysis of Variance (Factor VII: Learning Skills)

Source	SS	df	MSS	*F*
Lt	1.47	1	1.47	1.36@
S	2.46	1	2.46	2.26@
L	11.55	2	5.77	5.32**
E	8.27	2	4.14	3.81*
LtxS	0.00	1	0.00	0.00@
LtxL	1.85	2	0.92	0.85@
LtxE	5.17	2	2.59	2.38@
SxL	1.93	2	0.96	0.89@
SxE	6.93	2	3.47	3.19*
LxE	16.18	4	4.05	3.73**
LtxSxL	11.89	2	5.95	5.48**
LtxSxE	3.57	2	1.78	1.64@
LtxLxE	6.38	4	1.59	1.47@
SxLxE	2.26	4	0.56	0.52@
LtxSxLxE	13.21	4	3.30	3.04*
Error	514.57	474	1.09	
Total	**602.52**	**509**		

Note: See note under Table—6.2.

Table—6.119 Mean Scores of *Ss* Belonging to Different Localities and the Results of *t* Test (Factor VII: Learning Skills)

R	SU	U
6.12	6.45	6.59

Note: See note under Table—6.3.

Table—6.120 Mean Scores of *Ss* Belonging to Different Lengths of Experiences and the Results of *t* Test (Factor VII: Learning Skills)

1-15 yrs	16-25 yrs	26+yrs
5.75	6.62	6.84

Note: See note under Table—21.

The SxE and LxE interactions were also significant. Table 6.121a explains the significant SxE interaction. In the case of men teachers those with 1-15 years of experience differed significantly from the other two sub-groups, while in the case of women there was no significant difference between the three sub-groups of teachers.

Table—6.121 Mean Scores of Different Sub-groups of *Ss* Classified According to the Variables to Explain Corresponding Interaction Effect (Factor VII: Learning Skills)

	(6.121a) (SxE)				(6.121b) (ExS)	
	1-15 yrs	16-25 yrs	26+ yrs		M	W
M	5.64	6.61	6.87	1-15 yrs	5.64	5.94
	1-15 yrs	16-25 yrs	26+ yrs		W	M
W	5.94	6.05	6.77	16-25 yrs	6.05	6.61
					W	M
				26+ yrs	6.77	6.87

Note: See note under Table—6.3.

Table—6.122

	(6.122a) (LxE)			(6.122b) (ExL)			
	1-15 yrs	16-25 yrs	26+ yrs		SU	U	R
U	5.83	6.64	7.26	1-15 yrs	5.48	5.83	5.98
	1-15 yrs	26+ yrs	16-25 yrs		R	U	SU
SU	5.48	6.83	6.87	16-25 yrs	6.30	6.64	6.87
	26+ yrs	1-15 yrs	16-25 yrs		R	SU	U
R	5.83	5.98	6.30	26+ yrs	5.83	6.83	7.26

Note: See note under Table—6.3.

It could be seen from Table 6.122 that in the case of teachers of *U* localities, those with 1-15 years of experience (M = 5.83) differed significantly from the teachers with an experience of 26 or more years (M = 7.26). In the case of SU localities teachers with 1-15 years of experience (M = 5.48) differed significantly from the other two sub-groups, whereas in the case of *R* localities there was no significant difference between the three sub-groups. This explains the significant LxE interaction.

The three factor interaction LtxSxL was significant (*F* = 5.48) at 0.01 level, indicating that the effect of any two variables taken at a time was not independent of the level of the third variable. The four factor interaction, viz., LtxSxLxE was also significant (= 3.04) at 0.05 level.

(h) Factor VIII: Educational Policy

Table 6.123 shows the mean scores of different sub-groups of *Ss* on factor VIII, while Table 6.124 gives the results of analysis of variance on this factor.

From Table 6.123 it could be observed that all the sub-groups of teachers had a highly significant negative attitude towards the non-detention system.

Table—6.123 Means, SDs and *t* values of different sub-groups of teachers (Factor VIII: Educational policy)

Group	N	M	S.D	*t*
Whole group	510	8.02	1.87	6.41***
Sec. grades	170	7.75	1.94	8.42***
B. Eds.	340	8.15	1.83	8.59***
M	300	8.10	1.89	8.24***
W	210	7.90	1.84	8.70***
U	180	8.14	1.72	6.68***
SU	180	7.81	1.89	8.45***
R	150	8.11	2.01	5.41***
1-15	157	7.85	1.88	7.65***
16-25	232	8.07	1.89	7.53***
26+	121	8.13	1.83	5.22***

Note: See note under Table—6.2.

Table—6.124 Results of Analysis of Variance (Factor VIII: Educational Policy)

Source	SS	df	MSS	*F*
1	2	3	4	5
Lt	2.10	1	2.10	3.83@
S	0.43	1	0.43	0.78@
L	0.40	2	0.20	0.37@
E	0.31	2	0.16	0.29@
LtxS	0.00	1	0.00	0.00@
LtxL	0.005	2	0.002	0.005@
LtxE	0.03	2	0.02	0.03@
SxL	1.92	2	0.96	1.75@
LxE	0.87	4	0.22	0.40@

(Contd...)

1	2	3	4	5
SxE	0.22	2	0.11	0.20@
LtxSxL	2.06	2	1.03	1.88@
LtxSxE	0.12	2	0.06	0.11@
LtxLxE	1.22	4	0.30	0.56@
SxLxE	0.77	4	0.19	0.35@
LtxSxLxE	0.26	4	0.07	0.12@
Error	259.52	474	0.55	
Total	**270.23**	**509**		

Note: See note under Table—6.2.

The negative attitude towards the system as measured by this factor was due to the fact that teachers strongly feel that if the government had followed the correct educational principles, it would not have removed detentions. Once can easily visualise the encouragement indiscipline gets when automatic promotions are guaranteed. Further, students from backward classes who have less aptitude for education are worst affected by the new system, since they do not show interest in studies from the beginning and can not cope up with facing the common examination at the VII class and X class levels.

None of the *F* ratios was significant indicating no significant effect of any of the variables on the attitude of the teachers as measured by this factor.

(i) Factor IX: Freedom for the Teacher

Table 6.125 shows the mean attitude scores of different sub-groups of *Ss* on factor IX. This factor contained 3 items. Hence, the neutral point was 9. From the table it is revealed that all the sub-groups of *Ss* without any exception had a significantly negative attitude towards the system as measured by this factor.

When the non-detention system was introduced it was contended that the system would allow the schools, to try out better methods of teaching and evaluation, for achieving the desired development on the intellectual as well as many other aspects of the personality of the pupils (*Satyanarayana*, 1972). The highly negative attitude score of all the sub-groups of teachers on this factor suggest that the above assumption of the protagonists of the system was not upheld in practice.

Table—6.125 Means, SDs and *t* Values of Different Sub-groups of Teachers (Factor IX; Freedom for the Teacher)

Group	N	M	S.D	*t*
Whole group	510	7.34	3.09	12.12***
Sec. grades	170	7.33	2.93	7.18***
B.Eds.	340	7.32	3.16	9.82***
M	300	7.63	3.16	7.52***
W	210	6.92	2.95	10.23***
U	180	7.49	3.11	6.51***
SU	180	6.81	2.87	10.00***
R	150	7.73	3.26	4.77***
1-15	157	6.82	2.88	9.51***
16-25	232	7.40	3.17	7.69***
26+	121	7.89	3.11	3.91***

Note: See note under Table—6.2.

In fact, the teacher fell that they do not have much free time since they have to conduct unit tests, quarterly and half yearly examinations and value the papers. This probably is coupled with lack of discipline and abnormal strength of the classes especially in *U* and *SU* areas where it (the strength) may range between 60 to 80 pupils in any class and make the teachers fell over burdened. Further, many of them felt that the system was spoiling the academic career of the students. This was what was revealed in an examination of the responses of a sample of 100 teachers.

The scores of the *Ss* were further analysed by ANOVA as in the earlier cases, to examine the effect of the different variables on the attitude of the students towards the new system. The results of this analysis are presented in Table 6.126.

Table—6.126 Results of Analysis of Variance (Factor IX: Freedom for the Teacher)

Source	SS	df	MSS	*F*
Lt	6.58	1	6.58	4.70*
S	3.85	1	3.85	2.79@
L	16.73	2	8.37	5.98**
E	9.27	2	4.63	3.31*
LtxS	1.10	1	1.10	0.79@
LtxL	5.20	2	2.60	1.86@
LtxE	3.38	2	1.69	1.21@
SxL	7.68	2	3.84	2.75@
SxE	12.70	2	6.35	4.54@
LxE	6.83	4	1.71	1.22@
LtxSxL	5.16	2	2.58	1.84@
LtxSxE	4.75	2	2.37	1.70@
LtxLxE	2.54	4	0.63	0.45@
SxLxE	1.06	4	0.27	0.19@
LtxSxLxE	10.41	4	2.60	1.86@
Error	662.79	474	1.90	
Total	**757.02**	**509**		

Note: See note under Table—6.2.

It could be seen from the Table that the *F* ratio (4.70) for the level of teaching (Lt) was significant at 0.05 level for 1 and 474 df. This shows that there was a significant difference between B.Eds and Secondary grade assistants with regard to their attitude. The mean score of Secondary grade teachers was 7.38 while it was 7.02 for the B.Ed. Assistants.

The *F* ratio (5.98) for locality was also significant indicating a significant difference between the attitude of teachers belonging to different localities. Table 6.127 shows that the teachers of *SU* localities obtained the lowest mean score and they differed significantly from the teachers of the other two localities with regard to their attitude.

Table—6.127 Mean Scores of *Ss* Hailing from Different Localities and the Results of the *t* Test (Factor IX: Freedom for the Teacher)

SU	U	R
6.81	7.49	7.73

Note: See note under Table—6.3.

Table—6.128 Mean Scores of *Ss* Belonging to Different Durations of Experience and the Results of the *t* Test (Factor IX: Freedom for the Teacher)

1-15 yrs	16-25 yrs	26+ yrs
6.82	7.40	7.89

Note: See note under Table—6.3.

The *F* ratio (3.30) for the length of experience was also significant at 0.05 level. Table 6.128 shows that teachers with 1-15 years of experience (M = 6.82) differed significantly from those with an experience of 26 years or more (M = 7.89). Other differences between means were not significant.

Among the *F* ratios for interaction effects only that between SxE was significant. This shows that the difference between men and women teachers with regard to their attitude towards the new system was not of the same order for teachers with different levels of experience and vice versa. The mean scores presented in Table 6.129a and 6.129b explain the situation.

Table—6.129 Mean Scores of Different Sub-groups of *Ss* Classified According to Sex and Length of Experience of Teachers to Explain the SxE Interaction Effect (Factor IX: Freedom for the Teacher)

(6.129a) (SxE)				(6.129b) (ExS)		
	1-15 yrs	16-25 yrs	26+ yrs		M	W
M	6.79	7.82	8.34	1-15 yrs	6.79	6.86
	1-15 yrs	16-25 yrs	26+ yrs		W	M
W	6.86	6.87	7.11	16-25 yrs	6.87	7.82
					W	M
				26+ yrs	7.11	8.34

Note: See note under Table—6.3.

(j) Factor X: Emotional

Factor X also contained only three items. The mean scores of different sub-groups of *Ss* on this factor and the results of *t* test are presented in Table 6.130. It could be seen from the table that all the sub-groups of *Ss* had a significantly negative attitude towards the new system of evaluation as measured by this factor also.

Table—6.130 Means, SDs and *t* Values of Different Sub-groups of Teachers (Factor X: Emotional)

Group	N	M	S.D	*t*
Whole group	510	8.13	2.11	9.36***
Sec. grades	170	8.02	2.13	5.98***
B.Eds.	340	8.19	2.11	7.11***
M	300	8.11	2.12	7.26***
W	210	8.16	2.12	5.74***
U	180	8.12	1.96	6.03***
SU	180	8.04	2.28	5.65***
R	150	8.26	2.09	4.31***
1-15	157	7.69	1.99	8.24***
16-25	232	8.55	2.06	3.35***
26+	121	7.91	2.24	5.36***

Note: See note under Table—6.2.

Many teachers feel that lack of detentions hampered students' seriousness in studies and that they would study seriously for their progress if there were detentions and could boldly face the competitive examinations. A majority of teachers feel that occasional failures do not develop inferiority complexes among students. This explains the negative attitude of the teachers towards the non-detention system as measured by this factor.

From the results of ANOVA (Table 6.131) it could be observed that the *F* ratios for locality ($F = 3.67$) and that for experience ($F = 3.06$) were significant. From Table 6.132 it could be seen that the mean attitude scores of *SU, U* and *R* localities were 8.04, 8.12 and 8.26 respectively, the difference between any two means was however, not significant. Table 6.132 shows the mean scores of different sub-groups of teachers classified according to their experience. It could be seen that teachers with 16-25 years obtained the highest mean score and differed significantly from the other two groups of teachers.

Table—6.131 Results of Analysis of Variance (Factor X: Emotional)

Source	SS	df	MSS	*F*
Lt	0.01	1	0.01	0.01@
S	0.01	1	0.01	0.01@
L	4.87	2	2.43	3.67*
E	4.06	2	2.03	3.06*
LtxS	1.46	1	1.46	2.21@
LtxL	6.40	2	3.20	4.83*
LtxE	0.92	2	0.46	0.69@
SxL	1.81	2	0.90	1.36@
SxE	0.85	2	0.43	0.64@
LxE	2.68	4	0.67	1.01@
LtxSxL	0.54	2	0.27	0.41@
LtxSxE	2.40	2	1.20	1.82@
LtxLxE	3.01	4	0.75	1.13@
SxLxE	1.19	4	0.30	0.45@
LtxSxLxE	3.23	4	0.81	1.22@
Error	314.17	474	0.66	
Total	**347.60**	**509**		

Note: See note under Table—6.2.

Table—6.132 Mean Scores of *Ss* Hailing from Different Localities and the Results of *t* Test (Factor X: Emotional)

SU	U	R
8.04	8.12	8.26

Note: See note under Table—6.3.

Table—6.133 Mean Scores of *Ss* Belonging to Different Durations of Experience and the Results of *t* Test (Factor: X: Emotional)

1-15 yrs	26+ yrs	16-25 yrs
7.69	7.91	8.59

Note: See note under Table—6.3.

The two factor interaction between level of teaching and locality was also significant. Table 6.134 shows the mean scores of teachers classified according to the two variables. It could be seen from the table that in the case of Secondary grades, teachers from *R* localities scored highest (M = 8.62) and differed significantly from those of *SU* localities who scored the least (M = 7.77), whereas in the case of B.Ed. assistants, there was

Table—6.134 Mean Scores of *Ss* Classified According to the Variable Level of Teaching and Locality to Explain LtxL Interaction Effect (Factor X: Emotional)

(6.134a) (LtxL)				(6.134b) (LxLt)		
	SU	U	R		B.Eds.	Sec. grades
Sec. grades	7.77	8.38	8.62	U	7.98	8.38
	U	R	SU		Sec. grades	B. Eds.
B. Eds.	7.98	8.08	8.48	SU	7.77	8.48
					B. Eds.	Sec. grades
				R	8.08	8.62

Note: See note under Table—6.3.

no significant difference between the three groups of teachers. Further, considering difference between B.Eds and Secondary grades, the two categories of teachers differed significantly in the case of *SU* localities only, while there was no significant difference between them in the case of *U* and *R* localities.

(k) Factor XI: Dullards-Wastage and Stagnation

Table 6.135 shows the mean scores and SDs of different sub-groups of teachers on this factor which had 4 items with a neutral point of 12. It could be said that all the sub-groups of *Ss* without any exception had a highly negative attitude towards this system as measured by this factor.

Table—6.135 Mean, SDs and *t* Values of Different Sub-groups of Teachers (Factor XI: Dull Ards-Wastage and Stagnation)

Group	N	M	S.D	*t*
Whole group	510	9.96	2.58	17.90***
Sec. grades	170	9.98	2.62	10.07***
B.Eds.	340	9.96	2.56	14.70***
M	300	10.04	2.68	12.67***
W	210	9.85	2.43	12.79***
U	180	9.86	2.41	11.94***
SU	180	10.22	2.58	9.27***
R	150	9.78	2.76	9.82***
1-15	157	9.87	2.49	10.73***
16-25	232	10.01	2.80	10.82***
26+	121	9.99	2.25	9.81***

Note: See note under Table—6.2.

Teachers seem to hold the old belief that detaining a student in a class will help him learn better (though many studies—*McCullers* (1978), *McGraws* (1978), *Gayen* and *Lyle* (1971), *Glucksberg* (1962) and *Dornbush* (1965) have shown that it was not true). Because there were common examinations at the VII and X class levels, where the student has to pass the examination to go to the next higher class, there is rush for extra coaching and parents try to send their children for tutions under reputed teachers. Though teachers agree that in the non-detention system wastage and stagnation is reduced, they do not fully agree that detentions make learning a part-time activity as contended by the supporters of the non-detention system.

Table 6.136 gives the results of analysis of variance for this factor. From the table it may be seen that none of the *F* ratios was significant. This shows that the effect of any of the variables—level of teaching or sex, or locality or experience—on the attitude of teachers was not significant at 0.05 level.

Table—6.136 Results of Analysis of Variance (Factor XI: Dullards-Wastage and Stagnation)

Source	SS	df	MSS	*F*
Lt	0.07	1	0.07	0.07@
S	1.71	1	1.71	1.65@
L	1.09	2	0.55	0.53@
E	2.06	2	1.03	0.10@
LtxS	0.47	1	0.47	0.45@
LtxL	3.49	2	1.74	1.69@
LtxE	4.07	2	2.03	1.96@
SxL	0.59	2	0.29	0.28@
SxE	1.70	2	0.85	0.82@
LxE	1.15	4	0.29	0.28@
LtxSxL	0.18	2	0.09	0.09@
LtxSxE	1.25	2	0.63	0.61@
LtxLxE	3.84	4	0.96	0.93@
SxLxE	2.46	4	0.62	0.60@
LtxSxLxE	3.37	4	0.84	0.81@
Error	490.83	474	1.04	
Total	**518.34**	**509**		

Note: See note under Table—6.2.

(l) *Factor XII: Competence*

Table 6.137 shows the mean scores of different sub-groups of *Ss* on this factor which had 4 items with 12 as the neutral point. It could be seen that all the sub-groups of *Ss* irrespective of level of teaching or sex or locality or experience had a highly negative attitude towards the system as measured by this factor also.

In this system there was no discrimination between dull and intelligent students as the role of examinations was minised and the students did not evince real interest in the tests conducted as the marks in the tests were of no real value for them. The teachers probably feel because of lack of seriousness on the part of the students, and the scope for indulging in wasteful activities they may not become good citizens. This explains the negative attitude of the teachers towards this system as measured by this factor.

Table—6.137 Means, SDs and *t* Values of Different Sub-groups of Teachers (Factor XII: Competence)

Group	N	M	S.D	*t*
Whole group	510	8.61	3.17	24.21***
Sec. grades	170	8.56	3.31	13.52***
B.Eds.	340	8.63	3.10	20.04***
M	300	8.72	3.10	18.34***
W	210	8.45	3.27	15.73***
U	180	9.23	3.16	11.78***
SU	180	8.44	3.17	15.11***
R	150	8.05	3.09	15.59***
1-15	157	8.05	2.95	16.77***
16-25	232	8.69	3.21	15.69***
26+	121	9.16	3.29	9.50***

Note: See note under Table—6.2.

Table—6.138 Results of Analysis of Variance (Factor XII: Competence)

Source	SS	df	MSS	*F*
Lt	2.88	1	2.88	1.98@
S	2.74	1	2.74	1.88@
L	17.11	2	8.56	5.87**
E	21.38	2	10.69	7.33***
LtxS	0.62	1	0.62	0.43@
LtxL	5.95	2	2.98	2.04@
LtxE	3.95	2	1.98	1.35@
SxL	8.90	2	4.45	3.05*
SxE	5.05	2	2.53	1.73@
LxE	4.32	4	1.08	0.74@
LtxSxL	10.46	2	5.23	3.59*
LtxSxE	3.85	2	1.93	1.32*
LtxLxE	4.21	4	1.05	0.72@
SxLxE	24.77	4	6.19	4.25**
LtxSxLxE	22.15	4	5.54	3.80**
Error	691.47	474	1.46	
Total	**829.82**	**509**		

Note: See note under Table—6.2.

From Table 6.138 in which the results of ANOVA are presented, it may be seen that the *F* ratios for the main effects of locality (*F* = 5.87) and experience (F = 7.33) were significant. Table 6.139 shows that teachers from *R* localities had the lowest score. Teachers from *U* localities had the highest score and differed significantly from those belonging to *R* and *SU* localities. Table 6.140 shows that teachers with 1-15 years of experience obtained the least mean score and differed significantly from the other two groups of teachers.

Table—6.139 Mean Scores of *Ss* Belonging to Different Localities and the Results of *t* Test (Factor XII: Competence)

R	SU	U
8.05	8.44	9.23

Note: See note under Table—6.3.

Table—6.140 Mean Scores of *Ss* Belonging to Different Durations of Experiences and the Results of *t* Test (Factor XII: Competence)

1-15 yrs	16-25 yrs	26+ yrs
8.05	8.69	9.16

Note: See note under Table—6.3.

Table—6.141 Mean Scores of *Ss* Classified According to the Variables Sex and Locality to Explain SxL Interaction Effect (Factor XII: Competence)

	(6.141a) (SxL)				(6.141b) (LxS)	
M	U 7.77	SU 9.04	R 9.34	U	M 7.77	W 8.48
W	SU 8.26	U 8.48	R 8.84	SU	W 8.26	M 9.04
				R	W 8.84	M 9.34

Note: See note under Table—6.3.

The two factor interaction between sex and locality was significant (F = 3.50). Table 6.141 explains the significant SxL interaction effect. It may be observed that in the case of men teachers those from U localities scored the least (7.77) and differed significantly from the other two groups, while in the case of women none of the differences between the three means was significant. The remaining 2 factor interactions were not significant.

However, the three factor interactions Lt x S x L and S x L x E and the four factor interaction were significant.

(m) Factor XIII: Ethical Value

The mean attitude scores of different sub-groups of *Ss* for factor XIII are presented in Table 6.142. It could be observed from the table that all the sub-groups of *Ss* without any exception had a highly negative attitude towards the system as measured by this factor also, which had 3 items with a neutral point of 9.

The teachers seem to feel that in this system the students do not have an immediate goal (like passing the examination and getting promoted) which hampers their interest in studies. Teachers also probably tend to take their duty little easy, producing a negative orientation towards the system on their part.

Table 6.143 shows the results of ANOVA of the scores on this factor. From the table it could be observed that the main effect of locality was significant.

Table—6.142 Means, SDs and *t* Values of Different Sub-groups of Teachers (Factor XIII: Ethical Value)

Group	N	M	S.D	*t*
Whole group	510	5.71	2.83	26.32***
Sec. grades	170	5.40	2.86	16.39***
B.Eds.	340	5.86	2.81	20.67***
M	300	5.80	2.83	19.55***
W	210	5.57	2.83	17.61***
U	180	5.97	2.64	15.40***
SU	180	5.46	2.92	16.34***
R	150	5.69	2.93	13.80***
1-15	157	5.15	2.65	18.20***
16-25	232	5.95	2.95	15.74***
26+	121	5.96	2.73	12.27***

Note: See note under Table—6.2.

Table—6.143 Results of Analysis of Variance (Factor XIII: Ethical Value)

Source	SS	df	MSS	*F*
Lt	0.13	1	0.13	0.11[@]
S	3.91	1	3.91	3.34[@]
L	11.03	2	5.51	4.72**
E	5.68	2	2.84	2.43[@]
LtxS	0.35	1	0.35	0.30[@]
LtxL	2.73	2	0.37	1.17[@]
LtxE	0.46	2	0.23	0.20[@]
SxL	3.18	2	1.59	1.36[@]
SxE	1.84	2	0.92	0.79[@]
LxE	14.21	4	3.55	3.04[@]
LtxSxL	5.88	2	2.94	2.52[@]
LtxSxE	1.48	2	0.74	0.63[@]
LtxLxE	4.62	4	1.16	0.99[@]
SxLxE	3.93	4	0.98	0.84[@]
LtxSxLxE	15.43	4	3.86	3.30*
Error	553.63	474	1.17	
Total	**628.48**	**509**		

Note: See note under Table—6.2.

Table 6.144 shows that the *Ss* from *SU* localities scored the least (M = 5.46) whereas those from *U* localities scored the highest (M = 5.97) with teachers from *R* localities (M = 5.69) falling in between. However, the difference between any two localities was not significant. L x E interaction was significant, indicating that the effect of locality of the teachers was not independent of the level of experience of the teachers involved and vice versa. The mean scores presented in Table 6.145 explain the situation. It could be seen from the table that in the *U* localities teachers with 16-25 years of experience obtained the least score (M = 5.54) and differed significantly from the teachers with 26 or more years of experience. In the case of *SU* localities, teachers with 16-25 years scored the highest (M = 6.07) and differed significantly from the other two sub-groups of teachers. In the case of *R* localities, teachers with 1-15 years of experience scored the least (M = 4.64) and differed significantly from the other two sub-groups of teachers.

The *F* ratio (3.30) for the four factor interaction was significant, indicating that the effect of any three variables taken at a time was not independent of the level of the fourth variable involved.

Table—6.144 Mean Scores of *Ss* Belonging to Different Localities and the Results of *t* Test (Factor XIII: Ethical Value)

SU	R	U
5.46	5.69	5.97

Note: See note under Table—6.3.

Table—6.145 Mean Scores of *Ss* Classified According to the Variables Locality and Experience of the Teachers to Explain L x E Interaction Effect (Factor XIII: Ethical Value)

(6.145a) (xE)

	16-25 yrs	1-15 yrs	26+ yrs
U	5.54	5.89	6.58
	26+ yrs	1-15yrs	16-25 yrs
SU	4.90	4.91	6.07
	1-15 yrs	16-25 yrs	26+ yrs
R	4.64	6.18	6.30

(6.145b) (ExL)

	R	SU	U
1-15 yrs	4.64	4.91	5.89
	U	SU	R
16-25 yrs	5.54	6.07	6.18
	SU	R	U
26+ yrs	4.90	6.30	6.58

Note: see note under Table—6.3.

(n) Factor XIV: Natural Setting

Table 6.146 shows the mean scores of different sub-groups of *Ss* on this factor which had 3 items with a neutral point of 9.

Table—6.146 Means and SDs of Different Sub-groups of Teachers with the Results of *t* Value for the Neutral Point (Factor XIV: Natural Setting)

Group	N	M	S.D	*t*
Whole group	510	10.50	2.31	14.66***
Sec. grades	170	10.19	2.54	6.10***
B. Eds.	340	10.65	2.18	13.96***
M	300	10.44	2.27	11.02***
W	210	10.57	2.38	9.58***
U	180	10.66	2.24	9.92***
SU	180	10.33	2.34	7.63***
R	150	10.51	2.37	7.77***
1-15	157	10.61	2.39	8.47***
16-25	232	10.50	2.35	9.72***
26+	121	10.35	2.16	6.85***

Note: See note under Table—6.2.

From Table 6.147 it may be seen that the mean score of the whole group of *Ss* was 10.50 which was highly significant (t = 14.66) at 0.001 level. This shows that the group as a whole had a highly positive attitude towards the non-detention system as measured by this factor. Similar results were obtained for all the sub-groups of *Ss* also.

Because there were no detentions in the new system, there will not be much difference in the age of children in any class. Naturally this homogeneity makes the work of the teacher easier. Further, in the non-detention system there is scope for the student to learn in a natural setting without any fear of detentions. Teachers seem to endorse these points as indicated by the positive attitude score obtained by them on this factor.

Table—6.147 Results of Analysis of Variance (Factor XIV: Natural Setting)

Source	SS	df	MSS	*F*
Lt	0.51	1	0.51	0.61@
S	0.12	1	0.12	0.15@
L	2.04	2	1.02	1.23@
E	1.31	2	0.65	0.79@
LtxS	0.93	1	0.93	1.13@
LtxL	1.41	2	0.71	0.85@
LtxE	0.54	2	0.27	0.32@
SxL	4.30	2	2.15	2.59@
SxE	0.43	2	0.22	0.26@
LxE	1.16	4	0.29	0.35@
LtxSxL	2.55	2	1.28	1.54@
LtxSxE	0.21	2	0.11	0.13@
LtxLxE	1.99	4	0.50	0.60@
SxLxE	2.86	4	0.71	0.86@
LtxSxLxE	2.39	4	0.58	0.70@
Error	393.23	474	0.83	
Total	**415.94**	**509**		

Note: See note under Table—6.2.

The results of ANOVA presented in table 6.147 shows that none of the *F* values were significant. This shows that there was no significant difference between men and women teachers, or between B.Eds and Secondary grade teachers, or between those belonging to different localities or those with different levels of experience, with regard to their attitude towards the new system as measured by this factor. All sub-groups had a positive attitude.

PART III

Attitude of Administrators Towards the Non-detention System

The administrators—Headmasters, Gazetted Inspectors and District Educational officers—are the people who have to get any system implemented in the schools. As such it may be of interest to know their attitude towards the non-detention system. For this purpose, the attitude scores of the administrators were analysed. The results of this analysis are presented hereunder.

Table—6.148 Mean Scores, SDs and *t* Values of Different Factors (Administrators —N = 40)

S.No.	Factors	M	S.D	*t*
1.	Overall score	154.88	25.10	4.82***
2.	Policy implementation	34.10	8.71	7.92***
3.	Facility	8.70	2.86	0.66@
4.	Teaching learning	14.43	2.11	1.72@
5.	Personality	10.35	1.96	4.37***
6.	Discipline	9.15	2.34	0.41@
7.	Incentive for progress	9.95	2.36	2.54*
8.	Learning skills	7.46	2.66	3.81***
9.	Educational policy	8.63	2.12	1.12@
10.	Freedom for the teachers	7.83	3.61	2.06*
11.	Emotional	8.18	1.99	2.63*
12.	Dullards—Wastage and Stagnation	10.80	2.55	2.97**
13.	Competence	9.33	3.32	5.09***
14.	Ethical value	6.45	3.10	5.19***
15.	Learning in a natural setting	9.60	2.26	1.68@

Note: See note under Table—6.2.

The means and SDs of the attitude scores of the administrators on the different factors are presented in Table 6.148. The mean overall attitude scores of the administrators was 154.88 which is below the neutral point. When *t* test was applied to see whether it was significantly different from the neutral point, the t value obtained was 4.82 significant at 0.001 level.

An examination of the results of the analysis of the factor-wise scores shows that the administrators had a significant negative attitude towards the system as assessed by factors—Policy implementation (I), Learning skills (VII), Freedom for the teacher (IX), Emotional (X), Dullards—Wastage and Stagnation (XI), Competence (XII) and Ethical values (XIII). In the case of factors—Personality (IV) and Incentive for Progress (VI) the mean scores were significantly above the neutral point showing that the administrators had a positive attitude towards the new system of evaluation as measured by those factors. In the case of factors—Facility (II), Teaching learning (III), Discipline (V), Educational policy (VIII) and learning in a natural setting (XIV) the difference between the mean score and the neutral point was not significant indicating a neutral attitude of the administrators towards the system as measured by the above five factors.

The administrators, as in the case of teachers and students, seem to feel that in the non-detention system the role of malpractices in the examinations were reduced and the scope for corruption in the schools was curtailed. They also seem to endorse the view that in the new system the stimulus to work is within the system itself rather than from the threat of detentions and that teachers will have ample time and opportunity to develop the personality of the children.

However, like teachers and students, administrators too were against the new system of evaluation when they observe some of the ill effects of the system like eroding the moral values of teachers and Headmasters, spoiling the academic career of the students as they just attend the school for the sake of attendance alone and sometimes they do not even care to purchase their books. Administrators also seem to accept that in the system students who do not have mastery even in their mother tongue were getting promoted to the next class. They also seem to feel that since many students were able to come up to X class level due to the non-detention system, unemployment problem was getting aggrevated. Further, since the system failed to discriminate the intelligent and the dual, the intelligent lost confidence in the system of education itself.

From these results it could be said that in general the administrators were also not in favour of the new system.

PART IV

Comparison of Attitude of Students, Teachers and Administrators Towards the Non-detention System

It was observed in parts I, II and III that generally speaking students, teachers as well as administrators had a negative attitude towards the non-detention system. However, is there any significant difference between the three groups with regard to their reaction to the different aspects of the non-detention system? A comparative analysis of the attitude of the three groups may throw light on some salient issues related to the new system. Hence, the attitude scores of the three groups of *Ss* were analysed by applying one way analysis of variance.

The mean scores of the three groups of *Ss* and the results of ANOVA of the overall score and the factor-wise scores are presented in a summary or the Table 6.149 *in page 301* without using 30 different tables to conserve space, without loss of essential information.

(a) *Overall Score*

It may be seen from the table that the mean overall attitude scores of students, teachers and administrators were 156.36, 147.99 and 154.88 respectively. All the mean scores were significantly below the neutral point (174). This shows that all the groups had a negative attitude towards the non-detention system. (*see Fig. 6.20*).

Table—6.149 Means, Sds, *t* and *F* Values of Different Samples for Different Factors

S. No.	Name of Factors		Students (N = 1080)	Teachers (N = 510)	Adminis—tators (N = 40)	Neutral point	F (df = 2, 1627)	E.M.S.
1	2		3	4	5	6	7	8
1.	Overall score	M =	156.36***	147.99***	154.88***	174	52.41***	240.70
		SD =	14.72	18.87	25.10			
2.	Policy implementation	M =	31.31***	31.56***	34.10***			
		SD =	7.00	6.92	8.71	45	0.44@	343.30
3.	Facility	M =	9.37***	8.19***	8.70@			
		SD =	2.70	2.81	2.86	9	33.28***	7.45
4.	Teaching-learning	M =	14.17***	14.12***	14.43@			
		SD =	2.93	2.58	2.11	15	0.27@	7.75
5.	Personality	M =	9.83***	10.77***	10.35***	9	31.86***	4.66
		SD =	2.30	1.91	1.96			
6.	Discipline	M =	9.67***	9.09@	9.15@			
		SD =	2.42	2.23	2.34	9	11.34***	5.41
7.	Incentive for progress	M =	10.60***	9.60***	9.95*	9	28.29***	6.35
		SD =	2.49	2.64	2.36			
8.	Learning skills	M =	7.63***	6.40***	7.40***			
		SD =	2.57	2.70	2.66	9	38.61***	6.79

(Contd...)

Table—6.149 (Contd...)

1	2		3	4	5	6	7	8
9.	Educational policy	M =	7.95***	8.06***	8.63@	9	1.78@	5.04
		SD =	2.41	1.87	2.12			
10.	Freedom for the teachers	M =	9.76***	7.34***	7.83*	9	126.23***	8.32
		SD =	2.76	3.09	3.61			
11.	Emotional	M =	8.34***	8.13***	8.18**	9	1.64	5.13
		SD =	2.35	2.11	1.99			
12.	Dullards—Wastage and stagnation	M =	10.61***	9.96***	10.80**	9	11.59***	6.67
		SD =	2.60	2.58	2.55			
13.	Competence	M =	9.82***	8.61***	9.33***	12	25.79***	10.02
		SD =	3.17	3.17	3.32			
14.	Ethical value	M =	6.43***	5.71***	6.45***	9	11.33***	8.22
		SD =	2.88	2.83	3.11			
15.	Learning in a natural setting	M =	10.87***	10.50***	9.60@	9	8.32***	6.18
		SD =	2.59	2.31	2.26			

Note:

1. @ All the mean scores except those marked thus are significantly different from the neutral point.
2. All the F ratios except those marked significant at 0.001 level for 2 and 1627 df.
3. EMS = Error Mean Square.
4. The values of different sums of squares for any factor can be calculated as shown below, from which the complete ANOVA table can be constructed if required:

Between Groups Mean Squre (BGMS) = F value × EMS

Between groups sum of squres = BGMS x 2

Error Sum of Squares, EMS = 1627

Total Sum of Squares, BGSS + EMS

To examine whether there was any significant difference between the three groups of *Ss*, one way analysis of variance was applied. The obtained *F* ratio was 52.41, highly significant even at 0.001 level for 2 and 1627 df. This indicates that there was a significant difference between the attitude of the three groups towards the new system of evaluation.

To see which group of *Ss* differed significantly from the others *t* test was applied. The results of the *t* test presented in Table 6.150 shows that the mean score (147.99) of teaches was significantly lower than that (156.36) of students. The difference between teachers and administrators or that between administrators and students was not significant. All the sub-groups had a negative attitude towards the non-detention system. But teachers had a far more negative attitude than students.

Similar analysis was carried out for all the factors separately.

(b) Factor I: Policy Implementation

It may be seen from Table 6.149 that the mean scores of students, teachers and administrators on factor—Policy implementation (I) were 31.311, 31.51 and 34.10 respectively. As all the mean scores were significantly below the neutral point indicating a negative attitude of all the three groups towards the new system as measured by this factor. The *F* ratio (1.44) for the difference between the three groups was not significant. This shows that there was no significant difference between the attitude of students, teachers and administrators towards the non-detention system as measured by this factor.

(c) Factor II: Facility

The mean scores of students, teachers and administrators on factor—facility (II) were 9.37, 8.29 and 8.70 respectively. The mean attitude score of the students was significantly above the neutral point, while that of teachers was significantly below it. In the case of administrators the difference between the mean attitude score and the neutral point was not significant at 0.05 level. Thus students had a favourable attitude, teachers had an unfavourable attitude, while administrators had a neutral attitude towards the new system as measured by this factor.

Table—6.150 Mean Scores and the Results of *t* Tests for Different Factors of Different Samples.

S.No.	Names of factors	Results of t test		
1.	Overall score	T 147.99	A 154.88	S 156.36
2.	Facility	T 8.19	A 8.70	S 9.37
3.	Personality	S 9.83	A 10.35	T 10.77
4.	Discipline	T 9.09	A 9.15	S 9.67
5.	Incentive for Progress	T 9.60	A 9.95	S 10.60
6.	Learning skills	T 6.40	A 7.40	S 7.63
7.	Freedom for the teachers	T 7.34	A 7.83	S 9.76
8.	Dullards—Wastage and stangation	T 9.96	S 10.61	A 10.80
9.	Competence	T 8.61	A 6.33	A 9.82
10.	Ethical valueO	T 5.71	S 6.43	A 6.45
11.	Learning in a natural setting	A 9.60	T 10.50	S 10.87

Note: 1. See note under Table—6.3.

2. S = students; T = Teachers; A = Administrators

Analysis of variance of the attitude scores of the three groups yielded an *F* ratio of 33.28 significant at 0.001 level for 2 and 1627 df. The results of *t* test presented in Table 6.150 show that students differed significantly from teachers in attitude towards non-detention system as measured by this their factor. In this system when examinations are not conducted with its real spirit, naturally students feel free and happy. However, teachers do not feel so because in any educational set up teaching, learning and evaluation should go hand in hand each contributing to the other. Therefore, they seem to be averse to the new system and do not accept that in this system students learn freely under a natural set up.

(d) Factor III: Teaching Learning

With regard to factor III—Teaching learning, the mean scores of the three groups of *Ss*—students, teachers and administrators as were 14.17, 14.12 and 14.43 respectively which are all below neutral point. However, the difference between the mean scores and the neutral point was significant in the case of students and teachers only. The *F* ratio for the significance of the difference between the three groups was not significant.

(e) Factor IV: Personality

It may be observed from Table 6.149 that all the sub-groups had a significantly positive attitude towards the new system as measured by factor-Personality (IV). Analysis of variance yielded an *F* ratio of 31.86 which is highly significant even at 0.001 level for 2 and 1627 df. From the results of *t* test shown in Table 6.150 we find that the mean of teachers (M = 10.77) was significantly higher than that of students (M = 9.83). The non-detention system helped to reduce malpractices in examinations and promotions of students and provided the teachers with opportunities for developing the desired personality characteristics among the students. Teachers seemed to appreciate the facts better than students.

(f) Factor V: Discipline

The mean scores of students, teachers and administrators on factor—Discipline (V) were 9.67, 9.09 and 9.15 respectively. All the means were above the neutral point. However, the difference between the mean and the neutral point was significant only in the case of students. Teachers and administrators had a neutral attitude towards the non-detention system as measured by this factor.

F ratio obtained from analysis of variance on this factor was 11.34 significant at 0.001 level. Only the difference between the mean score of students and teachers was significant. Other differences between means were not significant at 0.05 level.

(g) Factor VI: Incentive for Progress

Mean scores of 10.60, 9.60 and 9.95 were obtained by students, teachers and administrators respectively on this factor. All the mean scores were significantly above the neutral point indicating that all the sub-groups had a positive attitude towards the new system of evaluation as measured by factor—Incentive for progress (VI). The *F* ratio obtained from analysis of variance on this factor was 28.29 significant at 0.001 level. The mean score (10.60) of students was significantly higher than that (9.60) of teachers (Table 6.150). Teachers accept the positive aspect of the new system as measured by this factor, like in the non-detention system the stimulation to learn comes from within the system, defects in the examinations are reduced, there is good scope for the capable to develop well in the new system. But their intensity of favouring the system is less than that of the students.

(h) Factor VII: Learning Skills

The mean scores of students, teachers and administrators on this factor were 7.63, 6.40, 7.40 respectively all of which were significantly below the neutral point. This shows a negative attitude of all the sub-groups of *Ss* towards this system as assessed by this factor. The significant *F ratio* and the results of *t* test show that teachers had a far more negative attitude than administrators and students. Students have to undergo the system, while teachers have to implement it and administrators have to supervise its implementation. As implementors teachers naturally feel the real brunt of the system and one more answer to the system than others as measured by this negative aspects of the factor. For example it is they who have to handle students who get promoted to higher classes without adequate knowledge even in the basic skills.

(i) Factor VIII: Educational Policy

The mean scores of all the sub-groups were below the neutral point on this factor also. However, the difference between the mean score of administrators and the neutral point was not significant. The *F* ratio (1.78) for the difference between the attitude of the three groups was not significant indicating that there was no significant difference between the attitude of students, teachers and administrators towards the non-detention system as measured by this factor.

(j) Factor IX: Freedom for the Teachers

It may be seen from Table 6.149 that the mean score of students (M = 9.76) was significantly above the neutral point indicating a positive attitude of the students towards the new system. However, the mean scores of teachers (M = 7.34) and administrators (M = 7.83) were significantly below the neutral point, revealing a negative attitude of both these groups towards the system as assessed by this factor. Analysis of variance of the attitude scores yielded a significant *F* ratio of 126.23. Evidently, the students had a more favourable attitude compared to administrators and teachers. Teachers and administrators do not seem to accept that teachers will have ample time and freedom to experiment with new methods of teaching and evaluation to develop desired intellectual skills among the students.

(k) Factor X: Emotional

With regard to factor—Emotional (X) the mean scores of students, teachers as well as administrators were significantly below the neutral point, indicating a negative attitude of all the groups towards the non-detention system. There was no significant difference between the three groups as indicated by the *F* ratio of 1.04 which was not significant at 0.05 level.

(l) Factor XI: Dullards—Wastage and Stagnation

The mean scores of all the three sub-groups were significantly above the neutral point for this factor, showing a positive attitude towards the system. The significant *F* ratio of 11.59, and the results of *t* test show that students and administrators were more favourable towards the new system. One of the aims of introducing the non-detention system is to root out wastage and stagnation, the two eroding agents of the education system. The teachers and administrators are very well aware of the magnitude of this problem and know how this problem of wastage and stagnation has been reduced to a minimum in the new system.

(m) Factor XII: Competence

The mean scores of students, teachers and administrators on factor—Competence (XII) were 9.82, 8.61 and 9.33 respectively. All the mean scores were significantly below the neutral point, indicating a negative attitude towards the system. From the results of ANOVA ($F = 25.79$) and the results of *t* test it may be seen that teachers and administrators expressed a more unfavourable attitude towards the system compared to students.

(n) Factor XIII: Ethical Value

With regard to factor—Ethical value (XIII) the mean scores of students, teachers and administrators were 6.43, 5.71 and 6.45 respectively all of which were significantly below the neutral point indicating a significant negative attitude of all the sub-groups towards the system. The *F* ratio for the significance of the difference between the three groups was 11.33 significant at 0.001 level. The results of *t* show that teacher's attitude was more unfavourable than that of students and administrators as in the case of earlier factors. Teachers seem to be very sensitive to the deterioration of educational standards and their moral values because of this system. even devoted teachers got slackened in this system because of lessening interest among the students.

(o) Factor XIV: Learning in a Natural Setting

Students, teachers and administrators obtained mean scores of 10.87, 10.50 and 9.60 respectively on this factor. All the mean scores were above the neutral point. However, the mean score of administrators was not significantly different from the neutral point, indicating a neutral attitude of administrators towards the system as assessed by this factor. The *F* ratio (8.32) for the difference between the three groups was significant at 0.001 level for 2 and 1627 df. The results of *t* test show that all the three sub-groups differed significantly from each other with regard to their attitude towards the new system as measured by this factor. Though students, teachers and administrators seem to agree on the aspects measured by this factor (like providing education under natural set up, incentives, discipline etc.) students and teachers seem to more strongly agree with them than the administrators.

Conclusions

From the above results the following conclusions may be drawn:

1. The overall attitude of the pupils towards the non-detention system was significantly negative. This was true irrespective of their sex, social class or locality.
2. It was found that the overall attitude of the teaches towards the new system of evaluation was also

negative. This was true irrespective of their sex, locality, level of the teaching or length of experience.

3. The overall attitude of the administrators towards the new system of evaluation was also negative.

4. There was no significant difference between the overall attitude of pupils, teachers and administrators towards the new system of evaluation.

□□□

7

Summary and Conclusions

I. THE PROBLEM

There is no gainsaying that it is the type of education of a country that makes or mars it. It is but natural therefore, that education and problems related to it are topics of deep concern today for the educationists in a developing like India.

Among the many problems, those connected with evaluation have assumed great importance since evaluation is part and parcel of any sound system of education and teaching, learning and evaluation go hand in hand each inseparable from the other. It is indeed in the fitness of things that Commission after Commission ever since the beginning of the 20th century made attempts to resurrect the evaluation system from all its lapses and to put it in the right gear.

The *University Education Commission* (1948) was quite categorical in its unequivocal condemnation of the present examination system when it said "if we were to suggest any single reform in Indian education, it should be that of examinations." The *Report of the Secondary Education Commission* (1954) was very critical of the system of examinations and remarked that the present examinations do not help us in evaluating the real intellectual achievements of the pupils. *The Education Commission* (1966) recommended for abolition of set syllabi and the external examination based upon them and emphasised that they should be replaced by a system of internal and continuous evaluation by teachers themselves. *The National Policy on Education* (1986) stressed that "assessment of performance is an integral part of any process of learning and teaching". As a part of sound educational strategy, examinations should be employed to bring about qualitative improvements in education. The objective will be to recast the examination system so as to ensure a method of assessment that is a valid and reliable measure of student development and a powerful instrument for improving teaching and learning. The policy laid great stress on de-emphasising the role of examination since, unfortunately in India, toady examinations dominate the field of education. Examination is the main object both for students and teachers and learning has become secondary. The efficiency of a school or a teacher is judged by the examination results. Thus the whole system of education, the teaching, the methods adopted for it, learning and the methods of study, all centre round the system of examinations.

According to *Bloom* (1962) "in India, an examination system has been created which has a powerful effect on all the students and teachers who come into contact with it. It has reduced learning to a part time activity, teaching to the coverage of particular material and education to a relatively drab and meaningless activity. This same system can, if improved, restore learning and teaching to the creative and powerful force it can and must be in an India that is coming to be".

The monarchical control and undifferentiated regimentation of the examination system as the sole measure of evaluation procedure has been bitterly denounced by many not only in India but also elsewhere. According to *Singha* (1984), "vexed with the faulty evaluation system many Western countries abolished examinations. In Canada Ontario abolished its examinations in 1967, Manitaba did so in 1970,

Queensland has announced plans to terminate all its secondary school examinations and other Australian states have given notice of similar moves. Sweden has abolished all external examinations and Norway is reported to be moving in the same direction. Great Britain is experimenting with school based examinations and reference tests, while the United States has for many years operated on elaborate system of aptitude and achievement testing not tied to any particular school prescription".

Due to the terror it creates among the pupils, it is no wonder, many feel that education without examinations and detentions will be tension free. Then the students will be able to learn in a natural set up (*Kabra,* 1971). P.V. Narasimha Rao (1971), the then Minister of Education, Government of Andhra pradesh, said that education is best imparted in an atmosphere of free progress where the incentive and urge to improve spring from within the educational process rather than from the terror of examinations and detentions. With this thinking he abolished detentions and introduced a system called non-detention system, which is also popularly known as the system of automatic promotions. Under this system the student will be automatically promoted to the next class provided he puts in a stipulated percentage of attendance. However, there will be two common/public examinations during the school career (between the I and X classes), one at the end of the upper primary stage, the other at the end of the secondary stage. The student may be detained if he does not secure the minimum stipulated percentage of marks in these examinations. In all other classes he will be automatically promoted if he has put in the required percentage of attendance.

This system has naturally evoked a mixed reaction from the educational elite of the state as well as of the entire nation. Some contended that examinations and detentions are necessary, if not essential, in any education system, while others denounced them in toto.

Krishnamoorthy (1971) observed that detentions are negative incentives. They do not promote learning on the other hand they lead to unlearning of what has been learnt. Further, they develop inferiority complexes and unfavourable attitude towards the school, the teachers and the system of education as a whole. According to *Kabra* (1971) education is best imparted in an atmosphere of free progress, when the fear of examinations and anxiety of detentions are removed from the total system of education.

Some felt that the teachers will be released from the cruel grip of yearly examinations under the new system (*Sarabachari,* 1971; *Satyanarayana,* 1971). Consequently, the new system of evaluation would allow ample time and freedom to the teachers to experiment with new methods of teaching and evaluation and also to develop the desired intellectual skills and personality aspects among the students (*Krishnamoorthy,* 1971; *Venkata Reddy,* 1971; *Kabra,* 1971; *Rao;* 1977).

It was also felt that this system would reduce wastage and stagnation (Kabra, 1971; *Krishnamoorthy,* 1977; *Rao,* 1977; *Spokesman, Government of Kerala,* 1973). It was contended by some that if a student who was regular to school had not attained the minimum expected level of attainment by the end of the year, the fault may not necessarily be with the student. It may be somewhere else. Such being the case it was not correct to detain him (*Rao,* 1977). Those who believed in the above line of thinking commended the Government of Andhra Pradesh when it introduced the non-detention system. They said it was 'a bold step in the right direction'.

However, the system was criticised by others. They said that the Government has taken the most unacademic decision on an academic matter, and abolished detentions with a stroke of the pen. They argued that this system would tell upon the standards of education, which were already low, because wile fear of examinations can not be commended, some compelling circumstance should be there to motivate the students, especially adolescents, to be regular and to work hard. This was naturally provided by examinations and detentions. Without them the students postpone and postpone their studies and accumulate arears and the net result would be a fall in the standards of education and not improvement of the same (*Editorial, Educational India,* 1971). Though examinations were there in the non-detention system also students would not evince any interest in them as the marks obtained in them were not going to matter much (*Editorial, Educational India,* 1971; *Editorial, The Educational Review,* 1971).

Thus there was a vast divergence of opinion among the educational elite with regard to the effect of the non-detention system. Yet, much of what is known or said about the system is only at the level of opinion and not based on any empirical evidence. A systematic study of the effect of the system in all aspects like achievement, rate of drop-outs, etc., should be made so that the system may be introduced in other States also if the results are commendable.

It will be worthwhile for Andhra Pradesh also to know where it stands, whether the scheme is working on right lines yielding the desired results, or whether drastic modifications are required, and if so in what direction.

II. STATEMENT OF THE PROBLEM

Hence, the present study was designed to evaluate the non-detention system in some important aspects like its effect on the achievement of students, percentage of passes, rate of drop-outs and the attitude of students, teachers and administrators towards the system.

III. OBJECTIVES OF THE STUDY

1. To make a comparative study of the achievement of students under the detention and non-detention systems.
2. To make a comparative study of the percentage of passes in the detention and non-detention systems.

3. To make a comparative study of the rate of drop-outs in the detention and non-detention systems.
4. To assess the attitude of pupils, teachers and administrators, towards the non-detention system.
5. To suggest remedies for the defects, if any, in the new system.

IV. HYPOTHESES

Based upon the above objectives, the following major hypotheses were set up for investigation:

1. There would not be any significant difference between the achievement of pupils under the detention and non-detention systems. This would be true irrespective of their sex, social class and locality to which they belong.

   This hypothesis was tested separately for each of the 6 school subjects and for the total of the marks in all subjects.
2. There would not be any significant difference between the percentage of passes in the two systems. This would be true irrespective of the sex or locality of the pupils.
3. The rate of drop-outs in the non-detention system would be significantly less than that in the detention system. This would be true irrespective of their sex or locality of the pupils.
4. Pupils would have a negative attitude towards the non-detention system. This would be true irrespective or their sex, social class or locality.
5. Teachers would have a negative attitude towards the new system of evaluation. This would be true irrespective of their sex, locality, level of teaching or length of experience.
6. Administrators would have a negative attitude towards the non-detention system.

7. There would not be any significant difference between the attitude of pupils, teachers and administrators towards the new evaluation system.

In addition to the above major hypotheses the following related hypotheses were also set up for investigation:

1. There would not be any significant difference between the achievement of boys and girls;
2. There would not be any significant difference between the achievement of pupils belonging to different social classes;
3. Pupils hailing from different localities would not differ significantly with regard to their achievement;

The above hypotheses were tested separately for each of the 6 subjects and for the total of the marks in all subjects.

V. VARIABLES STUDIED

Since the problem envisages an evaluation of the non-detention system with reference to achievement, percentage of passes, rate of drop-outs and attitude of pupils, teachers and administrators, the dependent and independent variables employed in the study were:

1. Dependent Variables

(a) Achievement

(b) Percentage of passes

(c) Rate of drop-outs

(d) Attitude towards the non-detention system.

2. Independent Variables

(a) System (detention/non-detention)

(b) Sex

(c) Social class

(d) Locality

(e) Level of teaching

(f) Length of experience

VI. DESIGN

The study was essentially of a 2X2X2X3 factorial design with 2 system (detention and non-detention), 2 sexes (boys and girls), 2 social classes (scheduled castes/schedule tribes and other communities) and 3 localities (urban, semi-urban and rural). This was the design employed for analysis of the achievement of students.

For the analysis of the attitude of the pupils towards the new system, 2X3X3 factorial design was employed with 2 sds (boys and girls), 3 social classes (forward castes, backward castes and scheduled castes/scheduled tribes) and 3 localities (urban, semi-urban and rural).

The design for the study of the attitude of teachers was 2X2X3X3 factoral design with 2 sexes (male and female), 2 levels of teaching (B. Ed. Assistants and Secondary Grade Assistants), 3 levels of experience (1-15 years, 16-25 years and 26 or more years of experience) and 3 localities (urban, semi-urban and rural).

VII. SAMPLE

1. ***Achievement:*** The sample for the study was selected by a multistage stratified random sampling procedure. At the outset from out of the 23 districts in Andhra Pradesh 3 districts were selected at random at the rate of one from each region, viz., Rayalaseema, Circar and Telangana. The secondary schools in each of the districts thus selected were divided as urban, semi-urban and rural depending upon the locality in which they were situated. From each district, four schools from urban areas, six schools from semi-urban areas and eight schools from rural areas were selected at random.

Students who took the X class public examination from the schools selected as above in March 1971 (the last batch of students under the detention system) and in March 1983 (students who had their education right from class I to X under non-detention system) constituted the sample of the study for the analysis of marks. The achievement scores of the above sample of students in the six subjects (Telugu, Hindi, English, Mathematics, Science and Social Studies) in which they take the X class public examination were recorded from the registers maintained in the office of the Commissioner for Government Examinations, Hyderabad, and were analysed. The total number of students whose marks were analysed was 7,740. The marks of these students in each of the six subjects mentioned above and the total of the marks in all the six subjects were analysed separately.

2. Percentage of Passes

The number of students who appeared for the X class public examination from the above schools during the above years and the number of those who passed were recorded from the registers maintained in the schools and the percentage of passes under the two systems was calculated and analysed. The size of the sample for this analysis was 7,740.

3. Rate of Drop-outs

Further, the number of students who were admitted into each class during the selected years viz., 1971 and 1983 and the number who dropped-out before the beginning of the next year were also recorded from the registers maintained in the schools and the rate of drop-outs under the two systems was analysed. The size of the sample for this analysis was 37,764.

4. Attitude

From each of the schools in urban, semi-urban and rural areas selected as mentioned earlier, 30, 20 and 15 X class students respectively were selected by adopting systematic sampling from among the students present in the school on the day of investigation. The total number of students thus selected was 1080. The attitude of these students towards the non-detention system was assessed and analysed.

Similarly 10 B.Ed. assistants and 5 secondary Grade teachers from each urban school and 6 B.Ed. and 4 Secondary Grades from each semi-urban school were selected by adopting systematic sampling from among the teachers present in the school on the day of the investigation. In the case of rural areas since the number of teachers was rather limited all the B.Ed. and Secondary Grade teachers were included in the study by adopting cluster sampling technique. 510 teachers were thus selected and their attitude towards the new system was analysed.

The Headmasters of the schools selected for the study, the Gazetted Inspectors and District Educational Officers of the three districts constituted the population of administrators. From this population a random sample of 40 administrators was selected and their attitude towards the new system of evaluation was analysed.

VIII. TOOLS USED

To assess the attitude of the pupils, teachers and administrators towards the non-detention system, an attitude scale was constructed based on Likert's method of summated ratings. At the outset a pilot form containing 67 items was prepared. Each of the item was arranged on a five point scale strongly agree, agree, doubtful, disagree and strongly disagree.

It was administered to a sample of 240 teachers and 240 students equally distributed between the two sexes and the three localities (urban, semi-urban and rural). The sample was selected by a multistage stratified random sampling procedure from schools located in Chittoor district. Item analysis was carried out by *Likert's* (1932) procedure of criterion of internal consistency, which is far simpler and less time consuming, but at the same time yields results which are as valid as those obtained by the traditional method of item analysis. Factor analysis was also carried out with a maximum of 15 factors by applying vary max rotation (*Overall* and *Klett,* 1972).

The split-half reliability of the attitude scale was 0.83 in the case of teachers, while it was 0.95 for students. Content, criterion and factorial validities of the attitude scale have been established for teachers as well as for students.

IX. DATA COLLECTION AND SCORING

The attitude scale was administered to the sample of students selected from each school in small groups not exceeding 20. At the outset they were well motivated by informing them about the nature and importance of the investigation. They were also explained briefly about the detention system to avoid any ambiguity about the concept of detention system (this was necessary since they had all their education under the non-detention system). The attitude scales were distributed and instructions were read to the students slowly as they read them for themselves. Doubts if any were clarified and they were asked to mark their responses. The time taken for administration of the attitude scale was about an hour.

The instrument was administered to the sample of teachers individually through personal contact during leisure hours in their respective schools, after establishing adequate rapport and explaining the purpose of the investigation. They were also explained how they had to answer the items as given in the instructions at the beginning of the attitude scale. The instrument itself was self-administering.

For the headmasters of the schools who were included in the sample of administrators the attitude scale was administered individually when the investigator visited the school for the collection of data from the school. For the sample of Gazetted Inspectors and DEOs selected for the study, the attitude scale was mailed. Since their number was small, the filled in attitude scales could be obtained from all of them after sending 2 or 3 reminders.

The attitude scale was scored by assigning numerical weights of 5, 4, 3, 2, and 1 respectively for the five alternatives: strongly agree, agree, doubtful, disagree, and strongly disagree in the case of positive items following *Likert* (1932). The scoring procedure was reversed in the case of negative items.

X. ANALYSIS OF DATA

The data thus collected was analysed using relevant statistical techniques like analysis of variance, *t* test, etc. The usual levels of significance, viz., 0.05, 0.01 and 0.001 were employed to test the significance of the obtained statistics.

XI. CONCLUSIONS

From the results obtained in this investigation the following conclusions appear warranted:

1. Students achieved significantly better in the non-detention system than in the detention system in all subjects. This was true irrespective of their sex, social class or locality to which they belonged.

Hence, the first hypothesis, 'there would not be any significant difference between the achievement of pupils under the detention and non-detention systems', was rejected.

2. The percentage of passes was significantly higher in the non-detention system than that in the detention system. This was also true irrespective of the sex or locality of the students.

Hence, the second hypothesis, viz., 'there would not be any significant difference between the percentage of passes in the two systems', was also rejected.

3. The rate of drop-outs among the students was significantly less in the non-detention system than that in the detention system. This was true for all classes (from VI to X class) irrespective of the sex or locality to which the students belonged leading to the

acceptance of the third hypothesis that, 'the rate of drop-outs in the non-detention system would be significantly less than that in the detention systems.

4. The overall attitude of the pupils towards the non-detention system was significantly negative. This was true irrespective of their sex, social class or locality.

So, the fourth hypothesis, 'pupils would have a negative attitude towards the non-detention system', was accepted.

5. It was found that the overall attitude of the teachers towards the new system of evaluation was also negative. This was true irrespective of their sex, locality, level of the teaching or length of experience.

As such, the fifth hypothesis, viz., 'teachers would have a negative attitude towards the new system of evaluation', was also accepted.

6. The overall attitude of the administrators towards the new system of evaluation was also negative, leading to the acceptance of the sixth hypothesis, viz., 'administrators would have a negative attitude towards the systems'.

7. There was no significant difference between the overall attitude of pupils, teachers and administrators towards the new system of evaluation.

Hence, the seventh hypothesis that, 'there would not be any significant difference between the attitude of pupils, teachers and administrators towards the new system of evaluation', was accepted.

Besides the above major hypothesis, certain related hypotheses were also tested and the following conclusions were drawn:

1. Generally, girls outperformed boys in all subjects. Hence, the hypothesis that, 'there would not be any

significant difference between the achievement of boys and girls' was rejected.

2. Pupils belonging to other communities (OCs) achieved better than those belonging to scheduled castes/scheduled tribes in all subjects without any exception.

This led to the rejection of the second related hypothesis, viz., 'there would not be any significant difference between the achievement of pupils belonging to different social classes.

3. Generally, children belonging to rural localities did better than those belonging to urban and semi-urban areas. Urban children were the poorest performers.

Therefore, the third related hypothesis, 'pupils hailing from different localities would not differ significantly with regard to their achievement', was also rejected.

However, some interaction effects between different variables were significant, setting limits of the conclusions that may be drawn from the *F* ratios for the main effects (*Edwards,* 1971; *Winer,* 1971).

For example, in the case of analysis of marks an examination of the system X sex interaction effect showed that girls performed better than boys in both the systems, in almost all subjects, except in Hindi, in which boys scored better in the detention system, while girls scored better in the non-detention system.

The system X locality interaction effect showed that children belonging to rural localities scored better in both the systems in all subjects without any exception. Children hailing from U localities were the poorest performers in all subjects except Telugu and Total marks. In the case of Telugu and total marks children from U localities were no doubt the poorest performers under the detention system, but under the non-detention system, SU children scored the least in Telugu and Total marks.

Similarly an examination of sex X locality interaction effect showed that children from R localities outperformed the children belonging to the other two localities in all the six subjects and the total. This was true for boys as well as for girls. Children from U localities were the least scores among both the sexes in all subjects except Telugu and Total marks. In the case of Telugu and Total marks those belonging to SU localities were the least scorers among girls, while those hailing from U localities were the least scores among boys.

An examination of the system X social class, sex X social class and locality X social class interaction effects showed that children belonging to other communities achieved better than SCs/STs. This was true for all subjects irrespective of the system or sex or locality to which the students belonged.

It may be noted from the above that in all cases performance in the non-detention system was better than that in the detention system.

Hence, the above limitations to the conclusions drawn from the *F* ratios for main effects pertain only to 'related' hypotheses (P. 316) i.e., those concerned with sex, locality or social class differences in achievement.

With regard to the attitude of students, teachers and administrators, factor-wise analysis of the attitude scores led to the following conclusions:

1. In the case of the factors: Policy implementation (I), Teaching-learning (III), Learning skills (VII), Educational policy (VIII), Emotional (X), Competence (XII) and Ethical value (XIII) all the sub-groups of students had a negative attitude towards the system.

Hence, the hypothesis that, 'students would have a negative attitude towards the non-detention system', was accepted in the case of the above factors.

2. With regard to the factors: Personality (IV), Incentive for progress (VI), Freedom for the teachers

(X), Dullards—Wastage and stagnation (XI) and Learning in a natural setting (XIV) all the sub-groups of students and had a positive attitude towards the system.

So the hypothesis that, 'students would have a negative attitude towards the non-detention system', was rejected in the case of the above factors.

With regard to Factor II—Facility, those belonging to R localities and SCs/STs had a negative attitude as assessed by this factor (while all the other sub-groups had a positive attitude). Similarly in the case of Factor V-Discipline, students belonging to U localities had a negative attitude (while all other sub-groups had a positive attitude).

Hence, the above hypothesis was accepted in the above cases and rejected in all other cases.

3. All the sub-groups of teachers had a negative attitude towards the system as measured by the factors: Policy implementation (I), Teaching-learning (III), Learning skills (VII), Educational policy (VIII), Freedom for the teachers (IX), Emotional (X), Competence (XII) and Ethical value (XIII).

Therefore, the hypothesis that, 'teachers would have a negative attitude towards the non-detention system', was accepted in the case of the above factors.

In the case of factor II-Facility, teachers with 26 or more years of experience had a positive attitude, while all other sub-groups had a negative attitude. Hence, the above-hypothesis that, 'teachers would have a negative attitude towards the non-detention system', was accepted for this factor also for all sub-groups of teachers except those who had 26 or more years of experience, in whose case the hypothesis was rejected.

4. All the sub-groups of teachers had a positive attitude towards the system as assessed by the factors:

Personality (IV), Dullards—Wastage and stagnation (XI) and Learning in a natural setting (XIV).

Hence, the hypothesis that, 'teachers would have a negative attitude towards the non-detention system', was rejected in the case of the above factors.

In the case of factor VI—Incentive for progress, except Secondary Grade assistants, teachers belonging to SU and R localities and teachers with 1-15 years of experience who had a neutral attitude all other sub-groups had a positive attitude towards the non-detention system.

Hence, the hypothesis that, 'teachers would have a negative attitude towards the non-detention system', was rejected in the case of all the sub-groups for this factor.

5. Considering factor V—Discipline, those belonging to U localities and those who had 26 or more years of experience had a positive attitude, and all other sub-groups of teachers had a neutral attitude towards the system.

Hence, the hypothesis that, 'teachers would have negative attitude towards the non-detention system', was rejected.

6. Administrators had a negative attitude towards the system as assessed by the factors: Policy implementation (I), Learning skills (VIII), Freedom for the teachers (IX), Emotional (X), Dullards—Wastage and stagnation (XI), Competence (XII) and Ethical value (XIII) leading to the acceptance of the hypothesis that, 'administrators would have a negative attitude towards the non-detention system', in the case of the above factors.

7. Administrators had a positive attitude towards the new system of evaluation in the case of the factors: Personality (IV) and Incentive for progress (VI).

Hence, the hypothesis that, 'administrators would have a negative attitude towards the non-detention system', was rejected in the case of the above factors.

8. Administrators had a neutral attitude towards the system as assessed by the factors: Facility (II), Teaching-learning (III), Discipline (VI), Educational policy (VIII) and Learning in a natural setting (XIV).

So, the hypothesis that, 'administrators would have a negative attitude towards the non-detention system', was rejected in the case of the above factors also.

9. In the case of the factors: Policy implementation (I), Teaching-leaning (III), Learning skills (VII), Emotion (X), Competence (XII) and Ethical value (XIII) all the three sub-groups of *Ss,* viz. pupils, teachers and administrators had a negative attitude.

With regard to the factors: personality (IV), Incentive for progress (VI), Dullards—Wastage and stagnation (XI) and Learning in a natural setting (XIV) all the three sub-groups of *Ss* had a positive attitude towards the new system of evaluation.

There was no significant difference between the attitude of the three groups in the case of the above 10 factors.

10. However, in the case of the factors: Facility (II) (where pupils had a positive attitude, teachers had a negative attitude and administrators had a neutral attitude), discipline (V) (where pupils had a positive attitude but teachers and administrators had a neutral attitude), Educational policy (VIII) (where students and teachers had a negative attitude and administrators had a neutral attitude) and Freedom for the teachers (IX) (where pupils had a positive attitude and teachers and administrators had a negative attitude) there was a significant difference between the attitude of the three groups of *Ss*.

Hence, the hypothesis that, "there would not be any significant difference in the attitude of pupils, teachers and administrators towards the non-detention system", was rejected in the case of the above 4 factors and accepted in the case of the other 10 factors.

8

Educational Implications, Limitations and Suggestions for Further Research

The Government of Andhra Pradesh introduced the non-detention system expecting that in this system the students will be free from anxiety, fear and tension, the concomitant feature of examinations coupled with detentions. It was expected therefore, that in this system students will be able to study in a natural setting which would stand them in good stead for better grasp of the subject matter leading to better achievement (*Narasimha Rao,* 1971; *Kabra,* 1971; *Krishnamoorthy,* 1971). *Experimental Studies by Keyes* (1911), *Klene* and Branson (1929), *Coffield* and *Bloomers* (1956), *Kowitz* and *Armstrong* (1961), *Gaite* 91969) and *Otto* and *Melby* (nd) also showed that students do achieve better when they were told that they would be promoted irrespective of their progress than when they were told that they would be failed if they were not diligent in their work and achieve well. Studies by *McCullers* (1978) *Gayen* and *Lyle* (1965), *Glucksberg* (1962) and *Dornbush* (1965) have shown that rewards rather than punishment facilitate performance.

The results of the present study not only corroborate the contention of the proponents of the system but also fall in line with the results of the studies mentioned above.

When the non-detention system was introduced it was felt by some that there will be a steep rise in the percentage of failures at the VII and X class levels at which common/public examinations were to be held (*Editorial, Educational India,* 1977; *Venkata Rao,* 1971). However, the results obtained in the present investigation do not support the above view. Under the non-detention system there was an increase in the percentage of passes at the X class level.

It was thought by *Kabra* (1971), *Narasimha Rao* (1971), *Sarabhachari* (1971) and *Satyanarayana* (1971) that the new system of evaluation would reduce drop-outs which is a menacing problem of our education system. The results of the present study support the opinion expressed by the above authors.

Thus the system seems to be conducive for better achievement and also for reducing the rate of drop-outs. However, the overall attitude of students, teachers and administrators towards the new system was negative pointing out some lapses in the system.

It is a common phenomenon that one seems to understand better when he is studying the material without any anxiety or tension of say getting good marks in an examination. But what about motivations to study? At the adolescent age where the individual is half-child-half-adult, one can not expect that all the students will develop on their own accord, the necessary motivation to study. They must be motivated. But not by threat of failure in the examination, but by a positive approach, where tests are conducted to assess one's strengths and weaknesses and not to declare him as a pass or fail. These tests should be followed up by remedial teaching to overcome the weaknesses of the students. This is the essence of the non-detention system. In the nondetnetion system motivation to study springs from within the system which is the right kind of motivation rather than trying to motivate him through external threats. It is needless to mention that intrinsic motivation is far superior to extrinsic motivation.

That the rate of drop-outs was reduced significantly in the non-detention system, is a significant contribution of the system. It also points out that failure or fear of failure is an important factor in the drop-out phenomenon. In the detention system the child might have dropped-out because of the usual economical, sociological and psychological causes plus failure in the examination, because in an agriculture oriented India where a vast majority of the parents are illiterate, the parents tend to withdraw the child from the school if he fails in an examination taking it as an indication of lack of capacity on the part of the child and also due to the fact that the child has to spend one more year in the same class. Though there is an increased awareness of the importance of education and more number of schools and colleges are opened and the enrollment in the schools has increased ever since the country attained Independence in 1947, there is no drastic change in the economic or sociological factors between 1971 and 1983. As such the reduction in the rate of dropouts must be largely due to removal of failure or fear of failure in the examination due to the introduction of non-detention system. The Government, however, should try to evolve schemes to further reduce the rate of drop-outs. For example ancillary services like mid-day meal programme, free supply of textbooks and note books, free supply of clothes, etc., can be introduced or strengthened. Attendance scholarships can also be instituted.

Though students, teachers and administrators in general had a negative attitude towards the non-detention system, there are certain aspects on which they had a positive attitude. Those aspects of the system should be further strengthened. From a peep into the detention system one can recall how teachers and Headmasters were under the clutches of politics and other unfair means for the promotion of children, which has been nullified in the new system. Moreover learning has been facilitated because of the scope to learn the subjects in the natural setting free from tension and fear where the incentive and urge for progress spring form within the system itself. Therefore, it provides ample opportunities for the students to develop their intellectual as well as various personality aspects. Further as the domination of examinations (for the purpose of deciding the promotion or otherwise of a students) is minised in the new system, it has done away with all sorts of unfair means adopted during the examinations.

It must be realised that the non-detention system does not mean no examination or no evaluation. It is not a tasteless system but a system where there is continuous evaluation of the student's progress, but without the threat of detention. It is a scheme which provides for systematic evaluation of student's progress and for pinpointing the strengths and weaknesses of both the teacher and the taught. It is a programme of continuous evaluation of students' performance in all the areas of school learning. If a student has not achieved upto the expected level in an area, follow-up measures like remedial teaching, extra class, etc., are to be instituted. Every opportunity must be given to the student to develop; there should be no threat of failure holding up his development.

The students' progress must be informed to their parents at regular intervals and the teachers and parents must cooperate in helping the child to achieve his educational goals. This will act as an immediate feedback both for the student and for the teacher. That is why it is said that in this system the incentive to learn springs from within the system rather than from the threat of detentions. In this system the responsibilities of teachers have increased since they are expected to do remedial teaching and try new methods to help the weak students. They must raise to the occasion, for whatelse can given more pleasure to the teacher than the progress of his students, especially those who are backward?

One undesirable and unfortunate features of present day classrooms is that they are overcrowded with unmanageable number of students. Another unfortunate aspect is many of the schools are understaffed. Further this optimal staff strength is determined on the basis of the number of sections in the school and not on the basis of the total strength of students or optimal teachers pupil ratio. As such with large classes the teachers work has abnormally increased. *Bullayya* (1972) rightly remarked that the new system of evaluation would not work well with understaffed schools and insincere teaches. So efforts should be taken by the government to reduce the size of the class and also appoint required number of teachers to each school.

To check insincerity and slackness on the part of the teaching staff and for the successful implementation of the system an annual plan should be drawn for the coverage of the syllabus and for conducting tests. This should be done before the beginning of the school year, and meticulously followed by every teacher. A teacher-wise performance register should be maintained and the inspecting officers should strictly watch the implementation of the programme by each of the teachers and the Headmasters. They should report back to the higher authorities about the performance of each teacher and Headmaster.

If such a procedure is adopted slackness on the part of the teachers can be overcome. If reports of the progress of the students are sent periodically to the parents both the students and the parents will know where they/their wards stand and also feel that this system is not a tasteless system. It helps the students to evince interest and parents also will take care of the slackness, if any, on the part of their wards. To encourage both the intelligent and the dull and to have some sort of distinction between them, methods like putting the names of those who performed well and those who laggeds behind on the notice board may be tried. This competition aspect, however should not be over emphasised since it has its own demerits and may even boomerang (*Morse* and *Wingo,*

1970). Growth charts depicting the rate of progress of the child from the beginning of the year may help as incentive especially for the backward.

In any sound system of education teaching, testing and reinforcement in the form of feedback are the essential ingredients. If teachers teach and conduct tests at regular intervals, value the papers promptly and make the results known, there will be immediate knowledge of results and feedback to the pupils as well as to the teachers, who can undertake remedial measures where necessary. If this is coupled with praise or reproof from the teachers and/or parents it will have tremendous influence on the progress of the students.

It is contended that the system encourages the students to indulge in unworthy activities as they can abscond from the schools immediately after giving attendance. To regulate this type of behaviour rules with regard to attendance may be modified. Teachers may take attendance for each period instead of taking it only once in the forenoon and once in the afternoon sessions. Further to make the students regular to the schools and to be with the school system, scholarships may be introduced for regularity of attendance. Today most of the socially and economically backward students get the EBC, or LBC scholarships. These scholarships should be linked with regularity of attendance. The percentage of attendance required for getting the scholarships should be kept at a higher level, say at 90 per cent with facility for condonation upto a maximum of 10 per cent for genuine reasons. Inspectorate should also be strengthened, so that they can properly watch the working of the system and remove any misconceptions among the teachers about the system.

All such efforts should be taken meticulously and a programme should be planned with care and sensitivity to eliminate all sorts of fissiparous tendencies among the students, teachers and administrators so as to create a proper and conducive atmosphere for its effective implementation, designed to yield the desired results.

An unfortunate aspect is that students, parents and also some of the teachers construe that the non-detention system is a tasteless system. For them it is just an administrative measure 'to keep the numbers in'. So it is necessary for the Government to organise programmes through the mass media and other channels, for the benefit of the parents, students and teachers, projecting the real idea underlying the new system of evaluation. This would go a long way in effective implementation of the new system.

When promotion of students is guaranteed irrespective of their learning, and if per iodical testing and sending progress reports is not properly done, there is no wonder if students do not show any interest in studies. They may be irregular to the school. They may not even care to purchase books. This melody spread rapidly from one student to the other because they are at vulnerable age, leading large scale Indisciline. Further, apathy for studies on the part of the students is like a contageous disease. It leads to disinterest, and apathy on the part of the teachers, making them sluggish and slack in their work. The slackness on the part of the teachers leads to further loss of interest and increased Indisciline on the part of the students. This is a vicious circle.

No wonder teachers, administrators and students have a negative attitude towards the new system.

The vicious circle can be broken by reducing the class strength, by appointing sufficient number of teachers in all schools, and by carefully monitoring the conduct of periodical tests, valuation of answer papers and despatch of progress reports to the parents.

According to *Seshadri* (1984) the scheme of non-detention is to be looked at against the overall perspective of the Nation's commitment to the universalisation of education, the national objectives of compulsory schooling, the long range educational purposes of examinations, viz., classification, promotion/detention in schools and the extent to which they are served by current practices and policies pertaining to school education. As mentioned earlier, the non-detention system has a salient effect on reducing wastage. Generally, this problem of wastage is more in the primary classes than in the higher forms. There are some states which have dispensed with detentions in the primary classes. The Government of Uttar Pradesh has this policy of non-detention upto V class, in Kerala and Goa standards I and II are considered as one unit and there is no detention in standard I. Further, in Goa there are no detentions in standards V, VI and VII (*Seshadri,* 1984). These states may introduce the system in higher classes also, with necessary safe guards as mentioned above.

Limitations and Suggestions for Further Research

Many experimental studies have shown that students do achieve better when they were told that they would be promoted irrespective of their progress than when they were told that they would be failed if they were not diligent in their work and achieve well. However, when the non-detention system was introduced, it was contended by the Editor, The *Educational Review* (1971) that the failures at the public examinations at VII and X classes will run into staggering proportions under the new system.

In this investigation, an attempt was made to analyse the achievement and percentage of passes at the X class Public Examination under the two systems and it was found that the achievement and percentage of passes were better in the non-detention system. Will these results hold good for the VII class level also? No attempt was made in the present investigation to study the effect of the system on the achievement and percentage of passes at the VII class level. A study may be conducted to examine the effect of the system at this level.

It was contended by *Kabra* (1971), *Krishnamoorthy* (1977), *Rao* (1977) and *Spokesman, Government of Kerala* (1973) that the non-detention system would reduce the problem of drop-out.

In the present investigation the class-wise drop-out rate was analysed for classes VI to X. No attempt was made to study the rate of drop-outs at the primary level. A study to examine the impact of the non-detention system on the rate of drop-out at primary level may be fruitful.

In this study the attitude of high school teachers towards the non-detention system was studied. A study of the attitude of primary school teachers, who lay the foundation for the education of the children may give fruitful results.

How do parents look at the system? It is needless to mention that parents also should bestow proper attention on the education of the children since they have to guide the children in their educational pursuits. As such an investigation into the attitude of parents towards this system may be conducted. Based upon the results of such an investigation, programmes may be evolved to educate the parents through parent-teacher associations (PTAs), circulars, etc., about the silent features of the non-detention system.

Studies of the type conducted by *Keyes* (1911), *Klene* and *Branson* (1929), *Coffield* and *Bloomers* (1955), *Kowitz* and *Armstrong* (19610, *Gaite* (1963) and *otto* and *Melby* (nd), where one group of students were told that they would pass irrespective of their progress and another parallel group were told that they would be failed if they do not achieve well, are not possible (or may look highly artificial) in Andhra Pradesh, since the students know that they cannot be failed if they have the necessary attendance. They also know that the teacher has very little role to play in determining their promotion (even if detentions were there) since it is the Headmaster of the school who prepares the promotion list based upon certain rules framed by the District Educational officer of the district concerned. Such a controlled study however, may be tried in other states where the detention system is in vogue. This type of study may throw light on the validity of the results of the studies mentioned above in the Indian setting.

In this study no attempt was made to compare the performance of the students belonging to schools coming under different managements (like private schools, government schools, municipal schools, zilla praja parishad schools). Will the system work better in private schools than in government schools or local body schools?

Similarly, a comparative analysis of the attitude of students and teachers selected from schools belonging to different managements may throw more light on the effect of management on the working of the new system.

Bibliography

Abraham, M. 1974. Some Factors Relating to Under-achievement in English of Secondary School Pupils. Ph.D. Education, Kerala University. (In) Buch, M.B. (Ed.) 1979. *Second Survey of Research in Education (1972-1978),* Society for Educational Research and Development, Baroda, 340.

Abramson, L.Y., Seligman, M.E.P., and Teasdale, J.L. 1978. Learned Helplessness in Humans: Critique and Reformation. *Journal of Abnormal Psychology,* 87, 49-74.

Agarwal, P.C. 1974. A Study of the Corrolation of Achievement Motivation. Unpublished Doctoral Dissertation, Kurukshetra University, (In) Sinha, S.P. and Alika Garg, 1987. Sex Difference in Achievement as Related to Risk Taking Behaviour in Adolescents. *Indian Educational Review,* 22, 4.

Aggarwal, J.C. and Agrawal, S.P. 1989. *National Policy on Education,* Concept Publishing Company, New Delhi.

Aiken, L.R. 1972. Junior Language Factors in Learning Mathematics. *Review of Education Research,* 42, 359-385.

Allport, G.W. 1929. The Composition of Political Attitudes. *American Journal of Sociology,* 35, 220-238.

Anand, C.L. 1973. A Study of Effects of Socio-economic Environment and Medium of Instruction Mental Abilities and the Academic Achievement of Children in Mysore State,

Ph.D. Edu. Mysore University. (In) Buch, M.B. (Ed.) 1979. *Second Survey of Research in Education (1972-1978)*, Society for Educational Research and Development, Baroda, 332.

Anfinson, R.D. 1941. School Progress and Pupil Adjustment. *Elementary School Journal*, 41, 6, 504-514.

Arthur, G. 1936. A Study of the Achievement of Sixty Grade One Repeaters as Compared with that of Non-repeaters of the Same Age. *Journal of Experimental Education*, 5, 203-205.

Aruna, N.S. 1981. A Study of the Factors Influencing the Achievement of Standard VII Students Belonging to Scheduled Caste and Scheduled Tribes whose Medium of Instruction is Kannada. (In) Buch, M.B. (Ed.) 1986. *Third Survey of Research in Education (1978-1983)*, NCERT, New Delhi, 658.

Asher, E.J. 1935. The Inadequacy of Current Intelligence Tests for Testing Kentucky Mountain Children. *Journal of Genetic Psychology*, 46, 480-486.

Asher, R., and Gottman, J.M. 1973. Sex of Teacher and Student Reading Achievement. *Journal of Educational Psychology*, 65, 168-171.

Akkinson, J. 1978. The Mainsprings of Achievement Oriented Activity (In) Atkinson, J. and Raynor, J. (Eds.) *Personality, Motivation and Achievement*, Halsted, New York, 11-39.

Atkinson, J.W., Bastin, J.R. et al., 1960. The Achievement Motivation, Goal Setting and Probability Preference. *Journal of Abnormal and Social Psychology*, 1, 27-36.

Atkinson, J.W., and Feather, N.T. 1966. *A Theory of Achievement Motivation*, Wiley, New York.

Ausubel, D.P., and Sullivan, E.V. 1970. *Theory and Problems of Child Development*, Grune and Stratton, New York, London, 669-680.

Ayres, I.P. 1909. *Laggards in our Schools*, Russel Sage Foundation, New York.

Backman, N.E. 1972. Patterns of Mental Abilities; Ethnic Socio-Economic and Sex Differences. *American Education Research Journal*, 9, 1-12.

Bala Girish, 1978. A Factor Analysis of Reasoning Ability of 13, 14, 15 years Old Children Studying in Delhi Higher Secondary School. (In) Buch, M.B. (Ed.) *Second Survey of Research in Education (1972-1978),* Society for Educational Research and Development, Baroda, 181.

Bala Renu, 1978. A Study of Reasoning Ability of X Grade Students in Relation to Intelligence and Academic Achievement. *M.Phil Dissertation,* Punjab University, Patiala.

Ballard, P.B. 1949. *New Examiner,* London Press, London.

Baratz, S.S., and Baratz, J.C. 1970. Early Childhood Intervention: The Social Science Base of Institutional Racism. *Harvard Educational Review,* 40, 29-50.

Barret, H.C. 1957,. Intensive Study of 32 Gifted Children. *Personnel and Guidance Journal,* 35, 194.

Basavayya, D. 1974. Effects of Bilinguism on Language Achievement, CIIL, Mysore. (In) Buch, M.B. (Ed.) 1979. *Second Survey of Research in Education (1972-1978),* Society for Educational Research and Development, Baroda, 342.

Bayley, N., and Jones, H.E. 1937, Environmental Correlates of Mental and Motor Development, *Children Development,* 8, 329-341.

Beedawat, S.S. 1976. A Study of Academic Under-achievement Among Students, Ph.D. Edu, Rajasthan University. (In) Buch, M.B. (Ed.) 1979. *Second Survey of Research in Education (1972-1978),* Society for Educational Research and Development, Baroda, 343.

Benson, C. 1985. Financing Education. (In) Torsten Husen and T. Neville Postelethwaite. (Eds.) 1986. *The International Encyclopaedia of Education,* Pergamon Press, Oxford, 4, 1880.

Bernette, W. Leslie (Jr.) 1957. Advanced Credit for the Superior High School Students. (In) Ebel, R.L. (Ed.) 1969. *Encyclopaedia of Educational Research,* 45h edition, The Macmillan Company, London, 7-9.

Bernstein, B. 1964. Elaborated and Restricted Codes: Their Social Origins and Some Consequences. (In) Torsten Husen and T. Neville Postelethwaite. (Eds.) 1986. *The Internaltional Encyclopaedia of Education,* Pergamon Press, Oxford, 9, 5401.

Bhatia, I. 1976-77. A study of Relationship Between n-Achievement Academic Competence and Level of Aspiration. *Research Journal of Educational Psychology,* 7, 9-14.

Bhatia, Hans Raj. 1969. *General Psychology,* Oxford and IBH Publishing House, Calcutta.

Bhatnagar, R.P., 1969. A Study of Relationship Between n-Achievement, Academic Competence and Level of Aspiration, *Research Journal of Educational Psychology,* 7, 9-14.

Bhola, V. 1978. Measurement of Achievement in Physics and Chemistry—A Critical Study of the Effectiveness of the Matriculation Examination in Physics and Chemistry Conducted by the Board of School Education, Haryana. (In) Buch, M.B. (Ed.) 1986. *Third Survey of Research in Education (1978-1983),* NCERT, New Delhi, 714.

Bhoodev Singh. 1987. Personality and Biographical Factors of School Drop-outs and Stayins. *Indian Educational Review,* 22, 4, 141-146.

Bir Singh, 1971. Failing in Examinations—Do Pupils gain? *The Education Quarterly,* 23, 2.

——— 1976. Examinees Explain their Failure, *The Educational Review,* 82, 11, 203.

Blan, P.M. and Duncan, D.M. 1967. *The American Occupational Structure,* Wiley, New York.

Blan, Z.S. 1981. *Black Children / While Children, Competence Socialization and Social Structure,* Free Press, New York.

Blattastein, Abraham, 1981. Sex and Ethnicity Affect School Out Cosmer Separately, *ERIC Resources in Education,* 16, 1, E.D. 191 859.

Bloom, B.S. 1961. *Evaluation in Higher Education* (A Report of the Seminars on Examination Reform Organised by the

University Grants Commission under the Leadership of Dr. B.S. Bloom), University Grants Commission, New Delhi.

———. 1964. *Stability and Change in Human Characteristics*, Wiley and Sons, New York.

Bloommers (n.d.) (In) Smith, E.W., et al., (Eds.) 1969. *The Educator's Encyclopaedia*. Prentice-Hall-Inc, Englewood Cliffs, N.J. 438-441.

Bogardus, E.W. 1941. *Fundamental Social Psychology*, Century, New York, 62.

Bokil, S.R. 1956a. (In) Buch, M.B. (Ed.) 1979, *Second Sruvey of Research in Education (1972-1978)*, Society for Educational Research and Development, Baroda, 374.

——. 1956b. School-wise Failure Analysis of the SSC Examination of March 1955 (Size and Location as Factors), Research and Investigation Section; Maharashtra State Board of Secondary Education, Poona, (In) Buch, M.B. (Ed.) 1979. *Second Survey of Research in Education (1972-1978)*, Society for Educational Research and Development, Baroda, 368.

——. 1963. A Statistical Analysis of Failures in English at the SSC Examiantion of March 1961 for Urban, Semi-urban and Rural Schools, Research and Investigation Second, Maharashtra State. (In) Buch, M.B. (Ed.) 1979. *Second Survey of Research in Education (1972-1978)*. Society for Educational Research and Development, Baroda, 373.

Bora, K.P. 1974. Action for Education Reform, *Quest in Education*, 11, 3.

Bowker, R., and Trafton, R.S. 1981. The Influence of Perceptional Speed on Performance Vs Paper and Pencil Measures of Spatial Ability (Paper Presented at the Annual Meeting of the American Educational Research Association). (In) Harold E. Mitzet et al., (Eds.) 1983. *Encyclopaedia of Educational Research*, 5th Edition, The Macmillan Company, London.

Bradley, R.A., Caldwell, B.M. and Elrado, R. 1977. Home Environment, Social Status and Mental Test Performance, *Journal of Educational Psychology,* 69, 6, 697-701.

Broadbent, W.A. 1975. An Inquiry into the Factors Underlying Class Schedule Changes at Lerward Community College, Honolulu: University of Hawaii, *ERIC Document Reproduction Service,* No. Ed 119 778.

Brody, B.E. and Brody, H. 1976. *Intelligence, Nature, Determinants and Consequences,* Academic Press, New York.

Broussard, V. 1978. Pre-requisities for Teaching the Disadvantaged. *Forum for the Discussion of New Trends in Education,* 20, 3.

Brown, B., Frank, 1963. The Non-graded High School. (In) Smith, E.D. et al., (Eds.) 1969. *The Educators Encyclopaedia,* Prentice Hall, INC, Englewood Cliffs, N.J. 216.

Blude, U. 1985. Rural Education Programmes. (In) Torsten Husen and T. Neville Postelethwaite. (Eds.) 1986. *The International Encyclopaedia of Education,* Pergamon Press, Oxford, 7, 4360.

Bulcock, J.W., Fagerlind, I., and Emanuelsson, I. 1974. Education and the Socio-Economic Carreer: U.S.—Swedish Comparisons. (In) Torsten Husen and T., Neville Postelethwaite. (Eds.) 1986. *The International Encyclopaedia of Education,* Pergamon Press, Oxcord, 8, 4820.

Bullayya, L. 1977. Pattern of Education in A.P. (10+2+3). Education in A.P. 1956-76. *Telugu Academy,* Hyderabad, 12-13.

Burt, C. 1949. Mental and Scholastic Test, Stamples. (In) Sharma, V.P. 1985. Effectiveness of Test Types on High and Low Achievers. *Indian Educational Review,* 20, 4.

Callahan, L.G. and Glennon, V.J. 1975. Elementary School Mathematics: A Guide to Current Research (4th Ed.), Association for Supervision and Curriculum Development. Washington, D.C. *ERIC Document Reproduction Service* No. ED 116 966.

Carlsmith, L. 1964. Effect of Early Father Absence Upon Scholastic Aptitude. *Harvard Educational Research,* 34, 3-21.

Chacho, T. 1964. *System of Examinations,* Proceedings of the Educational Conference and Seminars, 19-21 Dec. 1964, Hyderabad, 90-93.

Chapanis, A., and Williams, W.C. 1945. Results of a Mental Survey with the Kuhlmann Anderson Intelligence Tests in Williamson County, Tennessee, *Joural of Genetic Psychology,* 67, 27-55.

Chaplin, J.P. 1968. *Dictionary of Psychology,* Dell Publishing, New York.

Charwood, E. et al., 1959. Examinations in Indian Higher Education. (In) Sharma, V.P. 1985. Effectiveness of Test Types on High and Low Achievers. *Indian Educational Review,* 20, 4.

Chatterjee, S., Mukherjee, M. and Banerjee, S.N. 1971. Effect of Certain Socio-Economic Factors on the Scholastic Achievement of the School Children. (In) Buch, M.B. (Ed.) 1986. *Third Survey of Research in Education (1978-1983),* NCERT, New Delhi, 659-660.

Chaterjee, B.B. 1977. Pattern of School Achievement in Primary Grades. (In) Jagannathan, K. 1983. The Effects of Certain Socio-Psychological Factors on the Academic Achievement of Children Studying in Classes V to VII. *Unpublished Doctoral Thesis,* S.V. University, Tirupati, 78.

Chaterjee, V. 1977. A Comparison of Performance of Tribal and Non-tribal Boys of Tripura on Five Performance Tests. (In) Radheshyam et al., 1988. Cognitive Processing Differential Among Rural Tribals and Non-Tribals. *The Educational Review,* 441, 7, 101-103.

Chaudhary, N.E. 1972. The Relationship Between Achievement Motivation and Anxiety, Intelligence, Sex, Social Class and Vocational Aspiration. Unpublished Doctoral dissertation, Punjab University. (In) Sinha, S.P. and Alika Garg, 1987. *Indian Educational Review,* 22, 4.

Coffield, W.H., and Bloomers (n.d.) Factors Affecting Promotion and Retention. (In) Smith, E.D., et al., (Eds.) 1969. *The Educator's Encyclopaedia,* Prentic Hall, Inc, Englewood Cliffs, N.J. 436.

——. 1956. Effects of Non-promotion on Educational Achievement in Elementary School, *Journal of Educational Psychology,* 47, 235-250.

Coleman, J.S., Campbell, E.Q., Hobson, C.J., Mc Partlan, J. Mood, A.M., Weinfeld, R.L. and York, R.L. 1966. Equality of Educational Opportunities. (In) Torsten Husen and T. Neville Postlethwaite. (Eds.) 1986. *The International Encyclopaedia of Education,* Pergemon Press, Oxford, 9, 5126.

Combs, J. and Cooly, W. 1968. Drop-outs: In High School and After School. *American Educational Research Journal,* 5, 343-363.

Cook, W.W., and Kearney, N.E. 1940. Effects of Non-promotion on Achievement and Personality Traits. (In) Ebel, R.L. (Ed.) 1983. *Encyclopaedia of Educational Research,* 5th Edition, The Macmillan Company, London, 1469.

Cornelius, M.L., Cockburn, D. 1978. Influence of Pupil Peformance. *Educational Research,* 21, 1, 48-53.

Correspondent, 1980a. Automatic Promotionss: Teachers may Become More Slack in Work. *The Hindu,* 103, 145, (18 June, 1980), 16.

——. 1980b. Non-detention System: Merits and Demerits. *The Hindu,* 103, 151 (25 June 1980), 19.

Coster, J.K. 1958. Attitude Towrds School of High School Pupils from Three Income Levels. *Journal of Educational Psychology,* 49, 2, 61-66.

Curry, R.L. 1962. The Effect of the Socio-Economic Status on the School Achievement of 6th Grade Children. *British Journal of Educational Psychology,* 46-49.

Dale, H. Schunk. 1983. Reward Contingencies and the Development of Children Skills and Self Efficacy. *Journal of Educational Psychology,* 75, 4, 511-518.

Daly, R.F., and Bateman, H.H. 1978. The Grade W: Why students Drop Their Classes. *Community Junior College Research Quarterly,* 2, 353, 366.

Dandapani, 1969. An Examiantion of Examinations. *Educational India,* 36, 5, 161.

Dandekar, W.N., and Vidya Prakashan, 1972. Evaluation in Schools. *Educational India,* 39, 3 and 4, 103.

Dave, P.N. and Dave, J.P. 1971. Socio-Economic Environment as Related to Non-verbal intelligence of Rank and Failed Students, RCE, Mysore. (In) Buch, M.B. (Ed.) 1979. *Second Survey of Research in Education (1972-78)* Society for Educational Research and Development, Baroda, 345.

Deborah, J. Stipek and Joel, M. Hoffman, 1980. Children's Achievement—Related Expectancies as a Function of Academic Performance Histories and Sex. *Journal of Educational Psychology,* 72, 6, 861-865.

Deshpande, M.V. 1972. Reliability of External and Internal Marks of Vidarbha Board of Secondary Education Examination. (In) Buch, MB. (Ed.) 1986. *Third Survey of Research in Education (1978-83),* NCERT, New Delhi, 715.

Desai, D.B. 1971. Achievement Motivation in High School Pupils in Kaira District, NCERT Project Report, M.B. Patel College of Education, Vallabh Vidhyanagar (In) Buch, M.B. (Ed.) 1979. *Second Survey of Research in Education (1972-78),* Society for Educational Research and Development, Baroda, 169.

Deutsch M., and Brown, B. 1964. Social Influence in Negro-White Intelligence Differences. *Journal of Sociological Issues,* 20, 24-35.

Directorate of Extension Programme for Secondary Education (DEPSE). 1964. Sample Studies of Failures in Boards of Secondary Education. (In) Buch, M.B. (Ed.) 1986. *Third Survey of Research in Education (1978-83),* NCERT, New Delhi, 720.

Directorate of Higher Education. 1966. A Study of Incidence of High Percentage of Failure in Public Examiantion of H.S.C,

Hyderabad. (In) Buch, M.B. (Ed.) 1986. *Third Survey of Research in Education (1978-83),* NCERT, New Delhi, 720.

Dona, Johnson, 1981. Naturally Acquired Learned Helplessness: The Relationship of Failure to Achievement Behaviour, Attributions and Self Concept. *Journal of Educational Psychology,* 73, 2, 174-180.

Dornbush, R.L. 1965. Motivation and Positional Cues in Incidental Learning, Perceptual and Motor Skills. *Journal of Educational Psychology,* 20, 709, 714.

Dressel, P.L. (n.d.). *Evaluation in Higher Education,* The River Side Press, Cambridge, 3-26.

——. 1976. *Handbook of Academic Evaluation,* Jossey-Bass, Sanfrancisco, California.

Drouge, R.C. 1967. Sex-differences in Aptitude Maturation During High School. *Journal of Counselling Psychology,* 14, 407-411.

Dubois, P.H. 1965. A Test Dominated Society: China, 1115 B.C.—1905 A.D. (In) Ebel, R.L. (Ed.) 1969. *Encyclopaedia of Educational Research,* 4th Edition, The Macmillan Company, London 7-9.

Ebel, R.L. 1969, History of Achievement Testing. *Encyclopaedia of Educational Research,* 4th Edition, The Macmillan Company, London, 7-9.

Editorial. 1967. Undermining Examinations. *The Educational Review,* 73, 5, 122.

——. 1970. Examiantion Politics. *The Educational Review,* 76, 2, 48.

——. 1971. Automatic Promotions. *The Educational Review,* 77, 7, 168.

——. 1975. *The Educational Review,* 81, 8, 1961.

——. 1977. Need to Evaluate the A.P.'s New Evaluation Scheme. *Educational India,* 43, 7, 159-164.

——. 1980. Measurement in Education. *Educational India,* 44, 11 and 12, 255-256.

——. 1988. Continuous Comprehensive Evaluation, *Journal of Education and Psychology,* 46, 1-2.

Edwards, A.L. 1969. *Techniques of Attitude Scale Construction,* Vakils Feffer and Simons, Bombay.

——. 1971. *Experimental Design in Psychological Research,* New York, Holt, Rinchart and Winston, 215 and 264, 267.

Edwards, A.L. and Kilpatrick, F.P. 1948. A Technique for the Construction of Attituders Scales. *Journal of Applied Psychology,* 32, 374-384.

Eell, K., and Davis, A. 1951. *Intelligence and Cultural Differences: A Study of Cultural Learning and Problem Solving.* University of Chicago Press, Chicago.

Entwistle, N.J. and Welsh, J. 1969. Correlates of School Attainment at Different Ability Levels. *British Journal of Educational Psychology,* 39, 57-63.

Entwistle, N.J. 1972. Personality and Achievement. *British Journal of Educational Psychology,* 137-151.

Eysenck, A.J. and Cooksin, D. 1969. Personality in Primary School Children, Ability and Achievement. *British Journal of Educational Psychology,* 39, 2, 109-122.

Farmer, H., et al., 1981. *Career Motivation and Achievement Planning (C-MAP),* Measures Available with Scoring Manual and Interpretive Materials from Helen S. Farmer, Department of Educational Psychology, University of Illinois, Illinois.

Feather, N.T. 1961. The Relationship of Persistence at a Task to Expectation of Success and Achievement Releated Motives. *Journal of Abnormal and Social Psychology,* 63, 552-561.

Fennema, E. 1974. Sex Differences in Mathematics Achievement: A Review. *Journal of Research in Mathematics Education,* 5, 126-139.

——. 1975. Mathematics, Spatial Ability and the Sexes, (In) Fennema, E. (Ed.) *Mathematics Learning: What Research Says About Sex Differences.* ERIC Clearing House for

Science, Mathematics and Environmental Education, Columbio, Ohio.

Fennema, E. and Sherman, J. 1977a. Sex-related Differences in Mathematics Achievement, Spatial Visualization and Affective Factors. *American Educational Research Journal,* 14, 51-71.

——. (Eds.) 1976b. *Women and Mathematics: Research Perspectives for Change,* National Institute of Education, Washington, D.C.

Fenske, R.H. 1969. Who Selects Vocational Technical Post High School Education? (In) Torsten Husen and T. Neville Postlethwaite. (Eds.) 1986. *The International Encyclopaedia of Education,* Pergamon Press, Oxford, 9, 5532.

Finlayson, D.S. 1970. A Follow-up Study of School Achievement in Relation to Personality. *British Journal of Psychology,* 40, 344-348.

Finlayson, H.J. 1977. *Non-promotion and Self-Concept Development.* Phi Delta Kappan, 205-206.

Finn, J.D., Dulber, L., and Reis, J. 1979. Sex Differences in Educational Attainment: A Cross-national Perspective. *Harvard Educational Review*, 49, 477-503.

Flanagan, J.C. et al., 1961. *Project Talent Counsellor's Technical Manual for Interpreting Test Scores.* University of Pittsburgh Project Talent Office, Washington, D.C.

Fraser, E. 1969. *Home and School,* University of London Press, London.

Freeman, F.S. 1969. *Theory and Practice of Psychological Testing,* Oxford and IBH Publishing Co., New Delhi, 108-116.

Gaters, A.I. 1961. Sex Differences in Reading Ability. *Elementary School Journal,* 61, 431-434.

Garrett, H.E. 1973. *Statistics in Psychology and Education.* Vakils Feffer and Simons Pvt. Ltd., Bombay.

Gadgil, A.V. 1978. Study of the Causes of Large Failures in English at the S.S.C. Examiantion (Std. X) March 1977. (In)

Buch, M.B. (Ed.) 1986. *Third Survey of Educational Research (1978-83),* NCERT, New Delhi, 729.

——. 1979a. Study of the Causes of large Failures in Mathematics at the SSC Examiantion (St. X) of March 1977 (In) Buch, M.B. (Ed.) 1986. *Third Survey of Research in Education (1978-83),* NCERT, New Delhi, 730.

——. 1979b. Study of the Causes of Large Failures in Social Incidence at the SSC Examiantion (Std. X), of March 1979. (In) Buch, M.B. (Ed.) 1986. *Third Survey of Research in Education (1978-83),* NCERT, New Delhi, 730.

Gaite, A.J.H. 19690. On the Validity of Non-promotion as an Educational Procedure (Report to U.S. Office of Education). Madison: University of Wisconsin. *ERIC Document Reproduction Service No. ED 046 043.*

Ganapathy, M. and Raghuram Singh, M. 1981. The Impact of Socio-Economic Conditions on Achievement. *Experiments in Education,* 9, 8, 144-147.

Gautam, G.S. 1964. Improvement of Examinations. *The Educational Review,* 70, 2, 27.

Gaynor Cohen, 1981. Culture and Educational Achievement. *Harvard Educational Review,* 51, 2, 270.

Gayen, A.K., Nanda, P.B., Durai, P, Battacharya, N., Mukherjee, M.N., and Mathur, R.K. 1961-70. Measurement of Achievement in English, Some Indian Languages, Physics, and Chemistry, History, Civics and Economics, Geography, General Science and Biology. (In) Buch, M.B. (Ed.) 1986. *Third Survey of Research in Education (1978-83),* NCERT, New Delhi, 712.

Gayen, J.D. and Lyle, J.G. 1971. Effect of Incentive Upon Retarded and Normal Readers on a Visual Associative Learning Task. *Journal of Experimental Chld Psychology,* 11, 274-280.

Gluksberg, S. 1962. The Influence of Strength of Drive on Functional Fixedness and Perceptual Recognition. *Journal of Experimental Psychology,* 63, 36-41.

Gopala Krishna Moorthy, S. 1964. System of Examinations. Proceedings of the Collegiate Educational Conference and Seminars, 19-21 Dec. 1964, Hyderabad, 77-79.

Good, Carter, V. 1973. *Dictionary of Education,* McGraw-Hill Company, New York.

Goodlad, J.I. 1954. Some Effects of Promotion upon Social and Emotional Adjustment of Children. *Journal of Experimental Education,* 22, 4, 301-328.

Gorden and Elliott (n.d.). 100 percent Promotion and Social Promotion. (In) Smith, E.D. et al., (Eds.) 1969. *The Educator's Encyclopaedia,* Prentice-Hall, INC, Englewood Cliffs, N.J. 441.

Gottfredson, L. 1981. Circumscription and Compromise: A Developmental Theory of Occupational Aspirations. *Journal of Counselling Psychology,* 28, 545-579.

Government Central Pedagogical Institute (GCPI). 1964. An Investigation into the Causes of High Incidence of Failure at the High School Examiantion of the U.P. Board, Allahabad. (In) Buch, M.B. (Ed.) 1986. *Third Survey of Research in Education (1978-83),* NCERT, New Delhi, 720.

Grant, W.V. and Eiden, L.J. (Eds.) 1980. *Digest of Educational Statistics,* U.S. Government Printing Office, Washington, D.C.

Green, R.L., 1977. The Urban Challenge: Poverty and Race. (In) Torsten Husen and T. Neville Postlethwaite. (Eds.) 1986. *The International Encyclopaedia of Education,* Pergamon Press, Oxford, 9, 5401.

Grewal, S.S. and Bansbir Kaur, 1987. Verbal Reasoning of 10th Grade Urban and Rural Students. *Journal of Educational Research and Extension,* 24, 1, 11.

Griffiths, C.H. 1926. The Influence of Family on School Marks. *School and Society,* 24, 713-716.

Grunes, L.S. 1974. A Critical Study of the Attrition in the Mathematics Courses at Mercer Country Community College, *ERIC Document Reproduction Service No. ED* 089 824.

Guilford, J.P. 1954. *Psychometric Methdos,* McGraw Hill Publishing Company, New York.

——. 1965. *Fundamental Statistics in Psychology and Education,* McGraw-Hill, New York.

Gump, J., and Rivers, L. 1975. The Consideration of Race in Efforts to End Sex ais. (In) Diamon, E. (Ed.) *Issues of Sex Bias in Interest Measurement,* U.S. Government Printing Office, Washington, D.C. 123-139.

Gunasekaran, K., and Jayanthi, P. 1980. A study of the Continuous Internal Assessment and the university Examiantion Marks of the Undergraduate Semester Courses, (1976-77) Examiantion Reform Unit, Madras U. (In) Buch, M.B. (Ed.) 1986. *Third Survey of Education (1978-83),* NCERT, New Delhi, 733.

Gupta, V.P. 1968. Intelligence, Economic Status, Sex and Academic Success. *Journal of Educational Research and Extension,* 5, 2.

Gupta, S. 1982. Relationship Between Reading Ability and Fethers Profession and Birth Order. (In) Buch, M.B. (Ed.) 1986. *Third Survey of Research in Education, (1978-83),* NCERT, New Delhi, 652.

Gutman, L. 1947. A Basis for Scaling Qualitative Data. *American Social Review,* 9, 139-150.

Hall, L.H. 1969. Selective Variables in the Academic Achievement of Junior College Students from Different Socio-Economic Status Background. *The Journal of Educational Research,* 6, 3.

Hanusa, B.H. and Schulz, R. 1977. Attributional Mediators of Learned Helplessness. *Journal of Personality and Social Psychology,* 35, 602-611.

Harinder Nanda Mahajan. 1983. Question Banks and Construction of Tests and Reporting of Results for Internal Assessment and External Examinations. *Journal of Higher Education,* 9, 2, 243.

Harper Jr. A.E. 1970. Research on Examiantion in India. (In) Buch, M.B. (Ed.) 1986. *Third Survey of Research in Education (1978-83),* NCERT, New Delhi, 712.

Haris, L.J. 1978. Sex Differences in Spatial Ability: Possible Environmental, Genetic and Neurological Factors. (In) Kinshboune, M. (Ed.), *Assymetrical Function of the Brain,* Cambridge University Press, Cambridge.

Harris, D.L.B. 1979. The Relationship of School Behaviour and Family Background to Academic Achievement. *Dissertation Abstracts International,* 39, 10, 5819-A.

Harris, L.J. 1979. Sex Related Differences in Spatial Ability. A Developmental Psychological View. (In) Kopp, C.B. (Ed.), *Becoming Female: Perspectives on Development,* Plenun, New York.

Harris, L.J. 1981. Sex Related Variations in Spatial Skill. (In) Liben, L.S. Patterson, A.H. and New Combe, N. (Eds.), *Spatial Representation and Behaviour Across the Life Span,* Academic Press, New York.

Havighurst, R.J. and Breeze, F.H. 1947. Relation Between Ability and Social Status in a Mid-Western Community, III. Primary Mental Abilities, *Journal of Educational Psychology,* 38, 241-247.

Heckhausen, H. 1967. *The Anatomy of Achievement Motivation,* Academic Press Inc, New York.

Hema Kumari, T.A. 1977. Role of the Mother and Educational Achievement of the Child. *Education Quarterly,* 29, 16-21.

Hemalatha Natesan and Seetha, R. 1986. Achievement Motivation and Academic Achievement. *Journal of Educational Research and Extension,* 23, 2.

Henderson, R.W. and Merritt, C.B. 1968. Environmental Background of Mexican American Children with Different Potentials for School Success, *Journal of Social Psychology,* 75, 101-106.

Hill, W. 1964. Planning an Examiantion Paper. *The Progress of Education,* 39, 2-7.

Hill, W.H. 1972. *Improvement of Examinations,* University of Calicut, 1-6, 43-49.

Hobson, T.R. 1947. Sex Differences in Primary Mental Abilities. *Journal of Educational Research,* 41, 126-132.

Horny, A.S., Cowei, A.P. and Lewis, J.W. 1968. *Oxford Advanced Learner's Dictionary of Current English.* The English Language Book Society, Oxford University Press, London.

Horner, M. 1978. The Measurement and Behavioural Implications of Fear of Success in Women. (In) Atkinson, J. and Raynor, J. (Eds.), *Personality, Motivation and Achievement,* Halsted, New York, 41-70.

Howighurst, R.J., Bowman, P.H., Liddle, G.P., Mathews, C.V., and Pierce, J.V. 1962. *Growing up in River City,* Wiley, New York.

Hundal, P.S., and Jerarth, J.M. 1972. Personality Correlates of Projective Measures of Achievement Motivation and Their Factorial Structure. *Indian Journal of Psycology,* 47, 15-27.

Hunt, J. Mcv. 1961. *Intelligence and Experience,* Ronald Press, New York.

Hushak, Jheroy, 1977. The Role of Schools in Reducing the Variance of Cognitive Skills. *The Journal of Experimental Education,* 70, 3, 115-122.

Ilyukhin, A. and Tsimirinova, L. 1971. Examinations in Russia. *The Educational Review,* 77, 7. 152.

Inayat khan, 1971. Examiantion System—A Review. *Educational India,* 38, 3, 89.

Insubsong and John Hattie. 1984. Home Environment and Self Concept and Academic Achievement: A Casual Modelling Approach. *Journal of Educational Psychology,* 74, 6, 1269-1281.

Irwin, N. et al., 1978. The Relationship of Prior Ability and Final Characteristics of School Attendance and School Achievement in Rural Gautemala. *Child Development,* 49, 415-427.

Inaugural Address of V.C. of Gandhigram Rural institute. 1988. New Concepts in Teaching and Evaluation at the University Level. *University News,* 26, 46, 12.

Jabbar, S. 1968. A Study of Level of Aspiration Among High School Students in Co-educational and Non-Co-Educational Institutes. *unpublished Masters' Degree Dissertation,* Madras University, Madras.

Jachuck, K. and Das, J. 1982. Free Recall of Categorised Materials: A Cross Cultural Examinations of Jensen's Two Level Theory. *Indian Psychologist,* 1, 51-56.

Jacklin, C.N. Epilogue, 1979. Sex Related Differences in Cognitive Functioing. (In) Harold E. Mitzel, et al., (Eds.) 1983. *Encyclopaedia of Educational Research,* 5th edition, The Macmillan Company, London.

Jagadeesan, S. 1979. Assessment of Student's Performance, *The Hindu,* 102, 8 (9 Jan. 1979), 3.

Jaganatha Rao, C. 1977. Levels of Education in A.P. *Education in Andhra Pradesh 1956-76,* Telugu Academy, Hyderabad, 13-16.

Jagannathan, K. 1983. The Effects of Certain Socio-Psychological Factors on the Academic Achievement of Children Studying in Classes V to VII. *Unpublished Doctoral Theis,* S.V. University, Tirupati.

——. 1986. Home Environment and Academic Achievement. *Journal of Educational Research and Extension,* 23, 1, 18-24.

Jain Kagzi, M.C. 1984. *The Constitution of India,* Volume 2, Metropolitan Book Co., Private Ltd., New Delhi.

Jeffrey, G. Reed. 1981. Dropping a College Course; Factors Influencing Students' withdrawal Decisions. *Journal of Educational Psychology,* 73, 3, 376-385.

Jensen, A.R. 1968. Social Class in Verbal Learning. (In) Deutch, M., Katz, I., and Jensen, A.R. (Eds.), 1968. *Social Class Race and Psychological Development,* Holt, Rinehart and Winston, New York.

——. 1969. How much Can We Boost I.Q and Scholastic Achievement? *Harvard Educational Review,* 39, 1, 123.

Jensen, A.R. and Figueroq, R.A. 1975. Forward and Backward Digit Span, Interaction with Race and I.Q: Predictions from Jensen's Theory. *Journal of Educational Psychology,* 67, 887-893.

Jensen, A.R., and Inowye, A.R. 1980. Level I and Level II Abilities in Asian White and Black Children Intelligence. (In) Radha Shyam et al., 1988. Cognitive Processing Differential Amogn Rural Tribals and Non-Tribals. *The Educational Review,* 44, 7, 101-103.

John Hottie. 1984. Home Environment, Self Concept and Academic Achievement: A Causal Modelling Approach. *Journal of Educational Psychology,* 76, 6, 1269-1281.

Joseph, A. 1985. Educational Problems of Social Disadvantaged Children. *Journal of Indian Education,* 11, 1, 14-19.

Kabra, R.M. 1971. Doing Away with the *Examinations. Educational India,* 38, 3, 81.

Kamin, L.J. 1961. *Intelligence: The Battle for the Mind.* Macmillan, London.

Kandekar, M. 1974. A Study of Drop-outs. *Journal of Social Work,* 34, 367-385.

Kanna Babu, D. 1970. Reforms in Examinations. *The Educational Review,* 76, 11, 241.

Kathareene, O. 1975. Personality, Ability and Achievement in Primary School Children. *Educational Research,* 17, 3, 199-201.

Keeves, J.P. 1972. Educational Environment and Student Achievement. *Australian Council for Educational Research,* Melbourne.

——. 1973. Differences between the Sexes in Mathematics and Science Courses. *International Review of Education,* 19, 47-63.

Kelly, T.L. 1939. A Selection of Upper and Lower Group for the Validation of Test Items. *Journal of Educational Psychology,* 30, 17-24.

Kennedy, W.A., et al., 1963. A Normative Sample of Intelligence and Achievement of Negro Elementary School Children in the Southern United States, *Monogr. Soc. Res. Child Development,* 28, 6.

Kerlinger, F.N. 1959. *Statistical Analysis in Psychology and Education,* McGraw-Hill Book Co, Lec. New Delhi, 64-103.

Keyes, C.H. 1911. Progress Through Grades of City Schools (Contributions to Education, No. 4). Columbia University, Teachers College, Bureau of Publications, New York. (In) Ebel, R.L. (Ed.) 1983. *Encyclopaedia of Educational Research,* 5th Edition, Macmillan Company, London, 1471.

Khanna, M. 1980. A Study of the Relationship Between Students Socio-Economic Background and Their Academic Achievement at Junior School Level. (In) Buch, M.B. (Ed.) 1986. *Third Survey of Research in Education (1978-83),* NCERT, New Delhi, 671.

Klene, V., and Branson, E.P. 1929. Trail Promotion Versus Failure. *Education Research Bulletin,* 8, 6-11.

Knowles, A.S. 1977. *The International Encyclopaedia of Higher Education,* Jossey-Brass Publishers, London, 1481-1485.

Kochhar, S.K. 1982. *Pivotal Issues in Indian Education,* Sterling Publishers Private Limited, New Delhi, Bangalore, 265.

Kogan, J. 1977. On Cultural Deprivation. (In) Torsten Husen and T. Neville Postlethwaite. (Eds.) 1986. *The International Encyclopaedia of Education,* Pergamon Press, Oxford, 8, 4891.

Kohler, W. 1929. *Gestalt Psychology,* Liveright, New York.

Kowitz, G.T., and Armstrong, C.M. 1961. The Effect of Promotion Policy on Academic Achievement. *Elementary School Journal,* 61, 435-443.

Krech, D., Cruchfield, R.S. 1948. *Theory and Problems of Social Psychology,* McGraw-Hill, New York.

Krech, D., Cruchfield, R.S., and Ballachey, E.L. 1962. *Individual in Society,* McGraw-Hill, New York.

Krishna Murthy, S. 1971. Reform of Examinations. *The Educational Review,* 77, 11, 241-243.

Krishna Murthy, 1977. Examiantion Reforms in Andhra Pradesh. *Education in Andhra Pradesh (1956-76),* Telugu Academy, Hyderabad, 242-248.

Kuruville Jacob. 1964. System of Examinations. *Proceedings of the Collegiate Educational Conference and Seminars,* 19-21, Dec. 1964. Hyderabad, 77-78.

Laporte, R., and Voss, J. 1975. Retention of Prose Materials as a Function of Post-Acquisition Testing. *Journal of Educational Psychology,* 67, 259-266.

Lalithamma, K.N. 1975. Some Factors Affecting Achievement of Secondary School Pupils in Mathematics, Ph.D. Edu. Ker. U. (In). Buch, M.B. (Ed.) 1979. *Second Survey of Research in Education (1972-78),* Society for Educational Research and Development, Baroda, 332.

Lef Court, H.M. and Ladwing, G.W. 1965. The American Negro: A Problem in Expectancies. *Journal of Personality and Social Psychology,* 1, 377-380.

Leibovich De Figueroa, 1980. Intellectual Development and Scholastic Achievement. *Psychological Abstracts,* 64, 1, 4165.

Lele, T.P., Patel, P.M., Parikh, N.P., and Palkar, S.G. 1963. Qualitiative Analysis of Essay Questions (In) Buch, M.B. (Ed.) 1986. *Third Survey of Research in Education (1978-83),* NCERT, New Delhi, 714.

Lesser, G.S. et al., 1965, Mental Abilities of Children in Different Social and Cultural Groups, *Monogr. Soc. Res Child Develop,* 30, (4, Serial No. 120).

Likert, R. 1932. A Technique for the Measurement of Attitudes. Archieves of Psychology, No. 140. (In) Brayfield, A.H. and

Rothe, H.F. 1951. An Index of Job Satisfaction. *Journal of Applied Psychology,* 35, 5, 307-311.

Lindgren, Hendy Clay. 1979. *Introduction to Social Psychology,* Wiley Eastern Limited, New Delhi, 105-106.

Linn, C. Marcid and Steven Pulos. 1983. Male-Female Differences in Predicting Displaced Volume. *Journal of Educational Psychology,* 75(1), 86-96.

Lolyd, D.N. 1978. Prediction of School Failure from Third Grade Data. *Educational and Psychological Measurement,* 38, 1193-1200.

Lokesh Koul and Satish Chand Bhadwal. 1986. Effect of Interim Tests on the Academic Performance of High School Students. *Journal of Educational Research and Extension,* 23, 1, 1-7.

Maccoby, E.E. 1966. *The Development of Sex Differences,* Standford University Press, Standford.

Maccoby, E.E. and Jacklin, C.N. 1974. *The Psychology of Sex Differences,* Standford University Press, Standford.

Malhotra, R.K. 1972. Measurement of Achievement in English. (In) Buch, M.B. (Ed.) 1986. *Third Survey of Research in Education (1978-83),* NCERT, New Delhi, 718.

Marjoribanks, K. 1976. Sibsize, Family Environment, Cognitive Performance and Affective Characteristics. *The Journal of Psychology,* 94, 195-204.

Mathew, T. 1976. Some Personality Factors Related to Under-achievement in Science. Doctoral Dissertation, University of Kerala. (In) Buch, M.B. (Ed.) 1979. *Second Survey of Research in Education (1972-78),* Society for Educational Research and Development, Baroda, 350.,

Mathur, K. 1964. Effects of School Environment on the Achievement and Behaviour of Higher Secondary Schools, *Ph.D. Thesis,* Agra University, 1964.

McClelland, D.C. 1961. *The Achieving Society,* Princeton, D Van Nostrand.

McCullers, J.C. 1978. Issues in Learning and Motivation. (In) Lepper, M.R. and Greener, D. (Eds.), *The Hidden Costs of Reward: New Perspectives on the Psychology of Human Motivation,* Hillsdale, N.J., Erlbaum.

McElwee, E.W. 1932. A Comparison of Personality Traits of Accelerated, Normal, and Retarded Children. *Journal of Educational Research,* 26, 31-34.

McGehee, W., and Lewis, W.D. 1942. The Socio-Economic Status of the Homes of Mentally Superior and Retarded Children and the Occupational Rank of Their Parents. *Journal of Genetic Psychology,* 60, 375-380.

McGrath, J.E. 1964. *Social Psychology: A Brief Introduction.* Holt, New York.

McGraw, K.O. 1978. The Detrimental Effects of Reward on Performance: A Literature Review and a Prediction Model. (In) Lepper, M.R. and Greene, D. (Eds.), *The Hidden Costs of Reward: New Perspectives on the Psychology of Human Motivation,* Hillsdale, N.J., Erlbaum.

McGuiness, Dayand Pribram, K.H. 1978. The Origins of Sensory Bias in the Development of Gender Differences in Perception and Cognition. (In) Bortner, M. (Ed.), *Cognitive Growth and Development—Essays in Memory of Herbert G. Birch.* Bruner/Mazel, New York.

McNemer, G. 1962. *Psychological Statistics,* John Wiley and Sons, New York, 78-83.

Melby (n.d.). Non-promotion and the Mastery of Subject Matter, (In) Smith, E.D. et al., (Eds.), 1969. *The Educator's Encyclopaedia,* Prentice-Hall INC, Englewood Cliffs, N.J. 439.

Meonon, 1973. (In). Buch, M.B. (Ed.), 1979. *Second Survey of Research in Education (1972-78),* Society for Educational Research and Development, Baroda, 332.

Milner, D. 1977. Ethnic Identity and Preference in Minority Group Children. Unpublished Ph.D. Thesis, University of Bristol, Quoted by Singh, A.K. and Hansa, S. (In) Social Disadvantage. *A. Psychological Review,* Ranchi University.

Miner, B. 1968. Sociological Background Variables Affecting School Achievement. *Journal of Educational Research,* 61, 8.

Mishra, B.N. et al., 1968. An Investigation into the Influence of Home Environment on School Achievement. *Journal of Educational and Vocational Guidance,* 7, 72-76.

Morgan, J.J.B. 1934. *Keeping a Sound Mind,* MacMillan, New York.

Moritz, D.M. 1977. Socio-Economic and School Related Factors as Predictors of High School Drop-outs Cąṭegorized by Race and Sex. *Unpublished Doctoral Dissertation,* University of Kansas.

Morjoribanks, K. 1976. Sibsize Family Environment, Cognitive Performance and Affective Characteristics. *The Journal of Psychology,* 94, 195-204.

Morrison, I.E. and Perry, I.F. 1956. Acceptance of Average Children by Their Classmates. *Elementary School Journal,* 56, 217-220.

Morse, W.C. and Wingo, G.M. 1970. *Psychology of Teaching,* Tarapore Vala Sons and Co., Bombay, p. 375.

Moss, J.D. 1982. *Towards Equality: Progress by Girls in Mathematics in Australian Secondary Schools,* Australian Council for Educational Research, Hawthorn, Victoria.

Mostellar, F., and Moynihan, D.P. (Eds.) 1972. *On Equality of Educational Opportunities,* Random House, New York.

Mukerjee, R.K. 1951. *Ancient Indian Education,* Macmillan and Co., London.

Mukerjee, S.N. 1957. *Educational in India: Today and Tomorrow,* Acharya Book Dept, Baroda.

Mukerjee, B.N. 1965. Achievement Motivation and Goal Setting Behaviour in the Classroom. *British Journal of Educational Psychology,* 35, 262-265.

Mumbaver, C.C. and Miller, J.C. 1970. Socio-Economic Background and Cognitive Functioning in Pre-school Children. *Child Development,* 41, 471-480.

Murphy, G. and Likert, A. 1937. *Public Opinion and the Individual,* Harper; New York.

Muthaya, B.C. 1967. Certain Personal Data and Their Relation to Level of Aspiration. *Psychological Annual,* 2, 1-8.

Nagamani, T.S. and Raja Rajeswari, Y. 1988. Factors Responsible for Dropping-out of the School of 7 to 12 Year Girls. *Journal of Educational Research and Extension,* 24, 159-164.

Nath, B. 1980. University Examiantion—An Analytical Study of the Conduct of Pre-University Degree and Master Degree Examiantion of Gauhati University. (In) Buch, M.B. (Ed.) 1986. *Third Survey of Research in Education (1978-83),* NCERT, New Delhi, 712 and 715.

National Assessment of Educational Progress (NAEP), 1972. Reading Summary (Rep 02-4-00) Educational Commission of the States, Denvar. (In) Harold E. Mitzel, et al., (Eds.) 1983. *Encyclopaedia of Educational Research, (Vol. 4),* 5th Edition, The Macmillan Company, London.

National Assessment of Educational Progress (NAEP), 1976. News Letter, Educational Commission of the States, Denver, 4, 5. (In) Harold E. Mitzel, et al., (Eds.), 1983. *Encyclopaedia of Educational Research (Vol. 4),* 5th Edition, The Macmillan Company, London.

National Council of Educational Research and Training (NCERT) 1965. Sample Study of Failures in Boards of Secondary Examiantion, New Delhi. (In) Buch, M.B. (Ed.) 1986. *Third Survey of Research in Education (1978-83),* NCERT, New Delhi, 720.

Narasimha Rao, P.V. 1971. (In) Editorial, *Educational India,* 38, 3, 98a-98b.

Narayana Rao, S. 1970. Reforms in Evaluation Methods in Higher Education. *Evalution in Higher Education,* (Proceedings of Seminars Held on 22nd October and 23rd 1970), S.V. University, Tirupathi, 83-84.

New Comb, T.M., Turner, R.H. and Converse, P.E. 1965. *Social Psychology: The Study of Human Interaction,* Holt, New York.

Newhen (n.d.). 100 Per Cent Promotion and Social Promotion. (In) Smith, E.D., et al., (Eds.) 1969. *The Educator's Encyclopaedia,* Prentice Hall, INC Englewood Cliffs, N.J. 441.

Nongnuch, W., and Clements, M.A. 1982. Qualitative aspects of Sex-Related Differences in Performances on Pencil and paper Spatial Questions, Grades 7-9. *Journal of Educational Psychology,* 74 (6), 878-887.

Noreen, M. Webb. 1984. Sex Difference in Interaction and Achievement in Cooperative Small Groups. *Journal of Educational Psychology,* 76, 1, 33-44.

Northby, A.S. 1958. Sex-differences in high School Scholarship. (In) Ebel, R.L. 1969 (Ed.), *Encyclopaedia of Educational Research,* 4th Edition, The Macmillan Company, Co., London.

Nurul Hasan, 1975. *The Hindu,* 8 Aug. 1975, 8.

Oberlander, M., Jenkins, N., Henlihan, K. and Jackson, J. 1970. Family Size and Birth Order as Determinants of School Aptitutde and Achievement in a Sample of Eighth Graders. *Journal of Consulting and Clinical Psychology,* 34, 1, 19-21.

Ostle, B. 1966. *Statistics in Research,* Oxford and IBH Publishing Company, Bombay, 127.

Otto, H.J. 1951. *Findings in Child Psychology Should Affect Grading and Promotion Policies;* (In) Smith, E.D. et al., (Eds.), 1969. *The Educator's Encyclopaedia,* Prentice-Hall, Inc., Englewood Cliffs, N.J. 438-441.

Otto and Melby (n.d.). Non-promotion and the Mastery of Subject Matter. (In) Smith, E.D. et al., (Eds.), 1969. *The Educator's Encyclopaedia,* Prentice-Hall INC, Englewood Cliffs, N.J. 438-441.

Overall, J.E., and Klett, C.J. 1972. *Applied Multivariate Analysis,* McGraw Hill, New York.

Padmanabhaiah, S. 1972. A Study of the Attitudes of Teachers Towards the Present Examiantion System. *M.Ed. Dissertation,* S.V. University, Tirupati.

Pant, K.C. 1985. New Education Policy in 1986-87. *The Hindustan Times* (10th April, 1985).

Parthasarathy, R. 1980. Examinations: Their Role in Education, *The Hindu,* '103, 90, (15 April, 1980), 3.

Pathy, M.K. 1982. A Sample Study of High School Drop-outs in Rural Western Orissa. *Indian Educational Review,* 17, 3, 123-139.

Phares, E.J., and Rolter, J.B. 1956. An Effect of the Situation on Psychological Testing. *Journal of Consulting Psychology,* 20, 291-293.

Philippa Pattison and Norma Grieve. 1984. Do Spatial Skills Contribute to Sex Difference in Different Types of Mathematical Problems? *Journal of Educational Psychology,* 76, 4, 678-689.

Philips, T.K. 1979. An Investigation of the Relationship of Selected Demographic and School Related Variables to the Reading Achievement of Students in Grade 4th and 7th. *Dissertation Abstract International,* 39, 10, 6042-A.

Pillai, K.S. 1983. Achievement Motive in Relation to Masculanity and Femininity. *Psychological Studies,* 28, 2, 81-84.

Radhashyam, Omprakash Sharma, and Raghubir Singh, 1988. Cognitive Processing Differential Among Rural Tribals and Non-Tribals. *The Educational Review,* 44, 101-103.

Raghuram Singh, 1971. Examiantion Reform: Internal Assessment, *Educational India,* 38, 3, 79.

Ramoji Rao, Y. 1977. Socio-Economically Disadvantaged Children and Their Academic Achievement. *Journal of Educational Research,* 1, 2, 9-13.

Rani, B. 1980. Self Concept and Other Non-cognitive Factors Affecting the Academic Achievement of the Scheduled Caste Students in Instructions for Higher Technical Education. (In) Buch, M.B. (Ed.) 1986. *Third Survey of Research and Education (1978-83),* NCERT, New Delhi, 682.

Rao, C.R. 1962. *Advanced Statistical Methods in Biometric Research,* John Wiley and Sons, Inc., New York, 94-102.

Rao, D.G. 1965. A Study of Some Factors Related to Scholastic Achievement. Ph.D. Thesis, Delhi University. (In) Buch, M.B. (Ed.). *A Survey of Research in Education,* Centre for Advanced Study in Education, Baroda, 342.

Rao, K.V. 1977. Educational Innovations for Better Education. *Education in Andhra Pradesh 1956-76,* Telugu Academy, Hyderabad, 28-32.

Rasool, G., Sarpur, R. and Sharma, N.R. 1981. A Comparative Study of Internal and External Awards at the Postgraduate level in Jammu University. (In) Buch, M.B. (Ed.) 1986. *Third Survey of Research in Education (1978-83),* NCERT, New Delhi, 739 and 740.

Rathnaiah, E.V. 1977. *Structural Constraints in Tribal Education; A Regional Study,* Sterling Publishers, New Delhi.

Raymond, K.W. 1977. The Relationship Between Socio-Economic Status and Academic Achievement. *Dissertation Abstracts International,* 5067-A.

Reddy, M.V.S. and Basavanna, M. 1978. A Study of Self-Confidence and Achievement Motivation in Relation to Academic Achievement. (In) Buch, M.B. (Ed.) 1986. *Third Survey of Research in Education (1978-83),* NCERT, New Delhi.

Reddy, V.L.N. 1973. Study of Certain Factors Associated with Academic Achievement at First Year Degree Examination, Ph.D., Edu., M.S. University. (In) Buch, M.B. (Ed.) 1979. *Second Survey of Research in Education (1972-78),* Society for Educational Research and Development, Baroda.

Reissman, F. 1962. *The Culturally Deprived Child,* Harper, New York.

Renie, D. 1986. Factors Related to the Drop-outs of Freshman Students in a Venezulan Teachers College. *Dissertation Abstracts international,* 47, 8, Feb. 87, 106.

Report of the Calcutta University Commission. 1920. Government of India Press, New Delhi.

Report of the Hartog Committee. 1936. Hartog, Philip and Rhodes, K.C. 1936. An Examiantion of Examinations, Macmillan and Co., London, 10.

Report of the Norwood Committee on Curriculum and Examinations. 1943. (In) Breretons, J.C. 1944. The Case for Examinations, Cambridge University Press, 191.

Report of the University Education Commission. 1948. Government of India, Ministry of Education, New Delhi.

Report of the Secondary Education Commission. 1954. Government of India, Ministry of Education, New Delhi.

Report of the Bhopal Seminar on Examination. 1956. Government of India, Ministry of Education, New Delhi.

Report of the Committee on Examination Reform. 1962. University Grants Commission, New Delhi.

Report of the Education Commission. 1966. Government of India, Ministry of Education, New Delhi, 244-247.

Report of the Seminar. 1988. Curbing Malpractices at the Examinations, University News, 26, 17, 15.

Reynolds, C.R. and Gutkin, T.B. 1981. A Multivariate Comparison of the Intellectual Performance of Black and White Children Matched on Four Demographic Variables. *Personality and Intelligence Differences,* 2, 175-180.

Riley, D.M. 1981. Selected Classroom Behaviours as Predictors of Achievement in Introductory Accounting. *Dissertation Abstracts International,* 42, 3, 769-A.

Rosenberg, B.G., and Sutton, Smith, B. 1964. The Relationship of Ordinal Position and Sibling Sex Status to Cognitive Abilities. *Psychometric Science,* 1, 81-82.

——. 1969. Sibling Association, Family Size and Cognitive Abilities. *Journal of Genetic Psychology,* 109, 271-279.

Rotter, J.C., Chance, J.E., and Phares, E.J. 1972. *Applications of a Social Learning Theory of Personality,* Hold, Rinehart and Winston, New York.

Ruch, C.M. 1924. *The Improvement of the Written Examinations,* Scott Foresman and Co., Chicago.

Rychalk, J.F. 1975. Affective Assessment of Intelligence, Social Class and Racial Learning Style. *Journal of Personality and Social Psychology,* 6, 989-995.

Sachdeva, K. 1974. Etiology of Poor School Performance, *Growing Minds,* 3, 4, 15-20.

Saini, B.K. 1977. Academic Achievement as a Function of Economic Status and Educational Standard of Parents. *Psychological Studies,* 22, 2, 24-27.

Salamatullah. 1958. Improvement of Examinations: A Point of View. *The Education Quarterly,* 10, 38.

Sali, V.Z. 1978. Question-wise Analysis of Answer Books of Mathematics and English of the Secondary School Learning Examiantion: March 1977. (In) Buch, M.B. (Ed.) 1986. *Third Survey of Research in Education (1978-83),* NCERT, New Delhi, 741.

Sambaiah, P. 1964. System in Examinations. *Proceedings of the Collegiate Educational Conference and Seminars,* 19-21, Dec. 1964. Hyderabad, 77-79.

Sandin, et al., (n.d.). Non-promotion and the Mastery of Subject Matter. (In) Smith, E.D., et al., 1969 (Eds.) *The Educators Encyclopaedia,* Prentice-Hall INC, Englewood Cliffs, N.J. 439.

Sarabhachari, P. 1971. The Needed Examiantion Reform. *Educational India,* 38, 3, 86.

Sarala, P.M. 1975. Construction of Standardized Achievement Test in Mathematics (Part-I) for Standard VIII. *M.Ed. Dissertation,* University of Kerala, Kerala.

Satyamma Srinath, 1964. System of Examiantion, *The Proceedings of the Collegiate Educational Conference and Seminars,* 19-21, Dec. 1964, Hyderabad, 87-89.

Satyanarayana, K. 1972. Education in Andhra Pradesh (1947-72), *Educational India,* 39, 2, 35.

Scates, D.E. 1947. 50 years of Objective Measurement and Research in Education. (In) Ebel, R.L. (Ed.) 1969. *Encyclopaedia of Educational Research,* 4th edition, Macmillan Company, London, 7-9.

Schmuck, P.A. and Schmuck, R.W. 1961. Upward Mobility and IQ Performance. *Journal of Educational Research,* 55, 123-127.

Seashore, H.G. 1962. Women and More Predictable than Men. *Journal of Counselling Psychology,* 9, 261-70.

Seshadri, C. 1984. Non-detention in Schools: An Academic Exploration. *The Education Quarterly,* 36, 2, 10-23.

Sewell, W. and Hauser, R. 1975. *Education, Occupation and Earnings: Achievement in Early Career.* Academic Press, New York.

Shah, R.S. 1972. A Survey and Study of the Internal Evaluation System in the Colleges of Saurashtra and Evolving a Plan for it. (In) Buch, M.B. (Ed.) 1986. *Third Survey of Research in Education, (1978-83),* NCERT, New Delhi, 715.

Shah, J.H. 1982. Construction and Standardization of Primary School Achievement Tests (SAT) for Pupils of Grade VII in the State of Gujarat. (In) Buch, M.B. (Ed.) 1986. *Third Survey of Research in Education (1978-83),* NCERT, New Delhi.

Sharpe, S. 1976. Just Like a Girl: How Girls Learn to be Women. (In) Torsten Husen, and T. Neville Postlethwaite (Eds.) 1986. *The International Encyclopaedia of Education,* Pergamon Press, Oxford, 9, 5558-5567.

Sharma, V.P. 1967. Evaluation of Attainment in Federal Hindi at the Secondary School Level in West Maharashtra, Ph.D. Thesis, Poona University, Poona. (In) Buch, M.B. (Ed.) 1979. *Second Survey of Research in Education (1972-78),* Society for Educational Research and Development, Baroda, 374.

Sharma, R.C., and Sapra, C.L. 1969. *Wastage and Stagnation in Primary and Middle Schools,* NCERT, New Delhi.

Sharma, V.P. 1977. Achievement Norm Study of School Children of Ahmedabad. (In) Buch, M.B. (Ed.) 1979. *Second Survey of Research in Education (1972-78),* Society for Educational Research and Development, Baroda, 390.

Sharma, V.P. 1985. Effectiveness of Test-Types on High and Low Achievers. *Indian Educational Review,* 20, 4.

Sharma, V.P. and Bhagava, M. 1980. Academic Attainment and Prolonged Deprivation. *Journal of Education and Psychology,* 37, 4.

Shashidhar, B. 1981. A Study of the Relationship Between a Few School Variables and the Achievement of Scheduled Caste Students Studying in Secondary Schools of Karnataka. (In) Buch, M.B. (Ed.) 1986. *Third Survey of Research in Education (1978-83),* NCERT, New Delhi, 688-689.

Shaw, M.E. and Wright, J.M. 1967. *Scales for the Measurement of Attitudes,* McGraw-Hill Book Co., New York.

Sherman, J. 1977. Effects of Biological Factors on Sex-Related Differences in Mathematics Achievement. (In) Fox, L.H., Fennema, E., and Sherman, J. (Eds.) *Women and Mathematics Achievement; Research Perspectives for Change,* National Institute of Education, Washington, D.C.

——. 1980. Mathematics, Spatial Visualization and Related Factors: Changes in Girls and Boys, Grades 8-11, *Journal of Educational Psychology,* 72, 476-482.

Sherwood, Robert, Dan. 1980. The Effect of Selected Instructional Strategies on the Problem Solving Ability of High School Chemistry Students as Related to Their Proportional Reasoning Ability and Verbal Visual Preferences. *Dissertation Abstract International.* 4, 3, September.

Singh, M.K. 1969. Evaluation Versus Examinations. *The Educational Review,* 75, 3, 49.

Singha, H.S. 1984. Public Examinations in 2001, *Journal of Higher Education,* 9, 3, 315-322.

Sinha, S.P., and Alika, Garg, 1987. Sex Differences in Achievement as Related to Risk-Taking Behaviour in Adolescents. *Indian Educational Review,* 22, 4, 131-136.

Smith, C.P. 1964. Relationship Between Achievement Related Motives and Intelligence. Performance Level and Persistence, *Journal of Abnormal Psychology,* 68, 523-532.

Spokesman, Government of Kerala, 1973. Enmasse Promotion in Schools. *Educational India,* 39, 11 and 12, 316.

Srivastava, J.O. A Study of the Effect of Academic and Personality Characteristics on the Academic Achievement of Boys Reading in Class X. Ph.D. Education, Rajasthan University. (In) Buch, M.B. (Ed.) 1979. *Second Survey of Research in Education (1972-78),* Society for Educational Research and Development, Baroda, 360.

Srivastava, H.S. 1979. Examiantion and Employment, *The Hindu,* 102, 26 (30 Jan. 1979), 3.

Starch, D. 1913. Reliability and Distribution of Grades, Science, 38, 630-86. Quoted by Sharma, V.P. 1985. Effectiveness of Test Types on High and Low Achievers, *Indian Educational Review,* 20, 4.

Starch, D. and Eilliot, E.C. 1913. Reliability of Grading Work in Maths, *School Review,* 21, 954-59.

Stroud, J., and Lindguist, E. 1942. Sex Differences in Achievement in the Elementary and Secondary Schools. *Journal of Educational Psychology,* 33, 657-667.

Stroup, A.L. and Robins, L.N. 1973. Elementary School Preditors of School Drop-outs Among Black Males, *Sociology and Education,* 45, 212-222.

Subbaiah Naidu, V.C. 1964. System of *Examinations, Proceedings of the Collegiate Educational Conference and Seminars,* 19-21, Dec. 1964, Hyderabad.

Subramanyam, D.S. 1964. System of Examinations, *Proceedings of the Collegiate Educational Conference and Seminars,* 19-21 Dec. 1964, Hyderabad.

Sudhama, G.R. 1973. A Study of the Effect of Library Use on Academic Achievement of Post-graduate Students in the

M.S. University of Baroda. (In) Buch, M.B. (Ed.) 1979. *Second Survey of Research in Education (1972-78),* Society for Educational Research and Development, Baroda, 332.

Sudha Rao, K. 1987. Influence of Continuous Evaluation of Learning. *Indian Educational Review,* 22, 4, 150-51.

Sukhdev Singh, 1985. Internal Evaluation System Favoured. *University News,* 23, 7.

Svensson, A. 1972. Relative Achievement; School Performance in Relation to Intelligence, Sex and Home Environment. A Linguist and Wicksell 1971, p. 1976. Reviewed by Joan and Bissel, *Harvard Educational Review,* 42, 1, 151-152.

Taylor, H.J. 1963. Operation Pass Mark: An Account of the Methods Used in the Matriculation Examiantion of 1963. (In) Buch, M.B. (Ed.) 1986. *Third Survey of Research in Education (1978-83),* NCERT, New Delhi, 712.

——. 1964. An Examianation Examiners. (In) Buch, M.B. (Ed.) 1986. *Third Survey of Research in Education (1978-83),* NCERT, New Delhi, 712.

Terman, L.M. and Merill, M.A. 1937. *Measuring Intelligence,* Houghton Mifflin, Boston.

Terman, L.M. and Tyler, L.E.1954. Sex Differences. (In) Ebel, R.L. 1969. (Ed.) *Encyclopaedia of Educational Research,* 4th Edition, The Macmillan Company Co., London.

Texas Education Agency. 1977. Course Withdrawal Data Summary—Fall 1976. Austin: Texas 813 Follow-up Post Secondary, Student Follow-up Post Secondary, Student Follow-up Management Information System. Monograph 2, *ERIC Document Reproduction Service, No. ED 140 905.*

Thakur, R.S. 1972. A Study of the Scholastic Achievement of Secondary School Pupils in Bihar. D. Litt, Edu. Bih. U. (In) Buch, M.B. (Ed.) 1979. *Second Survey of Research in Education (1972-78),* Society for Educational Research and Development, Baroda, 362.

Thompson, J.R. 1969. Why Students Drop Courses, McComb Country Community College. *ERIC Document Reproduction Service No. ED 026 994.*

Through Different States. 1971. Seminar Opposes Abolition of Examiantion. *Educational India,* 38, 2, 63.

——. 1971. Reasons for Large Scale Failure in Public Examinations. *Educational India,* 38, 1, 28.

——. 1972. Abolition of Detentions to Create Proper Climate, *Educational India,* 39, 1, 23.

Thurstone, L.L. 1946. Comment. *American Journal of Sociology,* 5, 52.

Tluanga, L.N. 1974. Examiantion as a Mode of Management. (In) Buch, M.B. (Ed.) 1986. *Third Survey of Research in Education (1978-83),* NCERT, New Delhi, 712.

Trivedi, N.H., and Shinol, 1968. Examinations—Unavoidable. *The Educational Review,* 74, 1-3.

Trivedi, N. 1974. Social Determinants of Educational Backwardness. *Quest in Education,* 11, 2, 83-88.

Tyler, B.B. 1958. Expectancy for Eventual Success as a Factor in Problem-solving Behaviour. *Journal of Educational Psychology,* 49, 166-172.

Tyler, L.E. 1965. *The Psychology of Human Differences,* Appleton Century Crofts, New York.

Tyler, L.E. 1974. *Individual Differences: Abilities and Motivational Directions,* Prentice-Hall Inc, Englewood Cliffs, N.J.

Union Ministry of Education, 1984. *School Drop-outs: A Real Plague, Education Micellary (Special Issue),* 13, July 1982 to June 1984.

Upamanyu, V.V. 1973. Tests and Their Relative Importance. *Educational India,* 39, 8, 212.

Ushashri, S. 1978. A Comparative Study of the Socially Disadvantaged and Socially Non-disadvantaged Pupils with Regard to School Achievement and Academic Adjustment. *Unpublished Doctoral Thesis,* Department of Psychology, S.V. University, Tirupati.

Varma, D. 1971. Student Failure: Few Observations. *The Progress of Education,* XLVI, 3, 82-85.

Varma, O.P. 1982. The Home Environment of the Child. *The Educational Review,* 8 (6), 85-87.

Venkata Rami Reddy. A. 1976. Adjustment of Adolescents in Relation to the Occupation of Their Parents. *Journal of Educational Theory and Research—Shiksha,* 6-13.

——. 1977a. From the Traditional System to Internal Assessment. *The Educational Review,* 83, 9, 173.

——. 1977b. Parental Educational Status and Adjustment of Children. *Psychological Studies,* 32, 8-16.

——. 1978a. Attitude of Post-graduate Students Towards Internal Assessment. *Indian Educational Review,* 13, 3, 16-32.

——. 1978b. A Two Year Follow-up Study on Internal Assessment. *Journal of Higher Education,* 4, 47-56.

——. 1979. Student's Reactions Towards English and Regional Media: A Comparative Study. *Journal of Higher Education,* 5, 101-108.

——. 1980. Do Under-graduate Students Want Regional Medium? *Indian Psychological Review,* 19, 48-52.

——. 1984. Post-graduates want a Change over to Internal Assessment. *Asian Journal of Psychology and Education,* 13.

Venkata Rao, D. 1971. The New Remedy. *Educational India,* 38, 3, 89.

Verma, M. 1966. Significant Correlates of Secondary School Failures. (In) Buch, M.B. (Ed.) *A Survey of Research in Education,* Centre for Advanced Study in Education, Baroda, 349.

Vernon, P.A. 1981. Level I and Level II: A Review. Quoted by Radha Shyam et al., 1988. Cognitive Processing Differential Among Rural Tribals and Non-Tribals. *The Educational Review* 49, 7, 101-103.

Very, P.S. 1967. Differential Factor Structures Mathematical Abilities. *Genetic Psychology Monographs,* 75, 169-207.

Vital Rao, 1964. System of Examinations. *Proceedings of the Collegiate Educational Conference and Seminars,* 19-21, Dec. 1964, Hyderabad, 98-100.

Walker, D.A. 1976. *The IEA Six Subjects Surveys: An Empirical Study of Education in Twentyone Countries,* Almquist and Siksell, Stockholm.

Walter, C.M., and Mazolf, S.S. 1951. The Relation of Sex, Age and School Achievement to Level of Aspiration. *Journal of Educational Psychology,* 42, 285-292.

Watson, C.C. 1965. Cross Validation of Certain Background Variables as Predictors of Academic Achievement. *The Journal of Educational Research,* 59, 147-148.

Wangoo, M.L. 1972. On Examinations. *Educational India,* 39, 384-81.

Warren, H.C. 1934. *Dictionary of Psychology,* Mifflin Company, Houghton, Boston.

Wilson, J.R. et al., 1975. Cognitive Abilities: Use of Family Data as a Control to Assess Sex and Age Differences in Two Ethnic Groups. *International Journal of Aging and Human Development,* 6, 161-176.

Winer, B.J. 1971. *Statistical Principles in Experiments,* McGraw-Hill Book Co., New York, 445-449.

Wortman, C.B., Panciera, L., Shusterman, L. and Hibscher, J.A. 1976. Attribution of Causality and Reaction to Uncontrollable Outcomes. *Journal of Experimental Social Psychology,* 12, 301-316.

Wheeler, L.R. 1942. A Comparative Study of the Intelligence of East Tennesse Mountain Children. *Educational Psychology,* 33, 321-334.

Additional Reading

Bhaskara Rao, Digumarti (1994). *Scientific Aptitude.* New Delhi: Ashish Publishing House. pp: 100. Rs. 100. ISBN 81-7024-658-X.

Bhaskara Rao, Digumarti (1995), *Animal Kingdom*. New Delhi: Discovery Publishing House. pp: 135. Rs. 200. ISBN 81-7141-274-2.

Bhaskara Rao, Digumarti (1995). *Batracology*. New Delhi: Discovery Publishing House, pp: 174. Rs. 250 ISBN 81-7141-279-3.

Bhaskara Rao, Digumarti (1996). *Scientific Attitude vis-a-vis Scientific Aptitude*. New Delhi: Discovery Publishing House. pp: 143 Rs. 275. ISBN 81-7141-308-0.

Bhaskara Rao, Digumarti, ed. (1996). *Encyclopaedia of Education For All,* 5 Vols. New Delhi: APH Publishing Corporation. pp: 1460. Rs. 3000. ISBN 81-7024-759-4. (set).

Vol. I Education For All: The World Conference pp: 440. ISBN 81-7024-760-8.

Vol. II Education For All: The EPA-9 Summit. pp: 340. ISBN 81-7024-761-6.

Vol. III Education for All: Quality Education For All. pp: 250. ISBN 81-7024-762-4.

Vol. IV Education For All: Planning and Monitoring. pp: 170. ISBN 81-7024-763-2.

Vol. V Education For All: The Indian Scenario. pp: 260. ISBN 81-7024-764-0.

Bhaskara Rao, Digumarti, ed. (1996). *Global Perceptions on Peace Education,* 3 Vols. New Delhi: Discovery Publishing House, pp: 980 Rs. 1800. ISBN 81-7141-319-6.

Bhaskara Rao, Digumarti, ed. (1996). *National Policy on Education,* 2 Vols. New Delhi: Anmol Publications Pvt. Ltd. pp: 710. Rs. 1000. ISBN 81-7488-323-1.

Bhaskara Rao Digumarti, ed. (1997). *Care the Child,* 2 Vols. New Delhi: Discovery Publishing House. pp: 616. Rs. 1000. ISBN 81-7141-394-3.

Bhaskara Rao, Digumarti, ed. (1997). *Education for the 21st Century*. New Delhi: Discovery Publishing House. pp. 288. Rs. 500. ISBN 81-7141-389-7.

Bhaskara Rao, Digumarti, ed. (1997), *Reflections on Scientific Attitude*. New Delhi: Discovery Publishing House. pp: 310. Rs. 500. ISBN 81-7141-328-5.

Bhaskara Rao, Digumarti (1997). *Scientific Attitude*. New Delhi: Discovery Publishing House. pp: 120. Rs. 225 ISBN 81-7141-381-1.

Bhaskara Rao, Digumarti, ed. (1997). *Success Story of a Primary Education Project*. New Delhi: APH Publishing Corporation. pp. 260. Rs. 400. ISBN 81-7024-850-7.

Bhaskara Rao, Digumarti, ed. (1997). *World Food Summit*. New Delhi: Publishing House. pp. 153. Rs. 300. ISBN 81-7141-386-2.

Bhaskara Rao, Digumarti, ed. (1998). *Adolescence Education*. New Delhi: Publishing House. pp. 238. Rs. 350. ISBN 81-7141-432-X.

Bhaskara Rao, Digumarti, ed. (1998). *Community and School Nutrition Education*. New Delhi: Publishing House. pp. 425. Rs. 650. ISBN 81-7141-435-4.

Bhaskara Rao, Digumarti, ed. (1998). *District Primary Education Programme*. New Delhi: Publishing House. pp: 506. Rs. 650. ISBN 81-7141-396-X.

Bhaskara Rao, Digumarti, ed. (1998) *Earth Summit*. 2 Vols. New Delhi: Publishing House. pp. 930. Rs. 1500. ISBN 81-7141-435-4.

Bhaskara Rao, Digumarti, ed. (1998) *National Policy on Education: Towards an Enlightened and Humane Society*. New Delhi: Publishing House. pp. 542. Rs. 860. ISBN 81-7141-426-5.

Bhaskara Rao, Digumarti, ed. (1998). *Reforming School Education*. New Delhi: Publishing House. pp; 575 Rs. 750. ISBN 81-7141-403-6.

Bhaskara Rao, Digumarti, ed. (1998). *Teacher Education in India*. New Delhi: Publishing House. pp. 424. Rs. 600. ISBN 81-7141-406-0.

Bhaskara Rao, Digumarti, ed. (1998), *World Summit for Social Development*. New Delhi: Publishing House. pp: 278. Rs. 450. ISBN 81-7141-420-6.

Bhaskara Rao, Digumarti, ed. (2000). *Education For All: Achieving the Goal.* 3 vols. New Delhi: APH Publishing Corporation. pp: 830. Rs. 2000. ISBN 81-7648-152-1.

Vol. I The Global Consensus. pp: 285. ISBN 81-7648-153-X.

Vol. II Mid-Decade Review Reports of Regional Seminars. pp: 198. ISBN 81-7648-154-8.

Vol. III Issues and Trends. pp: 346. ISBN 81-7648-155-6.

Bhaskara Rao, Digumarti, ed. (2000). *International Encyclopaedia of AIDS,* 11 Vols in 13 parts. New Delhi: Discovery Publishing House, pp: 3676. Rs. 7500. ISBN 81-7141-465-6 (set).

Vol. 1. Introduction to HIV/AIDS. pp: 246 ISBN 81-4141-523-7 Rs. 500.

Vol. 2 HIV/AIDS—Issues and Challenges, 2 Parts. pp: 805. Rs. 1700. ISBN 81-7141-524-5.

Vol. 3 HIV/AIDS-Socio Economic Realities. pp: 436. Rs. 900. ISBN 81-7141-525-3.

Vol. 4 HIV/AIDS Law Ethics and Human Rights, 2 parts. pp: 859. Rs. 1800. ISBN 81-7141-526-1 Rs. 1800/-

Vol. 5 AIDS and NGOs. pp: 215 Rs. 450 ISBN 81-7141-527-X.

Vol. 6 AIDS and Home Care pp: 183 Rs. 400 ISBN 81-7141-528-8.

Vol. 7 STD Case Management pp: 223 Rs. 475 ISBN 81-7141-529-6.

Vol. 8 HIV Prevention and Care-Teaching Modules for Nurses and Midwives. p: 125 Rs. 275. ISBN 81-7141-530-X.

Vol. 9. HIV/AIDS Prevention Education for Educational Institutions. pp: 75. Rs. 150 ISBN 81-7141-531-8.

Vol. 10 Instructional Modules for AIDS Education. pp: 111. Rs. 250. ISBN 81-7141-532-6.

Vol. 11 School Health Education to Prevent AIDS and STD-A Pckage for Curriculum Planners. pp: 298. Rs. 600. ISBN 81-7141-533-4.

Bhaskara Rao, Digumarti, ed. (2000). *International Encyclopaedia of Science and Technology Education.* 11 Volumes. New Delhi: Discovery Publishing House. pp: 4892. Rs. 8500. ISBN 81-7141-548-2 (set).

Vol. 1 Science and Tchnology Education. pp: 557. Rs. 975 ISBN 81-7141-568-7.

Vol. 2 Science Education in Developing Countries. pp. 334. Rs. 600 ISBN 81-7141-570-9.

Vol. 3 Organsiational Structure of Science. pp: 334. Rs. 600 ISBN 81-7141-570-9.

Vo! 4 Science Education in Asia and the Pacific. pp: 429. Rs. 750 ISBN 81-7141-571-7.

Vol. 5 Science and Technology Education For All. pp: 464. Rs. 800 ISBN 81-7141-572-5.

Vol. 6. Values, Ethics, Talent and Girls in Science and Technology Education. pp: 463. Rs. 800 ISBN 81-7141-573-3.

Vol. 7 Popularization of Science and Technology Education. pp: 334. Rs. 600. ISBN 81-7141-574-1.

Vol. 8 Science, Power and Society. pp: 357. Rs. 625 ISBN 81-7141-575-X.

Vol. 9 Information Technology. pp: 442. Rs. 775. ISBN 81-7141-576-8

Vol. 10 Teacher Training in Science and Technology Education. pp: 536. Rs. 975. ISBN 81-7141-577-6.

Vol. 11 Science, Technology and Society: A Curriculum Framework. pp: 642. Rs. 1000. ISBN 81-7141-578-4.

Bhaskara Rao, Digumarti, ed. (2001). *Distance Education in Different Countries*. New Delhi: APH Publishing Corporation. pp: 574. Rs. 1500. ISBN 81-7648-229-3.

Bhaskara Rao, Digumarti, ed. (2001). *Decentralised Management of Education (Management of Education in Panchavati Raj and Municipal Bodies)*. New Delhi: Discovery Publishing House. pp: 116. Rs. 250. ISBN 81-7141-617-9.

Bhaskara Rao, Digumarti, ed. (2001). *Electrochemistry for Environmental Protection*. New Delhi: Discovery Publishing House. pp: 208. Rs. 400. ISBN 81-7141-619-5.

Bhaskara Rao, Digumarti, ed. (2001). *Global Educational Studies*. New Delhi: Discovery Publishing House. pp. 145. Rs. 300. ISBN 81-7141-616-0.

Bhaskara Rao, Digumarti, ed. (2001) *Global Synthesis of Educational Assessment*. New Delhi: Publishing House. pp: 152. Rs. 300. ISBN 81-7141-613-6.

Bhaskara Rao, Digumarti, ed. (2001). *International Encyclopaedia of Human Rights,* 7 volumes in 13 parts. New Delhi: Discovery Publishing House. pp: 6500 (Royal size). Rs. 22000. ISBN 81-7141-567-9 (set).

Vol. 1 International Instruments of Human Rights, 2 parts Rs. 3500. ISBN 81-7141-595-4.

Vol. 2 Regional Instruments of Human Rights. Rs. 1500 ISBN 81-7141-604-7.

Vol. 3 Human Rights and the United Nations, 2 parts. Rs. 2800. ISBN 81-7141-605-5.

Vol. 4 Fact Files of Human Rights, 2 parts. Rs. 3000. ISBN 81-7141-606-3.

Vol. 5 Study Stories of Human Rights, 3 parts. Rs. 5200. ISBN 81-7141-607-1.

Vol. 6 International Meetings on Human Rights, 2 parts. Rs. 3000. ISBN 81-7141-608-X.

Vol. 7 Professional Training in Human Rights. Rs. 2200. ISBN 81-7141-609-8.

Bhaskara Rao, Digumarti, ed. (2001). *Jomtein Decade of Education.* New Delhi: Discovery Publishing House. pp: 106. Rs. 225. ISBN 81-7141-618-7.

Bhaskara Rao, Digumarti, ed. (2001). *Nuclear Materials: Issues and Concerns,* 2 Vols. New Delhi: Discovery Publishing House. pp: 1100. Rs. 2200. ISBN 81-7141-611-X.

Bhaskara Rao, Digumarti, ed. (2001). *World Conference on Education for All.* New Delhi: APH Publishing Corporation. pp; 380. Rs. 995. ISBN 81-7648-274-9.

Bhaskara Rao, Digurmarti, ed. (2001). *World Conference on Higher Education.* New Delhi: Discovery Publishing House. pp: 306. Rs. 600. ISBN 81-7141-610-1.

Bhaskara Rao, Digumarti, ed. (2001). *World Conference on Science.* New Delhi: Discovery Publishing House. pp: 85. Rs. 200. ISBN 81-7141-612-8.

Bhaskara Rao, Digumarti, C.A.P. Swamy and B.S.V. Dutt (1997). *Self Evaluation in Student Techning.* New Delhi: Discovery Publishing House. pp: 762. Rs. 150. ISBN 81-7141-374-9.

Bhaskara Rao, Digumarti, C. Sridevi and K. Vijaya (1995). *Achievement in Social Studies.* New Delhi: Discovery Publishing House. pp: 102. Rs. 150. ISBN 81-7141-281-5.

Bhaskara Rao, Digumarti and Digumarti Pushpa Latha (1994). *Achievement in Biology.* New Delhi: Discovery Publishing House. pp: 102. Rs. 125. ISBN 81-7141-264-5.

Bhaskara Rao, Digumarti and Digumarti Pushpa Latha (1995). *Achievement in English.* New Delhi: Discovery Publishing House. pp: 214. Rs. 275. ISBN 81-7141-283-1.

Bhaskara Rao, Digumarti and Digumarti Pushpa Latha (1995). *Achievement in Science.* New Delhi: Discovery Publishing House. pp: 159. Rs. 225. ISBN 81-7141-280-7.

Bhaskara Rao, Digumarti and Digumarti Pushpa Latha (1995). *Achievement in Mathematics.* New Delhi: Discovery Publishing House. pp: 125. Rs. 175. ISBN 81-7141-278-5.

Bhaskara Rao, Digumrti and Digumarti Pushpa Latha, eds. (1998). *International Encyclopaedia of Women,* 5 Vols. New

Delhi: Discovery Publishing House. pp: 2172. Rs. 4000. ISBN 81-7141-410-9.

Vol.1 Status of World's Women pp: 427. Rs. 750. ISBN 81-7141-494-X.

Vol. 2 Women, Education and Empowerment. pp: 467. Rs. 875. ISBN 81-7141-498-2.

Vol. 3 Women Challenges and Advancement. pp: 354. Rs. 650. ISBN 81-7141-497-4.

Vol. 4 Women and Family Health. pp: 40. Rs. 875. ISBN 81-7141-497-4.

Vol. 5 Women and International Action. pp: 453. Rs. 850. ISBN 81-7141-498-2.

Bhaskara Rao, Digumarti, Digumarti Pushpa Latha and Digumarti Harshitha, eds. (2001). *Biological Warfare.* New Delhi: Discovery Publishing House. pp. 422. Rs. 800. ISBN 81-7141-597-0.

Bhaskara Rao, Digumarti, Digumarti Pushpa Latha and Digumarti Harshitha, eds. (2001). *Women as Educators.* New Delhi: Discovery Publishing House. pp. 112. Rs. 200. ISBN 81-7141-602-0.

Bhaskara Rao, Digumarti, Digumarti Pushpa Latha and Digumarti Harshitha, eds. (2000. *Education in India.* New Delhi: APH Publishing Corporation. pp. 280. Rs. 700. ISBN 81-7648-207-2.

Bhaskara Rao, Digumarti, Digumarti Pushpa Latha and Digumarti Harshitha, eds. (2001). *Assessing Learning Achievement.* New Delhi: Discovery Publishing House. pp. 128. Rs. 225. ISBN 81-7141-601-2.

Bhaskara Rao, Digumarti, Digumarti Pushpa Latha and Digumarti Harshitha, eds. (2000). *Energy Security.* New Delhi: Discovery Publishing House. pp: 564. Rs. 1000. ISBN 81-7141-598-9.

Bhaskara Rao, Digumarti, D. Harshitha and K.R.S.S. Rao, eds. (1999). *Advanced Bio-technology.* New Delhi: Discovery Publishing House. pp: 335. Rs. 550. ISBN 81-7141-516-4.

Bhaskara Rao, Digumarti and K.R.S. Sambasiva Rao, eds. (1996). *Current Trends in Indian Education.* New Delhi: Discovery Publishing House. pp: 234. Rs. 400. ISBN 81-7141-311-0.

Bhaskara Rao, Digumarti and K. Vijay (1995). *A. Text Book Evaluation.* Ambala Cantt: The Associated Publishers. pp: 100. Rs. 160.

Bhaskara Rao, Digumarti, V.V. Rao, V.V. Lakshmi and V.V. Krishna, eds. (2000). *Status and Advancement of Women.* New Delhi: APH Publishing Corporation. pp: 570. Rs. 1100. ISBN 81-7648-169-6.

Bhagya Lakshmi, Lingineni and Digumarti Bhaskara Rao, ed. (2000). *Reading and Comprehension.* New Delhi: Discovery Publishing House. pp: 108. Rs. 175. ISBN 81-7141-543-1.

Bhuvaneswara Lakshmi, G. and Digumarti Bhaskara Rao, ed. (2000). *Attitude Towards Science.* New Delhi: Discovery Publishing House. pp: 128. Rs. 250. ISBN 81-7141-541-6.

Devraj, T.A. S. and Digumarti Bhaskara Rao, ed. (1997). *Trace Analysis of Uranium and Thorium.* New Delhi: Discovery Publishing House. pp: 195. Rs. 350. ISBN 81-7141-375-7.

Durgani Rani, K. and Digumarti Bhaskara Rao, ed. (2000). *Educational Aspriations and Scientific Attitudes.* New Delhi: Discovery Publishing House. pp: 130. Rs. 250. ISBN 81-7141-55-55.

Dutt. B.S.V. and Digumarti Bhaskara Rao (2001). *Empowering Primary Teachers.* New Delhi: Discovery Publishing House. pp: 283. Rs. 475. ISBN 81-7141-615-2.

Ediger, Marlow and Digumarti Bhaskara Rao (1996). *Science Curriculum.* New Delhi: Discovery Publishing House. pp. 309. Rs. 450. ISBN 81-7141-321-8.

Editor, Marlow and Digumarti Bhaskara Rao (2000). *Teaching Mathematics Successfully.* New Delhi: Discovery Publishing House. pp: 279. Rs. 525. ISBN 81-7141-552-0.

Ediger, Marlow and Digumarti Bhaskara Rao (2000). *Teaching Reading Successfully.* New Delhi: Discovery Publishing House. pp. 386. Rs. 750. ISBN 81-7141-556-3.

Ediger Marlow and Digumarti Bhasakar Rao (2001). *Teaching Science Successfully*. New Delhi: Discovery Publishing House. pp. 320 Rs. 600. ISBN 81 7141-600-4.

Ediger, Marlow and Digumarti Bhaskara Rao (2001). *Teaching Social Studies Successfully*. New Delhi: Discovery Publishing House. pp. 296. Rs. 575. ISBN 81-7141-596-2.

Jayasree, Kandi and Digumarti Bhaskara Rao, ed. (1999). *Correlates of Socialisation*. New Delhi: Discovery Publishing House. pp: 160. Rs. 375. ISBN 81-7141-517-2.

John Babu, Ch., T.J.R. Prasad, G.M. Madhukar and Digumarti Bhaskara Rao, eds. (2001). *Problem Solving in Mathematics*. New Delhi: APH Publishing Corporation. pp: 125. Rs. 250. ISBN 81-7648-273-0.

Marja, Talvi and Digumarti Bhaskara Rao, eds. (1996). *Educational Leadership and Social Changes*. New Delhi: Discovery Publishing House, pp: 236. Rs. 400. ISBN 81-7141-320-X.

Prabhakaram, K.S. and Digumarti Bhasakra Rao, ed. (1998). *Concept Attainment Model in Mathematics Teaching*. New Delhi: Discovery Publishing House. pp: 122. Rs. 200. ISBN 81-7141-424-9.

Prasanth Kumar, J. and Digumarti Bhaskara Rao, ed. (1998). *Effectiveness of Distance Education System*. New Delhi: Publishing House. pp: 152. Rs. 275. ISBN 81-7141-437-0.

Prasanth Kumar, J. and Digumarti Bhasakara Rao and G. Sundara Rao, eds. (2000). *Open University Student Support Services*. New Delhi: Discovery Publishing House. pp: 100 Rs. 200. ISBN 81-7141-550-4.

Rama Krishnaiah, D. and Digumrti Bhaskara Rao, ed. (1998). *Job Satisfaction of College Teachers*. New Delhi: Discovery Publishing House. pp: 251. Rs. 400. ISBN 81-7141-438-9.

Ramesh, Gants and Digumarti Bhaskara Rao, eds. (1998). *Environmental Education: Problems and Prospects*. New Delhi: Discovery Publishing House. pp: 324. Rs. 525. ISBN 81-7141-423-0.

Rathaih, L. and Digumarti Bhaskara Rao, eds. (1997). *International Innovations in Education*. New Delhi: Discovery Publishing House. pp: 514. Rs. 750. ISBN 81-7141-359-5.

Rathaiah, Lavu, Digumarti Bhaskara Rao and Paturi Koteswara Rao. (1997). *Achievement Correlates*. New Delhi: Discovery Publishing House. pp: 116. Rs. 225. ISBN 81-7141-385-4.

Sanjeeva Rao, B.C. and Digumarti Bhaskara Rao, ed. (1996). *A Text Book of Geology*. New Delhi: Discovery Publishing House. pp: 320. Rs. 525 ISBN 81-7141-313-7.

Satya Narayana, V. and Digumarti Bhaskara Rao, ed. (2001). *Physical Education, Social Attitudes and Leadership Qualities*. New Delhi: Discovery Publishing House. pp: 296. Rs. 575. ISBN 81-7141-593-8.

Srinivasulu Reddy, M., K.R.S. Sambasiva Rao and Digumarti Bhaskara Rao, ed. (1999). *A Text Book of Aquaculture*. New Delhi: Discovery Publishing House. pp. 296. Rs. 525. ISBN 81-7141-482-6.

Vanaja, M. and Digumarti Bhaskara Rao, ed. (1999). *Inquiry Training Model*. New Delhi: Discovery Publishing House. pp: 189. Rs. 325. ISBN 81-7141-515-6.

Veena Kumari, Balusu and Digumarti Bhaskara Rao 91996). *Operation Black Board*. New Delhi: APH Publishing Corporation. pp: 140. Rs. 2000. ISBN 81-7024-711-X.

Veena Kuarmi, B. and Digumarti Bhaskara Rao, ed. (2000). *Psycho Social Correlates of Achievement*. New Delhi: Discovery Publishing House. pp: 136. Rs. 300. ISBN 81-7141-547-4.

Venkata Rao, P. and Digumarti Bhaskara Rao (1989). *A Text Book of Zoology—Junior Intermediate*. Guntur: Vignan Publishers. pp: 370. Rs. 57.

Venkata Rao, P. and Digumarti Bhaskara Rao (1989). *A Text Book of Zoology—Senior Intermediate*. Guntur: Vignan Publishers. pp: 480. Rs. 68.

Venugopala Rao, K. and Digumarti Bhaskara Rao, ed. (2000). *Teacher Morale in Secondary Schools*. New Delhi: Discovery Publishing House. pp. 300. Rs. 575. ISBN 81-7141-551-2.

Vidya, C. and Digumarti Bhaskara Rao, ed. (1996). *A Text Book of Nutrition*. New Delhi: Discovery Publishing House. pp: 438. Rs. 650. ISBN 81-7141-309-9.

Vijaya Bharathi, D. and Digumarti Bhaskara Rao, ed. (2000). *Educational Philosophies of Swami Vevekanand and John Dewey*. New Delhi: APH Publishing Corproation. pp: 200. Rs. 500. ISBN 81-7648-202-1.

Bhaskara Rao, Digumarti, (1986). *Dhrushya Sravana Bodhanapakaranalu* (Audio Visual Teaching Aids). Guntur: Nagarjuna Publishers.

Bhaskara Rao, Digumarti (1993). *Jeevasashtra Bodhana* (Teaching of Biology. Guntur: Nagarjuna Publishers.

Bhaskara Rao, Digumarti (1995). *Vignanasasthra Bodhana*. (Teaching of Science). Guntur: Nagarjuna Publishers.

Bhaskara Rao, Digumarti (1997). *Vidya Manovignana Sashtram*. (Educational Psychology). Guntur: Creative Press. pp. 434. Rs. 79.

Bhaskara Rao, Digumarti (1998). *DSC Study Material*. Guntur: Nagarjuna Publishers.

Bhaskara Rao, Digumarti (1998). *Upadhyayudu Vidya* (Teacher and Education). Guntur: Nagarjuna Publishers.

Bhaskara Rao, Digumarti (1998). *Vidya Dhrukpadhalu*. (Perspectives of Education). Guntur: Nagarjuna Publishers.

Bhaskara Rao, Digumarti (1999). *EdCET Teaching Aptitude*. Guntur: Nagarjuna Publishers.

Bhaskara Rao, Digumarti (2001). *Bharata Samajamulo Upadhayayudu Vidya* (Teahcer and Education in Emerging Indian Society). Guntur: Nagarjuna Publishers. pp: 256. Rs. 59.

Bhaskara Rao, Digumarti (2001). *Bhoutika Sastra Bodhana Padhatulu* (Methods of Teaching Physical Science). Guntur: Nagarjuna Publishers. pp: 324. Rs. 77.

Bhaskara Rao, Digumarti (2001). *Jeeva Sastra Bodhana Padhatulu* (Methods of Teaching Biological Science). Guntur: Nagarjuna Publishers. pp. 224. Rs. 59.

Bhaskara Rao, Digumarti (2001). *Vidya Manovignana Sastram* (Educational Psychology) Guntur: Nagarjuna Publishers. pp: 344. Rs. 77.

At the state level, state evaluation units have been established in different states which have been entrusted with the task of reforming examinations. These SEU's came into existence during the first part of the last decade.

In Andhra Pradesh the state evaluation unit was established in 1964, with the establishment of State Council of Educational Research and Training (SCERT) in 1967, it became one of its chief departments.

Type of Reform

Commenting on the haphazard way of tinkering with examination system in different parts of the country, the Editor, *The Educational Review* (1975) observed, no doubt examination reform is being debated all over the world. But here the pressure for reform has come not from psychologists and educationists, but from students who want an easy pass without adequate preparation or study. Education without evaluation is no education at all. What is needed, therefore, is a concrete drive to change the psychology of the students, to make them more responsive to discipline, to inculcate in them habits of regular study and a sense of examination ethics, and to make them understand that examination cannot be sabotaged or downgraded without hurting their own interests.

The reform of examinations is not a simple task. If it is to be successful, all the concerned agencies should develop a favourable attitude towards examinations, according to *Krishna Moorthy* (1971). The students should be educated as to the desirability of educational measurement in their own interests. Parents should also consider examinations as a necessary phase of the educational career of their children. Administrators should see that examination phobia is not developed in the students by imposing too many restrictions and too much rigidity. The administration of examinations should take pace in a calm, peaceful and graceful environment where mutual trust pervades all through. It should be remembered that examinations are a means for the end of acquisition of knowledge—and that they are not an end in themselves.